PM Practice Guide

Copyright Information

Copyright 2010

No part of this publication may reproduced, stored in a retrieval system, or transmitted in any form or by any means, electronic, mechanical, photocopying, recording, scanning, or otherwise, except as permitted under Sections 107 or 108 of the 1976 United States Copyright Act, without either the prior permission of the Publisher or author.

Many of the designations used by manufacturers and sellers to distinguish their products are claimed as trademarks. Where those designations appear in this book, and the publisher was aware of a trademark claim, the designations have been printed with initial capital letters or in all capitals.

PMP® and the PMP® Logo are certification marks of the Project Management Institute, which are registered in the United States and other nations.

PMI® is a service and trademark of the Project Management Institute, Inc., which is registered in the United States and other nations.

PMBOK® is a trademark of the Project Management Institute, Inc., which is registered in the United States and other nations.

PMI® did not participate in the development of this publication and has not reviewed the content for accuracy. PMI® does not endorse or otherwise sponsor this publication and makes no warranty, guarantee, or representation, expressed or implied, as to its accuracy or content. PMI® does not have any financial interest in this publication and has not contributed any financial resources.

The author and publisher have taken care in the preparation of this book, but make no expressed or implied warranty of any kind and assume no responsibility for errors or omissions. No liability is assumed for incidental or consequential damages in connection with or arising out of the use of the information or programs contained herein.

Published by: The Project Management Excellence Center, Inc.

Email: info@pmexam.com

ISBN 0-9787468-5-6 (paperback)

Manufactured in the United States of America

10 9 8 7 6 5 4 3 2 1

Table of Contents

Project Integration Management

The Project Integration Management section on the PMP® certification exam addresses critical project management functions that ensure coordination of the various elements of the project. As the PMBOK® Guide explains the processes in integration management are primarily integrative. Project integration management involves making trade-offs among competing objectives in order to meet or exceed stakeholder needs and expectations and addresses develop project charter, develop preliminary project scope statement, develop project management plan, direct and manage project execution, monitor and control project work, integrated change control and close project. These seven processes not only interact with each other but also interact with processes in the other eight knowledge areas. Noting PMI's view that integration occurs in other areas also is important. For example, project scope and product scope need to be integrated; project work needs to be integrated with the other work of the ongoing organization, and deliverables from various technical specialties need integration.

The Project Integration Management questions are straightforward. In the past, most people find them to be easy. Nevertheless, because they cover so much material, you do need to study them carefully to become familiar with PMI's terminology and perspectives. PMBOK® Guide Figure 4.1 provides an overview of the structure of Project Integration Management.

The Project Integration knowledge area is concerned with coordinating all aspects of the project and is highly interactive. Project planning, project execution, and change control occur throughout the project and are repeated continuously while working on the project. Project planning and execution involve weighing the objectives of the project against alternatives to bring the project to a successful completion. Change control impacts the project plan, which, in turn, impacts execution, so you can see that these three processes are very tightly linked. The processes in this area also interact with other processes in the remaining knowledge areas.

Project Integration Management - Questions

1. During project integration activities, a project sponsor's role can best be described as doing which one of the following?

   (A) Deflecting change requests for the project manager.
   (B) Showing management the project progress and status reports.
   (C) Acting as a sounding board for the project stakeholders.
   (D) Helping the project manager and stakeholders to resolve any issues as soon as possible.

2. You remember from your readings that the controlling process is necessary in project management to ensure planned actions are executed and measured for progress. The controlling process for the schedule will typically focus on which of the following?

   (A) Activities that start earlier than planned
   (B) Activities that vary on the plan, either early or late
   (C) Activities that never start
   (D) Activities that start later than planned

3. Where is the bulk of the project budget spent?

   (A) Labor and materials
   (B) Project plan execution
   (C) Scope management
   (D) Production

4. All of the following are true about change requests except:

    (A) They always require additional funding.
    (B) They can be requested by a stakeholder.
    (C) They can be written or verbal.
    (D) They happen while the project work is being done.

5. All of the following statements regarding configuration management is true except:

    (A) Configuration management is used to report the change and its implementation status.
    (B) Configuration management is used to identify the functional and physical characteristics of the product.
    (C) Configuration management defines the level of authority needed to approve changes.
    (D) Configuration management is used to audit the changes to verify conformance to requirements.

6. Your organization, a software development firm, has more project opportunities to pursue than resources available to complete them. You are leading a team to establish a project selection and prioritization method. The team is considering different management concerns, including financial return, market share, and public opinion. You told the team the most important of the various criteria for building a project selection model is?

    (A) Capability
    (B) Realism
    (C) Ease of use
    (D) Cost

7. At the end of each project, the project team should prepare a lessons learned summary that focuses on all the following except:

    (A) Warning others of potential problems.
    (B) Sharing best practices with other project teams in the organization.
    (C) Sharing only positive aspects of the project for future replication elsewhere in the organization.
    (D) Suggesting methods to mitigate risks effectively to ensure success.

8. You have recently been hired as a project manager and are implementing a project management methodology for your company based on your former employer. This methodology requires your company to establish a change control board. Which one of the following statements best describes a change control board?

    (A) Recommended for use on large projects
    (B) Recommended for use on projects that span more than 18 months
    (C) Used as required to approve or reject change requests
    (D) Composed of key project leaders

9. A project manager has just been assigned to a project that has been in progress for two months. A team member has requested more time on a task he is working on. The extra time needed will not delay the project, and the customer has emphasized the importance of completing the project on schedule. Who is responsible for approving this request?

    (A) Senior management
    (B) Functional manager
    (C) Project manager
    (D) The customer

10. As a result of a recent customer meeting, the customer requests a change in design that will affect the production schedules. The project manager should do which of the following?

(A) Do nothing
(B) Update resume
(C) Help the team to identify alternative schedules
(D) Provide much closer supervision

11. Earned Value Management (EVM) is used during the:

(A) Controlling processes
(B) Executing processes
(C) Closing processes
(D) Entire project

12. According to PMI® what are the outcomes of the activities performed to accomplish the project.

(A) Performance reports
(B) Change request
(C) Additional planning
(D) Work results

13. Progressive elaboration is a attribute of projects that integrate the concepts of temporary and unique. In project plan development, progressive elaboration also is important in terms of which of the following?

(A) Work breakdown structure
(B) Organizational policy development
(C) Assumptions
(D) Constraints

14. What is the difference between a project baseline and a project plan?

(A) Project plans and baselines do not change-they are amended.
(B) Baselines are control tools; project plans are execution tools.
(C) Project plans change as needed; baselines are snapshots of the project plan.
(D) Project plans change as needed, baselines change only at milestones.

15. You are the project manager for your organization. Management would like you to use a tool that can help you plan, schedule, monitor, and report your findings on your project. This tool is which one of the following?

(A) Earned Value Management (EVM)
(B) Project Management Information System (PMIS)
(C) Project team knowledge and skill set
(D) Status Review Meetings

16. The scope statement that is created in the develop preliminary project scope statement process should include which of the following:

(A) Project and project objectives
(B) Project boundaries
(C) Product assumptions
(D) All of the above

17. You are a member of your company's project office. The company is running many concurrent projects; most of them share a resource pool. Understanding how resources are utilized across projects is seen as being essential to cost effectiveness and profitability. You recently received an inquiry to assess the benefits of using project management software to manage the company's project portfolio. Which of the following is true?

(A) Supporting project portfolio management is not the project office's business.
(B) Evaluating project management software is not the project office's business.
(C) Project management software has the capability to help organize resource pools.
(D) Project management software will dramatically simplify the task of leveling resources across projects with different project management teams.

18. Your company president has asked you to implement a system to document what procedures are used to apply technical/administrative direction to identify control and record any changes to product characteristics. Which of the following methods would you use?

(A) Scope Change Control
(B) Schedule Change Control
(C) Contract Administration
(D) Configuration Management

19. A project management plan is:

(A) A formal, approved document used to guide both project execution and project control.
(B) A document issued by senior management that provides the project manager with the authority to apply organizational resources to project activities.
(C) A narrative description of products or services to be supplied.
(D) A document describing the organizational breakdown structure of the company.

20. Because you are the project manager on a sensitive project your project sponsor wants you to prepare a Monte Carlo analysis of your project's schedule risk. This requirement is part of your organizations

(A) Project execution methodology
(B) Project justification management plan
(C) Project design execution
(D) Project planning methodology

21. Your company president has asked you to implement a system to document what procedures are used to apply technical/administrative direction to identify control and record any changes to product characteristics. Which of the following methods would you use?

(A) Schedule Change Control
(B) Scope Change Control
(C) Configuration Management
(D) Contract Administration

22. Integrated change control requires all of the following except?

(A) Ensuring that changes to the product scope are reflected in the project scope
(B) Maintaining the integrity of the baseline
(C) Making process adjustments as a result of deficiencies
(D) Coordinating changes across knowledge areas

23. Integrated change control is concerned with all of the following except:

(A) Influencing factors that create change to ensure that changes are beneficial.
(B) Managing changes as they occur.
(C) Determining that a change has occurred.
(D) Creating change requests.

24. All of the following are inputs to the close project process except?

(A) Deliverables
(B) Project management methodology
(C) Project management plan
(D) Contract documentation

25. The project sponsor's role during integration activities is which of the following?

(A) Pressure the team to finish early
(B) Provide the project manager with formal authority over the line managers during conflict resolution
(C) Help clarify outstanding issues as quickly as possible
(D) Keep the project visible to the corporate board

26. A project management plan best described as which of the following?

(A) A document issued by senior management that provides the project manager with the authority to apply organizational resources to project activities.
(B) A formal, approved document used to guide both project execution and project control.
(C) A document describing the organizational breakdown structure of the company.
(D) A narrative description of products or services to be supplied.

27. The project manager has just received a change from the customer that does not affect project time and is easy to complete. What should the project manager do first?

(A) Make the change happen as soon as possible.
(B) Contact the project sponsor for permission.
(C) Go to the change control board.
(D) Evaluate the other components of the triple constraint.

28. One of the more important tasks of project managers can have is to identify the goals of each project. One approach that can help managers set up and achieve those goals is management by objectives (MBO). MBO specifically addresses all the following except?

(A) Evaluating whether project objectives have been achieved during review meetings
(B) Analyzing and reducing risk to determine how best to deal with it when it occurs
(C) Promoting participation and team building on the project
(D) Establishing realistic objectives

29. Who should contribute to the development of the project plan?

(A) Project manager
(B) Entire project team including project manager
(C) Senior management
(D) Development team

30. The customer has decided that he wants blue walls instead of gray. You have not painted the walls yet. What should you do?

        (A) Change the scope document to reflect the change
        (B) Document the change order and buy blue paint
        (C) See if the contract allows for a surcharge for changes
        (D) Update the schedule to reflect the change

31. The project plan provides what in regard to project changes?

        (A) A guide to all future project decisions
        (B) A methodology to approve or decline CCB changes
        (C) A fluid document that may be updated as needed based on the CCB
        (D) A vision of the project deliverables

32. You are managing a large project with 20 stakeholders in three continents. Sixteen different contractors are involved and all their work must be coordinated. With a project this size in scope you realize that you must devote a lot of attention to effective integrated change control. This means you are concerned primarily with

        (A) Establishing a change control board that oversees the overall project changes
        (B) Influencing factors that cause change, determining that change has occurred, and managing actual changes as they occur
        (C) Integrating deliverables from different functional specialties on the project
        (D) Maintaining baseline integrity, integrating product and project scope, and coordinating change across knowledge areas

33. You are managing a large project with 20 stakeholders in three continents. Sixteen different contractors are involved and all their work must be coordinated. With a project this size in scope you realize that you must devote a lot of attention to effective integrated change control. This means you are concerned primarily with:

        (A) Establishing a change control board that oversees the overall project changes.
        (B) Integrating deliverables from different functional specialties on the project.
        (C) Maintaining baseline integrity, integrating product and project scope, and coordinating change across knowledge areas.
        (D) Influencing factors that cause change, determining that change has occurred, and managing actual changes as they occur.

34. You are the project manager for your company project. This project is to design and implement a new application that will connect to a database server. Management of your company has requested that you create a method to document technical direction on the project and to document any changes or enhancements to the technical attributes of the project deliverable. Which one of the following would satisfy management's request?

        (A) Scope Control
        (B) Change Management Plan
        (C) Configuration management
        (D) Integrated Change Control

35. Great news, you have just been hired as a project manager and the new project is having problems. You come to realize that you are the project manager for a construction project with a team of highly skilled staff members. Many on the team like to do tasks when they want to, regardless of the order in which these tasks appear in a project schedule. You are concerned that this informal method of task completion will be detrimental to the project. With that in mind you call a team meeting to discuss which procedures to implement to ensure that work is done at the right time and in the right sequence. At this meeting, you put into place a

     (A) Work authorization system
     (B) Resource management plan
     (C) Resource authorization matrix
     (D) Change control system

36. Your project is struggling and you have just been assigned as the replacement project manager on a project where you will need to be both a leader and a manager. You're not sure how to proceed but realize from past project mistakes that leadership without management or management without leadership will produce poor results. Which one of the following key responsibilities represents project leadership?

     (A) Establishing direction, aligning people, and motivating/inspiring others on the team
     (B) Using positive reinforcement to get things done
     (C) Delegating power to motivate others into getting work done
     (D) Using all types of power as motivational tools

37. A project's culture can affect its success significantly during several life cycle phases. As manager of an international project with a team of people representing diverse cultures, you should create an environment that maximizes team efforts as the project progresses. Although most people view the values of other cultures in terms of their own culture, a project's cultural emphasis will change during different life cycle phases. During the closing project phase, the emphasis basically is:

     (A) Competitive
     (B) Cooperative
     (C) Focused on information transfer
     (D) Participative

38. You are trying to implement a project management methodology for your company based on upon recommendations from the PMBOK. This methodology recommends that your company establish a change control board. Based on that recommendation which one of the following statements best describes a change control board?

     (A) Recommended for use on large projects lasting more than 18 months
     (B) Used as required to approve or reject change requests
     (C) Managed by the project manager
     (D) Composed of key stakeholders

39. Your project is struggling and you have just been assigned as the replacement project manager on a project where you will need to be both a leader and a manager. You're not sure how to proceed but realize from past project mistakes that leadership without management or management without leadership will produce poor results. Which one of the following key responsibilities represents project leadership?

     (A) Using positive reinforcement to get things done
     (B) Establishing direction, aligning people, and motivating/inspiring others on the team
     (C) Using all types of power as motivational tools
     (D) Delegating power to motivate others into getting work done

40. Which of the following statements is true regarding scoring models, benefit contribution and economic models?

    (A) These are inputs to the project charter.
    (B) These are tools used when applying mathematical models.
    (C) These are benefit measurement methods.
    (D) These are constrained optimization methods.

41. You have just informed your project team that each team member will be contributing to the Lessons Learned documentation. Your team does not understand this approach and wants to know what the documentation will be used for. Which one of the following best describes the purpose of the Lessons Learned documentation?

    (A) Offers proof of concept for management.
    (B) Offers historical information for future projects.
    (C) Offers evidence of project progression as reported by the project team.
    (D) Offers input to team member evaluations at the project conclusion.

42. Out of the options below which one is a document or collection of documents that should be expected to change over time as more information becomes available about the project?

    (A) Additional work authorizations
    (B) Project monitoring plan
    (C) Change request
    (D) Project management plan

43. You have just been assigned as a project manager on a new project and have called your first team meeting. You are explaining the way you will run the project. You have just informed your team about lessons learned and told them that they are used for which of the following?

    (A) As reference for any future legal procedures
    (B) As an input to the staff management plan
    (C) As an input to individual evaluation appraisals
    (D) Provide historical information for upcoming projects

44. You have just finished reading the PMBOK and the PMP® Exam Guide and you now know that lessons learned are used for which of the following?

    (A) Historical information for upcoming projects
    (B) As reference for any future legal procedures
    (C) Input to individual evaluation appraisals
    (D) An input to the staff management plan

45. Your current project is moving slowly ahead and you have decided establish several change control boards for your project. Now your project team and certain members of management have become upset with you over the bureaucracy of boards. To help smooth things out you point out that some changes can be approved automatically without any involvement from the board. An example of such a change is one that is

    (A) Recommended by the project team
    (B) Made mandatory by a new government regulation
    (C) The result of an emergency
    (D) Recommended by the project sponsor

46. Configuration management is best described as?

    (A) The creation of the work breakdown structure
    (B) A mechanism to track budget and schedule variances
    (C) The set of procedures developed to assure that project design criteria are met
    (D) Used to ensure that the description of the product is correct and complete

47. You are preparing a project management plan. You have identified a key subject matter expert. Her experience will be invaluable to project success. But you do not know when she will be available to support the project. Therefore, you have assumed a start date. This shows that assumptions generally involve some risk because they:

    (A) Are based on lessons learned.
    (B) May not have any historical precedent.
    (C) Involve factors that limit the project management team's options.
    (D) Involve factors that are considered true, real, or certain.

48. You have just been hired as a project manager for a construction company that has few project management policies and procedures in place. Your twelve years experience has taught you that some controls are required. You would like to establish a change control system for your company, but must convince other management officials to use it. To be effective, the change control system must include which of the following?

    (A) Procedures that define how project documents should/will be changed
    (B) Specific change requests and who is responsible for making those changes
    (C) Work breakdown structure updates
    (D) A description of the functional characteristics of a component

49. You are the project manager for a company project. You and your project team are preparing the final project plan. Of the following, which one is a project plan development constraint you and your team must consider?

    (A) Project plans from similar projects.
    (B) The budget as assigned by management.
    (C) Interviews with Subject Matter Experts (SMEs) who have experience with the project work in your project plan.
    (D) Project plans from similar projects that have failed.

50. As project manager and you recently submitted a product plan which was approved by all stakeholders. Work is proceeding on the project according to schedule. Everyone seems pleased with the progress to date. You have just learned that the client needs to make a major scope change to comply with a new regulatory requirement going into effect. To ensure that this change is incorporated into the project plan, you should?

    (A) Prepare a change request
    (B) Immediately inform all stakeholders and wait for a go ahead
    (C) Call a meeting of the change control board
    (D) Update the work breakdown structure

51. According to the PMBOK Guide, what is the formal procedure for approving project work?

    (A) Organizational procedures
    (B) Work authorization system
    (C) Organizational policies
    (D) Status review

52. Which one of the following represents the vast majority of a project's budget?

    (A) Project plan execution
    (B) Project planning
    (C) Cost of goods and services
    (D) Labor

53. Integrated change control requires all of the following except:

    (A) Ensuring that changes to the product scope are reflected in the project scope.
    (B) Coordinating changes across knowledge areas.
    (C) Maintaining the integrity of the performance measurement baselines.
    (D) Auditing deliverables to verify conformance to requirements.

54. You are the project manager responsible for constructing a new 500-unit apartment building in downtown Los Angeles. As part of the construction project, you are planning to outsource a particular deliverable on your project. You have created a document that described the product and services required in detail and have included the necessary reporting requirements. Which of the following best describes the document you have just prepared?

    (A) Procurement management plan
    (B) Request for Quotation
    (C) Request for Proposal
    (D) Statement of Work

55. A project plan best described as which of the following?

    (A) A document issued by senior management that provides the project manager with the authority to apply organizational resources to project activities.
    (B) A document describing the organizational breakdown structure of the company.
    (C) A narrative description of products or services to be supplied.
    (D) A formal, approved document used to guide both project execution and project control.

56. A narrative description of products or services to be supplied under contract is called:

    (A) the project plan.
    (B) a statement of work.
    (C) an exception report.
    (D) Pareto report.

57. Which one of the following is not beneficial to the project manager during the project plan development process?

    (A) Project Management Information System (PMIS)
    (B) Gantt Charts
    (C) Stakeholder knowledge
    (D) Earned Value Management (EVM)

58. Project team members obtain new skills and increase proficiency with existing skills during the course of their project work. When this happens, it is important to update employee skills in the staff pool database. This should be done in which of the following processes?

    (A) Communications planning
    (B) Resource planning
    (C) Close project
    (D) Team development

59. Configuration management is a process for applying technical and administrative direction and surveillance of the project implementation. Which activity is not included in configuration management?

    (A) Automatic change request approvals
    (B) Identification of the functional and physical attributes of the project deliverables
    (C) Controlling changes to the project deliverables
    (D) Scope verification

60. The primary purpose of your project plan is:

    (A) To define the work needed in each phase of the project life cycle.
    (B) To define the work to be completed to reach the project end date.
    (C) To provide accurate communication for the project team, project sponsor, and stakeholders.
    (D) To prevent any changes to the scope.

61. You are the project manager for your organization. When it comes to Integrated Change Control, you must ensure which one of the following is present?

    (A) Approval of the change from the project team
    (B) Supporting detail for the change exists
    (C) Risk assessment for each proposed change
    (D) Approval of the change from an SME

62. You have just been hired as a project manger and have been given your first project. You are not sure where to start on project planning so you decided to rely on which of the following to help you plan your project?

    (A) Historical information
    (B) Staff management plan
    (C) Resource assignment matrix
    (D) Project management training

63. You are a project manager on a project that is developing a next-generation search engine for the Internet. Instead of using simple word or link analysis methods, your search engine will use a sophisticated algorithm based on latent semantic indexing. You have reviewed the scope statement for this project, and concluded that the scope statement is very ambiguous and poorly written. Which of the following statements are true based on this information?

    (A) A direct result of a poorly written scope statement is difficulty in assessing schedule estimates.
    (B) A direct result of a poorly written scope statement is difficulty in performing risk assessments.
    (C) A direct result of a poorly written scope statement is difficulty in assessing cost estimates.
    (D) A direct result of a poorly written scope statement is difficulty in assessing future project decisions.

64. You recently established a change control board that is responsible for approving, deferring, or rejecting proposed changes to your avionics project. When you set up the board, you established specific procedures to govern its operation. The procedures require all approved changes to be reflected in which of the following:

    (A) Work breakdown structure
    (B) Performance measurement baseline
    (C) Project management plan
    (D) Quality assurance plan

65. The risk management plan is a major component of the?

    (A) Communications plan
    (B) Project plan
    (C) Contingency plan
    (D) Procurement plan

66. You believe that a rolling wave type of planning is appropriate because your highway project is going to last for seven years. It provides information about the work to be done

    (A) Throughout all major project phases
    (B) For successful completion of the current project phase
    (C) For successful completion of the current project phase and subsequent project phases
    (D) For the upcoming project phases

67. As project manager you have decided to establish a change control board that will be responsible for approving or rejecting proposed changes to your project. When you set up the board, you established specific procedures that will hopefully govern its operation. The procedures require all approved changes to be reflected in the?

    (A) Work breakdown structure
    (B) Project management plan
    (C) Quality assurance plan
    (D) Scope change baseline

68. Of the following, which one is an input to project plan development?

    (A) Project planning methodology
    (B) Business needs
    (C) Earned Value Management (EVM)
    (D) Assumptions

69. Project planning is defined in the PMBOK as:

    (A) A structured approach used to guide a project team during development of a project plan
    (B) General management skills
    (C) Organizational policies
    (D) Using planning techniques to achieve a desired end goal

70. There are several tools and techniques that are useful with integrated change control. Which of the following is used to assess whether variances from the plan require corrective action?

    (A) A project management information system (PMIS)
    (B) Earned value management
    (C) Project review meetings with key stakeholders
    (D) A configuration information system (CIS)

71. You are trying to explain to your project team how PMI® defines the project planning methodology. You tell them it is defined as:

    (A) General project management skills
    (B) Using planning techniques to achieve a desired end goal
    (C) A structured approach used to guide a project team during development of a project plan
    (D) Organizational management policies

72. Your project is moving ahead of schedule. Management elects to incorporate additional quality testing into the project to improve the quality and acceptability of the project deliverable. This is an example of which one of the following?

    (A) Scope Creep
    (B) Change Control
    (C) Quality Assurance
    (D) Integrated Change Control

73. You have just been hired as a project manager and have been given your first assignment. You discover that part of the scope is not defined and you decide to?

    (A) Immediately inform management of the error
    (B) Do what you can to get the scope work defined
    (C) Continue with project and update the work breakdown structure
    (D) Wait until that part of development is needed

74. According to PMI configuration management includes procedures for applying technical and administrative direction and surveillance. Which one of the following tasks is performed in configuration management?

    (A) Corrective action
    (B) Preparing the work authorization system
    (C) Preventive action
    (D) Control any changes to such characteristics

75. You have just established a project office and your first order of business was to issue a project management methodology that emphasizes the importance of integrated change control. You state in your report that the change requests can occur in all the following forms except?

    (A) Legally mandated by government regulations
    (B) Oral or written, although written was preferred
    (C) Externally or internally initiated
    (D) Formal or informal

76. You are a project manager for your organization. Management has asked you to help them determine which projects should be selected for implementation. In a project selection model, the most important factor is which one of the following?

    (A) Type of constraints
    (B) Business needs
    (C) Schedule
    (D) Budget

77. You realize as a project manager that one of the more important tasks a project managers can have is to identify the goals of each project. One approach that can help managers set up and achieve those goals is management by objectives (MBO). Which of the following specifically addresses MBO?

    (A) Evaluating project objectives to make sure they are in line with the company rather than the client
    (B) Trying to stop team building so the team can refocus on the project objectives
    (C) Analyzing and reducing risk to determine how best to deal with it when it occurs
    (D) Establishing realistic objectives

78. Which one of the following is a formal document to manage and control project execution?

(A) Project Management Plan
(B) Work Breakdown Structure
(C) Work Authorization System
(D) Organizational Management Plan

79. As project manager and you recently submitted a product plan which was approved by all stakeholders. Work is proceeding on the project according to schedule. Everyone seems pleased with the progress to date. You have just learned that the client needs to make a major scope change to comply with a new regulatory requirement going into effect. To ensure that this change is incorporated into the project plan, you should:

(A) call a meeting of the change control board.
(B) update the work breakdown structure.
(C) prepare a change request.
(D) immediately inform all stakeholders and wait for a go ahead.

80. When an organization chooses a project selection model, the most important criteria is?

(A) Cost
(B) Capability
(C) Realism
(D) Ease of use

81. The PMBOK™ clearly states that change control requests:

(A) Provide the baseline against which changes will be controlled
(B) Must be relayed in writing
(C) Are inputs to integrated change control
(D) Are always initiated externally

82. The project plan provides a baseline for several things. Which one of the following does the project plan not provide a baseline for?

(A) Cost
(B) Scope
(C) Control
(D) Schedule

83. One of the requirements of project management in your organization is to describe your project management approach and methodology in the project plan. You can best accomplish this requirement through which one of the following actions?

(A) Establishing a project office
(B) Establishing a program office
(C) Compiling the management plans from each of the knowledge areas
(D) Creating a Project Management Information System (PMIS) and documenting its inputs, tools and techniques, and outputs

84. The risk management plan is a major component of the?

(A) Communications plan
(B) Project management plan
(C) Contingency plan
(D) Procurement plan

85. Status review meetings are best defined by which of the following?

    (A) Regularly scheduled meetings held to exchange information about the project
    (B) Held to update departmental staff of project status
    (C) Held to update departmental staff of project status
    (D) Held to notify stakeholders of critical information

86. You have just been hired as a project manager and you want to review your organization's informal and formal policies. A team member has suggested a list items to possible review. Four items are on the list. Which one of the following is not an organizational policy whose effects on the project must be considered?

    (A) Continuous improvement targets
    (B) Resource assignment matrix
    (C) Employee performance reviews
    (D) Time reporting

87. The role of the change control board is to:

    (A) represent top management interests in initiating innovation.
    (B) issue change requests.
    (C) identify new areas of project work.
    (D) review the impact of change requests on project costs, schedule, and specifications.

88. Out of the list below what is an applicable restriction that will affect project performance?

    (A) An organizational policy
    (B) A Performance guideline
    (C) A constraint
    (D) Some additional planning requirements

89. Which of the following best describes a change control board?

    (A) An informal or formal group of team members responsible for changes to a project.
    (B) A formally constituted group of stakeholders responsible for approving or rejecting changes to the project baseline.
    (C) An informal group which has oversight of project implementation.
    (D) A formally constituted group of stakeholders responsible for ensuring that only a minimal amount of changes occur on the project.

90. Your company currently has no project management policies or procedures in place and you have decided as project manager to draft up some polices to be set in place. Your ten years experience has taught you that some controls are required. You would like to establish a change control system for your company, but must convince other management officials to use it. If management does approve your polices which if the following is to be included for the change control system to effective?

    (A) Specific change requests and who is responsible for making those changes
    (B) Procedures that define how project documents should/will be changed
    (C) A description of the functional characteristics of a component
    (D) Updated project management information system (PMIS)

91. According to PMI® and the PMBOK Guide the project management plan is used to?

(A) Provide project inputs, tools and techniques, and outputs
(B) Guide project execution, document project planning assumptions, and facilitate communication among stakeholders
(C) Provide general management, product knowledge, and project management information
(D) Create organized policies using stakeholder's skills and knowledge

92. At the outset of a project you should define the processes necessary to account for change. Which of the following is not a standard inclusion in a change control system?

(A) Performance reports.
(B) Procedures to handle changes that may be approved without prior review.
(C) How to handle changes in emergencies.
(D) The responsibilities of the change control board.

93. Which of the following can best help a project manager during project execution?

(A) Change control boards
(B) Stakeholder analysis
(C) Scope verification
(D) Project Management Information System (PMIS)

94. Your company operates a large chemical processing plant, has been convicted of illegally dumping toxic substances into a local town lake causing most fish to die. The court has mandated that the required cleanup activities be completed by within 45 days. Such a constraint is an example of:

(A) A major milestone.
(B) A key event.
(C) An external dependency.
(D) An imposed date.

95. Another project manager in your organization is going around talking about how the project charter is a collection of formal, documented procedures that defines how project performance will be monitored and evaluated. You realize he is wrong from your own work experience. You want to correct him and tell him which of the following is actually what he should be referring to?

(A) Lessons learned
(B) Configuration management
(C) Change control system
(D) Concurrent engineering

96. Baseline variances, a documented plan to management variances, and a proven methodology to offer corrective actions to the project plan are all part of which process?

(A) Change Control System
(B) Integrated Change Control
(C) Scope Change Control
(D) Change management

97. Which set of the following tools is part of the project plan execution?

(A) General management skills, status review meetings, Earned Value Management (EVM)
(B) Project Management Information System (PMIS), Work Breakdown Structure (WBS), Earned Value Management (EVM)
(C) General management skills, status review meetings, Earned Value Management (EVM)
(D) General management skills, status review meetings, Work Authorization Systems

98. Your project has a budget of $2 million for the first 3 years, and $3 million for the fourth year. Most of the project budget will be spent during?

(A) Project plan development
(B) Scope change control
(C) Project plan execution
(D) Performance measurement baseline

99. As project manager you are creating a project plan and you and a co-worker are discussing what should be done to limit changes to the project. You both decide that all of the following are acceptable ways by which project documents may be changed except?

(A) Written scope detail changes
(B) Tracking systems
(C) Approval from authorized management
(D) Oral communication from key stakeholders

100. On any project, the lessons learned document is created by which one of the following?

(A) Project Sponsor
(B) Stakeholders
(C) Project Team
(D) Customers

Sample Answer Sheet

	T F															

1 (A)(B)(C)(D)(E)   26 (A)(B)(C)(D)(E)   51 (A)(B)(C)(D)(E)   76 (A)(B)(C)(D)(E)

2 (A)(B)(C)(D)(E)   27 (A)(B)(C)(D)(E)   52 (A)(B)(C)(D)(E)   77 (A)(B)(C)(D)(E)

3 (A)(B)(C)(D)(E)   28 (A)(B)(C)(D)(E)   53 (A)(B)(C)(D)(E)   78 (A)(B)(C)(D)(E)

4 (A)(B)(C)(D)(E)   29 (A)(B)(C)(D)(E)   54 (A)(B)(C)(D)(E)   79 (A)(B)(C)(D)(E)

5 (A)(B)(C)(D)(E)   30 (A)(B)(C)(D)(E)   55 (A)(B)(C)(D)(E)   80 (A)(B)(C)(D)(E)

6 (A)(B)(C)(D)(E)   31 (A)(B)(C)(D)(E)   56 (A)(B)(C)(D)(E)   81 (A)(B)(C)(D)(E)

7 (A)(B)(C)(D)(E)   32 (A)(B)(C)(D)(E)   57 (A)(B)(C)(D)(E)   82 (A)(B)(C)(D)(E)

8 (A)(B)(C)(D)(E)   33 (A)(B)(C)(D)(E)   58 (A)(B)(C)(D)(E)   83 (A)(B)(C)(D)(E)

9 (A)(B)(C)(D)(E)   34 (A)(B)(C)(D)(E)   59 (A)(B)(C)(D)(E)   84 (A)(B)(C)(D)(E)

10 (A)(B)(C)(D)(E)   35 (A)(B)(C)(D)(E)   60 (A)(B)(C)(D)(E)   85 (A)(B)(C)(D)(E)

11 (A)(B)(C)(D)(E)   36 (A)(B)(C)(D)(E)   61 (A)(B)(C)(D)(E)   86 (A)(B)(C)(D)(E)

12 (A)(B)(C)(D)(E)   37 (A)(B)(C)(D)(E)   62 (A)(B)(C)(D)(E)   87 (A)(B)(C)(D)(E)

13 (A)(B)(C)(D)(E)   38 (A)(B)(C)(D)(E)   63 (A)(B)(C)(D)(E)   88 (A)(B)(C)(D)(E)

14 (A)(B)(C)(D)(E)   39 (A)(B)(C)(D)(E)   64 (A)(B)(C)(D)(E)   89 (A)(B)(C)(D)(E)

15 (A)(B)(C)(D)(E)   40 (A)(B)(C)(D)(E)   65 (A)(B)(C)(D)(E)   90 (A)(B)(C)(D)(E)

16 (A)(B)(C)(D)(E)   41 (A)(B)(C)(D)(E)   66 (A)(B)(C)(D)(E)   91 (A)(B)(C)(D)(E)

17 (A)(B)(C)(D)(E)   42 (A)(B)(C)(D)(E)   67 (A)(B)(C)(D)(E)   92 (A)(B)(C)(D)(E)

18 (A)(B)(C)(D)(E)   43 (A)(B)(C)(D)(E)   68 (A)(B)(C)(D)(E)   93 (A)(B)(C)(D)(E)

19 (A)(B)(C)(D)(E)   44 (A)(B)(C)(D)(E)   69 (A)(B)(C)(D)(E)   94 (A)(B)(C)(D)(E)

20 (A)(B)(C)(D)(E)   45 (A)(B)(C)(D)(E)   70 (A)(B)(C)(D)(E)   95 (A)(B)(C)(D)(E)

21 (A)(B)(C)(D)(E)   46 (A)(B)(C)(D)(E)   71 (A)(B)(C)(D)(E)   96 (A)(B)(C)(D)(E)

22 (A)(B)(C)(D)(E)   47 (A)(B)(C)(D)(E)   72 (A)(B)(C)(D)(E)   97 (A)(B)(C)(D)(E)

23 (A)(B)(C)(D)(E)   48 (A)(B)(C)(D)(E)   73 (A)(B)(C)(D)(E)   98 (A)(B)(C)(D)(E)

24 (A)(B)(C)(D)(E)   49 (A)(B)(C)(D)(E)   74 (A)(B)(C)(D)(E)   99 (A)(B)(C)(D)(E)

25 (A)(B)(C)(D)(E)   50 (A)(B)(C)(D)(E)   75 (A)(B)(C)(D)(E)   100 (A)(B)(C)(D)(E)

Project Integration Management - Answers

1. (D) Helping the project manager and stakeholders to resolve any issues as soon as possible. The project sponsor can help the project manager and the stakeholders resolve issues during project integration management.

2. (B) Activities that vary on the plan, either early or late. A project management function that involves comparing actual performance with planned performance and taking corrective action (or directing or motivating others to do so) to yield the desired outcome when significant differences exist.

3. (B) Project plan execution. The vast majority of the project's budget will be expended in performing the Executing Process Group processes.

4. (A) They always require additional funding. Change requests do not always require more money. Approved changes may require more funds, but not always. The change request may be denied, so no additional funds are needed for the project.

5. (C) Configuration management defines the level of authority needed to approve changes. Configuration management is used to identify and document the functional and physical characteristics of the product / project. Configuration management controls and manages any changes to such characteristics, including reporting the change and its status and auditing the change to verify conformance to requirements.

6. (B) Realism. Project selection methods are used to determine which project the organization will select. These methods generally fall into one of two broad categories: (1) benefit measurement methods that are comparative approaches, scoring models, benefit contribution, or economic models and (2) mathematical models that use linear, nonlinear, dynamic, integer, or multiobjective programming algorithms.

7. (C) Sharing only positive aspects of the project for future replication elsewhere in the organization. The lessons learned summary should document the major positive and negative aspects of the project so that future projects can benefit from the team's successes and failures, by replicating the good things about the project and avoiding the mistakes.

8. (C) Used as required to approve or reject change requests. Change Control Board ("CCB") - A group of people responsible for providing a central control mechanism to ensure that every change request is properly considered, authorized and coordinated.

9. (D) The customer. Customer - The person or group that is/are the recipient(s) of a product or service, the direct beneficiary(ies) of a project's product or service. The people for whom the project is being undertaken.

10. (C) Help the team to identify alternative schedules. Change control system - defines procedures by which the project scope may be changed. Includes the paperwork, tracking systems, and approval levels necessary for authorizing changes. Should be integrated with the Integrated Change Control Process and any system(s) in place to control product scope. Must comply with all relevant contractual obligations.

11. (D) Entire project. Earned Value Management (EVM) is used throughout the project processes. Earned Value Management is a management methodology for integrating scope, schedule, and resources, and for objectively measuring project performance and progress. Performance is measured by determining the budgeted cost of work performed (i.e., earned value) and comparing it to the actual cost of work performed (i.e., actual cost). Progress is measured by comparing the earned value to the planned value.

12. (D) Work results. Work results are outcomes of the activities performed to accomplish the project.

13. (C) Assumptions. Progressive Elaboration. Continuously improving and detailing a plan as more detailed and specific information and more accurate estimates become available as the project progresses, and thereby producing more accurate and complete plans that result from the successive iterations of the planning process.

14. (B) Baselines are control tools; project plans are execution tools. A project baseline serves as a control tool. Project plan execution and work results are measured against the project baselines.

15. (B) Project Management Information System (PMIS. An information system consisting of the tools and techniques used to gather, integrate, and disseminate the outputs of project management processes. It is used to support all aspects of the project from initiating through closing, and can include both manual and automated systems.

16. (D) All of the above. The project scope statement is the definition of the project—what needs to be accomplished. The Develop Preliminary Project Scope Statement process addresses and documents the characteristics and boundaries of the project and its associated products and services, as well as the methods of acceptance and scope control. A project scope statement includes: Project and product objectives; Product or service requirements and characteristics; Product acceptance criteria; Project boundaries; Project requirements and deliverables; Project constraints; Project assumptions; Initial project organization; Initial defined risks; Schedule milestones; Initial WBS; Order of magnitude cost estimate and the Project configuration management requirements.

17. (C) Project management software has the capability to help organize resource pools. Project Management Software. A class of computer software applications specifically designed to aid the project management team with planning, monitoring, and controlling the project, including: cost estimating, scheduling, communications, collaboration, configuration management, document control, records management, and risk analysis.

18. (D) Configuration Management. Configuration Management System - A subsystem of the overall project management system. It is a collection of formal documented procedures used to apply technical and administrative direction and surveillance to: identify and document the functional and physical characteristics of a product, result, service, or component; control any changes to such characteristics; record and report each change and its implementation status; and support the audit of the products, results, or components to verify conformance to requirements. It includes the documentation, tracking systems, and defined approval levels necessary for authorizing and controlling changes. In most application areas, the configuration management system includes the change control system.

19. (A) A formal, approved document used to guide both project execution and project control. The Project Management Plan is a formal, approved document that defines how the projected is executed, monitored and controlled. It may be summary or detailed and may be composed of one or more subsidiary management plans and other planning documents.

20. (D) Project planning methodology. The identification of the project objectives and the ordered activity necessary to complete the project. The identification of resource types and quantities required to carry out each activity or task.

21. (C) Configuration Management. Configuration Management - Technical and administrative activities concerned with the creation, maintenance and controlled change of configuration throughout the life of the product.

22. (C) Making process adjustments as a result of deficiencies. Integrated Change Control. The process of reviewing all change requests, approving changes and controlling changes to deliverables and organizational process assets.

23. (A) Influencing factors that create change to ensure that changes are beneficial. Integrated Change Control - The process of reviewing all change requests, approving changes and controlling changes to deliverables and organizational process assets.

24. (B) Project management methodology. Inputs to the close project process are: project management plan; contract documentation; enterprise environmental factors; organizational process assets; work performance information; and deliverables.

25. (C) Help clarify outstanding issues as quickly as possible. Sponsor. The person or group that provides the financial resources, in cash or in kind, for the project.

26. (B) A formal, approved document used to guide both project execution and project control. Project Management Plan - a formal, approved document that defines how the projected is executed, monitored and controlled. It may be summary or detailed and may be composed of one or more subsidiary management plans and other planning documents.

27. (D) Evaluate the other components of the triple constraint. Triple Constraint - The term used to describe the three key project objectives that must be simultaneously accomplished, namely, the performance specification, the time schedule, and the monetary budget.

28. (B) Analyzing and reducing risk to determine how best to deal with it when it occurs. Management By Objectives - A system of managerial leadership that defines individual managerial responsibilities in terms of corporate objectives.

29. (B) Entire project team including project manager. The project plan is developed with the project team, stakeholders, and management. It is the guide to how the project should flow and how the project will be managed, and it reflects the values, priorities, and conditions influencing the project.

30. (B) Document the change order and buy blue paint. Integrated change control is concerned with (a) influencing the factors which create changes to ensure that changes are agreed upon, (b) determining that a change has occurred, and (c) managing the actual changes when and as they occur.

31. (A) A guide to all future project decisions. The project plan serves as a guide to all future project decisions.

32. (B) Influencing factors that cause change, determining that change has occurred, and managing actual changes as they occur. Integrated Change Control. The process of reviewing all change requests, approving changes and controlling changes to deliverables and organizational process assets.

33. (D) Influencing factors that cause change, determining that change has occurred, and managing actual changes as they occur. The process of reviewing all change requests, approving changes and controlling changes to deliverables and organizational process assets.

34. (C) Configuration management. Configuration Management is a subsystem of the overall project management system. It is a collection of formal documented procedures used to apply technical and administrative direction and surveillance to: identify and document the functional and physical characteristics of a product, result, service, or component; control any changes to such characteristics; record and report each change and its implementation status; and support the audit of the products, results, or components to verify conformance to requirements. It includes the documentation, tracking systems, and defined approval levels necessary for authorizing and controlling changes. In most application areas, the configuration management system includes the change control system.

35. (A) Work authorization system. Work Authorization System. A subsystem of the overall project management system. It is a collection of formal documented procedures that defines how project work will be authorized (committed) to ensure that the work is done by the identified organization, at the right time, and in the proper sequence. It includes the steps, documents, tracking system, and defined approval levels needed to issue work authorizations.

36. (A) Establishing direction, aligning people, and motivating/inspiring others on the team. Leadership in the context of a project, e.g. leading with a focus on the project's goals and objectives and the effectiveness and efficiency of the process.

37. (C) Focused on information transfer. Projects wind down during the close project phase, and team members start leaving the project. Project managers must show leadership during this phase and maintain the same efficiency and performance standards as in other phases. The closing phase emphasizes information transfer, and this advances the project management profession.

38. (B) Used as required to approve or reject change requests. Change Control Board - A formally constituted group of stakeholders responsible for approving or rejecting changes to the project baselines.

39. (B) Establishing direction, aligning people, and motivating/inspiring others on the team. Project leadership in the context of a project, e.g. leading with a focus on the project's goals and objectives and the effectiveness and efficiency of the process.

40. (C) These are benefit measurement methods. According to the PMI, there are two categories of project selection methods: constrained optimization methods and benefit measurement methods. Constrained optimization methods are complicated mathematical models "using linear, non-linear, dynamic, integer, and multi-objective programming algorithms", and are often referred to as decision models. On the other hand, benefit measurement methods are "comparative approaches, scoring models, benefit contribution, or economic models."

41. (B) Offers historical information for future projects. Lessons learned is a document that offers historical information. The learning gained from the process of performing the project. Lessons learned may be identified at any point. Also considered a project record, to be included in the lessons learned knowledge base.

42. (D) Project management plan. Project Management Plan. A formal, approved document that defines how the projected is executed, monitored and controlled. It may be summary or detailed and may be composed of one or more subsidiary management plans and other planning documents.

43. (D) Provide historical information for upcoming projects. Lessons Learned - The capture of what went well as well as past errors of judgment resulting in material failures, wrong timing or other mistakes, all for the purposes of improving future performance.

44. (A) Historical information for upcoming projects. Lessons Learned - The capture of what went well as well as past errors of judgment resulting in material failures, wrong timing or other mistakes, all for the purposes of improving future performance.

45. (C) The result of an emergency. Change Control Board ("CCB") - A group of people responsible for providing a central control mechanism to ensure that every change request is properly considered, authorized and coordinated.

46. (D) Used to ensure that the description of the product is correct and complete. Configuration Management System. A subsystem of the overall project management system. It is a collection of formal documented procedures used to apply technical and administrative direction and surveillance to: identify and document the functional and physical characteristics of a product, result, service, or component; control any changes to such characteristics; record and report each change and its implementation status; and support the audit of the products, results, or components to verify conformance to requirements. It includes the documentation, tracking systems, and defined approval levels necessary for authorizing and controlling changes. In most application areas, the configuration management system includes the change control system.

47. (D) Involve factors that are considered true, real, or certain. Assumptions - are factors that, for planning purposes, are considered to be true, real, or certain without proof or demonstration. Assumptions affect all aspects of project planning, and are part of the progressive elaboration of the project. Project teams frequently identify, document, and validate assumptions as part of their planning process. Assumptions generally involve a degree of risk.

48. (A) Procedures that define how project documents should/will be changed. Change Control - The process of implementing procedures which ensure that proposed changes are properly assessed and, if approved, incorporated into the project plan. Uncontrolled changes are one of the most common causes of delay and failure.

49. (B) The budget as assigned by management. If management has assigned the project constraint of a fixed budget, the project manager and the project team must determine how the project can operate within the constraint.

50. (A) Prepare a change request. Change Request. Requests to expand or reduce the project scope, modify policies, processes, plans, or procedures, modify costs or budgets, or revise schedules. Requests for a change can be direct or indirect, externally or internally initiated, and legally or contractually mandated or optional. Only formally documented requested changes are processed and only approved change requests are implemented.

51. (B) Work authorization system. Work Authorization System. A subsystem of the overall project management system. It is a collection of formal documented procedures that defines how project work will be authorized (committed) to ensure that the work is done by the identified organization, at the right time, and in the proper sequence. It includes the steps, documents, tracking system, and defined approval levels needed to issue work authorizations.

52. (A) Project plan execution. The project plan execution represents the majority of the project budget.

53. (D) Auditing deliverables to verify conformance to requirements. According to the PMBOK, Integrated Change Control requires all of the following: (1) maintaining the integrity of the performance measurement baselines; (2) ensuring that changes to the product scope are reflected in the project scope; and (3) coordinating changes across knowledge area.

54. (D) Statement of Work. The statement of work (SOW) is a narrative description of products or services to be supplied by the project. For internal projects, the project initiator or sponsor provides the statement of work based on business needs, product, or service requirements. For external projects, the statement of work can be received from the customer as part of a bid document, for example, request for proposal, request for information, request for bid, or as part of a contract.

55. (D) A formal, approved document used to guide both project execution and project control. Project plan - The project plan is a formal, approved document used to manage project execution.

56. (B) a statement of work. The statement of work (SOW) is a narrative description of products or services to be supplied by the project.

57. (B) Gantt Charts. Gantt charts are excellent tools to measure and predict the project progress, but are not needed during the project plan development process.

58. (C) Close project. The Close Project process involves performing the project closure portion of the project management plan. Two procedures are developed to establish the interactions necessary to perform the closure activities across the entire project or for a project phase: (1) administrative closure procedure and (2) contract closure procedure. Administrative closure procedure - details all the activities, interactions, and related roles and responsibilities of the project team members and other stakeholders involved in executing the administrative closure procedure for the project. Performing the administrative closure process also includes integrated activities needed to collect project records, analyze project success or failure, gather lessons learned, and archive project information for future use by the organization.

59. (A) Automatic change request approvals. Automatic change request approvals are not a part of configuration management.

60. (C) To provide accurate communication for the project team, project sponsor, and stakeholders. A formal, approved document that defines how the projected is executed, monitored and controlled. It may be summary or detailed and may be composed of one or more subsidiary management plans and other planning documents.

61. (B) Supporting detail for the change exists. Integrated Change Control requires detail for implementing the change. Without evidence of the need for the change, there is no reason to implement it.

62. (A) Historical information. Historic Records - Project documentation that can be used to predict trends, analyze feasibility and highlight problem areas/pitfalls on future similar projects.

63. (D) A direct result of a poorly written scope statement is difficulty in assessing future project decisions. The scope statement provides the basis for making future project decisions. A poorly written scope statement will make it difficult to assess future project decisions from the scope statement.

64. (C) Project management plan. Project Management Plan - a formal, approved document that defines how the projected is executed, monitored and controlled. It may be summary or detailed and may be composed of one or more subsidiary management plans and other planning documents. The project management plan must be updated continually to reflect project modifications, and those changes must be communicated to appropriate stakeholders on a timely basis.

65. (B) Project plan. Project Plan - A management summary document that gives the essentials of a project in terms of its objectives, justification, and how the objectives are to be achieved. It should describe how all the major activities under each project management function are to be accomplished, including that of overall project control. The project plan will evolve through successive stages of the project life cycle. Prior to project implementation, for example, it maybe referred to as a Project Brief.

66. (C) For successful completion of the current project phase and subsequent project phases. Rolling Wave Planning - Cost and schedule planning where details are developed for the near term and general allocations are made for the out periods. Detail is developed for the out periods as information becomes available to do so.

67. (B) Project management plan. Project Management Plan. A formal, approved document that defines how the projected is executed, monitored and controlled. It may be summary or detailed and may be composed of one or more subsidiary management plans and other planning documents.

68. (D) Assumptions. Of the choices, assumptions are the only inputs to the project plan development.

69. (A) A structured approach used to guide a project team during development of a project plan. Project planning is the identification of the project objectives and the ordered activity necessary to complete the project. The identification of resource types and quantities required to carry out each activity or task.

70. (B) Earned value management. Earned Value Management (EVM). A management methodology for integrating scope, schedule, and resources, and for objectively measuring project performance and progress. Performance is measured by determining the budgeted cost of work performed (i.e., earned value) and comparing it to the actual cost of work performed (i.e., actual cost). Progress is measured by comparing the earned value to the planned value.

71. (C) A structured approach used to guide a project team during development of a project plan. Project Planning - Developing the basis for managing the project, including the planning objectives, procedure, organization, routines, finance and chain of activities.

72. (D) Integrated Change Control. Additional quality testing will require additional time and resources for the project. This is an example of Integrated Change Control.

73. (B) Do what you can to get the scope work defined. Scope Definition - Breaking down a deliverable in to smaller manageable parts to ensure better control.

74. (D) Control any changes to such characteristics. Configuration Management System. A subsystem of the overall project management system. It is a collection of formal documented procedures used to apply technical and administrative direction and surveillance to: identify and document the functional and physical characteristics of a product, result, service, or component; control any changes to such characteristics; record and report each change and its implementation status; and support the audit of the products, results, or components to verify conformance to requirements. It includes the documentation, tracking systems, and defined approval levels necessary for authorizing and controlling changes. In most application areas, the configuration management system includes the change control system.

75. (D) Formal or informal. Change Request - A request needed to obtain formal approval for changes to the scope, design, methods, costs or planned aspects of a project. Change requests may arise through changes in the business or issues in the project. Change requests should be logged, assessed and agreed on before a change to the project can be made.

76. (B) Business needs. Projects are and should be selected based on business needs first.

77. (D) Establishing realistic objectives. Management by Objectives ("MBO") - A management theory that calls for managing people based on documented work statements mutually agreed to by manager and subordinate. Progress on these work statements is periodically reviewed, and in a proper implementation, compensation is tied to MBO performance.

78. (A) Project Management Plan. The project plan is the formal document used to manage and control project execution. The Project Management Plan is a formal, approved document that defines how the projected is executed, monitored and controlled. It may be summary or detailed and may be composed of one or more subsidiary management plans and other planning documents.

79. (C) prepare a change request. Change Request are requests to expand or reduce the project scope, modify policies, processes, plans, or procedures, modify costs or budgets, or revise schedules. Requests for a change can be direct or indirect, externally or internally initiated, and legally or contractually mandated or optional. Only formally documented requested changes are processed and only approved change requests are implemented.

80. (C) Realism. Project selection methods involve measuring value or attractiveness to the project owner or sponsor and may include other organizational decision criteria. Project selection also applies to choosing alternative ways of executing the project.

81. (C) Are inputs to integrated change control. Integrated Change Control – reviewing all change requests, approving changes, and controlling changes to the deliverables and organizational process assets.

82. (C) Control. Control does and is not a baseline.

83. (C) Compiling the management plans from each of the knowledge areas. The management approach is best described as a compilation of the individual plans in the project plan.

84. (B) Project management plan. The project management plan contains the schedule management plan, cost management plan, project scope management plan, and risk management plan. These plans guide the schedule development, as well as components that directly support the Schedule Development process.

85. (A) Regularly scheduled meetings held to exchange information about the project. Status review meetings are an examination of the project to discuss variances and approve corrective action.

86. (B) Resource assignment matrix. A resource assignment matrix shows who is responsible for the various tasks in your WBS and who are the other participants working on the task.

87. (D) review the impact of change requests on project costs, schedule, and specifications. The Change Control Board (CCB) is a formally constituted group of stakeholders responsible for reviewing, evaluating, approving, delaying, or rejecting changes to the project, with all decisions and recommendations being recorded.

88. (C) A constraint. Constraint. The state, quality, or sense of being restricted to a given course of action or inaction. An applicable restriction or limitation, either internal or external to the project, that will affect the performance of the project or a process. For example, a schedule constraint is any limitation or restraint placed on the project schedule that affects when a schedule activity can be scheduled and is usually in the form of fixed imposed dates. A cost constraint is any limitation or restraint placed on the project budget such as funds available over time. A project resource constraint is any limitation or restraint placed on resource usage, such as what resource skills or disciplines are available and the amount of a given resource available during a specified time frame.

89. (B) A formally constituted group of stakeholders responsible for approving or rejecting changes to the project baseline. Change Control Board (CCB). A formally constituted group of stakeholders responsible for approving or rejecting changes to the project baselines.

90. (B) Procedures that define how project documents should/will be changed.

91. (B) Guide project execution, document project planning assumptions, and facilitate communication among stakeholders. Project Management Plan. A formal, approved document that defines how the projected is executed, monitored and controlled. It may be summary or detailed and may be composed of one or more subsidiary management plans and other planning documents.

92. (A) Performance reports. Performance Reports - provides organized and summarized work performance information, earned value management parameters and calculations, and analyses of project work progress and status. Common formats for performance reports include bar charts, S-curves, histograms, tables, and project schedule network diagram showing current schedule status.

93. (D) Project Management Information System (PMIS). A PMIS can assist the project manager the most during project execution. It does not replace the role of the project manager, but only serves as an assistant.

94. (D) An imposed date. Constraint - the state, quality, or sense of being restricted to a given course of action or inaction. An applicable restriction or limitation, either internal or external to the project, that will affect the performance of the project or a process. For example, a schedule constraint is any limitation or restraint placed on the project schedule that affects when a schedule activity can be scheduled and is usually in the form of fixed imposed dates. A cost constraint is any limitation or restraint placed on the project budget such as funds available over time. A project resource constraint is any limitation or restraint placed on resource usage, such as what resource skills or disciplines are available and the amount of a given resource available during a specified time frame.

95. (C) Change control system. Change Control System. A collection of formal documented procedures that define how project deliverables and documentation will be controlled, changed, and approved. In most application areas the change control system is a subset of the configuration management system.

96. (B) Integrated Change Control. Integrated Change Control is a system to document changes, their impact, response to changes, and performance deficits.

97. (D) General management skills, status review meetings, Work Authorization Systems. General management skills, status review meetings, and Work Authorization Systems are the best tools described here that serve as part of the project plan execution.

98. (C) Project plan execution. Project Plan Execution - The act of carrying out activities as stated in the project plan.

99. (D) Oral communication from key stakeholders. Change Request. Requests to expand or reduce the project scope, modify policies, processes, plans, or procedures, modify costs or budgets, or revise schedules. Requests for a change can be direct or indirect, externally or internally initiated, and legally or contractually mandated or optional. Only formally documented requested changes are processed and only approved change requests are implemented.

100. (C) Project Team. The project team contributes to the lessons learned document. The project manager also contributes, if not leads, the creation of this document.

Project Scope Management

The Project Scope Management questions on the PMP® exam cover a diverse, yet functional set of project management topics: project planning, work breakdown structures, project charter, scope statement, scope verification, scope management plan, and the scope changes are among the topics covered.

PMI® views project scope management as a five-step process that consists of scope planning, scope definition, create WBS, scope verification, and scope control. In the PMBOK® Guide figure 5.1 provides an overview of the structure.

The project scope management questions on the exam are straightforward. In the past most people have found them to be easy; do not be lulled into a full sense of security by past results. These questions cover a wide range of material, and you must be familiar with the terminology and perspectives adopted by PMI®.

Project Scope Management is concerned with the work of the project. All of the processes involved with the work of the project, and only the work that is required to complete the project are found in this knowledge area. All of the scope management processes involve detailing the requirements of the project and the activities that will eventually comprise the project plan, verifying those details using measurements techniques, and controlling changes to these processes.

Project initiation occurs when an individual or group recognizes that a project should begin. Although project initiation is not always a clearly defined process, it frequently includes determining what the project should accomplish, defining the goal of project, and developing a project charter. These actions might vary depending on the organization for which the project is done.

PMI® defines initiation as the process that formally recognizes the beginning of a new project or the continuation of an existing project into its next phase. Note that projects are authorized in different ways in different organizations. PMBOK® Guide section 5.1 lists typical reasons to authorize projects, including market demand, business needs, customer request, technological advance, or social need.

The PMBOK® Guide notes the importance of relating the product description to the business need or other stimuli that gave rise to the product. The PMBOK® Guide states that the product description will generally have fewer details in early phases and more details in later phases as the product characteristics are progressively elaborated. The PMBOK® Guide also notes the need for projects to support an organization's strategic plan. In the initiation process, the PMBOK® Guide identifies the identification and assignment of the project manager as a key output and suggests that the project manager be assigned as early as possible in the project but always before project plan execution begins.

Initiation is where we get our work. This is a concept that is important, since it is where the project manager is assigned and where he/she can point to the beginning of the project. This is challenging, since many projects might be born out of thin air and do not often have a clear beginning point.

Project Scope Management - Questions

1. A project manager has just become the manager of a project. The document that recognizes the existence of the project is called:

      (A) The statement of work.
      (B) The project assignment.
      (C) The project charter.
      (D) The product description.

2. Which of the following is done during scope verification?

    (A) Create work breakdown structure.
    (B) Verify product correctness.
    (C) Performance measurement.
    (D) Inspection.

3. The change management plan should be included in which of the following?

    (A) Configuration management plan
    (B) Quality management plan
    (C) Scope management plan
    (D) Communications management plan

4. Management by objectives of a project works only if:

    (A) The project does not impact the objectives.
    (B) The project includes the objectives in the charter.
    (C) It is supported by management.
    (D) The rules are written down.

5. A project manager decides to bring expected future schedule performance in line with the project plan. What is this a definition of?

    (A) Lessons learned
    (B) Corrective action
    (C) Scope planning
    (D) Scope verification

6. The greatest degree of uncertainty is encountered during which phase of the project life cycle?

    (A) Concept
    (B) Planning
    (C) Implementation
    (D) Closeout

7. A temporary endeavor undertaken to create a new product or service is called a:

    (A) Project.
    (B) Enterprise.
    (C) Program.
    (D) New product development.

8. The process that includes managing the actual changes if and when they occur is known as:

    (A) Scope change control
    (B) Scope methodology
    (C) Work breakdown structure
    (D) The project plan

9. Detailed information about the tasks and components found in the work breakdown structure can be stored in the?

    (A) Scope statement
    (B) Work breakdown structure dictionary
    (C) Scope database
    (D) Schedule database

10. A project team member has asked you what a scope statement is. Which of the following is a characteristic of a scope statement?

     (A) Defines the requirements for each project within the organization.
     (B) Defines the baseline for project acceptance.
     (C) Defines the functional managers assigned to the project.
     (D) Defines the cost, schedule, and quality metrics.

11. Your company is marketing textbooks to college business departments. Marketing believes that these books could be used at corporate training seminars and management has asked you to determine whether a project should be initiated to study this suggestion. Consequently you need to prepare which of the following?

     (A) Work breakdown structure
     (B) Feasibility study
     (C) Project charter
     (D) Project scope

12. You recently joined a state agency after working in private industry for 10 years. Your previous employer, a defense contractor, had a detailed project management methodology requiring multiple in-progress reviews. Although project management is fairly new to the state agency, it has a project life cycle with four phases: concept, definition, execution, and finish. Although the agency's project life cycle does not mandate when or how many project reviews should be conducted, you believe it is important to review project performance at the conclusion of each project phase. The objective of such a review is to:

     (A) Determine how many resources are required to complete the project according to the project baseline
     (B) Adjust the schedule and cost baselines based on past performance
     (C) Obtain customer acceptance of project deliverables
     (D) Determine whether the project should continue to the next phase

13. What is the decomposition process used to develop?

     (A) Communication plan
     (B) Project management plan
     (C) Earned value
     (D) Work breakdown structure

14. Contribution, scoring models, and economic models are all examples of:

     (A) Management models
     (B) Benefit measurement models
     (C) Execution measurement
     (D) Project models

15. Your firm has been hired by the State of California to build a major portion of a new highway. Because you indicated that you were a minority owned firm the state will require one important contractual term, that 20% of all good be purchased from minority owned companies. This is an example of which type of the following constraints?

     (A) Environmental
     (B) Legal
     (C) Social
     (D) Economical

16. Your company has just received approval to purchase a company that offers complementary services to your company. As the project manager on the acquisition, you develop a deliverable-oriented grouping of project elements that organizes and defines the total scope of the project. This output is called?

    (A) Scope definition.
    (B) Work breakdown structure.
    (C) Scope management plan.
    (D) Organizational breakdown structure.

17. Because you were finance major in college, you have been asked to be an active participant in your company's project selection process. The project selection committee chair has asked you to describe ground rules and possible approaches for project selection. You know that organizations usually will not approve a project if its costs exceed its benefits, so you recommend using a discounted cash-flow approach. This approach is based in part on the economic theory that a dollar today generally is worth more than a dollar a year from now. Using this approach, the project is acceptable if the:

    (A) Sum of the net present value of all estimated cash flow during the life of the project equals the profit
    (B) Net present value of the inflow is greater than the net present value of the outflow by a specified amount or percentage
    (C) Gross present value of all future expected cash flow divided by the initial cash investment is greater than one
    (D) Payback period occurs by the second year of the project

18. The tool that defines the procedures by which project scope may be changed is _____.

    (A) The project plan
    (B) Scope change control
    (C) Work breakdown structure
    (D) Scope methodology

19. A project manager is managing a project during the planning phase. She chooses to use a precedence network diagram as a graphic planning tool to assist in making the project schedule. The most important reason for using the network diagram as a graphic planning tool is that it makes it easier to see which aspect of the project plan better than the other tools available?

    (A) The logical relationships between activities in the schedule.
    (B) The probability that the tasks will be completed on time.
    (C) The float between activities.
    (D) The start and finish dates of the activities.

20. You are the project manager for a large company project creating a new product for your industry. You have recently learned your competitor is also working on a similar project but their offering will include a computer-aided program and web-based tools, which the project does not offer. You have implemented a change request to update your project. This is an example of which of the following?

    (A) A change due to an external event.
    (B) A change due to an error and omission in the initiation phase.
    (C) A change due to a legal issue.
    (D) A change due to an error or omission in the planning phase.

21. Of the following, which does the scope statement not provide?

    (A) Project product
    (B) Project objective
    (C) Project manager authority
    (D) Project justification

22. During the planning phase of your project, your project team has discovered another method to complete a portion of the project scope. This method is safer for the project team, but may cost more for the customer. This is an example of:

(A) Alternative identification
(B) Risk assessment
(C) Product analysis
(D) Alternative selection

23. The principal sources of project failure are:

(A) Lack of a projectized or strong matrix structure, poor scope definition, and lack of a project plan
(B) Lack of commitment or support by top management, disharmony on the project team, and lack of leadership by the project manager
(C) Poorly identified customer needs, a geographically dispersed project team, and little communication with the customer until the project is delivered
(D) Organizational factors, poorly identified customer needs, inadequately specified project requirements, and poor planning and control

24. Upon delivery, a software system fails to give expected results, but was formally accepted by the customer. Which of the following best describes the activity involved here?

(A) Rework
(B) Inspection
(C) Scope verification
(D) Quality audit

25. You are the project manager for a pharmaceuticals company. A new government regulation will change your project scope. For the project to move forward and be in accordance with the new regulation, your next action should be?

(A) Notify management.
(B) Create a feasibility study.
(C) Present the change to the Change Control Board (CCB).
(D) Prepare a new baseline to reflect the government changes.

26. When selecting a project, it is always important to measure value or attractiveness to the project owner. Your company uses multiple criteria for project selection but combines them into a single value function. You also have established a way to determine value under uncertainty. This is known as the:

(A) Choice of alternative methods to perform the project
(B) Decision model and calculation method
(C) Logical framework analysis
(D) Analytic hierarchy process

27. The project justification is found in the Charter, which is a part of the:

(A) Scope Statement
(B) Planning cycle
(C) Management plan
(D) Stakeholder guide

28. Identifying alternative approaches is part of what step of the scope management process?

    (A) Scope planning
    (B) Initiation
    (C) Scope verification
    (D) Scope definition

29. What is the lowest level in a work breakdown structure is called?

    (A) Work unit
    (B) Project task
    (C) Work activity
    (D) Work package

30. A project manager is assigned to a project early in the project life cycle. One of the things that must be done is to do a justification for the project. Since very little information is known about the project, the estimates are considered to be rough estimates. The following table is the project manager's estimate of the cash flows that will take place over the next five years. What is the net cash flow at the end of five years?

    (A) -$50,000
    (B) $50,000
    (C) $100,000
    (D) $850,000

31. A connection between the product being created and the overall strategy of the organization is created by the _____.

    (A) Project plan
    (B) Sponsor requirements
    (C) Product description
    (D) Quality plan

32. Scope verification deals with _____ of the scope while quality control deals with the _____ of the scope.

    (A) Acceptance, correctness
    (B) Correctness, acceptance
    (C) Acceptance, quality
    (D) Quality, correctness

33. During the full life cycle of the project, a plot of the projects expected expenditures will usually follow a characteristic "S" shape. This indicates that:

    (A) There is a cyclic nature to all projects.
    (B) Problems will always occur in the execution phase.
    (C) There are high expenditures during closeout.
    (D) The bulk of the project budget will be spent in the execution phase.

34. You are lying in bed, listening to the air-conditioning system pump lukewarm air into your motel room. You are dreading the next day because you must face an extremely tough client. Suddenly, the phone rings: it is your senior partner from Milkem & Fleecem, Inc. He is pulling you off your current project and has assigned you to another project. Based on your project management experience, you know that, ideally, a project manager should be selected and assigned:

    (A) During the project planning process
    (B) During the initiating process
    (C) Prior to the beginning of the development phase of the project life cycle
    (D) At the end of the concept phase of the project life cycle

35. A project manager is trying to convince management to use project management and has decided to start with a project charter. Why would the project charter help the project?

(A) It lists the names of all team members.
(B) It describes the details of what needs to be done.
(C) It describes the project's history.
(D) It gives the project manager authority.

36. Your technical team leader has prepared a request for a value-adding change on your project that will result in expanding the project scope. To help assess the magnitude of any variations as the work to implement the change proceeds, you have mandated that earned value analysis be used. This approach represents a:

(A) Performance measurement technique
(B) Configuration management process
(C) Cost accounting procedure
(D) Scope reporting mechanism

37. You are working in the pharmaceutical industry. Your project has been defined as clinical trials for the drug Fantastica, which improves human memory and stimulates hair growth. As the project proceeds, the product is described more explicitly as four Phase I trials, five Phase II trials, and six Phase III trials. This situation provides an example of:

(A) Quality function deployment
(B) Close alignment of project activities with the work breakdown structure
(C) Value analysis
(D) Progressive elaboration of the product description

38. A project is proposed to a customer. Price and schedule for delivery are agreed upon. The work breakdown structure is agreed to as well. The customer requests that one of the milestones of the project be completed by a certain date. The project schedule is reviewed, and it is found that the expected completion date for this milestone is considerably earlier than the date requested by the customer. The date for this milestone is which of the following?

(A) Consideration
(B) Summary activity
(C) Constraint
(D) Suggestion

39. You are setting up a PMO for a large multinational company, which currently has 21 different projects in different levels of completion. The PMO will have a project management information system. This system will be an on-line repository of all program data. You will collect descriptions of all work components for each of the 21 projects. This information will form an integral part of which of the following items?

(A) Chart of accounts
(B) WBS dictionary
(C) WBS structure template
(D) Earned value management reports

40. A project manager is managing a fixed price contract. She thinks that a large customer requested change might impact the schedule of the project. What should she do first?

(A) Meet with the stakeholders
(B) Meet with the team
(C) Renegotiate the remainder of the contract
(D) Follow the change control system

41. A new project manager is about to begin creating the project's scope of work. One stakeholder wants to add many items to the scope of work. Another stakeholder only wants to describe the functional requirements. The project is important for the project manager's company but a seller will do the work. Which of the following would you advise the project manager to do?

(A) The scope of work should be general to allow the seller to make its own decisions.
(B) The scope of work should be general to allow clarification later.
(C) The scope of work should be detailed to allow clarifications later.
(D) The scope of work should be as detailed as necessary for the type of project.

42. On an environmental remediation project, an example of a value-adding change is a change that:

(A) Takes advantage of cost-reducing technology that was not available when the scope originally was defined
(B) Is caused by a new or revised government regulation, necessitating that the design be resubmitted
(C) Corrects omission of a required feature in the design of a system
(D) Uses a bill of materials to define the scope of the project, including all assemblies and subassemblies

43. A market demand, a technological advance, or a legal requirement are all examples of:

(A) Management concerns in terms of corporate strategy
(B) Reasons to become a project manager
(C) Incredible amounts of hard work
(D) Reasons for authorizing a project

44. You have been placed in charge of a group of people that is selecting one of three possible projects. The project is to develop an antidote to prickly heat. As you gather in the conference room, many of the team members already have decided which project selection technique to use. Some prefer IRR, and others argue for BCR. In deciding which method to use, your first step should be to:

(A) Identify the technique used most often in the company and determine if it is appropriate for this project
(B) Compare and contrast selection techniques, and identify the advantages and disadvantages of each
(C) Determine the philosophy and wishes of management
(D) Select the method that most team members are knowledgeable of

45. Rather than use a WBS as you suggested, your team developed a bill of materials to define the project's work components. A customer review of this document uncovered that a scope change was needed, and a change request was subsequently written. This is an example of a change request that was the result of:

(A) An external event
(B) An error or omission in defining the scope of the product
(C) A value-adding change
(D) An error or omission in defining the scope of the project

46. A project team member has, on his own initiative, added extra vents to an attic to increase air circulation in the attic. The project plan did not call for these extra vents, but the team member decided they were needed based on the geographical location of the house. The project team's experts concur with this decision. This is an example of:

(A) Cost control
(B) Ineffective change control
(C) Self-led teams
(D) Value added change

47. You are the project manager for a large company project. This project has over 50 key stakeholders and will span the globe in implementation. Management has deemed the project's completion should not cost more than $25 million. Because of the global concerns, the final budget must be in U.S. dollars. This is an example of which of the following?

     (A) Internationalization
     (B) Budget constraint
     (C) Management constraint
     (D) Hard logic

48. The chart of accounts is an important input to the cost estimating processes because it:

     (A) Must be included in the supporting detail which is an output of this process.
     (B) Reflects the financial reporting structure which has been defined in the WBS.
     (C) Describes the coding structure used by the performing organization to report financial information in its general ledger.
     (D) Forms the basis for the control aspects of the cost management plan.

49. Any numbering system that is used to monitor project costs by category such as labor, supplies, or materials, for example, is called:

     (A) Work breakdown structure.
     (B) Standard accounting practices.
     (C) Universal accounting standard.
     (D) Chart of accounts.

50. A work breakdown structure numbering system allows project staff to:

     (A) Systematically estimate costs of work breakdown structure elements.
     (B) Provide project justification.
     (C) Identify the level at which individual elements is found.
     (D) Use it in project management software.

51. Because of a new government regulation, you had to change the scope of your telecommunications project. Several changes were made to the project's objectives. You have updated the project's technical and planning documents as needed. Your next step should be to:

     (A) Notify stakeholders as appropriate
     (B) Revise the company's knowledge management system
     (C) Obtain formal acceptance from your sponsor and customer
     (D) Prepare a performance report

52. Completion of the product scope is measured against _____, and completion of the project scope is measured against the _____.

     (A) Technical requirements, schedule
     (B) Charter requirements, Scope Statement
     (C) Project plan, project execution plans
     (D) Product requirements, project plan

53. Project success depends on a number of interrelated factors, including time, cost, and scope control. However, the success of any project depends primarily on:

     (A) Customer satisfaction
     (B) Customer acceptance
     (C) Exceeding customer requirements through gold-plating
     (D) Customer compromise in defining its needs

54. A project is an idea! environment in which to use the management-by-objectives technique because:

(A) Projects generally are handled through a matrix management environment
(B) All projects should be strongly oriented toward goals and objectives
(C) Project managers' responsibilities are defined in terms of corporate objectives
(D) Project management involves setting organizational objectives

55. Which of the following is done during scope definition?

(A) Product analysis
(B) Project selection
(C) Decomposition
(D) Alternative definition

56. The coordinated undertaking of interrelated activities directed toward a specific goal that has a finite period of performance is a:

(A) Set of project objectives.
(B) Program.
(C) Project charter.
(D) Project.

57. You are working on a product development project under contract to an automotive company that is building the "next-millennium Yugo." Initially, the product was defined as "a state-of-the-art personal transportation vehicle." Later it was described as "a state-of-the-art personal transportation vehicle that requires no gasoline." Finally, after an all-night hot tub party with the design engineers, it was described as "a state-of-the-art personal transportation vehicle that requires no gasoline, costs less than USD $15,000, and does not make any noise." This shows the progressive elaboration of product characteristics. But, although the product characteristics are elaborated progressively, they must be coordinated carefully with the:

(A) Proper project scope definition
(B) Project stakeholders
(C) Scope change control system
(D) Customer's strategic plan

58. You are the project manager for a major company project. You recently assigned a scope of work to a subcontractor. The subcontractor needs to plan and manage that specific scope of work in a more detailed manner. Your friend Michele is the new project manager for the subcontractor. She also is new to the project management profession. You suggest that she first:

(A) Follow the work breakdown structure that you developed for the project and use the work packages you identified
(B) Develop a subproject work breakdown structure for the work package that is her company's responsibility
(C) Establish a similar coding structure to facilitate use of a common project management information system
(D) Develop a work breakdown structure dictionary to show specific staff assignments

59. The first document produced on a project should be the:

(A) Scope Statement
(B) Risk management plan
(C) Charter
(D) Quality plan

60. The letters RBS stand for both Resource Breakdown Structure and the _____ Breakdown Structure.

    (A) Real
    (B) Random
    (C) Risk
    (D) Ratified

61. Which of the following is an output of scope change control?

    (A) Corrective action
    (B) Workarounds
    (C) Risk assessment
    (D) Transference

62. A person who is involved in or may be affected by the activities or anyone who has something to gain or lose by the activity of the project is called a:

    (A) Customer.
    (B) Team member.
    (C) Supporter.
    (D) Stakeholder.

63. Of the following, which is not part of project scope management?

    (A) Scope planning
    (B) Scope verification
    (C) Quality assurance
    (D) Initiation

64. You can determine whether requirements have been met by using _____.

    (A) Templates
    (B) Inspection
    (C) Work breakdown structure
    (D) Scope Statement

65. The control points in the work breakdown structure that are used for assignments to work centers are referred to as:

    (A) Subtasks.
    (B) Work packages.
    (C) Integration points.
    (D) Tasks.

66. Last week you were lying on the beach in Key West. Today you are examining a pile of scope change requests on a project you were asked to take over because the previous project manager decided to resign and open a catfish farm in Arkansas. To assess the degree to which the project scope will change, you need to compare the requests to which project document?

    (A) WBS
    (B) Scope management plan
    (C) Project plan
    (D) Scope statement

67. Your company's project review committee (PRO meets quarterly to review any project with a budget exceeding $2 million. You recently were promoted to senior project manager and were assigned one of these large projects, the development of a next-generation, computer-aided manufacturing process. The PRC asked you to present the project's objectives, work content, and deliverables at its next meeting. Accordingly, you need to prepare which one of the following documents:

(A) Product description
(B) Project charter
(C) WBS
(D) Scope statement

68. The responsibility for a clear product description in a project where the project manager will be supplied by a vendor lies with the:

(A) General management
(B) Project manager
(C) Buyer
(D) Seller

69. You are a personnel management specialist for the human resources department. You recently were assigned to a new project team. The team is working on a project to establish a team-based reward and recognition system for all company projects that last more than 1 year and that have some team members committed to work on the project at least half-time. The other team members also work in the human resources department. The project charter should be issued by:

(A) The head of the human resources department
(B) The project manager
(C) A member of the program management office (PMO) who has jurisdiction over human resources
(D) A manager external to the project

70. During the concept phase of your project, management indicated that it wants the expected benefit of each new product to outweigh its development costs. This is an example of:

(A) A constraint
(B) An assumption
(C) A technical requirement
(D) Use of the constrained-optimization method of project selection

71. Your company, HealtNut, Inc., is a leading marketer of dietary supplements that can be produced quickly and without regulatory approval. Management wants to explore new markets and new products to boost revenue and profits. You are leading a team to identify potential products. Because of your background and interest in information technology, you recommended developing wireless communications products. But when you submitted the idea for review, executive management informed you that this product would not fit with the organization's core competencies. You need to go back to the drawing board and recommend other products using management's guideline

(A) A constraint
(B) An assumption
(C) A technical requirement
(D) A specification

72. The project plan is important in change control because it:

(A) Provides information on project performance
(B) Provides the baseline against which changes are managed
(C) Is expected to change throughout the project
(D) Alerts the project team to issues that may cause problems in the future

73. Which of the following is an output of scope verification?

    (A) Rework
    (B) SOW Acceptance
    (C) Formal Acceptance
    (D) Work Breakdown Structure Templates

74. The most complex type of project selection method is called the:

    (A) Constrained methodology method
    (B) Constrained optimization methods
    (C) Optimistic random method
    (D) Random choice method

75. You have prepared the scope statement and the WBS for your project. You also have an approved project plan. Your project is now under way, but you recognize that, given the nature of project work, scope change is inevitable. You also are aware of the danger of scope creep, having suffered the consequences of it recently. To avoid a similar experience, you meet with your team and decide to establish a project scope change control system. This is:

    (A) A collection of formal, documented procedures to define the steps by which official project documents may be changed.
    (B) A documented process used to apply technical and administrative direction and surveillance to identify and document functional and physical characteristics of items, record and report change, control change, and audit the items and system to verify conformance to requirements.
    (C) A set of procedures by which project scope may be changed, including the paperwork, tracking systems, and approval levels necessary for authorizing change.
    (D) Mandatory for use on projects so that the scope management plan cannot be changed without prior review and sign-off.

76. The U.S. Bureau of Indian Affairs awarded your firm a contract to renovate an elementary school on a Navajo reservation. One contractual term, Indian preference, requires you to hire Native American laborers and subcontractors from the reservation. This is an example of which type of the following constraints?

    (A) Social
    (B) Economical
    (C) Environmental
    (D) Legal

77. What is the major aspect of scope verification?

    (A) It makes sure the project is on track by ensuring the customer's acceptance of the deliverable.
    (B) It ensures the project deliverable is completed on time.
    (C) It provides a chance for differences of opinion to come to light.
    (D) It shows the deliverable meets specifications.

78. You are the project manager of a large company project and would like to meet with a stakeholder for scope verification. Which of the following is typical of scope verification?

    (A) Reviewing the performance of the project deliverables
    (B) Reviewing changes to the project scope with the stakeholders
    (C) Reviewing the EVM results of the project to date
    (D) Reviewing the performance of the project team to date

79. A project manager is assigned to a project early in the project life cycle. One of the things that must be done is to do a justification for the project. Since very little information is known about the project, the estimates are considered to be rough estimates. The following table is the project manager's estimate of the cash flows that will take place over the next five years. If the net present value for each of the cash flows were calculated at a 10% interest rate, the net present value cash flow at the end of five years would be:

(A) Less than the total cash flow without the net present value applied.
(B) Greater than the total cash flow without the net present value applied.
(C) Unable to be calculated with the information supplied.
(D) The same as the total cash flow without the net present value applied.

80. You have finished the project scope according to plan. For the customer to accept the project what must happen next?

(A) Lessons learned should be finalized.
(B) Proof-of-concept should be implemented.
(C) Nothing. The plan is complete so the project is complete.
(D) Scope verification should be conducted.

81. Your team decided to develop a bill of materials to define the project's work components rather than the work breakdown structure you initially suggested. A stakeholder review of this document uncovered that a scope change was needed, and a change request was subsequently written. This is an example of a change request that was the result of

(A) An error or omission in defining the scope of the product
(B) An external event
(C) An error or omission in defining the scope of the project
(D) A value-adding change

82. Formal authorization of advancement to the next project phase is generally not found in:

(A) Small projects
(B) Government projects
(C) Large projects
(D) The project plan

83. Technical associations and consultants are two examples of:

(A) Internal resources
(B) Expert judgment
(C) Scope managers
(D) Expensive additions

84. Work results, product documentation, Work breakdown structure, Scope Statement, and the project plan are all _____ of scope verification.

(A) Techniques
(B) Tools
(C) Inputs
(D) Outputs

85. You are the project manager for an airplane manufacturer. Your project concerns the development of lighter, stronger material for commercial jets. As the project moves towards completion, the material is defined in more detail after each phase of materials testing. This is an example of which of the following?

    (A) Program management
    (B) Progressive elaboration
    (C) Quality assurance
    (D) Regulatory guidelines

86. Performance reports are used to provide information to stakeholders on project scope, schedule, cost, and quality. Which statement most accurately describes this process?

    (A) Performance reporting focuses on examining earned value analysis to determine whether cost overruns will require budget revisions.
    (B) The configuration control board receives performance reports and generates change requests to modify aspects of the project.
    (C) Performance reporting includes histograms, flow charts, and bar charts to show network dependencies and relationships.
    (D) Performance reporting includes status reports, which detail where the project is now; progress reports, which describe accomplishments; and forecasts, which predict future status and progress.

87. Benefit measurement and constrained optimization are examples of:

    (A) Benefit cost ratios.
    (B) Variable costs.
    (C) Types of depreciation.
    (D) Project selection methods.

88. ROI and payback period are examples of _____ project analysis.

    (A) Financial
    (B) Management
    (C) Professional
    (D) Quantitative

89. One of the stakeholders of the project you are managing asks why you consider the scope statement so important in your project management methodology. You answer her question with which of the following?

    (A) It is mandatory to consult the plan before authorizing any change.
    (B) Project managers must document any changes before approving or declining them.
    (C) The project scope serves as a reference for all future project decisions.
    (D) The project plan and EVM work together to assess the risk involved with proposed changes.

90. Generally, the largest unit that you can mange in the WBS is _____ hours.

    (A) 10
    (B) 20
    (C) 50
    (D) 40

91. Which of the following which is a tool and technique of scope verification?

    (A) Inspection.
    (B) Sensitivity analysis.
    (C) Product reviews.
    (D) Audits.

92. Which of the following is a key attribute of scope verification?

    (A) Improved schedule estimates.
    (B) Improved project management information system.
    (C) Improved cost estimates.
    (D) Customer acceptance of project efforts.

93. A list of the summary-level subproducts whose full and satisfactory delivery marks completion of the project describes:

    (A) Project scope
    (B) Project Charter
    (C) Project management
    (D) Project deliverables

94. A project manager is managing a project. The original scope baseline of the project was budgeted at $100,000. Since works on the project started there have been seventeen authorized and approved changes to the project. The changes have a value of $17,000 and the cost of investigating them prior to their approval was $2,500. What is the current budget for the project?

    (A) $117,000
    (B) $119,500
    (C) $100,000
    (D) $114,500

95. An example of scope verification is:

    (A) Managing changes to the project schedule.
    (B) Reviewing the performance of an installed software module.
    (C) Performing a benefit-cost analysis to determine if we should proceed.
    (D) Decomposing the WBS to a work package level.

96. Function analysis is best done by:

    (A) The project sponsor
    (B) The project team
    (C) The project manager
    (D) Professional engineers

97. You are the project manager for a company project and Nick, the project manager you are mentoring, does not know which plan he should reference for guarding the project scope. Which of the following plans does Nick need?

    (A) The scope management plan
    (B) The scope change control system
    (C) The scope verification
    (D) The scope charter

98. You are a project manager for your organization. Jake, a project manager in training, wants to know when the project manager is assigned to a project. Your answer should be:

    (A) During the initiation stage
    (B) During the planning stage
    (C) When the stakeholders approve the budget
    (D) After the project is proven feasible

99. A project team has made up the work breakdown structure for a project. Senior management for the company and all of the stakeholders including the client have approved the WBS. The client later requests that a change be made in the project, which will cost a considerable amount of money. The client says that the company's salesman promised this feature prior to sign-off on the WBS. Who should pay for the change?

    (A) Both the company and the client should pay part of the cost.
    (B) The change should not be implemented.
    (C) The client should pay.
    (D) The company managing the project should pay.

100. The construction phase of a new software product is near completion. The next phase is testing and implementation. The project is two weeks ahead of schedule. What should the project manager be most concerned with before moving onto the final phase?

    (A) Quality control
    (B) Scope verification
    (C) Cost control
    (D) Performance reports

Sample Answer Sheet

	T F		T F		T F		T F
1	Ⓐ Ⓑ Ⓒ Ⓓ Ⓔ	26	Ⓐ Ⓑ Ⓒ Ⓓ Ⓔ	51	Ⓐ Ⓑ Ⓒ Ⓓ Ⓔ	76	Ⓐ Ⓑ Ⓒ Ⓓ Ⓔ
2	Ⓐ Ⓑ Ⓒ Ⓓ Ⓔ	27	Ⓐ Ⓑ Ⓒ Ⓓ Ⓔ	52	Ⓐ Ⓑ Ⓒ Ⓓ Ⓔ	77	Ⓐ Ⓑ Ⓒ Ⓓ Ⓔ
3	Ⓐ Ⓑ Ⓒ Ⓓ Ⓔ	28	Ⓐ Ⓑ Ⓒ Ⓓ Ⓔ	53	Ⓐ Ⓑ Ⓒ Ⓓ Ⓔ	78	Ⓐ Ⓑ Ⓒ Ⓓ Ⓔ
4	Ⓐ Ⓑ Ⓒ Ⓓ Ⓔ	29	Ⓐ Ⓑ Ⓒ Ⓓ Ⓔ	54	Ⓐ Ⓑ Ⓒ Ⓓ Ⓔ	79	Ⓐ Ⓑ Ⓒ Ⓓ Ⓔ
5	Ⓐ Ⓑ Ⓒ Ⓓ Ⓔ	30	Ⓐ Ⓑ Ⓒ Ⓓ Ⓔ	55	Ⓐ Ⓑ Ⓒ Ⓓ Ⓔ	80	Ⓐ Ⓑ Ⓒ Ⓓ Ⓔ
6	Ⓐ Ⓑ Ⓒ Ⓓ Ⓔ	31	Ⓐ Ⓑ Ⓒ Ⓓ Ⓔ	56	Ⓐ Ⓑ Ⓒ Ⓓ Ⓔ	81	Ⓐ Ⓑ Ⓒ Ⓓ Ⓔ
7	Ⓐ Ⓑ Ⓒ Ⓓ Ⓔ	32	Ⓐ Ⓑ Ⓒ Ⓓ Ⓔ	57	Ⓐ Ⓑ Ⓒ Ⓓ Ⓔ	82	Ⓐ Ⓑ Ⓒ Ⓓ Ⓔ
8	Ⓐ Ⓑ Ⓒ Ⓓ Ⓔ	33	Ⓐ Ⓑ Ⓒ Ⓓ Ⓔ	58	Ⓐ Ⓑ Ⓒ Ⓓ Ⓔ	83	Ⓐ Ⓑ Ⓒ Ⓓ Ⓔ
9	Ⓐ Ⓑ Ⓒ Ⓓ Ⓔ	34	Ⓐ Ⓑ Ⓒ Ⓓ Ⓔ	59	Ⓐ Ⓑ Ⓒ Ⓓ Ⓔ	84	Ⓐ Ⓑ Ⓒ Ⓓ Ⓔ
10	Ⓐ Ⓑ Ⓒ Ⓓ Ⓔ	35	Ⓐ Ⓑ Ⓒ Ⓓ Ⓔ	60	Ⓐ Ⓑ Ⓒ Ⓓ Ⓔ	85	Ⓐ Ⓑ Ⓒ Ⓓ Ⓔ
11	Ⓐ Ⓑ Ⓒ Ⓓ Ⓔ	36	Ⓐ Ⓑ Ⓒ Ⓓ Ⓔ	61	Ⓐ Ⓑ Ⓒ Ⓓ Ⓔ	86	Ⓐ Ⓑ Ⓒ Ⓓ Ⓔ
12	Ⓐ Ⓑ Ⓒ Ⓓ Ⓔ	37	Ⓐ Ⓑ Ⓒ Ⓓ Ⓔ	62	Ⓐ Ⓑ Ⓒ Ⓓ Ⓔ	87	Ⓐ Ⓑ Ⓒ Ⓓ Ⓔ
13	Ⓐ Ⓑ Ⓒ Ⓓ Ⓔ	38	Ⓐ Ⓑ Ⓒ Ⓓ Ⓔ	63	Ⓐ Ⓑ Ⓒ Ⓓ Ⓔ	88	Ⓐ Ⓑ Ⓒ Ⓓ Ⓔ
14	Ⓐ Ⓑ Ⓒ Ⓓ Ⓔ	39	Ⓐ Ⓑ Ⓒ Ⓓ Ⓔ	64	Ⓐ Ⓑ Ⓒ Ⓓ Ⓔ	89	Ⓐ Ⓑ Ⓒ Ⓓ Ⓔ
15	Ⓐ Ⓑ Ⓒ Ⓓ Ⓔ	40	Ⓐ Ⓑ Ⓒ Ⓓ Ⓔ	65	Ⓐ Ⓑ Ⓒ Ⓓ Ⓔ	90	Ⓐ Ⓑ Ⓒ Ⓓ Ⓔ
16	Ⓐ Ⓑ Ⓒ Ⓓ Ⓔ	41	Ⓐ Ⓑ Ⓒ Ⓓ Ⓔ	66	Ⓐ Ⓑ Ⓒ Ⓓ Ⓔ	91	Ⓐ Ⓑ Ⓒ Ⓓ Ⓔ
17	Ⓐ Ⓑ Ⓒ Ⓓ Ⓔ	42	Ⓐ Ⓑ Ⓒ Ⓓ Ⓔ	67	Ⓐ Ⓑ Ⓒ Ⓓ Ⓔ	92	Ⓐ Ⓑ Ⓒ Ⓓ Ⓔ
18	Ⓐ Ⓑ Ⓒ Ⓓ Ⓔ	43	Ⓐ Ⓑ Ⓒ Ⓓ Ⓔ	68	Ⓐ Ⓑ Ⓒ Ⓓ Ⓔ	93	Ⓐ Ⓑ Ⓒ Ⓓ Ⓔ
19	Ⓐ Ⓑ Ⓒ Ⓓ Ⓔ	44	Ⓐ Ⓑ Ⓒ Ⓓ Ⓔ	69	Ⓐ Ⓑ Ⓒ Ⓓ Ⓔ	94	Ⓐ Ⓑ Ⓒ Ⓓ Ⓔ
20	Ⓐ Ⓑ Ⓒ Ⓓ Ⓔ	45	Ⓐ Ⓑ Ⓒ Ⓓ Ⓔ	70	Ⓐ Ⓑ Ⓒ Ⓓ Ⓔ	95	Ⓐ Ⓑ Ⓒ Ⓓ Ⓔ
21	Ⓐ Ⓑ Ⓒ Ⓓ Ⓔ	46	Ⓐ Ⓑ Ⓒ Ⓓ Ⓔ	71	Ⓐ Ⓑ Ⓒ Ⓓ Ⓔ	96	Ⓐ Ⓑ Ⓒ Ⓓ Ⓔ
22	Ⓐ Ⓑ Ⓒ Ⓓ Ⓔ	47	Ⓐ Ⓑ Ⓒ Ⓓ Ⓔ	72	Ⓐ Ⓑ Ⓒ Ⓓ Ⓔ	97	Ⓐ Ⓑ Ⓒ Ⓓ Ⓔ
23	Ⓐ Ⓑ Ⓒ Ⓓ Ⓔ	48	Ⓐ Ⓑ Ⓒ Ⓓ Ⓔ	73	Ⓐ Ⓑ Ⓒ Ⓓ Ⓔ	98	Ⓐ Ⓑ Ⓒ Ⓓ Ⓔ
24	Ⓐ Ⓑ Ⓒ Ⓓ Ⓔ	49	Ⓐ Ⓑ Ⓒ Ⓓ Ⓔ	74	Ⓐ Ⓑ Ⓒ Ⓓ Ⓔ	99	Ⓐ Ⓑ Ⓒ Ⓓ Ⓔ
25	Ⓐ Ⓑ Ⓒ Ⓓ Ⓔ	50	Ⓐ Ⓑ Ⓒ Ⓓ Ⓔ	75	Ⓐ Ⓑ Ⓒ Ⓓ Ⓔ	100	Ⓐ Ⓑ Ⓒ Ⓓ Ⓔ

Project Scope Management - Answers

1. (C) The project charter. A project charter is a document that formally recognizes the existence of a project. It should include, either directly or by reference to other documents, the business need that the project was undertaken to address and the product description.

2. (D) Inspection. Scope verification is the process of obtaining the stakeholders' formal acceptance of the completed project scope and associated deliverables. Verifying the project scope includes reviewing deliverables to ensure that each is completed satisfactorily. If the project is terminated early, the project scope verification process should establish and document the level and extent of completion. Scope verification differs from quality control in that scope verification is primarily concerned with acceptance of the deliverables, while quality control is primarily concerned with meeting the quality requirements specified for the deliverables. Quality control is generally performed before scope verification, but these two processes can be performed in parallel.

3. (C) Scope management plan. The change management plan is generally a document or procedure that is normally found in the scope management plan.

4. (C) it is supported by management. Management by Objectives is a management theory that calls for managing people based on documented work statements mutually agreed to by manager and subordinate. Progress on these work statements is periodically reviewed, and in a proper implementation, compensation is tied to MBO performance.

5. (B) Corrective action. Corrective action are changes made to bring expected future performance of the project into line with the plan.

6. (A) Concept. The greatest degree of uncertainty about the future is encountered during the concept phase. The direction of the project is determined in this phase, and the decisions made have the greatest influence on scope, quality, time, and cost of the project.

7. (A) Project. A project is a temporary endeavor undertaken to create a new product or service.

8. (A) Scope change control. Both the tool within the process and the process itself are called the same thing according to the PMBOK.

9. (B) Work breakdown structure dictionary. The work breakdown structure dictionary is a narrative document which describes the effort to accomplish all work contained in each WBS element. The WBS Dictionary will often result in the project or contract statement of work (SOW).

10. (D) Defines the cost, schedule, and quality metrics. Scope statements must at least include the quantifiable criteria of cost, schedule, and quality metrics.

11. (B) Feasibility study. Feasibility Study - The methods and techniques used to examine technical and cost data to determine the economic potential and the practicality of project applications. It involves the use of techniques such as the time value of money so that projects may be evaluated and compared on an equivalent basis. Interest rates, present worth factors, capitalization costs, operating costs, depreciation, etc., are all considered.

12. (D) Determine whether the project should continue to the next phase. The review at the end of a project phase is called a phase exit, stage gate, or kill point. The purpose of this review is to determine whether the project should continue to the next phase, to detect and correct errors while they are still manageable, and to ensure that the project remains focused on the business need it was undertaken to address.

13. (D) Work breakdown structure. Decomposition is the process of subdividing the major project deliverables into smaller, more manageable components until the deliverables are defined in sufficient detail to support development of project.

14. (B) Benefit measurement models. Benefit measurement measures one project against another and gives the organization information with which to select projects by comparing the benefits of each. Only in the case of a mandated project is there little concern about the benefits derived from the project.

15. (B) Legal. Constraint - The state, quality, or sense of being restricted to a given course of action or inaction. An applicable restriction or limitation, either internal or external to the project, that will affect the performance of the project or a process. For example, a schedule constraint is any limitation or restraint placed on the project schedule that affects when a schedule activity can be scheduled and is usually in the form of fixed imposed dates. A cost constraint is any limitation or restraint placed on the project budget such as funds available over time. A project resource constraint is any limitation or restraint placed on resource usage, such as what resource skills or disciplines are available and the amount of a given resource available during a specified time frame.

16. (B) Work breakdown structure. Work Breakdown Structure - is a deliverable-oriented hierarchical decomposition of the work to be executed by the project team to accomplish the project objectives and create the required deliverables. It organizes and defines the total scope of the project. Each descending level represents an increasingly detailed definition of the project work. The WBS is decomposed into work packages. The deliverable orientation of the hierarchy includes both internal and external deliverables.

17. (B) Net present value of the inflow is greater than the net present value of the outflow by a specified amount or percentage. The discounted cash-flow approach, or the present value method, determines the net present value of all cash flow by discounting it by the required rate of return. The impact of inflation can be considered. Early in the life of a project, net cash flow is likely to be negative because the major outflow is the initial investment in the project. If the project is successful, cash flow will become positive.

18. (B) Scope change control. This procedure defines how project scope can be changed.

19. (A) The logical relationships between activities in the schedule. The precedence network diagramming tool is used because it best shows the logical relationships between the activities in the schedule. The Gantt chart shows the project schedule graphically indicating the start and finish for each activity. The milestone chart shows the start or completion for specific groups of activities on a summarized chart.

20. (A) A change due to an external event. The change is requested to remain competitive with the competition-an external event.

21. (C) Project manager authority. The project charter provides the project manager with authority.

22. (A) Alternative identification. Alternative identification is a planning process to find alternatives to completing the project scope.

23. (D) Organizational factors, poorly identified customer needs, inadequately specified project requirements, and poor planning and control. Organizational problems, such as separation of responsibility and authority, can hinder the work being done and lead to poor quality; poorly identified customer needs and inadequately specified project requirements can result in a product that is unusable or grossly underused; and poor planning and control can create a chaotic environment and poor project results.

24. (C) Scope verification. Scope verification is the process of obtaining the stakeholders' formal acceptance of the completed project scope and associated deliverables. Verifying the project scope includes reviewing deliverables to ensure that each is completed satisfactorily. If the project is terminated early, the project scope verification process should establish and document the level and extent of completion.

25. (C) Present the change to the Change Control Board (CCB). Presenting the change to the Change Control Board is the best choice.

26. (B) Decision model and calculation method. Use of a decision criterion is one part of project selection. If multiple criteria are used, the criteria should be combined into a single value function and a means of calculating value under uncertainty. This is known as the decision model and calculation method.

27. (A) Scope Statement. The Charter is a separate document done before the Scope Statement, but its contents should be a part of the overall Scope Statement.

28. (A) Scope planning. Scope Planning - this is the process necessary for creating a project scope management plan that documents how the project scope will be defined, verified and controlled, and how the work breakdown structure will be created and defined.

29. (D) work package. Work Package - a deliverable or project work component at the lowest level of each branch of the work breakdown structure. The work package includes the schedule activities and schedule milestones required to complete the work package deliverable or project work component.

30. (A) -$50,000. The net cash flow is the total of all the cash flows in and out of the company caused by the project. In this example 850,000 in and 900,000 out for a negative 50,000.

31. (C) Product description. Unless this connection is made, the project will almost always be unsuccessful.

32. (A) Acceptance, correctness. The stakeholders accept what is being done during scope verification, and the correctness of the results is determined during the quality control process.

33. (D) The bulk of the project budget will be spent in the execution phase. Most of the project money will be spent during the execution phase. At the beginning of execution the rate of expenditures rises as people and materials are brought into the project. Later the expenditures peak and slow down. By the end of the execution phase expenditures are approaching a minimum.

34. (B) During the initiating process. If the project manager is selected and assigned to the project during initiation, several of the usual start-up tasks of the project are simplified. In addition, becoming involved with project activities from the beginning helps the project manager understand where the project fits within the organization in terms of its priority relative to other projects and the ongoing work of the organization.

35. (D) It gives the project manager authority. The project charter is a formal document providing authority to a project manager to conduct a project within scope, quality, time and cost and resource constraints as laid down in the document.

36. (A) Performance measurement technique. Performance Measurement Techniques - The methods used to estimate earned value. Different methods are appropriate to different work packages, either due to the nature of the work or to the planned duration of the work package. Another term for Performance Measurement Techniques is Earned Value Methods.

37. (D) Progressive elaboration of the product description. The product description documents the characteristics of the product or service that the project was undertaken to create. This description will generally have less detail in early phases and more detail in later ones as the product characteristics are elaborated progressively.

38. (C) Constraint. The request for an agreement to a specific date for completion of a particular milestone in the project is called a constraint. Constraints for project tasks and activities that do not put them on the critical path are not necessarily a problem as long as delays in the schedule do not ultimately place them on the critical path. Some process constraints may be predefined as constraints. For example, management may specify a target completion date rather than allowing it to be determined by the planning process. Constraints are factors that will limit the project management team's options. For example, a predefined budget is a constraint that is highly likely to limit the team's options regarding scope, staffing, and schedule.

39. (B) WBS dictionary. Work Breakdown Structure Dictionary - a document that describes each component in the work breakdown structure (WBS). For each WBS component, the WBS dictionary includes a brief definition of the scope or statement of work, defined deliverable(s), a list of associated activities, and a list of milestones. Other information may include: responsible organization, start and end dates, resources required, an estimate of cost, charge number, contract information, quality requirements, and technical references to facilitate performance of the work.

40. (D) Follow the change control system. A change control system is a collection of formal, documented procedures that defines the steps by which official project documents may be changed. It includes the paperwork, tracking systems, and approval levels necessary for authorizing changes. The change control system must also include procedures to handle changes, which may be approved without prior review (e.g., changes that occur as the result of an emergency). These changes must still be documented and captured so that they do not cause problems later in the project.

41. (D) The scope of work should be as detailed as necessary for the type of project. Project scope is the way that we describe the boundaries of the project. It defines what the project will deliver and what it will not deliver. For larger projects, it can include the organizations affected, the transactions affected, the data types included, etc.

42. (A) Takes advantage of cost-reducing technology that was not available when the scope originally was defined. Most changes are the result of external events or errors or omissions in scope definition, or they are value-adding, that is, they add value to the project while reducing costs.

43. (D) Reasons for authorizing a project. There are many reasons for authorizing a project. The PMBOK lists several others under section 5.1. Remember that the reasons for authorizing a project are most often market-driven and usually contain the constraints of cost and schedule. For instance, just because there is a market demand for a particular product doesn't mean your organization should authorize a project to plan and build it if the product is not in the organization's strategic plan.

44. (C) Determine the philosophy and wishes of management. Any selection technique must be evaluated based on the degree to which it will meet the organization's objective for the project. Management generally establishes the organization's objective. Therefore, management's wishes must be identified first. Then the most appropriate model to support management's wishes should be selected.

45. (D) An error or omission in defining the scope of the project. The bill of materials presents a hierarchical view of the physical assemblies, subassemblies, and components needed to fabricate a manufactured product, whereas the WBS is a deliverable-oriented grouping of project components used to define the total scope of the project. Using a bill of materials where a WBS would be more appropriate may result in an ill-defined scope and subsequent change requests.

46. (B) Ineffective change control. The project team member did not follow the change management plan's method of incorporating changes into the scope.

47. (B) Budget constraint. This is an example of a budget constraint. The budget must not exceed $34 million. In addition, the metric for the values to be in U.S. dollars can affect the budget if most of the product is to be purchased in a foreign country.

48. (C) Describes the coding structure used by the performing organization to report financial information in its general ledger. A Chart of Accounts is any numbering system used to monitor project costs by category (e.g., labor, supplies, materials, and equipment). The project chart of accounts is usually based upon the corporate chart of accounts of the primary performing organization.

49. (D) Chart of accounts. The chart of accounts is the system used to monitor project costs as defined by PMI.

50. (C) identify the level at which individual elements are found. WBS elements are usually numbered, and the numbering system may be arranged any way you choose. However, the conventional numbering system is 1.2.3.4, where each digit represents the task subdivision level.

51. (A) Notify stakeholders as appropriate. Scope changes are fed back through the planning process and may require modifications to cost, time, quality, or other project objectives. Once technical and planning documents are updated, stakeholders should be notified.

52. (D) Product requirements, project plan. It is helpful to know both of these definitions. You will see them on the test. Both scope types must be integrated to ensure successful completion of the project. That means that the product outlined in the product requirements is successfully delivered against the schedule and full project plan.

53. (A) Customer satisfaction. Customer satisfaction, not time or cost, is the primary criterion for measuring project success.

54. (B) All projects should be strongly oriented toward goals and objectives. Management by objectives focuses on the goals of an activity rather than on the activity itself, so managers are held responsible for obtaining results rather than performing certain activities. These results can be used to help evaluate project performance.

55. (C) Decomposition. Decomposition is subdividing the major project deliverables into smaller, more manageable components until the deliverables are defined in sufficient detail to support development of project.

56. (D) Project. This is the definition of a project.

57. (A) Proper project scope definition. Progressive elaboration of product characteristics must be coordinated carefully with proper scope definition, particularly when the project is performed under contract. When properly defined, the project scope, the work to be done, should remain constant even when the product characteristics are elaborated progressively.

58. (B) Develop a subproject work breakdown structure for the work package that is her company's responsibility. Work packages are items at the lowest level of the work breakdown structure. A subproject work breakdown structure breaks down work packages into greater detail. A subproject work breakdown structure generally is used if the project manager assigns a scope of work to another organization, and the project manager at that organization must plan and manage the scope of work in greater detail.

59. (C) Charter. As discussed previously, this document does not always get done. But the areas is it supposed to control are ones that a project manager should view and manage for the project to be successful.

60. (C) Risk. Risk identification often produces nothing more than a long list of risks, which can be hard to understand or manage. The list can be prioritized to determine which risks should be addressed first, but this does not provide any insight into the structure of risk on the project. Traditional qualitative assessment cannot indicate those areas of the project which require special attention, or expose recurring themes, concentrations of risk, or 'hot-spots' of risk exposure. The best way to deal with a large amount of data is to structure the information to aid comprehension. For risk management, this can be achieved with a Risk Breakdown Structure (RBS) — a hierarchical structuring of risks on the project. The RBS can assist in understanding the distribution of risk on a project or across a business, aiding effective risk management.

61. (A) Corrective action. Corrective actions are outputs of change control.. Corrective Action are the documented direction for executing the project work to bring expected future performance of the project work in line with the project management plan.

62. (D) Stakeholder. A stakeholder is an individual or organization that is involved in or may be affected by project activities.

63. (C) Quality assurance. Quality Assurance is not part of project scope management. It is the quality assurance program of the entire organization.

64. (B) Inspection. Inspection tells you whether the requirements have been met or whether there is compliance with other planning documents.

65. (B) work packages. Work Package is a generic term for a unit within a work breakdown structure (WBS) at the lowest level of its branch, not necessarily at the lowest level of the whole WBS. It may be used to refer to a unit of work performed within the organization, while 'Commitment Package' may be used for work contracted or purchased outside the organization.

66. (A) WBS. The WBS defines the project's scope baseline, which provides the basis for any changes that may occur on the project.

67. (D) Scope statement. The scope statement provides stakeholders with a common understanding of the scope of the project and is a source of reference for making future project decisions.

68. (C) Buyer. Before an organization engages an outside project manager, a clear product description should be constructed.

69. (D) A manager external to the project. The project charter should be issued by a manager outside the project but at a level appropriate to the project's needs. Because it provides the project manager with the authority to apply organizational resources to project activities, the project charter should not be issued by the project manager. Functional managers should have approval authority.

70. (A) A constraint. Constraints are factors that will limit the team's options.

71. (B) An assumption. Assumptions are factors that, for planning purposes, are considered to be true, real, or certain. They are an output of the initiating process and are an input into scope planning.

72. (B) Provides the baseline against which changes are managed. The project plan is a key input to integrated change control.

73. (C) Formal Acceptance. Scope verification results in one thing: formal acceptance.

74. (B) Constrained optimization methods. Although these are important methods only for a limited number of projects, they can be very valuable. You certainly do not have to know how to run these methods for the exam.

75. (C) A set of procedures by which project scope may be changed, including the paperwork, tracking systems, and approval levels necessary for authorizing change. A project scope change control system, documented in the project scope management plan, defines the procedures by which the project scope and product scope can be changed. The system includes the documentation, tracking systems, and approval levels necessary for authorizing changes. The scope change control system is integrated with any overall project management information system to control project scope.

76. (D) Legal. The terms and conditions in any contract are legal requirements that must be adhered to by the parties entering into the agreement.

77. (A) It makes sure the project is on track by ensuring the customer's acceptance of the deliverable. Scope verification is the process of obtaining the stakeholders' formal acceptance of the completed project scope and associated deliverables. Verifying the project scope includes reviewing deliverables to ensure that each is completed satisfactorily. If the project is terminated early, the project scope verification process should establish and document the level and extent of completion.

78. (A) Reviewing the performance of the project deliverables. Where scope verification is concerned, the customer is concerned with the performance of the product.

79. (A) Less than the total cash flow without the net present value applied. Calculating the net present value of the cash flows for the project involves adjusting the future cash flows to allow for diminishing value due to the time that we must wait to get them. Money received today is more valuable to us than money that is received in the future.

80. (D) Scope verification should be conducted. Scope verification concerns itself with the formal acceptance of the product.

81. (C) An error or omission in defining the scope of the project. Change Request - A request needed to obtain formal approval for changes to the scope, design, methods, costs or planned aspects of a project. Change requests may arise through changes in the business or issues in the project. Change requests should be logged, assessed and agreed on before a change to the project can be made.

82. (A) Small projects. For the most part, small projects do not include formal authorization of advancement to each phase as a part of the overall scope management of the project.

83. (B) Expert judgment. Expert judgment is often the most effective way of dealing with questions concerning choices of projects. Experts should save time for you but will cost something. Use them; they are worth it.

84. (C) Inputs. These are all inputs into scope verification.

85. (B) Progressive elaboration. Progressive Elaboration is continuously improving and detailing a plan as more detailed and specific information and more accurate estimates become available as the project progresses, and thereby producing more accurate and complete plans that result from the successive iterations of the planning process.

86. (D) Performance reporting includes status reports, which detail where the project is now; progress reports, which describe accomplishments; and forecasts, which predict future status and progress. Performance Reporting - the process of collecting and distributing performance information. This includes status reporting, progress measurement, and forecasting.

87. (D) project selection methods. The project-selection method(s) used by an organization should be relevant to the objectives of the company and its managers and should be consistent with the capabilities and resources of the organization. The two methods of project selection are benefit measurement (comparative approach) and constrained optimization (mathematical approach).

88. (A) Financial. Although these are also quantitative types of analysis, the answer that is looked for on the exam is financial.

89. (C) The project scope serves as a reference for all future project decisions. The scope statement serves as a point of reference for all future project decisions.

90. (D) 40. If the tasks listed in the WBS are longer than this, it will be very difficult to have control over them.

91. (A) Inspection. Inspection includes activities such as measuring, examining, and verifying to determine whether work and deliverables meet requirements and product acceptance criteria. Inspections are variously called reviews, product reviews, audits, and walkthroughs. In some application areas, these different terms have narrow and specific meanings.

92. (D) Customer acceptance of project efforts. A person is writing a document identifying the business need for a project and is including a description of the product created by the project. She provides objectives and goals for the project in his document. What is the role of this person on the project?

93. (D) Project deliverables. Deliverables are the mark of a controlled project and as such should be planned early on in the project.

94. (B) $119,500. The current budget of the project contains all of the authorized funding for the project including additions to the project since the setting of the original baselines. This includes any and all authorized work done on the project, including the investigation of work that may be done to investigate the feasibility of changes.

95. (B) Reviewing the performance of an installed software module. Verifying scope is the process of verifying that the project made or delivered is what was asked for.

96. (D) Professional engineers. Only people trained in the major engineering types of product analysis should attempt to use these techniques to gain a better understanding of the product of the project. These techniques are not easily learned and require a good background in a variety of mathematical analytics. In other words, if you do not understand how to use them, do not even try.

97. (A) The scope management plan. The scope management plan provides details about how the project scope may be changed.

98. (A) During the initiation stage. Project managers are assigned during the initiation process of the project.

99. (C) The client should pay. The client should pay, because the signing of the WBS constituted an agreement between the company managing the project and the client. Work that is not specified in the WBS is not part of the project scope. In reality this is sometimes not the case. Companies will frequently do work that is outside of the project scope as defined by the WBS in order to ensure the goodwill of the client.

100. (B) Scope verification. Scope verification is the process of obtaining the stakeholders' formal acceptance of the completed project scope and associated deliverables. Verifying the project scope includes reviewing deliverables to ensure that each is completed satisfactorily. If the project is terminated early, the project scope verification process should establish and document the level and extent of completion.

Project Time Management

The Project Time Management questions on the PMP® exam focus heavily on the Critical Path Method (CPM) and the Precedence Diagramming Method (PDM), and the differences between these techniques. The exam tests your knowledge of how these networks are constructed, how schedules are computed, what the critical path is, and how networks are used to analyze and solve project scheduling, and resource allocation and leveling issues.

The exam may also contain some scheduling exercises. There is a focus on fast tracking as a method to accelerate the project schedule. You must know the advantages offered by networks over bar charts and flow diagrams and understand the two ways in which networks can be represented (activity-on-arrow and activity-on-node). You should also understand the notion of float (or slack) and how it presents challenges and opportunities to project schedulers.

In the PMBOK® Guide, the functions of Project Time Management are separated into six phases: activity definition, activity sequencing, activity resource estimating, activity duration estimating, schedule development, and schedule control. Review PMBOK® Guide figure 6.1.

This knowledge area is concerned with estimating the duration of the project plan activities, devising a project schedule, and monitoring and controlling deviations from the schedule. Collectively, this knowledge area deals with completing the project in a timely manner.

In many cases, all of the activity processes described here along with schedule development are completed as one activity. Sometimes, only one person is needed to complete these six processes, and they're all worked on at the same time. Time management is an important aspect of project management as it concerns keeping the project activities on track and monitoring those activities against the project plan to assure the project is completed on time.

As you go through this section of the exam, you do not want to spend quite as much time as you might anticipate studying the calculations associated with the whole network. Instead, what you want to look at are some unusual relationships—start-start, finish-finish, and lag and lead times, and examining the issues associated with the classical representations of schedules. That includes CPM, PDM, AOA (activity-on-arrow), and AON (activity-on-node).

Project Time Management - Questions

1. Your project is roughly two months behind schedule due to conflict between several key team members. After resolving the conflict by reassigning several of the members of your project, you should consider _____ to try and bring the project up to schedule.

    (A) leveling the resources
    (B) reassigning resources
    (C) crashing the schedule
    (D) reducing resource loads

2. A project is nearly 33% complete according to the earned value reporting method. An identified risk has occurred, and the project manager has chosen to draw funds from the contingency fund and add the activities necessary to deal with the problems associated with the risk. What should he do next?

    (A) The budget money set aside for the risk should be released, but there is not a need for a schedule change.
    (B) The schedule should not be change because the original plans should have allowed for this delay.
    (C) The budget baseline should be changed, but the work should be done within the schedule as it is.
    (D) The schedule and budget baselines should be changed, to show the new work.

3. What does "resource leveling" mean in project management?

   (A) Making the most efficient use of the available resources.
   (B) Shortening the time it takes to complete the project.
   (C) Reducing the project costs.
   (D) Hiring contractors to fill in during peak times on the project schedule.

4. The term activity resource estimating refers to?

   (A) Persons
   (B) Material
   (C) Equipment
   (D) All of the above.

5. The work on the foundation framework before the placement of the concrete for the foundation would be an example of what type of dependency?

   (A) Mandatory
   (B) Discretionary
   (C) Soft logic
   (D) External

6. You met with your project team to discuss the best ways to control the schedule. You want to influence the factors that can change the schedule. You also want to recognize when the schedule has changed so you can manage changes as they occur. Working with your team to provide the basis for measuring and reporting schedule progress, you agree to use the:

   (A) Project schedule.
   (B) Technical baseline.
   (C) Schedule management plan.
   (D) Network diagram.

7. You work for one of the leading manufacturers of country and western apparel. You are managing a project to redesign retail store layout to improve customer throughput and efficiency. Much of the project work must be done on site and will require the active participation of store employees. Many of these employees are lifelong members of a powerful union that has a reputation for labor unrest. One important component of your schedule must be:

   (A) Buffers and reserves
   (B) A resource capabilities matrix
   (C) A resource histogram
   (D) A resource calendar

8. Several types of float are found in project networks. Float that is used by a particular activity and does not affect the float in later activities is called:

   (A) Free float
   (B) Expected float
   (C) Total float
   (D) Extra float

9. In attempting to complete the project faster, the project manager looks at the cost associated with crashing each task. The most appropriate approach to crashing would also include looking at the:

(A) risk impact of crashing each task.
(B) customer's opinion of what tasks to crash.
(C) boss's opinion of what tasks to crash and in which order.
(D) project phase the task is due to occur in.

10. The main difference between the two types (ADM, arrow diagramming method, and PDM, precedence diagramming method) of the critical path method (CPM) of scheduling is:

(A) Arrow diagramming method (ADM) is a deterministic method, whereas the precedence diagramming method (PDM) is a probabilistic method.
(B) Precedence diagramming method (PDM) is a more accurate method.
(C) Precedence diagramming method (PDM) is a deterministic method, whereas the arrow diagramming method (ADM) is a probabilistic method.
(D) Placement of the activity on the logic diagram line.

11. What is another name for the waiting time between two tasks?

(A) Lag
(B) Total float
(C) Slack
(D) Float

12. In crashing the project schedule the project manager would or should focus on?

(A) Accelerating as many tasks as possible.
(B) Accelerating just the non-critical tasks.
(C) Accelerating the performance of tasks on the critical path.
(D) Cut the scope of the project.

13. You are the project manager for a large company project. This project has 32 stakeholders and will require implementation activities in North and South America. You have been requested to provide a duration estimate for the project. Of the following, which will offer the best level of detail in your estimate?

(A) Order of Magnitude
(B) Work Breakdown Structure
(C) Stakeholder Analysis
(D) Requirements Document

14. You are remodeling your kitchen and decide to prepare a network diagram for this project. Your appliances must be purchased and available for installation by the time the cabinets are completed. In this example, these relationships are:

(A) Finish to start
(B) Start to finish
(C) Finish to finish
(D) Start to start

15. You are preparing your project schedule on a sheet of paper. You abandoned the use of project scheduling software long ago, deciding that it is too feature rich, convoluted, and complex. To keep your life simple, you decided to calculate a single, deterministic early and late start date and an early and late finish date for each activity. Accordingly, you decide to use:

(A) Gantt charts (GC)
(B) Schedule analysis (SA)
(C) Critical path method (CPM)
(D) Monte Carlo analysis (MCA)

16. Jake is the project manager for a large company project. This project requires several members of the project team to complete a certification class for another project the week of March 5. This class causes some of the project activities on Jake's activities to be delayed from his target schedule. This is an example of which of the following?

(A) Soft logic
(B) Conflict of interest
(C) Hard logic
(D) External dependencies

17. You need to assess the implications of crashing a project. What is the first thing you should do?

(A) The cost and time slope for each critical activity that can be expedited.
(B) The cost of additional resources to be added to the project's critical path.
(C) The time that will be saved in the overall schedule when tasks are expedited on the critical path.
(D) The resource cost for each person involved on the project.

18. Activity A has a duration of 3 days and begins on the morning of Monday the 4th. The successor activity, B, has a finish-to-start relationship with A. The finish-to-start relationship has 3 days of lag, and activity B has a duration of 4 days. Sunday is a non-workday. What can be determined from these data?

(A) The finish date of B is Wednesday the 13th.
(B) Calendar time between the start of A to the finish of B is 14 days.
(C) The total duration of both activities is 8 days.
(D) Calendar time between the start of A to the finish of B is 11 days.

19. The competitive, complex project management environment has increased pressure for on-time performance. Schedule control is one important way of avoiding schedule delays. Time management corrective action often involves expediting certain activities to ensure that they are completed in a timely manner or to ensure that they are completed with the least possible delay. To plan and execute schedule recovery, corrective action frequently requires:

(A) Making unpopular decisions
(B) Immediately rebaselining
(C) Root cause analysis
(D) Resource leveling

20. You are planning to conduct the team-building portion of your new project management training curriculum outdoors. Participants will engage in a survival scenario to weed out the "weakest" team members. Winners will receive the company "Survivor" Award. You are limited to scheduling the course at certain times of the year because it will be conducted in Iceland. The best time for the course to begin is mid-July. One of the more common date constraints to use as you develop your project schedule is:

(A) Finish no later than
(B) Fixed early finish
(C) Fixed late start
(D) Start no earlier than

21. A project manager is managing a project and is considering the reschedule of an activity because one of the project engineers must work on this activity and another activity at the same time. Each of the activities is scheduled to have a duration of two weeks. One of the activities is on the critical path and the other activity has eighteen days of free float. The project manager should:

    (A) Ask the engineer to work overtime.
    (B) Reschedule both activities to take advantage of the float on each.
    (C) Reschedule the activity that has no float.
    (D) Reschedule the activity with float.

22. We cannot test the software until we develop the software. This expression describes which of the following dependencies?

    (A) Preferential
    (B) Mandatory or hard
    (C) Discretionary
    (D) Rational

23. The overall duration of the project schedule is not influenced by:

    (A) Using discretionary dependencies as constraints.
    (B) Using mandatory dependencies as constraints.
    (C) Using the arrow diagramming method instead of the precedence diagramming method (PDM) of scheduling.
    (D) The availability of the resources that are assigned to perform the work.

24. According to the Guide to the PMBOK, work packages can be divided into:

    (A) Tasks.
    (B) Smaller work packages.
    (C) Subprojects.
    (D) Activities.

25. A schedule was developed for a project to install windows in an apartment building. The project is a rush job, and the contractor has agreed to schedule the work on a single shift basis but will work seven days per week until the job is done. The project is to begin on May 1. (See image) What is the early finish date of activity A?

    (A) May 3
    (B) May 4
    (C) May 1
    (D) May 2

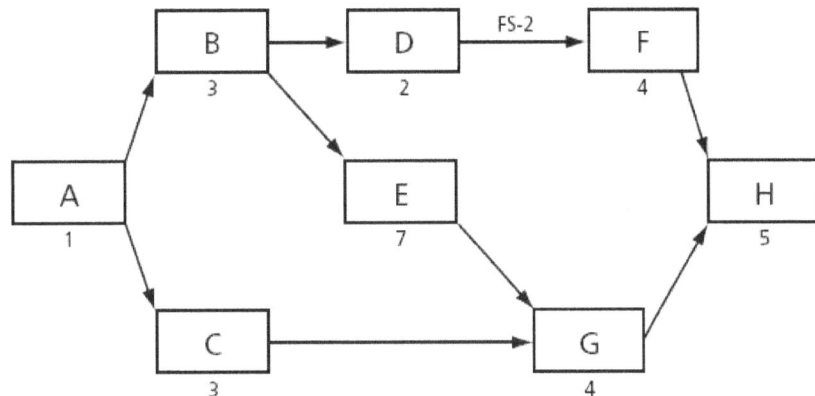

26. You work for an architectural-engineering firm and are responsible for designing the world's most advanced chicken coop. The project is highly complex and will require hundreds of drawings. You multiply the number of drawings by the hours needed to produce each drawing to estimate how long the coop will take to design. This results in which one of the following estimate types?

(A) Expert
(B) Three-point
(C) Parametric
(D) Analogous

27. Which of the following may be employed to shorten a schedule without changing the scope of the task?

(A) Releasing resources earlier from tasks which were scheduled with a late start
(B) Alter the task priorities
(C) Fast tracking
(D) Crashing

28. A method of shortening the duration of the project by doing activities in parallel is referred to as:

(A) Creating milestones.
(B) Leading.
(C) Fast tracking.
(D) Leveling.

29. Which of the following is true?

(A) The critical path is the list of activities that have zero float.
(B) The critical path is the list of activities that have critical risks associated with them.
(C) The critical path is the path through the network that has the highest total duration.
(D) The critical path is the path with the least amount of free float.

30. If project time and cost are not as important as the number of resources used each month, which of the following is the most appropriate course of action?

(A) Fast track the project.
(B) Analyze the life-cycle costs.
(C) Perform resource leveling.
(D) Perform a Monte Carlo analysis.

31. Which of the following is considered to be a simulation technique?

(A) PDM analysis
(B) GERT analysis
(C) Monte Carlo analysis
(D) Critical path method

32. You are managing a construction project for a new state water system. The contract requires you to use special titanium piping equipment that is guaranteed not to corrode. It also requires the use of titanium bolts to assemble the piping system. Because titanium has a mass density that is 50 times its weight, the pipe must be resting in the ground a total of 10 days before the bolts can be installed. In this example, the 10-day period is defined as:

(A) Lead
(B) Lag
(C) Slack
(D) Float

33. You are a project manager for a new product development project that has four levels in the work breakdown structure, and has been sequenced using the arrow diagramming technique. The activity duration estimates have been received. What is the next time management activity you would do?

      (A) Duration compression
      (B) Collect historical records
      (C) Create an activity list
      (D) Update the work breakdown structure

34. You are working on a new company project that will enable faxing through a sophisticated voice recognition system. Your company's marketing department just informed you that a major competitor is developing a similar product. Initially you decided to use resource leveling because your early-start schedule indicated that more resources were required during certain time periods than during others and because you were not under any great time pressure to complete the project. Now that you are pressured to beat your competitor to market, you need to develop a project schedule that is as close to the original one as possible. To do this, you should use:

      (A) Reverse resource allocation
      (B) Resource manipulation
      (C) Resource reallocation
      (D) Critical chain scheduling

35. Your company, which operates a large chemical processing plant, has been convicted of illegally dumping toxic substances into a local town lake causing most fish to die. The court has mandated that the required cleanup activities be completed by within 45 days. Such a constraint is an example of

      (A) A key event
      (B) A major milestone
      (C) An imposed date
      (D) An external dependency

36. It is important to rebaseline the project schedule carefully because:

      (A) Historical data will be lost for the project schedule.
      (B) Schedule recovery cannot be planned for activities delineated later in the schedule.
      (C) Root-cause analysis must be performed.
      (D) Revisions require management approval.

37. You have issued several revisions to your project's schedule. In some cases, your schedule delays are now severe. To ensure accurate performance measurement information, you should:

      (A) Rebaseline your schedule.
      (B) Initiate a change request.
      (C) Prepare a master schedule.
      (D) Issue a schedule update.

38. Decomposition is a technique used for both scope and activity definition. Which statement best describes the role decomposition plays in activity definition as compared to scope definition?

      (A) Final output is described in terms of work packages in the WBS.
      (B) Final output is described as deliverables or tangible items.
      (C) Final output is described as activities or action steps.
      (D) Decomposition is used the same way in scope definition and activity definition.

39. To best practice effective schedule control you inform your project team to be alert to any issues that may cause problems in the future. To best accomplish this, you tell the team to?

(A) Review performance reports.
(B) Update the schedule management plan on a continuous basis.
(C) Hold status reviews.
(D) Allow no changes to the schedule.

40. Which of the following would normally not result in an increased duration for an activity relative to its base estimate?

(A) The activity requires extensive interaction with various end-users.
(B) The assigned resource has other concurrent responsibilities and cannot work continuously on the task.
(C) The activity has three people assigned who must all work together to complete the task.
(D) The activity involves the performance of very detailed and accurate work.

41. Your company is adopting the management-by-projects approach for conducting its business. It now has more than 50 ongoing projects throughout the country instead of one or two major projects at a time. You are a program manager. Four project managers work for you. Each project manager is responsible for at least two projects. You must schedule and allocate resources for the projects that comprise your program. Which one of the following parameters should concern you primarily?

(A) Resource use and resource leveling.
(B) Duration compression and simulation.
(C) Activity lists and the WBS.
(D) Schedule slippage and in-process inventory.

42. The completion of a local government study resides on your critical path. This would most likely be referred to as?

(A) Soft logic
(B) Hard logic
(C) An external dependency
(D) A mandatory dependency

43. You are working on a new company project that will enable faxing through a sophisticated voice recognition system. Your company's marketing department just informed you that a major competitor is developing a similar product. Initially you decided to use resource leveling because your early-start schedule indicated that more resources were required during certain time periods than during others and because you were not under any great time pressure to complete the project. Now that you are pressured to beat your competitor to market, you need to develop a project schedule that is as close to the original one as possible. To do this, you should use:

(A) Reverse resource allocation
(B) Resource reallocation
(C) Critical chain scheduling
(D) Resource manipulation

44. All of the following statements are true regarding Monte Carlo analysis except?

(A) Monte Carlo is used to determine potential project outcomes by simulating the project under different scenarios.
(B) Monte Carlo analysis can be used during the schedule development and qualitative risk analysis process.
(C) Monte Carlo computes project costs by using possible costs.
(D) Monte Carlo Analysis is a simulation technique that can help quantify risks associated with the project.

45. You have issued several revisions to your project's schedule. In some cases, your schedule delays are now severe. To ensure accurate performance measurement information, you should:

    (A) Prepare a master schedule.
    (B) Initiate a change request.
    (C) Issue a schedule update.
    (D) Rebaseline your schedule.

46. Which of the following is usually a result of fast tracking a project?

    (A) Activities will have to be removed from the critical path.
    (B) Increased risk.
    (C) Potential cost overrun.
    (D) Activity durations will have to be compressed.

47. You are working to close out your project. During these hectic final days of the project, most conflict arises from:

    (A) Technical problems
    (B) Lack of customer acceptance
    (C) Schedule problems
    (D) Cost overruns

48. Which of the following provides the best definition for lag?

    (A) Activity waiting time.
    (B) The product of a forward and backward pass.
    (C) The amount of time a task can be delayed without delaying the project.
    (D) The amount of time a task can be delayed without delaying the early start date of its successor.

49. To practice effective schedule control, your project team must be alert to any issues that may cause problems in the future. To best accomplish this, the team should:

    (A) Review performance reports.
    (B) Allow no changes to the schedule.
    (C) Update the schedule management plan on a continuous basis.
    (D) Hold status reviews.

50. A schedule performance index (SPI) of less than 1.0 indicates that the:

    (A) Project is running behind the monetary value of the work it planned to accomplish.
    (B) Earned value physically accomplished thus far is 100%.
    (C) Project has experienced a permanent loss of time.
    (D) Project may not be on schedule, but the project manager need not be concerned.

51. As an advisor to a new project manager you inform the project manager to create lessons learned at the end of a project. Lessons learned include which of the following?

    (A) Reports from management.
    (B) All the plans used in the project.
    (C) Variances and their causes.
    (D) Reports from the customer.

52. A project manager looks at her schedule and sees that there has been a delay in completing a task. It seems practical to move a person from another task who is an expert on the work that is being done. There is a choice of using two different persons who are working on two different tasks. One person is working on a task that has five days of free float and the other is working on a task that has eight days of total float and no free float. Which person should be used to help out?

(A) The person working on the task with total float of eight days.
(B) The person working on the task with free float of five days.
(C) A person should be brought in from outside the project.
(D) Either person can be used.

53. Management has informed you that the resources for your project are to be reduced. Management wants to know how long the project will take if nine resources per month are committed to your project. What is this activity called?

(A) Resource leveling
(B) Fast tracking
(C) Crashing
(D) Resource floating

54. You are working on a product that will enable e-mail use through a sophisticated voice recognition system. Your company's marketing department just informed you that a major competitor is developing a similar product. Initially you decided to use resource leveling because your early-start schedule indicated that more resources were required during certain time periods than during others and because you were not under any great time pressure to complete the project. Now that you are pressured to beat your competitor to market, you need to develop a project schedule that is as close to the original one as possible. To do this, you should use:

(A) Critical chain scheduling
(B) Resource reallocation
(C) Resource manipulation
(D) Reverse resource allocation

55. Resource leveling will generally:

(A) Increase the total time necessary to do all the tasks.
(B) Reduce the time needed to do the project.
(C) Reduce resources to the lowest skill that is possible.
(D) Reduce the overutilization of resources.

56. You work for one of the leading manufacturers of country and western apparel. You are managing a project to redesign retail store layout to improve customer throughput and efficiency. Much of the project work must be done on site and will require the active participation of store employees. Many of these employees are lifelong members of a powerful union that has a reputation for labor unrest. One important component of your schedule must be:

(A) Buffers and reserves
(B) A resource capabilities matrix
(C) A resource histogram
(D) A resource calendar

57. As the project manager for a large company project, you are reviewing your project's network diagram (as shown in the following in the image), given the diagram, what is the relationship between tasks F and G?

(A) FS
(B) SS
(C) FF
(D) SF

58. Management has decided to crash a project to avoid penalty payments for late deliveries. Additional costs are expected. To crash the project, either overtime or additional resources should be assigned to:

(A) Those activities with the greatest degree of risk.
(B) Those activities on the critical path beginning with the longest time duration activities.
(C) Those activities with the longest time duration.
(D) All activities.

59. To assess the implications of crashing a project, a project manager should first compute:

(A) The cost of additional resources to be added to the project's critical path.
(B) The cost and time slope for each critical activity that can be expedited.
(C) The time estimates for each critical path activity.
(D) The time that will be saved in the overall schedule when tasks are expedited on the critical path.

60. Several years ago, you were involved in a prior project where a team of 7 developers were able to create a similar software application in 100 days. Therefore, in estimating the duration for this new project, you decide to use 100 days as an estimate. This is an example of which type of estimating technique?

(A) Analogous estimating
(B) Decomposition
(C) Qualitatively based durations
(D) Three point estimates

61. Project managers should pay attention to critical and subcritical activities when evaluating project time performance. One way to do this is to analyze 10 subcritical paths in order of ascending float. This approach is part of:

(A) Earned value management
(B) Trend analysis
(C) Variance analysis
(D) Simulation

62. You are the project manager for a project with the following network diagram (see image). Studying the diagram, which path is the critical path?

(A) E B C D
(B) A B C D
(C) E G H
(D) E F H

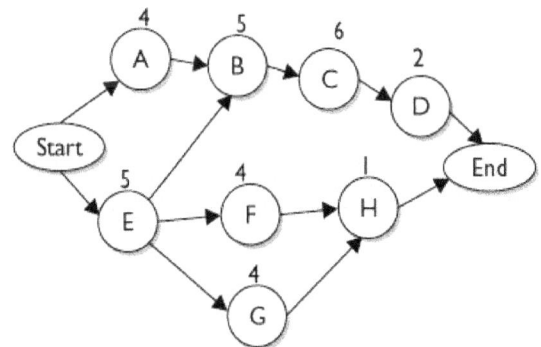

63. Your customer wants your project, a process to help eliminate all bad meat before it reaches consumers, to be completed 6 months earlier than planned. You believe you can meet this target by overlapping project activities. The approach you plan to use is known as:

(A) Fast-tracking
(B) Crashing
(C) Leveling
(D) Concurrent engineering

64. Five tasks are scheduled to be completed in sequence. Each task has a finish-start relationship with the next task. Each has one day of total float. As of today, task one and two have been completed on schedule. How many days of float remain in the schedule for these tasks?

    (A) Two
    (B) One
    (C) Zero
    (D) Four

65. Your company, which operates one of the region's largest chemical processing plants, has been convicted of illegally dumping toxic substances into the town's river killing all the fish. The court has mandated that the required cleanup activities be completed by December 30. Such a constraint is an example of:

    (A) A major milestone
    (B) A key event
    (C) An external dependency
    (D) An imposed date

66. Fast tracking requires greater project control because it is a practice that increases _____, while shortening the _____ of the project.

    (A) Budgeted cost of work performed, scheduled end date.
    (B) Level of effort, late finish date.
    (C) Risk, duration.
    (D) Benefit cost ratio, actual cost of work performed.

67. A project manager has increased project costs by $100,000, but completed the project four weeks earlier than planned. What tool is best described here?

    (A) Crashing
    (B) Fast tracking
    (C) Resource leveling
    (D) Duration compression

68. You need to assess the implications of crashing a project. What is the first thing you should do?

    (A) The cost of additional resources to be added to the project's critical path.
    (B) The cost and time slope for each critical activity that can be expedited.
    (C) The resource cost for each person involved on the project.
    (D) The time that will be saved in the overall schedule when tasks are expedited on the critical path.

69. All of the following are outputs of the activity definition process except?

    (A) Decomposition
    (B) Activity list
    (C) Activity attributes
    (D) Requested changes

70. Your project is behind schedule due to conflict among team members. After resolving the conflict, you should consider?

    (A) Reassigning resources.
    (B) Crashing the schedule.
    (C) Leveling the resources.
    (D) Reducing resource loads.

71. Crashing the schedule means:

    (A) Running the project team on overtime.
    (B) Making the project shorter by any economic means.
    (C) Getting out of town before the project is in trouble.
    (D) Doing activities that were in sequence in parallel.

72. An activity that consumes no time or resources and shows only that a dependency exists between two activities is called?

    (A) A milestone
    (B) A hammock
    (C) A dummy activity
    (D) A hanger

73. Which of the following statements is false regarding various activity scheduling tools?

    (A) ADM approach uses arrows to represent activities, and is an example of a activity-on-arrow (AOA) network.
    (B) ADM allows for conditional branching and iteration of activities.
    (C) PDM allows for conditional branching and iteration of activities.
    (D) PDM is also known as an activity on arrow (AOA) network.

74. All of the following are advantages to using templates to create activity lists except:

    (A) Saving planning time.
    (B) Encouraging creative thinking.
    (C) Reducing risk.
    (D) Indicating required resource skills.

75. In the past, you used bar charts when presenting project status to management because they are easy for everyone, even senior management, to understand. The project office issued a new procedure today requiring project managers to prepare milestone charts and to update them every 2 weeks. Unlike bar charts, milestone charts show:

    (A) Activity start and end dates.
    (B) Dependencies.
    (C) Expected durations.
    (D) Scheduled start or completion of major deliverables and key events.

76. Fast tracking requires more sophisticated schedule and control methods because it is a practice that _____ the schedule to place the system in operation at _____?

    (A) increases; minimum cost.
    (B) compresses; an earlier date.
    (C) moderates; the first opportunity.
    (D) stabilizes; an earlier date.

77. A precedence diagram and an arrow diagram are both examples of networks. The primary difference between them is that the:

    (A) Precedence diagram represents activities as nodes.
    (B) Arrow diagram incorporates standard deviation in the activity duration.
    (C) Precedence diagram uses float as part of the activity duration.
    (D) Arrow diagram does not indicate critical path.

78. All of the following are outputs of the activity definition process except?

   (A) Decomposition
   (B) Requested changes
   (C) Activity list
   (D) Activity attributes

79. The customer increased your project scope by 65%. This increased your cost estimate fivefold. Now you must change the scheduled start and finish dates in your approved project schedule. Your first step should be to:

   (A) Rebaseline the schedule.
   (B) Modify the contract.
   (C) Use a new target schedule.
   (D) Add resources.

80. An activity has an early start date of the 10th and a late start date of the 19th. The activity has a duration of 4 days. There are no non-workdays. From the information given, what can be concluded about the activity?

   (A) The late finish date is the 25th.
   (B) The activity can be completed in 2 days if the resources devoted to it are doubled.
   (C) Total float for the activity is 9 days.
   (D) The early finish date of the activity is the end of the day on the 14th.

81. A benefit of using a schedule change control system is that it includes the:

   (A) Requirements for reporting schedule performance.
   (B) Requirements for measuring schedule performance.
   (C) Methods for assessing the magnitude of schedule variations.
   (D) Approval levels necessary for authorizing schedule changes.

82. In performance reports related to schedule performance, which of the following items are unique to activities in progress?

   (A) Actual start date.
   (B) Forecast remaining time.
   (C) Baseline finish date.
   (D) Baseline start date.

83. A completion of a local government study resides on your critical path. This would most likely be referred to as:

   (A) hard logic.
   (B) soft logic.
   (C) a mandatory dependency.
   (D) an external dependency.

84. A task was scheduled to use two persons, full time, and take two weeks to complete. Instead, the project manager was only able to assign one person to this task. At the end of two weeks, the person assigned to the task was 75% complete. What is the cost performance index?

   (A) 1.5
   (B) .75
   (C) .5
   (D) 1.33

85. In project development, schedule information such as who will perform the work, where the work will be performed, activity type, and WBS classification are examples of:

    (A) Constraints
    (B) Activity attributes
    (C) Refinements
    (D) Data in the WBS repository

86. In the first attempt at resource leveling the project schedule, what would you expect to occur?

    (A) The number of required resources will increase during certain time periods of the project.
    (B) The number of required resources will decrease during certain time periods of the project.
    (C) The overall project duration will increase.
    (D) The overall project duration will decrease.

87. The project schedule is not used to determine:

    (A) The start and finish dates of the activities.
    (B) Occasional changes to the activity listing.
    (C) The total float of the activities.
    (D) The project's budget.

88. After analyzing the status of your project you determine that the project is two weeks behind schedule. You want to recover the original schedule if possible, and there is plenty of remaining budget in the current plan. Which of the following your best option?

    (A) Inform the team that overtime will be required for a short time to recover the schedule.
    (B) Crash the schedule.
    (C) Compress the testing and quality management portion of the project.
    (D) Reduce the scope of work with a change request.

89. If, when developing a project schedule, you want to define a distribution of probable results for each activity and use it to calculate a distribution of probable results for the total project, the most common technique to use is:

    (A) Resource leveling
    (B) Monte Carlo analysis
    (C) Critical path method
    (D) Concurrent engineering

90. Project schedule development is an iterative process. If the start and finish dates are not realistic, the project probably will not finish as planned. Because you realize the importance of schedule control, you are working with your team to define how to manage schedule changes. You documented your decisions in which one of the following:

    (A) Schedule change control procedures.
    (B) Schedule management plan.
    (C) Schedule risk plan.
    (D) Service-level agreement.

Sample Answer Sheet

	T F		T F		T F		T F
1	Ⓐ Ⓑ Ⓒ Ⓓ Ⓔ	26	Ⓐ Ⓑ Ⓒ Ⓓ Ⓔ	51	Ⓐ Ⓑ Ⓒ Ⓓ Ⓔ	76	Ⓐ Ⓑ Ⓒ Ⓓ Ⓔ
2	Ⓐ Ⓑ Ⓒ Ⓓ Ⓔ	27	Ⓐ Ⓑ Ⓒ Ⓓ Ⓔ	52	Ⓐ Ⓑ Ⓒ Ⓓ Ⓔ	77	Ⓐ Ⓑ Ⓒ Ⓓ Ⓔ
3	Ⓐ Ⓑ Ⓒ Ⓓ Ⓔ	28	Ⓐ Ⓑ Ⓒ Ⓓ Ⓔ	53	Ⓐ Ⓑ Ⓒ Ⓓ Ⓔ	78	Ⓐ Ⓑ Ⓒ Ⓓ Ⓔ
4	Ⓐ Ⓑ Ⓒ Ⓓ Ⓔ	29	Ⓐ Ⓑ Ⓒ Ⓓ Ⓔ	54	Ⓐ Ⓑ Ⓒ Ⓓ Ⓔ	79	Ⓐ Ⓑ Ⓒ Ⓓ Ⓔ
5	Ⓐ Ⓑ Ⓒ Ⓓ Ⓔ	30	Ⓐ Ⓑ Ⓒ Ⓓ Ⓔ	55	Ⓐ Ⓑ Ⓒ Ⓓ Ⓔ	80	Ⓐ Ⓑ Ⓒ Ⓓ Ⓔ
6	Ⓐ Ⓑ Ⓒ Ⓓ Ⓔ	31	Ⓐ Ⓑ Ⓒ Ⓓ Ⓔ	56	Ⓐ Ⓑ Ⓒ Ⓓ Ⓔ	81	Ⓐ Ⓑ Ⓒ Ⓓ Ⓔ
7	Ⓐ Ⓑ Ⓒ Ⓓ Ⓔ	32	Ⓐ Ⓑ Ⓒ Ⓓ Ⓔ	57	Ⓐ Ⓑ Ⓒ Ⓓ Ⓔ	82	Ⓐ Ⓑ Ⓒ Ⓓ Ⓔ
8	Ⓐ Ⓑ Ⓒ Ⓓ Ⓔ	33	Ⓐ Ⓑ Ⓒ Ⓓ Ⓔ	58	Ⓐ Ⓑ Ⓒ Ⓓ Ⓔ	83	Ⓐ Ⓑ Ⓒ Ⓓ Ⓔ
9	Ⓐ Ⓑ Ⓒ Ⓓ Ⓔ	34	Ⓐ Ⓑ Ⓒ Ⓓ Ⓔ	59	Ⓐ Ⓑ Ⓒ Ⓓ Ⓔ	84	Ⓐ Ⓑ Ⓒ Ⓓ Ⓔ
10	Ⓐ Ⓑ Ⓒ Ⓓ Ⓔ	35	Ⓐ Ⓑ Ⓒ Ⓓ Ⓔ	60	Ⓐ Ⓑ Ⓒ Ⓓ Ⓔ	85	Ⓐ Ⓑ Ⓒ Ⓓ Ⓔ
11	Ⓐ Ⓑ Ⓒ Ⓓ Ⓔ	36	Ⓐ Ⓑ Ⓒ Ⓓ Ⓔ	61	Ⓐ Ⓑ Ⓒ Ⓓ Ⓔ	86	Ⓐ Ⓑ Ⓒ Ⓓ Ⓔ
12	Ⓐ Ⓑ Ⓒ Ⓓ Ⓔ	37	Ⓐ Ⓑ Ⓒ Ⓓ Ⓔ	62	Ⓐ Ⓑ Ⓒ Ⓓ Ⓔ	87	Ⓐ Ⓑ Ⓒ Ⓓ Ⓔ
13	Ⓐ Ⓑ Ⓒ Ⓓ Ⓔ	38	Ⓐ Ⓑ Ⓒ Ⓓ Ⓔ	63	Ⓐ Ⓑ Ⓒ Ⓓ Ⓔ	88	Ⓐ Ⓑ Ⓒ Ⓓ Ⓔ
14	Ⓐ Ⓑ Ⓒ Ⓓ Ⓔ	39	Ⓐ Ⓑ Ⓒ Ⓓ Ⓔ	64	Ⓐ Ⓑ Ⓒ Ⓓ Ⓔ	89	Ⓐ Ⓑ Ⓒ Ⓓ Ⓔ
15	Ⓐ Ⓑ Ⓒ Ⓓ Ⓔ	40	Ⓐ Ⓑ Ⓒ Ⓓ Ⓔ	65	Ⓐ Ⓑ Ⓒ Ⓓ Ⓔ	90	Ⓐ Ⓑ Ⓒ Ⓓ Ⓔ
16	Ⓐ Ⓑ Ⓒ Ⓓ Ⓔ	41	Ⓐ Ⓑ Ⓒ Ⓓ Ⓔ	66	Ⓐ Ⓑ Ⓒ Ⓓ Ⓔ	91	Ⓐ Ⓑ Ⓒ Ⓓ Ⓔ
17	Ⓐ Ⓑ Ⓒ Ⓓ Ⓔ	42	Ⓐ Ⓑ Ⓒ Ⓓ Ⓔ	67	Ⓐ Ⓑ Ⓒ Ⓓ Ⓔ	92	Ⓐ Ⓑ Ⓒ Ⓓ Ⓔ
18	Ⓐ Ⓑ Ⓒ Ⓓ Ⓔ	43	Ⓐ Ⓑ Ⓒ Ⓓ Ⓔ	68	Ⓐ Ⓑ Ⓒ Ⓓ Ⓔ	93	Ⓐ Ⓑ Ⓒ Ⓓ Ⓔ
19	Ⓐ Ⓑ Ⓒ Ⓓ Ⓔ	44	Ⓐ Ⓑ Ⓒ Ⓓ Ⓔ	69	Ⓐ Ⓑ Ⓒ Ⓓ Ⓔ	94	Ⓐ Ⓑ Ⓒ Ⓓ Ⓔ
20	Ⓐ Ⓑ Ⓒ Ⓓ Ⓔ	45	Ⓐ Ⓑ Ⓒ Ⓓ Ⓔ	70	Ⓐ Ⓑ Ⓒ Ⓓ Ⓔ	95	Ⓐ Ⓑ Ⓒ Ⓓ Ⓔ
21	Ⓐ Ⓑ Ⓒ Ⓓ Ⓔ	46	Ⓐ Ⓑ Ⓒ Ⓓ Ⓔ	71	Ⓐ Ⓑ Ⓒ Ⓓ Ⓔ	96	Ⓐ Ⓑ Ⓒ Ⓓ Ⓔ
22	Ⓐ Ⓑ Ⓒ Ⓓ Ⓔ	47	Ⓐ Ⓑ Ⓒ Ⓓ Ⓔ	72	Ⓐ Ⓑ Ⓒ Ⓓ Ⓔ	97	Ⓐ Ⓑ Ⓒ Ⓓ Ⓔ
23	Ⓐ Ⓑ Ⓒ Ⓓ Ⓔ	48	Ⓐ Ⓑ Ⓒ Ⓓ Ⓔ	73	Ⓐ Ⓑ Ⓒ Ⓓ Ⓔ	98	Ⓐ Ⓑ Ⓒ Ⓓ Ⓔ
24	Ⓐ Ⓑ Ⓒ Ⓓ Ⓔ	49	Ⓐ Ⓑ Ⓒ Ⓓ Ⓔ	74	Ⓐ Ⓑ Ⓒ Ⓓ Ⓔ	99	Ⓐ Ⓑ Ⓒ Ⓓ Ⓔ
25	Ⓐ Ⓑ Ⓒ Ⓓ Ⓔ	50	Ⓐ Ⓑ Ⓒ Ⓓ Ⓔ	75	Ⓐ Ⓑ Ⓒ Ⓓ Ⓔ	100	Ⓐ Ⓑ Ⓒ Ⓓ Ⓔ

Project Time Management – Answers

1. (C) crashing the schedule. Crashing - is a schedule compression technique in which cost and schedule tradeoffs are analyzed to determine how to obtain the greatest amount of compression for the least incremental cost. Crashing does not always produce a viable alternative and can result in increased cost.

2. (D) The schedule and budget baselines should be changed, to show the new work. When a risk is identified, budget and schedule time are identified and put into the contingency reserve. If the risk actually occurs the money is used from the contingency reserve and added to the operating budget of the project. The total project budget contains the operating project budget or baseline, contingency reserve, and the management reserve. The project budget baseline is increased by the amount of the risk although the total project budget stays the same. The schedule baseline is changed to reflect the new activities that have to be done.

3. (A) Making the most efficient use of the available resources. Resource Leveling - any form of schedule network analysis in which scheduling decisions (start and finish dates) are driven by resource constraints (e.g., limited resource availability or difficult-to-manage changes in resource availability levels).

4. (D) All of the above. Estimating schedule activity resources involves determining what resources (persons, equipment, or materiel) and what quantities of each resource will be used, and when each resource will be available to perform project activities.

5. (A) Mandatory. Mandatory dependencies are those that are inherent in the nature of the work being done. They often involve physical limitations. (On a construction project, it is impossible to erect the superstructure until after the foundation has been built; on an electronics project, a prototype must be built before it can be tested.) Mandatory dependencies are also called hard logic.

6. (A) Project schedule. The approved project schedule is a key input to schedule control. It is the schedule baseline, and it provides the basis for measuring and reporting schedule performance.

7. (D) A resource calendar. Project and resource calendars identify periods when work is allowed. Project calendars affect all resources. Resource calendars affect a specific resource or a resource category, such as a labor contract that requires certain workers to work on certain days of the week.

8. (A) Free float. Free Float (FF) - the amount of time that a schedule activity can be delayed without delaying the early start of any immediately following schedule activities.

9. (A) risk impact of crashing each task. Crashing - a specific type of project schedule compression technique performed by taking action to decrease the total project schedule duration* after analyzing a number of alternatives to determine how to get the maximum schedule duration compression for the least additional cost. Typical approaches for crashing a schedule include reducing schedule activity durations and increasing the assignment of resources on schedule activities.

10. (D) Placement of the activity on the logic diagram line. Precedence diagramming method (PDM). This is a method of constructing a project network diagram using nodes to represent the activities and connecting them with arrows that show the dependencies. This technique is also called activity-on-node (AON) and is the method used by nearly all project management software packages.

11. (A) Lag. Lag - a modification of a logical relationship that directs a delay in the successor activity. For example, in a finish-to-start dependency with a ten-day lag, the successor activity cannot start until ten days after the predecessor activity has finished.

12. (C) Accelerating the performance of tasks on the critical path. Crashing - is a schedule compression technique in which cost and schedule tradeoffs are analyzed to determine how to obtain the greatest amount of compression for the least incremental cost. Crashing does not always produce a viable alternative and can result in increased cost.

13. (B) Work Breakdown Structure. The Work Breakdown Structure is the best choice for this scenario.

14. (C) Finish to finish. Finish-to-Finish - the completion of the successor activity depends upon the completion of the predecessor activity.

15. (C) Critical path method (CPM). Critical Path Method - a schedule network analysis technique used to determine the amount of scheduling flexibility (the amount of float) on various logical network paths in the project schedule network, and to determine the minimum total project duration. Early start and finish dates are calculated by means of a forward pass, using a specified start date. Late start and finish dates are calculated by means of a backward pass, starting from a specified completion date, which sometimes is the project early finish date determined during the forward pass calculation.

16. (D) External dependencies. Before the work can begin, the certification class must be completed.

17. (A) The cost and time slope for each critical activity that can be expedited. Crashing - is a schedule compression technique in which cost and schedule tradeoffs are analyzed to determine how to obtain the greatest amount of compression for the least incremental cost. Crashing does not always produce a viable alternative and can result in increased cost. (PMBOK Guide - page 145)

18. (D) Calendar time between the start of A to the finish of B is 11 days. The duration of A, which is 3, is added to the duration of B, which is 4, for a total of 7. The 3 days between the activities is lag and not duration. The lag is a constraint and must be taken into account as part of the network calculations, but it does not consume resources. The total time by the calendar is 11 days as counted from the morning of Monday the 4th. The lag occurs over Thursday, Friday, and Saturday. Sunday is a non-workday, so activity B does not start until Monday the 11th. Therefore, the calendar time is 11 days, and activity B ends on Thursday the 14th.

19. (C) Root cause analysis. Corrective action frequently requires root cause analysis to identify the cause of the variation. The analysis may address schedule activities other than the schedule activity actually causing the deviation; therefore, schedule recovery from the variance can be planned and executed using schedule activities delineated later in the project schedule.

20. (D) Start no earlier than. Imposed dates on activity starts or finishes can be used to restrict the start or finish to occur either no earlier than a specified date or no later than a specified date. Although all four date constraints typically are available in project management software, start no earlier than and finish no later than constraints are used most commonly.

21. (D) Reschedule the activity with float. The activity that has eighteen days of free float can be rescheduled without having to reschedule any other activity in the project. If this activity is rescheduled to start two weeks later, the resource will not be overutilized, and the project will remain on schedule.

22. (B) Mandatory or hard. Mandatory dependencies often involve physical limitations, such as on a construction project, where it is impossible to erect the superstructure until after the foundation has been built, or on an electronics project, where a prototype must be built before it can be tested. Mandatory dependencies are also sometimes referred to as hard logic.

23. (C) Using the arrow diagramming method instead of the precedence diagramming method (PDM) of scheduling. Mandatory dependencies are those which are inherent in the nature of the work being done. Discretionary dependencies are those which are defined by the project management team. They should be used with care (and fully documented) since they may limit later scheduling options. Resource requirements. The resources assigned to them will significantly influence the duration of most activities and the project itself. Resource capabilities. The duration of most activities will be significantly influenced by the capabilities of the humans and material resources assigned to them.

24. (A) Tasks. The Guide to the PMBOK defines the lowest level of the work breakdown structure as the work package. It goes on to say that the work package is a unit of work that can be assigned to a person or organization. It also says that the work package can be broken down into tasks, and that tasks can be broken down into activities.

25. (C) May 1. The early finish date of activity A is the same as its start date and the start of the project. Activities start on the beginning of the time period that work begins and end on the end of the time period that work finishes. This activity takes one day beginning in the morning of May 1 and finishing in the afternoon of May 1.

26. (C) Parametric. Estimating the basis for activity durations can be quantitatively determined by multiplying the quantity of work to be performed by the productivity rate. For example, productivity rates can be estimated on a design project by the number of drawings times labor hours per drawing, or a cable installation in meters of cable times labor hours per meter. The total resource quantities are multiplied by the labor hours per work period or the production capability per work period, and divided by the number of those resources being applied to determine activity duration in work periods.

27. (C) Fast tracking. Fast tracking - A schedule compression technique in which phases or activities that normally would be done in sequence are performed in parallel.

28. (C) Fast tracking. Fast tracking - is a schedule compression technique in which phases or activities that normally would be done in sequence are performed in parallel. An example would be to construct the foundation for a building before all the architectural drawings are complete. Fast tracking can result in rework and increased risk. This approach can require work to be performed without completed detailed information, such as engineering drawings. It results in trading cost for time, and increases the risk of achieving the shortened project schedule.

29. (A) The critical path is the list of activities that have zero float. The critical path activities are those activities that have zero float. There are exceptions. When activities are forced to be done on specific dates (date constraints), it is possible to create negative float. When the project is resource constrained the critical path may change due to resource constraints.

30. (C) Perform resource leveling. Resource Leveling - any form of schedule network analysis in which scheduling decisions (start and finish dates) are driven by resource constraints (e.g., limited resource availability or difficult-to-manage changes in resource availability levels).

31. (C) Monte Carlo analysis. Monte Carlo analysis is a simulation technique that assigns durations to tasks in a schedule and then calculates the schedule information. It repeats this assignment and calculation many times and then reports statistical results, including the percent of time a task is on the critical path.

32. (B) Lag. A lag directs a delay in the successor activity. For example, to account for a ten-day curing period for concrete, a ten-day lag on a finish-to-start relationship could be used, which means the successor activity cannot start until ten days after the predecessor is completed.

33. (A) Duration compression. Duration Compression - shortening the project schedule with reducing the project scope. Compression is not always possible and often requires an increase in cost. (Crashing utilizes duration compression)

34. (C) Resource reallocation. Resource leveling often results in a project duration that is no longer than the preliminary schedule. Resource reallocation from non-critical to critical activities is a common way to bring the project back on track, or as close as possible, to its originally intended overall duration.

35. (C) An imposed date. Imposed Date - A fixed date imposed on a schedule activity or schedule milestone, usually in the form of a "start no earlier than" and "finish no later than" date.

36. (A) Historical data will be lost for the project schedule. Some schedule delays are so severe that rebaselining is needed to provide realistic data in which to measure performance. Rebaselining should be used as a last resort, however, and should be used with care because historical data will be lost. It also is important to document lessons learned in the schedule control process.

37. (A) Rebaseline your schedule. In some cases, schedule delays may be so severe that rebaselining is needed for accurate performance measurement. Such cases demonstrate the importance of integrating schedule control with the integrated project change control system.

38. (C) Final output is described as activities or action steps. The technique of decomposition, as it is applied to activity definition, involves subdividing the project work packages into smaller, more manageable components called schedule activities. The Activity Definition process defines the final outputs as schedule activities rather than as deliverables, as is done in the Create WBS process.

39. (A) Review performance reports. Performance Reports - documents and presentations that provide organized and summarized work performance information, earned value management parameters and calculations, and analyses of project work progress and status. Common formats for performance reports include bar charts, S-curves, histograms, tables, and project schedule network diagram showing current schedule status.

40. (D) The activity involves the performance of very detailed and accurate work. This is an example of a question where you must select the best answer, not one that is necessarily always true. Presumably the nature of the detailed and accurate work would be known at the time the base estimate was made. All the other choices involve the uncertainties of coordinating with other team members which is inherently uncertain.

41. (D) Schedule slippage and in-process inventory. Schedule slippage occurs when the project's actual due or delivery date falls beyond its planned, or scheduled, date. This parameter may result in penalty costs that reduce profits, and slippage of one project may cause slippage in others. In-process inventory is the amount of work waiting to be processed. A shortage of project resources can affect this parameter by creating costly inventory backups.

42. (C) An external dependency. External dependencies are those that involve a relationship between project activities and non-project activities.

43. (B) Resource reallocation. Resource leveling often results in a project duration that is no longer than the preliminary schedule. Resource reallocation from non-critical to critical activities is a common way to bring the project back on track, or as close as possible, to its originally intended overall duration.

44. (B) Monte Carlo analysis can be used during the schedule development and qualitative risk analysis process. Monte Carlo Analysis - a technique that computes, or iterates, the project cost or project schedule many times using input values selected at random from probability distributions of possible costs or durations, to calculate a distribution of possible total project cost or completion dates.

45. (D) Rebaseline your schedule. In some cases, schedule delays may be so severe that rebaselining is needed for accurate performance measurement. Such cases demonstrate the importance of integrating schedule control with the integrated project change control system.

46. (B) Increased risk. Fast tracking - is a schedule compression technique in which phases or activities that normally would be done in sequence are performed in parallel. An example would be to construct the foundation for a building before all the architectural drawings are complete. Fast tracking can result in rework and increased risk. This approach can require work to be performed without completed detailed information, such as engineering drawings. It results in trading cost for time, and increases the risk of achieving the shortened project schedule.

47. (C) Schedule problems. Any schedule slippage during project execution will become apparent in the final phase of the project. During closeout, projects with firm deadlines often become hectic, with activity focused on completing the project on time and to specification.

48. (A) Activity waiting time. Lag - a modification of a logical relationship that directs a delay in the successor activity. For example, in a finish-to-start dependency with a ten-day lag, the successor activity cannot start until ten days after the predecessor activity has finished.

49. (A) Review performance reports. Performance reports provide information on schedule performance, such as which planned dates have been met and which have not. Performance reports may also alert the project team to issues that may cause schedule performance problems in the future.

50. (A) Project is running behind the monetary value of the work it planned to accomplish. Schedule Performance Index (SPI) - The schedule efficiency ratio of earned value accomplished against the planned value. The SPI describes what portion of the planned schedule was actually accomplished. SPI = EV/PV.

51. (C) Variances and their causes. Lessons learned documentation of the causes of variance, the reasoning behind the corrective actions chosen, and other types of lessons learned from schedule control are documented in the organizational process assets (Section 4.1.1.4), so that they become part of the historical database for both the project and other projects of the performing organization.

52. (B) The person working on the task with free float of five days. The person who is working on the task that has free float of five days can be used on the task that is in trouble for five days without affecting the other task schedules in the project. The person working on the task that has total float of eight days can be used on the task that is in trouble, but since there is zero free float for this task, there will have to be a rescheduling of other tasks to allow this.

53. (A) Resource leveling. Resource Leveling - any form of schedule network analysis in which scheduling decisions (start and finish dates) are driven by resource constraints (e.g., limited resource availability or difficult-to-manage changes in resource availability levels).

54. (B) Resource reallocation. Resource leveling is a schedule network analysis technique applied to a schedule model that has already been analyzed by the critical path method. Resource leveling is used to address schedule activities that need to be performed to meet specified delivery dates, to address the situation where shared or critical required resources are only available at certain times or are only available in limited quantities, or to keep selected resource usage at a constant level during specific time periods of the project work. This resource usage leveling approach can cause the original critical path to change.

55. (D) Reduce the overutilization of resources. Resource leveling is a tool in most project management software and can also be done manually. In resource leveling an attempt is made to reduce overutilization of resources to their normal utilization.

56. (D) A resource calendar. Project and resource calendars identify periods when work is allowed. Project calendars affect all resources. Resource calendars affect a specific resource or a resource category, such as a labor contract that requires certain workers to work on certain days of the week.

57. (A) FS. G is slated to start immediately after F, so this is a finish-to-start relationship. In other words, F must finish so G may start.

58. (B) Those activities on the critical path beginning with the longest time duration activities. Crashing is a schedule compression technique in which cost and schedule tradeoffs are analyzed to determine how to obtain the greatest amount of compression for the least incremental cost. Crashing does not always produce a viable alternative and can result in increased cost.

59. (B) The cost and time slope for each critical activity that can be expedited. Slope - (Crash cost - Normal cost)/(Crash time - Normal time). This calculation shows the cost per day of crashing the project. The slope is negative to indicate that as the time required for a project or task decreases, the cost increases. If the costs and times are the same regardless of whether they are crashed or normal, the activity cannot be expedited.

60. (A) Analogous estimating. Analogous duration estimating means using the actual duration of a previous, similar schedule activity as the basis for estimating the duration of a future schedule activity. It is frequently used to estimate project duration when there is a limited amount of detailed information about the project for example, in the early phases of a project. Analogous estimating uses historical information and expert judgment.

61. (C) Variance analysis. Performing the schedule variance analysis during the schedule monitoring process is a key function of schedule control. Comparing target schedule dates with the actual/forecast start and finish dates provides useful information for the detection of deviations, and for the implementation of corrective actions in case of delays. The total float variance is also an essential planning component to evaluate project time performance.

62. (A) E B C D. The critical path is E B C D as it is the longest path to completion at 18 days.

63. (A) Fast-tracking. Fast Tracking - a specific project schedule compression technique that changes network logic to overlap phases that would normally be done in sequence, such as the design phase and construction phase, or to perform schedule activities in parallel.

64. (B) One. Although total float is assigned to each of the tasks in the sequence, the total float can be used by any of them and it can be used only one time by any of them. If the tasks are A B C D E and each has one day of float, if A is delayed by one day, the total float at B C D E reduces to zero.

65. (D) An imposed date. Dates that are required by the project sponsor, customer, or other external factors for the completion of certain deliverables are considered imposed dates.

66. (C) Risk, duration. Fast tracking - is a schedule compression technique in which phases or activities that normally would be done in sequence are performed in parallel. An example would be to construct the foundation for a building before all the architectural drawings are complete. Fast tracking can result in rework and increased risk. This approach can require work to be performed without completed detailed information, such as engineering drawings. It results in trading cost for time, and increases the risk of achieving the shortened project schedule.

67. (D) Duration compression. Duration Compression - shortening the project schedule with reducing the project scope. Compression is not always possible and often requires an increase in cost. (Crashing utilizes duration compression)

68. (B) The cost and time slope for each critical activity that can be expedited. Crashing - is a schedule compression technique in which cost and schedule tradeoffs are analyzed to determine how to obtain the greatest amount of compression for the least incremental cost. Crashing does not always produce a viable alternative and can result in increased cost.

69. (A) Decomposition. The outputs of the activity definition process are: activity list, activity attributes, milestone list and requested changes.

70. (B) Crashing the schedule. Crashing - is a schedule compression technique in which cost and schedule tradeoffs are analyzed to determine how to obtain the greatest amount of compression for the least incremental cost. Crashing does not always produce a viable alternative and can result in increased cost.

71. (B) Making the project shorter by any economic means. Crashing a schedule is improving the project completion date by any means that is economical and feasible. In crashing a schedule an effort is made to find the largest schedule reduction for the least additional cost.

72. (C) A dummy activity. Dummy Activity. A schedule activity of zero duration used to show a logical relationship in the arrow diagramming method. Dummy activities are used when logical relationships cannot be completely or correctly described with schedule activity arrows. Dummy activities are generally shown graphically as a dashed line headed by an arrow.

73. (A) ADM approach uses arrows to represent activities, and is an example of a activity-on-arrow (AOA) network. The ADM (Arrow Diagramming Method) approach uses arrows to represent activities, and is also known as a Activity-On-Arrow (AOA) network. On the other hand, PDM (Precedence Diagramming Method) approach uses boxes (nodes) to represent activities, and arrows represent the relationship and dependencies of work packages. PDM is also known as a Activity-On-Nodes (AON) network, and NOT a Activity-On-Arrow (AOA) network.

74. (B) Encouraging creative thinking. The activities in templates can also contain a list of resource skills and their required hours of effort, identification of risks, expected deliverables, and other descriptive information. There is, however, a tendency to assume that the template list is already complete and thus to not think freshly about what might be different in the current project.

75. (D) Scheduled start or completion of major deliverables and key events. A milestone is a significant point or event in the project.

76. (B) compresses; an earlier date. Fast tracking. A schedule compression technique in which phases or activities that normally would be done in sequence are performed in parallel.

77. (A) Precedence diagram represents activities as nodes. Both diagramming methods show the logical relationships of project activities. The arrow diagram represents activities as arrows.

78. (A) Decomposition. The outputs of the activity definition process are: activity list, activity attributes, milestone list and requested changes.

79. (C) Use a new target schedule. Revisions are a special category of schedule updates that result in changes to the project's scheduled start or finish dates. These dates generally are revised in response to scope or estimate changes. Rebaselining may be required if schedule delays are so severe that realistic data is required to measure performance. Rebaselining should be used as a last resort in schedule control. New target schedules should be the usual mode of schedule revision.

80. (C) Total float for the activity is 9 days. Total float is computed by subtracting the early start date from the late start date, or 19-10 = 9. To compute the early finish date given a duration of 4, we would start counting the activity on the morning of the 10th; therefore, the activity would be completed at the end of day 13, not 14 (10, 11, 12, 13). If we started the activity on its late start date on the morning of the 19th, we would finish at the end of day 22, not 25. Insufficient information is provided to determine whether this activity can be completed in 2 days if the resources are doubled.

81. (D) Approval levels necessary for authorizing schedule changes. The schedule change control system defines the procedures by which the project schedule can be changed. It includes the paperwork, tracking systems, and approval levels necessary for authorizing changes. The schedule change control system is operated as part of the Integrated Change Control process.

82. (B) Forecast remaining time. All activities have baseline start and finish dates once project execution begins. Completed tasks also have an actual start date. Forecast remaining time only has meaning in the context of an activity in progress.

83. (D) an external dependency. The project management team identifies external dependencies during the process of establishing the sequence of activities. External dependencies are those that involve a relationship between project activities and non-project activities. For example, the testing schedule activity in a software project can be dependent on delivery of hardware from an external source, or governmental environmental hearings may need to be held before site preparation can begin on a construction project. This input can be based on historical information from previous projects of a similar nature or from seller contracts or proposals.

84. (A) 1.5. At the end of two weeks this task is 75% complete. The PV was to be 4 person-weeks, two people working full time for two weeks. The EV is therefore 3 person-weeks, .75 X 4. The AC is 2 person-weeks. The cost performance index is the EV / AC. CPI = 3 person-weeks / 2 person-weeks = 1.5.

85. (B) Activity attributes. Identifying activity attributes is helpful for further selection and sorting of planned activities.

86. (C) The overall project duration will increase. The logical analysis of the schedule often produces a preliminary schedule that requires more resources during certain time periods than are available, or requires changes in resource levels that are not manageable. Heuristics such as "allocate scarce resources to critical path activities first" can be applied to develop a schedule that reflects such constraints. Resource leveling, because of the limited availability of the resources, often results in a project duration that is longer than the preliminary schedule.

87. (D) The project's budget. The project schedule includes at least planned start and expected finish dates for each detail activity. A schedule update is any modification to the schedule information that is used to manage the project. Float is the amount of time that an activity may be delayed from its start without delaying the project finish date. Although the project's budget is the time phased expenditure of the project funds, it is not the project schedule and therefore the best answer.

88. (B) Crash the schedule. Crashing - a specific type of project schedule compression technique performed by taking action to decrease the total project schedule duration* after analyzing a number of alternatives to determine how to get the maximum schedule duration compression for the least additional cost. Typical approaches for crashing a schedule include reducing schedule activity durations and increasing the assignment of resources on schedule activities.

89. (B) Monte Carlo analysis. Simulation is a tool and a technique for schedule development. It involves calculating multiple project durations with different sets of activity assumptions. Monte Carlo analysis is the most commonly used simulation technique.

90. (B) Schedule management plan. The schedule management plan is a subsidiary element of the overall project plan. It defines how schedule changes will be managed. It may be formal or informal, highly detailed or broadly framed, or based on the specific project needs.

Project Cost Management

Project cost management includes the processes required to ensure that the project is completed within the approved budget. It is primarily concerned with the cost of the resources required to complete project activities.

A broader view of project cost management is often referred to as life-cycle costing. It involves including acquisition, operating, and disposal costs when evaluating various project alternatives. A creative approach used to optimize life cycle costs, save time, increase profits, improve quality, expand market share, use resources more effectively, and solve problems is called value engineering.

Life cycle costing and value engineering techniques are used together to reduce cost and time, improve quality and performance, and optimize the decision-making. In many application areas, predicting and analyzing the prospective financial performance of the project's product is done outside the project.

In some areas such as capital facilities projects, project cost management includes predicting and analyzing the prospective financial performance of the project's product. In these situations, project cost management will include general management techniques such as:

- Return on investment
- Discounted cash flow
- Payback analysis

Should consider the information needs of the project stakeholders and the different ways and times stakeholders measure project cost. For example, the cost of a procurement item may be measured when committed, ordered, delivered, incurred, or recorded for accounting purposes. When project costs are used as a component of a reward and recognition system, controllable and uncontrollable costs should be estimated and budgeted separately to ensure that rewards reflect actual performance.

The ability to influence cost is greatest at the early stages of the project. Early scope definition and requirements identification are critical to reducing costs in a project.

Project Cost Management - Questions

1. The difference between the Earned Value (EV) and the Planned Value (PV) is referred to as?

   (A) Cost variance
   (B) Actual cost of the work performed
   (C) Estimate of completion
   (D) Schedule variance

2. It is likely that the _____ estimate is the one that people remember most.

   (A) Last
   (B) First
   (C) Summary
   (D) Capital

3. To distinguish top-down estimates from bottom-up estimates, it would be correct to say that the bottom-up estimate would be:

    (A) Less accurate.
    (B) About equal in accuracy to the top-down estimate.
    (C) More accurate.
    (D) No different to perform than the top-down estimate.

4. The CPI used in the above formula is a(n) _____.

    (A) Cost schedule
    (B) Performance factor
    (C) Actual cost
    (D) Cost control

5. Which of the following is true in regard to the Code of Accounts?

    (A) It allows one to easily identify the breakdown level of the item in the resource structure.
    (B) It describes the coding structure used by the performing organization to report financial information in its general ledger.
    (C) It is the collection of unique identifiers generally assigned to WBS items.
    (D) It defines ethical behavior in the project and the responsibilities to the customer and the profession.

6. For a project with original assumptions that are no longer relevant to a change in conditions, Estimated at Completion is most likely determined by which technique?

    (A) ETC + AC
    (B) AC + BAC - EV
    (C) AC + (BAC - EV)/CPI
    (D) ETC + EV

7. Because you were a finance major in college, you have been asked to be an active participant in your company's project selection process. The project selection committee chair has asked you to describe ground rules and possible approaches for project selection. You know that organizations usually will not approve a project if its costs exceed its benefits, so you recommend using a discounted cash-flow approach. This approach is based in part on the economic theory that a dollar today generally is worth more than a dollar a year from now. Using this approach, the project is acceptable if the:

    (A) Net present value of the inflow is greater than the net present value of the outflow by a specified amount or percentage.
    (B) Sum of the net present value of all estimated cash flow during the life of the project equals the profit.
    (C) Payback period occurs by the second year of the project.
    (D) Gross present value of all future expected cash flow divided by the initial cash investment is greater than one.

8. If you think that the costs you have incurred up to now are in some way atypical of the project and that the rest of the project will cost the original estimate, the formula for finding the EAC is:

    (A) EAC=AC + ETC
    (B) EAC = (AC + (BAC-EV)/CPI)
    (C) EAC=AC + EV
    (D) EAC=AC + BAC-EV.

9. The difference between the Earned Value (EV) and the Planned Value (PV) is referred to as?

        (A) Actual cost of the work performed.
        (B) Estimate of completion.
        (C) Cost variance.
        (D) Schedule variance.

10. When you are choosing a certain level of skills or mechanical efficiency, you are trading _____ for time.

        (A) Quality
        (B) Cost
        (C) Ideas
        (D) People

11. Developing an approximation of the costs of the resources needed to complete project activity is _____.

        (A) Accounting
        (B) Cost control
        (C) Cost estimating
        (D) Budgeting

12. Historical information is a _____, not a _____.

        (A) Guideline, blueprint
        (B) Panacea, problem
        (C) Fact, guess
        (D) Nuisance, fact

13. If you are using models that look at project characteristics to do cost estimating, you are doing _____.

        (A) Parametric modeling
        (B) Analytical thinking
        (C) Acute cost analysis
        (D) Model characterization

14. A project is formed to produce a product that will be used for transporting people. Costs that are associated with the project that occur after the delivery of the product to the customer are considered to be what kind of cost?

        (A) Expenses
        (B) Prorated costs
        (C) Expected value
        (D) Life cycle cost

15. The inputs to Cost Budgeting includes all of the following except?

        (A) WBS dictionary
        (B) Work breakdown structure
        (C) Project schedule
        (D) Cost baseline

16. Equipment, materials, and people are three types of choices in _____.

        (A) Work Breakdown Structure
        (B) Resource pool description
        (C) State of Work
        (D) Scope Statements

17. If a project is to employ three people each for 40 hours at a labor rate of $40 per hour with overhead included and a fourth person for 30 hours during the same period but at a loaded labor rate of $60 per hour, the PV for the week is:

        (A) $1,800
        (B) $4,800
        (C) $5,600
        (D) $6,600

18. The term activity resource estimating refers to?

        (A) Labor
        (B) Capital equipment
        (C) Materials
        (D) All of the above

19. If you think that the costs to be incurred for the rest of the project were incorrectly estimated and use a new estimate for your EAC, the formula is:

        (A) EAC = (AC + (BAC-EV)/CPI)
        (B) EAC=AC + ETC
        (C) EAC=AC + BAC-EV.
        (D) EAC=AC +EV

20. You are using earned value progress reporting for your current project in an effort to teach your software developers the benefits of earned value. You plan to display project results so that the team knows how the project is progressing.

        PV = $5,300
        EV = $4,700
        AC = $5,900
        BAC = $10,000

What is the EAC for this project?

        (A) $4,100
        (B) $12,500
        (C) $10,000
        (D) $10,600

21. To determine the final number of resources needed for a large task, you _____ the _____ levels to get the next level higher.

        (A) Divide, average
        (B) Sum, higher
        (C) Multiply, higher
        (D) Sum, lower

22. Detail of the Work breakdown structure for doing your budgeting is found in the _____.

    (A) Work breakdown structure dictionary
    (B) State of Work
    (C) Charter
    (D) Schedule

23. Developing an approximation of the costs of the resources needed to complete project activity is _____.

    (A) Accounting
    (B) Cost control
    (C) Cost estimating
    (D) Budgeting

24. A project manager is using the earned value reporting system to manage his project. At this point in time the EV is $24,000, the BAC is $97,000, the PV is $29,000, and the AC is $45,000. What is the percent complete?

    (A) 25%
    (B) 53%
    (C) 46%
    (D) 30%

25. You are using earned value progress reporting for your current project in an effort to teach your software developers the benefits of earned value. You plan to display project results so that the team knows how the project is progressing.

    PV = $8,500
    EV = $6,000
    AC = $8,500
    BAC = $13,000

What is the CPI for this project, and what does it tell us about cost performance thus far?

    (A) 0.71; actual costs are exactly as planned
    (B) 0.71; actual costs have exceeded planned costs
    (C) 0.71; actual costs are less than planned costs
    (D) 0.71; actual costs have exceed planned costs

26. An estimate that has the range of 25% to +75 is called a(n) _____ estimate.

    (A) Order of magnitude
    (B) Strategic
    (C) Definitive
    (D) Budget

27. The budget that has the range of 10% to +25% is called a(n) _____ estimate.

    (A) Definitive
    (B) Capital
    (C) Budget
    (D) Order of magnitude

28. Value analysis and value management are other names for:

      (A) Life cycle management
      (B) Profitability
      (C) Value engineering
      (D) Life cycle costing

29. A project manager is assigned to a project early in the project life cycle. One of the things that must be done is to do a justification for the project. Since very little information is known about the project, the estimate is considered to be a rough estimate. See the image for the table that is the manager's estimate of the cash flows that will take place over the next five years.

If the net present value for each of the cash flows were calculated at a 10% interest rate, the net present value cash flow at the end of five years would be:

      (A) Less than the total cash flow without the net present value applied.
      (B) Greater than the total cash flow without the net present value applied.
      (C) Unable to be calculated with the information supplied.
      (D) The same as the total cash flow without the net present value applied.

30. A project team has a programmer on the team. The programmer will work on the project for twenty-six weeks as a full-time team member. Her utilization is 72%, productivity is 80%, basic wages are $50 per hour, fringe benefits are 30%, and overhead costs are 50% of wages plus fringe benefits. Use a forty-hour work week. What is the cost of this employee for the project?

      (A) $136,760
      (B) $126,750
      (C) $176,041
      (D) $101,400

31. Choosing to do a task in house or to outsource it may be an example of a(n) _____.

      (A) Tactical decision
      (B) Strategic decision
      (C) Management decision
      (D) Organizational policy

32. You are using earned value progress reporting for your current project in an effort to teach your software developers the benefits of earned value. You plan to display project results so that the team knows how the project is progressing.

      PV = $5,300
      EV = $2,700
      AC = $6,900
      BAC = $15,000

What is the EAC for this project?

      (A) $15,000
      (B) $29,900
      (C) $38,460
      (D) $32,000

33. Analogous estimating is also known as _____ estimating.

    (A) Bottom-up
    (B) Parametric
    (C) Top-down
    (D) Top-to-bottom

34. The project manager can have control over _____ costs.

    (A) Strategic
    (B) Tactical
    (C) Direct
    (D) Indirect

35. A project manager wants to make a trip to California by car. The project manager knows how many miles it will be to drive to California, the current price of gasoline, and how many miles the car will go on a gallon of gasoline. From this information he or she can calculate the estimated cost of the gasoline for the trip. This is a form of what kind of estimating technique?

    (A) Definitive
    (B) Analogous
    (C) Parametric
    (D) Quantitative

36. The _____ gives the detail you need to correctly estimate costs for the project.

    (A) Scope Statement
    (B) Charter
    (C) State of Work
    (D) Work Breakdown Structure

37. The budget that has the range of 5% to +10% is called a(n) _____ estimate.

    (A) Order of magnitude
    (B) Capital
    (C) Definitive
    (D) Budget

38. You are using earned value progress reporting for your current project in an effort to teach your software developers the benefits of earned value. You plan to display project results so that the team knows how the project is progressing.

    PV = $7,500
    EV = $5,000
    AC = $5,500
    BAC = $13,000

According to earned value analysis, the SV and status of the project described above is?

    (A) +$7,500; the project is on schedule
    (B) -$2,500; and the project is behind schedule
    (C) +$500; the project is ahead of schedule
    (D) -$2,500; the project is ahead of schedule

39. If EV is US $300,000, AC is US $350,000, and PV is US $375,000, what does the schedule performance index (SPI) indicate?

(A) You are progressing at 125% of the rate originally planned.
(B) You are only progressing at 86% of the rate originally planned.
(C) You are only progressing at 80% of the rate originally planned.
(D) You are progressing at 116% of the rate originally planned.

40. Historical information can be used as a guide, not as a blueprint because each project is _____.

(A) Important
(B) Tactical
(C) Planned
(D) Unique

41. What characteristic best describes the cost baseline?

(A) Time-phased budget for the project.
(B) Total budget for the project including the contingency budget and the management reserve.
(C) Total budget for the project including the contingency budget.
(D) Total budget for the project.

42. You are managing a 3-year project with a $3 million budget. If project requirements change, you expect additional funds to become available toward the end of each fiscal year. You may use these funds for your project. You decide to establish a cost change control system to:

(A) Determine why a cost variance has occurred.
(B) Determine whether a budget update is required.
(C) Define when to add contingency funds to the project.
(D) Define the procedures by which the cost baseline may be changed.

43. The reason that cost management is so difficult in project management is that?

(A) There are no tools for identifying project tasks.
(B) Projects by definition and nature are non-recurring events and are therefore difficult to predict.
(C) There are no tools for identifying project costs or the associated risks.
(D) Project managers do not care about tracking costs, as only schedules are important to all.

44. A construction company is being measured by the earned value reporting method. During the project one of the tasks, installing ten elm trees, was complete. The planned value for this task was $4,000, and it was completed two weeks ago. Unfortunately for the contractor, maple trees should have been planted. The customer insists that maple trees be planted and that the elm trees be removed. As of this time the elm trees are still in the ground, but the contractor has agreed to do the work of replacing them. What action should be taken on the earned value report?

(A) Reduce EV by $4,000
(B) Make no changes since the vendor has agreed to fix the problem.
(C) Reduce PV by $4,000
(D) Reduce AC by $4,000

45. You are the controller on your project. Your project manager has requested that you provide him with a forecast of project costs for the next 12 months. He needs this information to determine if the budget should be increased or decreased on this major construction project. In addition to the usual information sources, which of the following should you also consider?

    (A) Cost estimates from similar projects
    (B) Work breakdown structure
    (C) Project schedule
    (D) Existing change requests

46. Estimating cost by looking at previous projects is known as _____ estimating.

    (A) Analogous
    (B) Analytical
    (C) Bid
    (D) Strategic

47. During the full life cycle of the project, a plot of the project's expected expenditures will usually follow a characteristic ''S'' shape. This indicates that:

    (A) Problems will always occur in the execution phase.
    (B) There is a cyclic nature to all projects.
    (C) The bulk of the project budget will be spent in the execution phase.
    (D) There are high expenditures during closeout.

48. One common way to compute estimated at completion (EAC) is to take the project budgeted-at-completion and:

    (A) multiply it by the schedule performance index.
    (B) divide it by the schedule performance index.
    (C) divide it by the cost performance index.
    (D) multiply it by the cost performance.

49. You are using earned value progress reporting for your current project in an effort to teach your software developers the benefits of earned value. You plan to display project results so that the team knows how the project is progressing.

    PV = $7,500
    EV = $5,000
    AC = $5,500
    BAC = $13,000

What is the CPI for this project, and what does it tell us about cost performance thus far?

    (A) 0.91; actual costs have exceeded planned costs
    (B) 0.09; actual costs are exactly as planned
    (C) 0.09; actual costs have exceed planned costs
    (D) 0.91; actual costs are less than planned costs

50. Your manager asks you to take over one of four projects. If you had the following information, which project would you select?

    (A) Project A with an IRR of 10%.
    (B) Project B with an IRR of 12%.
    (C) Project C with an IRR of 15%.
    (D) Project D with an IRR of 21%.

51. You recently were appointed vice president of project management. As such, you will participate in performance reviews

for all projects that last more than 1 year, involve major clients, or are estimated to cost more than $1 million. To prepare for these reviews and to ensure they are meaningful and can be used to determine future project direction, you believe project managers must ensure that:

(A) Earned value analysis is used for all projects.
(B) The focus is on cost and schedule variances rather than scope, resources, quality, and risks.
(C) All project documents are available to meeting attendees before the meeting.
(D) Accurate, uniform information about work results is provided.

52. A cost management plan is best described as?

(A) A subsidiary element of the project charter.
(B) A plan for describing how cost variances will be managed.
(C) Includes identifying and considering various costing alternatives.
(D) An input to the cost estimating process.

53. In order to use a consultant well, you need to have your own _____ and _____ clearly understood as you engage the consultants.

(A) Tasks, strategy
(B) Requirements, hopes
(C) People, managers
(D) Expectations, requirements

54. Heating and electricity are examples of _____ costs.

(A) Tactical
(B) Strategic
(C) Indirect
(D) Direct

55. Which of the following estimating techniques most accurately reflects the actual cost of the project?

(A) Order of magnitude estimates.
(B) Bottom-up estimates.
(C) Conceptual estimates.
(D) Preliminary estimates.

56. A project manager is using the earned value reporting method to manage his project. The following table shows the data collected to date. The plan is for the project to be complete after eight weeks. The earned value report shows data collected for the first four weeks of the project. The figures shown in the table are cumulative. What is the EAC at week 4?

(A) 15,555
(B) 20,000
(C) 17,717
(D) 25,740

Week	PV	AC	EV
1	$1,000	$1,000	$1,000
2	$3,000	$2,000	$2,500
3	$5,000	$5,000	$6,000
4	$7,000	$9,000	$7,000
5	$13,000		
6	$17,000		
7	$19,000		
8	$20,000		

57. The first place to look for expert judgment is often in _____.

     (A) The Yellow Pages
     (B) Relatives
     (C) Your own organization
     (D) A vendor's organization

58. A project manager and the project team identify several specific risks in a project. The expected value of these risks is estimated at $10,000. The impact on the project brought about by these risks is estimated at $40,000. What value should be entered into the contingency reserve for these risks?

     (A) $40,000
     (B) $10,000
     (C) $25,000
     (D) $0

59. The abbreviation for costs actually incurred is:

     (A) AC
     (B) EV
     (C) DC
     (D) PV

60. Which of the following involves developing an approximation of the costs of the resources needed to complete project activities?

     (A) Cost control.
     (B) Cost budgeting.
     (C) Cost estimating.
     (D) Cost reporting.

61. A company is attempting to select the best project from a list of possible choices. If the information they have are the following benefit cost ratios, which project should they pick?

     (A) 2.2
     (B) 1.3
     (C) -0.8
     (D) -1.4

62. Using the formula: Present value = S / (1 = i)n where i is the interest rate in percentage, n is the number of periods, and S is the starting amount. Based on the table in the image, what is the value of an annual income flow of $1,300 each year over the next three years at 12%?

     (A) $3,900.00
     (B) $3,122.60
     (C) 36%
     (D) $3,497.00

Periods	10%	12%	14%
1	0.909	0.893	0.877
2	0.826	0.797	0.769
3	0.751	0.712	0.675
4	0.683	0.636	0.592
5	0.621	0.597	0.519

63. You are using earned value progress reporting for your current project in an effort to teach your software developers the benefits of earned value. You plan to display project results so that the team knows how the project is progressing.

      PV = $5,300
      EV = $4,700
      AC = $5,900
      BAC = $10,000

What is the CV?

      (A) $1,200
      (B) -$1,200
      (C) $4,100
      (D) -$4,100

64. The best way to get a good bid from the vendor is to write a good _____ document.

      (A) Request
      (B) Quality
      (C) Risk Statement
      (D) Letter

65. Cost, time, and quality are known as:

      (A) Value base indicators
      (B) Triple constraints
      (C) Project indicators
      (D) Tactical measurements

66. You are using earned value progress reporting for your current project in an effort to teach your software developers the benefits of earned value. You plan to display project results so that the team knows how the project is progressing.

      PV = $8,500
      EV = $6,000
      AC = $8,500
      BAC = $13,000

What is the CV?

      (A) $4,500
      (B) -$4,500
      (C) $2,500
      (D) -$2,500

67. Which of the following processes is involved with allocating the overall cost estimate to the individual work activities?

      (A) Cost budgeting
      (B) Resource planning
      (C) Cost control
      (D) Cost estimating

68. A project manager decides that for this point in the project life cycle she will use an analogous estimate. One of the things that the project manager will not have to worry about in preparing this estimate is:

    (A) Quantifying the estimate.
    (B) Historical support for the figures used.
    (C) Activity listings.
    (D) Scaling the estimate.

69. Calculate the SPI if PV = 8 and EV = 6?

    (A) 1.33
    (B) 2.0
    (C) 1.0
    (D) .75

70. You can go from _____ to accelerated depreciation from one year to the following year but not the reverse.

    (A) Capital expenditure methodology
    (B) Straight line depreciation
    (C) Intermediate depreciation
    (D) Direct cost capitalization

71. You are using earned value progress reporting for your current project in an effort to teach your software developers the benefits of earned value. You plan to display project results so that the team knows how the project is progressing.

    PV = $5,200
    EV = $5,000
    AC = $5,500
    BAC = $13,000

According to earned value analysis, the SV and status of the project described above is?

    (A) +$7,500; the project is on schedule
    (B) -$200; the project is ahead of schedule
    (C) -$200; and the project is behind schedule
    (D) +$500; the project is ahead of schedule

72. You are a project manager for a company that sells online music. Your project is to develop a new content management system that will not only manage all users purchases and downloads, but will automatically learn the users' music interests in order to make future product recommendations. In addition, your content management system must scale to support millions of concurrent music downloads a day. Your team has made significant progress on the project. You are preparing the performance of the project to date and have calculated the following measurements:
PV = 4000, EV = 3500, AC = 3000. What is the CPI of this project?

    (A) 1.16
    (B) 1.14
    (C) 1.333
    (D) 0.75

73. A project manager is assigned to a project early in the project life cycle. One of the things that must be done is to do a justification for the project. Since very little information is known about the project, the estimate is considered to be a rough estimate. See the image for the table that is the manager's estimate of the cash flows that will take place over the next five years.

What is the net cash flow at the end of five years?

(A) $50,000
(B) -$50,000
(C) $850,000
(D) $100,000

End of Year	Cash Flow In	Cash Flow Out
1	0	500,000
2	300,000	90,000
3	400,000	100,000
4	100,000	175,000
5	50,000	35,000

74. Summing the total of Work breakdown structure tasks to find the total cost is known as _____ estimating.

(A) Parametric
(B) Bottom-up
(C) Top-down
(D) Analytical

75. A project manager is considering applying learning curve theory to his project. The project involves designing a number of software modules that are very similar. According to the cost figures that have been collected the first unit required 100 person hours to design and test. The second unit required 90 person-hours to design and test. How many person-hours will the eighth module take to design and test?

(A) 73
(B) 172
(C) 90
(D) 100

76. Cost control is easiest to do _____ the project.

(A) Early in
(B) Late in
(C) In the middle of
(D) After

77. The amount of time it takes to recover the expenditure for the project before you begin to actually generate revenue is known as the _____.

(A) Payback period
(B) Return on investment
(C) Return period
(D) Selection period

78. In the work breakdown structure, _____ hours is the suggested longest task duration.

(A) 8
(B) 20
(C) 60
(D) 40

79. Looking at a broad overview of the project costs is known as:

    (A) Life cycle engineering
    (B) Auditing
    (C) Value engineering
    (D) Life cycle costing

80. In general, _____ estimating gives the most accurate picture of costs for doing cost estimating.

    (A) Analogous
    (B) Parametric modeling
    (C) Bottom-up
    (D) Top-down

81. A project team receives an approved change request from the customer. The team has previously estimated that the cost to implement this change is $10,000. The customer has agreed to pay this amount for the additional work. The customer realizes that there is a 50 percent chance that this change will not work and will later be removed. What change, if any, should be made in the budget?

    (A) The project budget should not be increased.
    (B) The project budget should be increased by $15,000.
    (C) The project budget should be increased by $10,000.
    (D) The project budget should be increased by $5,000.

82. When using Earned Value Management, the difference between what has been accomplished and what was scheduled is called the:

    (A) Schedule Variance
    (B) Cost Variance
    (C) Labor Variance
    (D) Projected Variance at completion

83. The major output of cost budgeting is the _____.

    (A) Summary of costs
    (B) Capital budget
    (C) Cost baseline
    (D) Capital baseline

84. Evaluating _____ is part of cost estimating.

    (A) Schedules
    (B) Personnel
    (C) Assignments
    (D) Risks

85. If you think that the costs you have incurred up to now are an indicator of what will happen for the rest of the project your formula for finding the EAC is:

    (A) EAC=AC + ETC
    (B) EAC = (AC + (BAC-EV)/CPI)
    (C) EAC=AC + EV
    (D) EAC=AC + BAC-EV.

86. You are using earned value progress reporting for your current project in an effort to teach your software developers the benefits of earned value. You plan to display project results so that the team knows how the project is progressing.

PV = $7,500
EV = $5,000
AC = $5,500
BAC = $13,000

According to earned value analysis, the SV and status of the project described above is?

    (A) +$7,500; the project is on schedule
    (B) -$2,500; and the project is behind schedule
    (C) +$500; the project is ahead of schedule
    (D) -$2,500; the project is ahead of schedule

87. Change requests should be noted _____ when they occur and become a part of the project record.

    (A) Tactically
    (B) Often
    (C) Orally
    (D) Permanently

88. When using either associations or industry groups, it is always important to know what _____ went into the final numbers.

    (A) Data
    (B) Thinking
    (C) Skills
    (D) Tactics

89. ROI and discounted cash flow are two examples of:

    (A) General management cost evaluation
    (B) Value management cost techniques
    (C) Project management cost evaluation
    (D) General cost techniques

90. Which of the following best describes how cost variances will be managed?

    (A) Cost estimate
    (B) Chart of accounts
    (C) Cost management plan
    (D) Cost baseline

91. The abbreviation for the amount that was budgeted in order for work to be performed is:

    (A) PV
    (B) DC
    (C) EV
    (D) AC

92. Although the stakeholders thought there was enough budget, halfway through the project the CPI was 0.7. To determine the root cause, several stakeholders audit the project and discover tasks were estimated analogously. Although the task estimates add up to the project estimate, the stakeholders think something was missing in how the estimate was completed. Which of the following best describes what was missing?

       (A) SPI should be used, not CPI.
       (B) Past history was not taken into account.
       (C) Bottom up estimating should have been used.
       (D) Estimated costs should be used to measure CPI.

93. A project manager is preparing the budget for the project. There are several inputs to the budgeting process that the project manager will use. One of the things that the project manager will not use is the:

       (A) Project schedule.
       (B) Work breakdown structure.
       (C) Cost baseline.
       (D) Cost estimates.

94. Project team knowledge, commercial cost-estimating databases, and project files are all part of _____ used as an input into cost estimating.

       (A) Estimating software
       (B) Resource requirements
       (C) Public information
       (D) Historical information

95. The document that shows the correct accounting category to list various cost estimates is called the _____.

       (A) Chart of accounts
       (B) Accounting system
       (C) Standard accounts
       (D) Accounting method

96. Estimating cost by looking at previous projects is known as _____ estimating.

       (A) Analytical
       (B) Analogous
       (C) Strategic
       (D) Bid

97. During the full life cycle of the project, a plot of the project's expected expenditures will usually follow a characteristic ''S'' shape. This indicates that:

       (A) There is a cyclic nature to all projects.
       (B) Problems will always occur in the execution phase.
       (C) There are high expenditures during closeout.
       (D) The bulk of the project budget will be spent in the execution phase.

98. The project manager of a project must buy a large piece of equipment costing $1,543,256. He meets with the accounting department representative to the project team and reviews the different depreciation methods that can be used to depreciate the equipment over the useful life of the equipment. Which of the following is an accelerated depreciation method?

    (A) Multiplication of the years' digits
    (B) Straight line
    (C) Sum of the years' digits
    (D) Average deflation

99. The act of doing anything that will help to bring future project performance into line with the project plan is called:

    (A) Corrective action.
    (B) Contingency planning.
    (C) Budget update.
    (D) Revised cost estimate.

100. Costs that are expected to occur but the time when they will occur is not known are called?

    (A) Indirect
    (B) Tactical
    (C) Direct
    (D) Known unknowns

Sample Answer Sheet

	T F		T F		T F		T F
1	Ⓐ Ⓑ Ⓒ Ⓓ Ⓔ	26	Ⓐ Ⓑ Ⓒ Ⓓ Ⓔ	51	Ⓐ Ⓑ Ⓒ Ⓓ Ⓔ	76	Ⓐ Ⓑ Ⓒ Ⓓ Ⓔ
2	Ⓐ Ⓑ Ⓒ Ⓓ Ⓔ	27	Ⓐ Ⓑ Ⓒ Ⓓ Ⓔ	52	Ⓐ Ⓑ Ⓒ Ⓓ Ⓔ	77	Ⓐ Ⓑ Ⓒ Ⓓ Ⓔ
3	Ⓐ Ⓑ Ⓒ Ⓓ Ⓔ	28	Ⓐ Ⓑ Ⓒ Ⓓ Ⓔ	53	Ⓐ Ⓑ Ⓒ Ⓓ Ⓔ	78	Ⓐ Ⓑ Ⓒ Ⓓ Ⓔ
4	Ⓐ Ⓑ Ⓒ Ⓓ Ⓕ	29	Ⓐ Ⓑ Ⓒ Ⓓ Ⓔ	54	Ⓐ Ⓑ Ⓒ Ⓓ Ⓔ	79	Ⓐ Ⓑ Ⓒ Ⓓ Ⓔ
5	Ⓐ Ⓑ Ⓒ Ⓓ Ⓔ	30	Ⓐ Ⓑ Ⓒ Ⓓ Ⓔ	55	Ⓐ Ⓑ Ⓒ Ⓓ Ⓔ	80	Ⓐ Ⓑ Ⓒ Ⓓ Ⓔ
6	Ⓐ Ⓑ Ⓒ Ⓓ Ⓔ	31	Ⓐ Ⓑ Ⓒ Ⓓ Ⓔ	56	Ⓐ Ⓑ Ⓒ Ⓓ Ⓔ	81	Ⓐ Ⓑ Ⓒ Ⓓ Ⓔ
7	Ⓐ Ⓑ Ⓒ Ⓓ Ⓔ	32	Ⓐ Ⓑ Ⓒ Ⓓ Ⓔ	57	Ⓐ Ⓑ Ⓒ Ⓓ Ⓔ	82	Ⓐ Ⓑ Ⓒ Ⓓ Ⓔ
8	Ⓐ Ⓑ Ⓒ Ⓓ Ⓔ	33	Ⓐ Ⓑ Ⓒ Ⓓ Ⓔ	58	Ⓐ Ⓑ Ⓒ Ⓓ Ⓔ	83	Ⓐ Ⓑ Ⓒ Ⓓ Ⓔ
9	Ⓐ Ⓑ Ⓒ Ⓓ Ⓔ	34	Ⓐ Ⓑ Ⓒ Ⓓ Ⓔ	59	Ⓐ Ⓑ Ⓒ Ⓓ Ⓔ	84	Ⓐ Ⓑ Ⓒ Ⓓ Ⓔ
10	Ⓐ Ⓑ Ⓒ Ⓓ Ⓔ	35	Ⓐ Ⓑ Ⓒ Ⓓ Ⓔ	60	Ⓐ Ⓑ Ⓒ Ⓓ Ⓔ	85	Ⓐ Ⓑ Ⓒ Ⓓ Ⓔ
11	Ⓐ Ⓑ Ⓒ Ⓓ Ⓔ	36	Ⓐ Ⓑ Ⓒ Ⓓ Ⓔ	61	Ⓐ Ⓑ Ⓒ Ⓓ Ⓔ	86	Ⓐ Ⓑ Ⓒ Ⓓ Ⓔ
12	Ⓐ Ⓑ Ⓒ Ⓓ Ⓔ	37	Ⓐ Ⓑ Ⓒ Ⓓ Ⓔ	62	Ⓐ Ⓑ Ⓒ Ⓓ Ⓔ	87	Ⓐ Ⓑ Ⓒ Ⓓ Ⓔ
13	Ⓐ Ⓑ Ⓒ Ⓓ Ⓔ	38	Ⓐ Ⓑ Ⓒ Ⓓ Ⓔ	63	Ⓐ Ⓑ Ⓒ Ⓓ Ⓔ	88	Ⓐ Ⓑ Ⓒ Ⓓ Ⓔ
14	Ⓐ Ⓑ Ⓒ Ⓓ Ⓔ	39	Ⓐ Ⓑ Ⓒ Ⓓ Ⓔ	64	Ⓐ Ⓑ Ⓒ Ⓓ Ⓔ	89	Ⓐ Ⓑ Ⓒ Ⓓ Ⓔ
15	Ⓐ Ⓑ Ⓒ Ⓓ Ⓔ	40	Ⓐ Ⓑ Ⓒ Ⓓ Ⓔ	65	Ⓐ Ⓑ Ⓒ Ⓓ Ⓔ	90	Ⓐ Ⓑ Ⓒ Ⓓ Ⓔ
16	Ⓐ Ⓑ Ⓒ Ⓓ Ⓔ	41	Ⓐ Ⓑ Ⓒ Ⓓ Ⓔ	66	Ⓐ Ⓑ Ⓒ Ⓓ Ⓔ	91	Ⓐ Ⓑ Ⓒ Ⓓ Ⓔ
17	Ⓐ Ⓑ Ⓒ Ⓓ Ⓔ	42	Ⓐ Ⓑ Ⓒ Ⓓ Ⓔ	67	Ⓐ Ⓑ Ⓒ Ⓓ Ⓔ	92	Ⓐ Ⓑ Ⓒ Ⓓ Ⓔ
18	Ⓐ Ⓑ Ⓒ Ⓓ Ⓔ	43	Ⓐ Ⓑ Ⓒ Ⓓ Ⓔ	68	Ⓐ Ⓑ Ⓒ Ⓓ Ⓔ	93	Ⓐ Ⓑ Ⓒ Ⓓ Ⓔ
19	Ⓐ Ⓑ Ⓒ Ⓓ Ⓔ	44	Ⓐ Ⓑ Ⓒ Ⓓ Ⓔ	69	Ⓐ Ⓑ Ⓒ Ⓓ Ⓔ	94	Ⓐ Ⓑ Ⓒ Ⓓ Ⓔ
20	Ⓐ Ⓑ Ⓒ Ⓓ Ⓔ	45	Ⓐ Ⓑ Ⓒ Ⓓ Ⓔ	70	Ⓐ Ⓑ Ⓒ Ⓓ Ⓔ	95	Ⓐ Ⓑ Ⓒ Ⓓ Ⓔ
21	Ⓐ Ⓑ Ⓒ Ⓓ Ⓔ	46	Ⓐ Ⓑ Ⓒ Ⓓ Ⓔ	71	Ⓐ Ⓑ Ⓒ Ⓓ Ⓔ	96	Ⓐ Ⓑ Ⓒ Ⓓ Ⓔ
22	Ⓐ Ⓑ Ⓒ Ⓓ Ⓔ	47	Ⓐ Ⓑ Ⓒ Ⓓ Ⓔ	72	Ⓐ Ⓑ Ⓒ Ⓓ Ⓔ	97	Ⓐ Ⓑ Ⓒ Ⓓ Ⓔ
23	Ⓐ Ⓑ Ⓒ Ⓓ Ⓔ	48	Ⓐ Ⓑ Ⓒ Ⓓ Ⓔ	73	Ⓐ Ⓑ Ⓒ Ⓓ Ⓔ	98	Ⓐ Ⓑ Ⓒ Ⓓ Ⓔ
24	Ⓐ Ⓑ Ⓒ Ⓓ Ⓔ	49	Ⓐ Ⓑ Ⓒ Ⓓ Ⓔ	74	Ⓐ Ⓑ Ⓒ Ⓓ Ⓔ	99	Ⓐ Ⓑ Ⓒ Ⓓ Ⓔ
25	Ⓐ Ⓑ Ⓒ Ⓓ Ⓔ	50	Ⓐ Ⓑ Ⓒ Ⓓ Ⓔ	75	Ⓐ Ⓑ Ⓒ Ⓓ Ⓔ	100	Ⓐ Ⓑ Ⓒ Ⓓ Ⓔ

Project Cost Management - Answers

1. (D) Schedule variance. Schedule Variance (SV). A measure of schedule performance on a project. It is the algebraic difference between the earned value (EV) and the planned value (PV). SV = EV minus PV.

2. (B) First. The first estimate that people see is often the one that they remember the most. Even if you explain the major caveat that you are simply showing a first estimate, it always seems that people remember the first information they receive.

3. (C) More accurate. A bottom-up estimate is a detailed estimate taking into consideration a number of small estimates and summarizing them to a total for the project or subproject being estimated. A top-down estimate is usually a less accurate method that estimates the cost of the entire project by means of parametric, analogous, or some other estimating method.

4. (B) Performance factor. The cost performance index is used in this case as an indicator of how the rest of the project will progress in terms of cost. This leads to an estimate at completion.

5. (C) It is the collection of unique identifiers generally assigned to WBS items. Code of Accounts - any numbering system used to uniquely identify each component of the work breakdown structure. Contrast with chart of accounts.

6. (A) ETC + AC. Estimate at Completion (EAC) - the expected total cost of a schedule activity, a work breakdown structure component, or the project when the defined scope of work will be completed. EAC is equal to the actual cost (AC) plus the estimate to complete (ETC) for all of the remaining work. EAC = AC plus ETC. The EAC may be calculated based on performance to date or estimated by the project team based on other factors, in which case it is often referred to as the latest revised estimate. See also earned value technique and estimate to complete.

7. (A) Net present value of the inflow is greater than the net present value of the outflow by a specified amount or percentage. The discounted cash-flow approach-or the present value method- determines the net present value of all cash flow by discounting it by the required rate of return. The impact of inflation can be considered. Early in the life of a project, net cash flow is likely to be negative because the major outflow is the initial investment in the project. If the project is successful, cash flow will become positive.

8. (D) EAC=AC + BAC-EV. You take the actual costs of the project and add the original estimate at completion to that number to get your estimate at completion.

9. (D) Schedule variance. Schedule variance (SV). SV equals earned value (EV) minus planned value (PV). Schedule variance will ultimately equal zero when the project is completed because all of the planned values will have been earned. Formula: SV = EV – PV

10. (B) Cost. The triple constraints of cost, quality, and time are always in play in a project. You must choose between the three constantly as you go through resource planning. You will probably not be the final arbiter of who to use or what equipment to use on the project because those choices will be made in organizational meetings leading to organizational policy. You should know that there are tradeoffs to be made between the triple constraints, and you should give good information to sponsors and stakeholders about your decisions in choosing resources.

11. (C) Cost estimating. This is the directly from the PMBOK.

12. (A) Guideline, blueprint. Historical information will not be the exact blueprint you need for your current project. People change, technologies change, situations change. All of these factors mean that although you can look at historical information as a guide, do not use it as your plan.

13. (A) Parametric modeling. Parametric modeling looks at parameters specific to your project and measures the new project against ones that have been done in the past.

14. (D) Life cycle cost.

15. (D) Cost baseline. Inputs to Cost Budgeting include: project scope statement, work breakdown structure, WBS dictionary, activity cost estimates, activity cost estimate supporting detail, project schedule, resource calendars, contract and the cost management plan.

16. (B) Resource pool description. All three of these elements are choices you will have to make to successfully plan the project.

17. (D) $6,600. Planned Value (PV) - The physical work scheduled plus the authorized budget to accomplish the scheduled work. 40 hours x $40 per hour x 3 = $4,800; 30 hours x $60 per hour x 1 =$1,800; PV = $4,800 + $1,800 = $6,600

18. (D) All of the above. Activity Resource Estimating - the process of estimating the types and quantities of resources required to perform each schedule activity.

19. (B) EAC=AC + ETC. You take the actual costs and add your new estimates to that to get your new estimate at completion.

20. (B) $12,500. EAC is calculated as BAC/CPI in this case $10,000 / .80 or $12,500.

21. (D) Sum, lower. You sum up the lower levels of the WBS to get the final number for the resources needed in the summary task at the top.

22. (A) Work breakdown structure dictionary. Use the dictionary as a tool to look at detail in the overall project task system. This will help give you better figures for use in your cost budgeting.

23. (C) Cost estimating. This is the directly from the PMBOK.

24. (A) 25%. The percent complete is the work completed, or the earned value divided by the total work to be done. EV / BAC = percent complete; PC = 24 / 97 = 25%.

25. (B) 0.71; actual costs have exceeded planned costs. CPI is calculated as EV/AC. $6,000 (EV) / $8,500 (AC) = .705 or .71 (CPI). EV measures the budgeted dollar value of the work that has actually been accomplished, whereas AC measures the actual cost of getting that work done. If the two numbers are the same, work on the project is being accomplished for exactly the budgeted amount of money. In this example, an index of 0.71 means that for every dollar spent on the project only 71 cents worth of work is actually being accomplished.

26. (A) Order of magnitude. This is the estimate with the largest variance and is often the first budget done.

27. (C) Budget. This is the middle of the three estimates, and it gives a smaller range than the order of magnitude but a large range than the definitive estimate.

28. (C) Value engineering. The planning of the engineering tasks to reduce cost, improve quality and maximize performance of the product is value engineering. Value engineering also helps to give clear data from which good decisions can be made.

29. (A) Less than the total cash flow without the net present value applied. Calculating the net present value of the cash flows for the project involves adjusting the future cash flows to allow for diminishing value due to the time that we must wait to get them. Money received today is more valuable to us than money that will be received in the future.

30. (D) $101,400. The programmer will be paid for twenty-six weeks of work. The productivity and utilization factors affect the amount of time that someone is paid in comparison to the hours of effort required to complete the work. In this case the utilization and productivity are not required to calculate the cost: 26 weeks X 40 hours per week X $50 per hour X 1.3 fringe benefits X 1.5 overhead = $101,400.

31. (D) Organizational policy. The organization will often have policies that are used to determine how resources are selected. As a professional project manager you should make every effort to be aware of any organizational policies that will affect you resource planning.

32. (C) $38,460. EAC is calculated as BAC/CPI in this case $15,000 / .39 or $38,460

33. (C) Top-down. This type of estimating looks at the large picture first and gives an overall view of the potential costs.

34. (C) Direct. Costs that are directly incurred because the project is being executed are directs costs. In some cases the project manager has control over the costs and in some cases the organization itself will control the costs. In any case, the costs occur only when the project is going on.

35. (C) Parametric. Both the cost and accuracy of parametric models vary widely. They are most likely to be reliable when the historical information used to develop the model was accurate, the parameters used in the model are readily quantifiable, and the model is scalable (i.e., it works as well for a very large project as for a very small one).

36. (D) Work Breakdown Structure. This is the document where the Scope Statement is decomposed and will give you the task detail necessary to make resource planning possible.

37. (C) Definitive. This is the final estimate you will use when executing the project. Although it is extremely difficult to create estimates that are this exact, it is a best practice to try to make the final estimate as close as possible to the actual cost.

38. (B) -$2,500; and the project is behind schedule. SV is calculated as EV – PV; $5,000 (EV) - $7,500 (PV) = $-2,500 (SV). A negative variance means that the work completed is less than what was planned for that point in time in the project.

39. (C) You are only progressing at 80% of the rate originally planned. Schedule performance index (SPI) - the SPI is used, in addition to the schedule status to predict the completion date and is sometimes used in conjunction with the CPI to forecast the project completion estimates. SPI equals the ratio of the EV to the PV. Formula: SPI = EV/PV.

40. (D) Unique. The basic definition of a project includes the fact that each project is unique. Something, often times many things, will be different between projects. So do not accept historical information as your final plan. It can guide you to get there, but it is not the final answer.

41. (A) Time-phased budget for the project. The cost baseline is the time-phased budget for the project. It is usually shown as the PV curve on the earned value report and is usually shown as a cumulative value of the project budget over time. It will usually have a characteristic "S" shape to it. The contingency reserve and the management reserve are added to the project budget and baseline when and if they are needed to resolve risks that have actually taken place.

42. (D) Define the procedures by which the cost baseline may be changed. A cost change control system, documented in the cost management plan, defines the procedures by which the cost baseline can be changed. It includes the forms, documentation, tracking systems, and approval levels necessary for authorizing changes. The cost change control system is integrated with the integrated change control process. (PMBOK Guide - page 172)

43. (B) Projects by definition and nature are non-recurring events and are therefore difficult to predict. The cost management plan describes how cost variances will be managed. A cost management plan may be formal or informal, highly detailed or broadly framed, based on the needs of the project stakeholders. It is a subsidiary element of the project plan.

44. (A) Reduce EV by $4,000. The EV should be reduced by the amount of the $4,000 already credited to the earned value report for planting the trees. The AC should not be reduced, and since there is no increase in budget the PV will not be changed. When the vendor installs the new trees, the $4,000 will be added to the EV once again.

45. (D) Existing change requests. A change request is likely to have an impact on costs and may result in either an increase or a decrease in the project budget.

46. (A) Analogous. Analogous estimating uses previous projects as a benchmark for estimating cost.

47. (C) The bulk of the project budget will be spent in the execution phase. Most of the project money will be spent during the execution phase. At the beginning of execution the rate of expenditures rises as people and materials are brought into the project. Later the expenditures peak and slow down.

48. (C) Divide it by the cost performance index. EAC using CPI. EAC equals actual costs to date plus the budget required to complete the remaining project work, which is the BAC minus the EV, modified by a performance factor. This approach is most often used when current variances are seen as typical of future variances.
Formula: EAC = AC + ((BAC – EV) / CPI)

49. (A) 0.91; actual costs have exceeded planned costs. CPI is calculated as EV/AC; $5,000 (EV) / $5,500 (AC) = .909 or .91 (CPI); EV measures the budgeted dollar value of the work that has actually been accomplished, whereas AC measures the actual cost of getting that work done. If the two numbers are the same, work on the project is being accomplished for exactly the budgeted amount of money. In this example, an index of 0.91 means that for every dollar spent on the project only 91 cents worth of work is actually being accomplished.

50. (D) Project D with an IRR of 21%. Internal Rate of Return (IRR) - average rate of return earned over the life of the project, expressed as a percentage. The discount rate that equates the present value of the expected future cash flows to the present value of the costs of the project.

51. (D) Accurate, uniform information about work results is provided. Work results are an output of project plan execution and an input to performance reporting (for example, what deliverables have been fully or partially completed, and what costs and resources have been incurred or committed). Work results should be reported within the framework of the project communications management plan. Accurate, uniform information about work results is essential to performance reporting.

52. (B) A plan for describing how cost variances will be managed. Cost Management Plan - The document that sets out the format and establishes the activities and criteria for planning, structuring, and controlling the project costs. A cost management plan can be formal or informal, highly detailed or broadly framed, based on the requirements of the project stakeholders. The cost management plan is contained in, or is a subsidiary plan, of the project management plan.

53. (D) Expectations, requirements. The clearer you are concerning your own expectations and requirements, the better you will be at engaging consultants effectively.

54. (C) Indirect. The costs of heating are not controllable by the project manager and do not occur because the project is begin executed. This makes them indirect costs.

55. (B) Bottom-up estimates. Bottom-up Estimating - a method of estimating a component of work. The work is decomposed into more detail. An estimate is prepared of what is needed to meet the requirements of each of the lower, more detailed pieces of work, and these estimates are then aggregated into a total quantity for the component of work. The accuracy of bottom-up estimating is driven by the size and complexity of the work identified at the lower levels. Generally smaller work scopes increase the accuracy of the estimates.

56. (D) 25,740. The EAC is calculated by dividing the BAC by the CPI for the week being calculated. It is the estimated cost of the project that is expected at the end of the project based on what we know about cost performance today. EAC = BAC / CPI; EAC = 20,000 / .7777 = 25,740.

57. (C) Your own organization. If someone in your organization has been through a project similar to yours, that person can be an excellent source of information. In addition, that person will have the same constraints on him or her that you have and will have made decisions on resources based on those constraints.

58. (B) $10,000. The contingency reserve is money that is set aside for dealing with known risks. These known risks can be specifically identified. The risks mentioned in the question are identified and therefore money should be put into the contingency reserve for them. It would not make sense to budget for the impact of every risk, since all risks have a probability associated with them that means that there is some chance that the impact will not occur; therefore, the expected value should be used.

59. (A) AC. The letters stand for "actual costs," which are the real costs that have been incurred during the project. Your accounting department may give this number to you.

60. (C) Cost estimating. Cost Estimating - the process of developing an approximation of the cost of the resources needed to complete project activities.

61. (A) 2.2. Benefit Cost Ratio (BCR) - benefit cost ratio (BCR) provides a measure of the expected profitability of a project by dividing the expected revenues by the expected costs. BCR of 1.0 indicates that the project is break-even, expected benefits equal expected costs. BCR of less than 1.0 indicates that the project is not financially attractive, expected costs exceed expected benefits. BCR of greater than 1.0 indicates that project is profitable, expected benefits exceed expected costs. Target Revenue should be at least 1.3X the cost. Does not indicate when you make a profit or loss.

62. (B) $3,122.60. The calculation for the present value is done by consecutively taking the appropriate factor from the table and multiplying it by the money flowing for the year. In this example $1,300 X .893 + $1,300 X .797 + $1,300 X .712, since there is a $1,300 payment each year.

63. (B) -$1,200. CV is calculated as EV - AC in this case $4,700 (EV) - $5,900 (AC) = .$-1,200 (CV). A negative CV means that accomplishing work on the project is costing more than was budgeted.

64. (A) Request. The better you are at framing the requirements of the project, the better the vendor should be in giving you a response.

65. (B) Triple constraints. Although these are also three chapter headings in PMBOK, they are known together as the triple constraints.

66. (D) -$2,500. CV is calculated as EV - AC in this case $6,000 (EV) - $8,500 (AC) = .$-2,500 (CV). A negative CV means that accomplishing work on the project is costing more than was budgeted.

67. (A) Cost budgeting. Cost budgeting involves aggregating the estimated costs of individual schedule activities or work packages to establish a total cost baseline for measuring project performance.

68. (C) Activity listings. Listings of activities are usually not part of an analogous estimate. In analogous estimates large portions of the project are estimated by comparing and scaling similar parts of other projects.

69. (D) .75. EV = 6 and PV = 8, and the formula reads SPI=6/8, which is .75.

70. (B) Straight line depreciation. You can switch from straight line depreciation as your means of accounting to accelerated depreciation the next year, but you cannot do the reverse.

71. (C) -$200; and the project is behind schedule. SV is calculated as EV – PV. $5,000 (EV) - $5,200 (PV) = $-200 (SV). A negative variance means that the work completed is less than what was planned for that point in time in the project.

72. (A) 1.16. The cost performance index (CPI) is calculated as follows: CPI = EV (earned value) / AC (actual costs) = 3500 / 3000 = 1.16

A CPI > 1 indicates the cost performance is better than expected. A CPI < 1 indicates that cost performance is worse than expected.

73. (B) -$50,000. The net cash flow is the total of all the cash flows in and out of the company caused by the project. In this example there was a flow of $850,000 in and $900,000 out for a negative $50,000.

74. (B) Bottom-up. By starting with the lowest tasks and then rolling up the costs, you will arrive at the final cost estimate.

75. (A) 73. According to learning curve theory, the cost of a unit of production, the software module, will decrease by a fixed percentage for each doubling of the units produced. Since from unit 1 to unit 2 there was a 10% change in cost, the fixed percentage of reduction in cost was 90%. For unit 4, cost would be 81 person-hours, 90% of 90 person-hours. For unit 8, it would be 90% of 81, or 73 person-hours.

76. (A) Early in. The earlier you have good plans from which to work the easier it is to control your costs and get good cost planning. If there is no clarity about the work to be done, there will be no clarity about the costs to be incurred.

77. (A) Payback period. Some projects are chosen because the payback period is shorter than on other projects being considered.

78. (D) 40. If you have a task that is larger than this is terms of time, it is very difficult to assess resources needed to execute the task. You can certainly have tasks that are shorter than this; they will be useful for many of the resource planning activities. But you will not be able to plan well if the task is over 40 hours in length. There are too many unknowns in a task over the 40 hours to do good resource planning.

79. (D) Life cycle costing. Life cycle costing looks at the entire project and is a technique that helps determine the most cost effective ways of managing the project.

80. (C) Bottom-up. This is true because you start with a breakdown that gives you the most accurate cost estimate possible.

81. (C) The project budget should be increased by $10,000. The project budget should be increased by $10,000 because the only work actually approved at this time is the change notice for the work to be done. If the work done must be undone at a later time and additional work is required to do it, another change notice must be approved and funding added to the project budget.

82. A) Schedule Variance. Schedule Variance (SV) - a measure of schedule performance on a project. It is the algebraic difference between the earned value (EV) and the planned value (PV). SV = EV minus PV.

83. (C) Cost baseline. The cost baseline is the budget that will be your measurement of costs for the project. It is usually time-phased so that you can look at a specific point in time and measure how you are doing against the baseline for that particular time.

84. (D) Risks. The occurrence of risks within a project will change the cost of the project. It is important for the project manager to calculate as well as possible the costs involved in managing the various risk events that might occur on a project. These costs are as critical as any of the other costs.

85. (B) EAC = (AC + (BAC-EV)/CPI). You use a cost performance index to determine what your final estimate at completion will be.

86. (B) -$2,500; and the project is behind schedule. SV is calculated as EV – PV; $5,000 (EV) - $7,500 (PV) = $-2,500 (SV). A negative variance means that the work completed is less than what was planned for that point in time in the project.

87. (D) Permanently. You should keep permanent records of every change made from the original approved plan. This is just as true in cost control as it is in any other type of control in a project.

88. (A) Data. The data are only useful to you when you know how they were derived. It is possible that one case in the data may be so far away from the average data that in fact the entire set of information is not truly useful. This would be the case when a very large company's data was blended in with several companies that were less than one tenth the size of the big company. Ask how the data were derived, and you can save yourself a lot of grief later.

89. (A) General management cost evaluation. There are other techniques used in general management to make decisions about use of capital. These techniques are two of them.

90. (C) Cost management plan. The cost management plan describes how cost variances will be managed, for example, having different responses to major or minor problems.

91. (C) EV. Earned value is the value of work that you have already done on the project. This is the concept that is not used in standard accounting and one that you will have to explain to management if you want to report using the earned value analysis technique.

92. (C) Bottom up estimating should have been used. Bottom-up Estimating - this technique involves estimating the cost of individual work packages or individual schedule activities with the lowest level of detail. This detailed cost is then summarized or "rolled up" to higher levels for reporting and tracking purposes. The cost and accuracy of bottom-up cost estimating is typically motivated by the size and complexity of the individual schedule activity or work package. Generally, activities with smaller associated effort increase the accuracy of the schedule activity cost estimates.

93. (C) Cost baseline. The cost baseline is not available when the budget is created, since it is the result of taking the completed budget and allocating it over the time of the project. The project budget can be calculated without being time phased, but the cost baseline must be time phased.

94. (D) Historical information. All three of these can be used to help estimate cost.

95. A) Chart of accounts. If the organization has a chart of accounts, the various estimates should be assigned to the correct category.

96. (B) Analogous. Analogous estimating uses previous projects as a benchmark for estimating cost.

97. (D) The bulk of the project budget will be spent in the execution phase. Most of the project money will be spent during the execution phase. At the beginning of execution the rate of expenditures rises as people and materials are brought into the project. Later the expenditures peak and slow down.

98. (C) Sum of the years' digits. Sum of the years' digits is an accelerated depreciation method. Each year of the useful life of the asset is given a sequential number; the numbers are summed and used as the denominator for a fraction of the asset's book value to be taken each year as depreciation. The numerator of the fraction for each year is the reverse of the years' sequence numbers. $1 + 2 + 3 + 4 + 5 + 6 + 7 + 8 + 9 + 10 + 55$; First year use 10/55; second year use 9/55, and so on.

99. (A) Corrective action. Anything that is done to help bring the project closer to its project plan is called corrective action. Updating the budget and revising the cost estimate are possible corrective actions. Contingency planning is not used to adjust project performance; it is used to budget money for known risks that may occur.

100. (D) Known unknowns. You expect that there is a high probability that a cost will occur but you are not sure when it will happen.

Project Quality Management

The Project Quality Management questions on the PMP® exam are straightforward. The exam reflects the current emphasis on customer satisfaction and continuous improvement through quality tools such as Pareto analysis and cause-and-effect diagrams. You must know the difference among quality planning, performing quality assurance, and performing quality control.

PMBOK® Guide includes all quality-related activities under the term Project Quality Management, which compromise the three quality processes mentioned above. Review PMBOK® Guide figure 8.1 for an overview of the Project Quality Management structure.

The Project Quality Management knowledge area assures that the project meets the requirements that the project was undertaken to produce. These processes measure overall performance, monitor the project's results, and compare them to the quality standards set out in the project planning process to assure that the customer will receive the product or service they thought they purchased.

Project Quality Management is composed of the following three processes:

- Quality Planning - involves defining quality standards and deciding how to achieve them.
- Perform Quality Assurance - consists of measuring project progress to ensure the product meets quality standards.
- Perform Quality Control - involves supervising project activity completion and correcting any errors.

The purpose of quality management during the project management process is to identify customers' needs, to develop goals based on those needs, and to identify factors that impede achievement of project goals. Another aim of quality management is to keep a project on schedule, which helps avoid sacrificing quality in the interest of time and cost.

Before beginning a project, it is important for you the project manager to have a solid understanding of quality management and how its components are integrated into the project management process.

The components of quality management fit into these steps of the project management process:

- Quality planning is part of the planning step of the project management process.
- Quality improvement is part of the executing step of the project management process.
- Quality control is part of the controlling step of the project management process.

The PMBOK® Guide defines quality as the totality of characteristics of an entity that bears on its ability to satisfy stated or implied needs.

Stated and implied needs are the inputs to developing project requirements. A critical aspect of quality management in the project context is turning implied needs into requirements through Project Scope Management.

It is important to recognize the difference between quality and grade. Grade is a category or rank given to entities having the same functional use but different technical characteristics. Low quality is always a problem; low grade may not be. For example:

- A software product may be of high quality (very few defects, a readable user's manual) but of low grade meaning it has a limited number of features.
- Or, a software product may be of low quality but of high grade meaning it has many defects but lots of customer features.

The project manager and team must determine and deliver the required levels of quality and grade.

One important area that is emphasized in the PMBOK® Guide is the growing attention to customer requirements as the basis for managing quality. Another concept that may appear on the test, which is not specifically mentioned in the PMBOK®

Guide, is "gold-plating." Simply defined, gold-plating gives the customer more than what was required. Exceeding the specified requirements is a waste of time and money, with no value added to the project. The customer should expect and receive exactly what was specified. This is the underlying philosophy of project quality management espoused by PMI®; it is the process required to ensure that the project will satisfy the needs for which it was undertaken.

Project Quality Management - Questions

1. Which of the following best describes benchmarking?

 (A) Calculating the benefit to cost of purchasing a new piece of equipment.
 (B) Determining the scope of work and measures to ensure the scope is met.
 (C) Performing a root cause analysis on the quality problems that have occurred on the project.
 (D) Reading a project management magazine each month and looking for past projects to help determine quality measures for future projects.

2. Which of the following charts or diagrams would help a project manager determine possible causes of potential problems and actual problems?

 (A) A fishbone diagram
 (B) A histogram diagram
 (C) A Pareto chart
 (D) A control chart

3. Providing confidence that the project will satisfy relevant quality standards is part of:

 (A) Quality planning.
 (B) Quality control.
 (C) Quality management.
 (D) Quality assurance.

4. When the quality management discipline is implemented, the benefits to costs ratio should at least be:

 (A) Unable to be evaluated.
 (B) Less than one.
 (C) Of little importance.
 (D) Greater than one.

5. Quality checklists are used to:

 (A) Ensure that Quality Assurance steps were followed
 (B) Keep quality inspectors busy
 (C) Inform upper management where failures occur
 (D) Prevent project audits

6. When a process is considered to be in control, it:

 (A) Should not be adjusted
 (B) May not be changed to provide improvements
 (C) Shows differences caused by expected events or normal causes
 (D) Should not be inspected or reworked for any reason

7. The quality function deployment process is used to:

  (A) Help identify processes that are under way in other organizations that should be emulated
  (B) Support production planning and the just-in-time approach
  (C) Provide better product definition and product development
  (D) Help products succeed in the marketplace

8. Management wants to be sure that the project is following defined quality standards. Which of the following would they look at?

  (A) Statement of work
  (B) Quality audit
  (C) Risk management plan
  (D) Work breakdown structure

9. The project team should have a working knowledge of statistical process control to help conduct quality control activities. Of all the topics involved, which of the following is the most important for the team to understand?

  (A) Tolerances and control limits
  (B) Special causes and random causes
  (C) Sampling and probability
  (D) Attribute sampling and variable sampling

10. The testing results for the new computer modulation project have arrived from the seller. The results indicate the project is not meeting the overall quality requirements. If the project manager meets with team members to analyze the problem, the project manager is involved in:

  (A) Quality assurance.
  (B) Quality management.
  (C) Quality control.
  (D) Quality planning.

11. Non-random data points that are grouped together on one side of the mean of a control chart are called:

  (A) Specification limits.
  (B) In control.
  (C) Rule of seven.
  (D) 6-sigma.

12. A control chart controls a manufacturing process. Measurements are taken while the process is operating one time each hour. At each hour five sample parts are measured, and the results are recorded and plotted on a control chart. During the last five hours the following data was observed for X bar and R. The upper control limit for X bar values is 142 and the lower control limit is 102. The value on the control chart for X bar is 122 and the value for R bar is 3. What can be said about this process?

	9 A.M.	10 A.M.	11 A.M.	12 P.M.	1 P.M.
X bar	125	126	127	128	129
R	2	1	4	2	3

  (A) The process is not in control and should be adjusted.
  (B) The process is in control and should not be adjusted.
  (C) The value of R is too high at 11.
  (D) The value for X bar is outside the control limits.

13. Work results, quality checklists, operational definitions, and the management plan are:

    (A) Outputs from quality control.
    (B) Outputs from quality assurance.
    (C) Inputs to quality assurance.
    (D) Inputs to quality control.

14. Senior management regularly evaluates project performance to maintain confidence in quality product standards. Which of the following best describes this?

    (A) Quality assurance
    (B) Quality control
    (C) Quality management
    (D) Quality planning

15. When the quality management discipline is implemented, the benefits to costs ratio should at least be:

    (A) Unable to be evaluated.
    (B) Less than one.
    (C) Of little importance.
    (D) Greater than one.

16. Decisions as to the types of projects that should be accomplished and strategic plans as to the quality of the projects that are required should be the decision of which of the following?

    (A) Procurement manager
    (B) Project manager
    (C) Stakeholders
    (D) Upper management

17. Traditional thinking (before Crosby, Juran, Deming, and others) on quality performance standards held that error is:

    (A) Inevitable
    (B) Beneficial because we all learn from our mistakes
    (C) More costly than the sophisticated design work required to prevent it
    (D) Unlikely if a sufficient number of inspectors are used in the process

18. A project manager is using a cause-and-effect diagram with the team to determine how various factors might be linked to potential problems. In what step of the quality management process is the project manager involved?

    (A) Quality assurance
    (B) Quality analysis
    (C) Quality planning
    (D) Quality control

19. Which of the following charts is based on the 80/20 rule?

    (A) The 50/50 rule.
    (B) A fishbone chart.
    (C) A control chart.
    (D) A Pareto diagram.

20. The project has had a major defect and the project manager has gotten the project team and the process engineers involved in analyzing the situation. Two groups disagree where the fault lies. One of the groups says that the real fault is the age of the equipment. Another says it is the lack of a material for the correct quality. The project manager decides to use a fishbone diagram to help the process. Which of the following would best describe what the group is involved in?

(A) Quality assurance
(B) Quality control
(C) Quality analysis
(D) Quality planning

21. Recently your company introduced a new set of "metal woods" to its established line of golfing equipment. The "metal woods" are made from a combination of titanium, uranium, and manganese. Your company claims the clubs will add 80 yards to any drive. The product launch was spectacular. Every major money-winner on the PGA tour bought a set. However, in the past weeks things have gone horribly wrong. The clubs are causing golfers to hook, slice, and hit the ball "fat." One golfer even claims they have given him the "yips." You decide to conduct a failure mode and criticality analysis to:

(A) Evaluate failure modes and causes associated with the design and manufacture of an existing product
(B) Analyze the product development cycle after product release to determine strengths and weaknesses
(C) Help management set priorities in its existing manufacturing processes to avoid failures
(D) Evaluate failure modes and causes associated with the design and manufacture of a new product

22. You are managing a major international project to organize off-track betting in your client's hotels. Your client recently won the Malcolm Baldrige Award and emphasizes quality in all its endeavors. Your contract requires you to prepare both a project plan and a quality management plan. Your core team is preparing a project quality management plan. Your first step in developing this plan is to:

(A) Develop a quality policy for the project
(B) Identify specific quality management roles and responsibilities for the project
(C) Determine specific metrics to use in the quality management process
(D) Identify the quality standards for the project

23. Which of the following statements concerning quality planning is correct?

(A) Quality planning is done only during project planning.
(B) Quality planning is not considered during project execution.
(C) Quality planning should be performed regularly throughout the project.
(D) Quality planning is done to compile a risk management plan.

24. Which of the following involves comparing actual or planned project practices to those of other projects in order to generate ideas for improvement and to provide a standard by which to measure performance?

(A) Operational definitions.
(B) Benchmarking.
(C) Benchline parameters.
(D) Process adjustments.

25. The primary benefits of meeting quality requirements are:

(A) Cost and delays are reduced, production improves, market share increases, and profits go up.
(B) Cost and delays are reduced, production improves, cost to customer goes up, and profits go up.
(C) Cost and delays are reduced, production improves, market share increases, and profits are maintained.
(D) Cost and delays are reduced, capital expenditures go down, market share increases, and profits go up.

26. It was decided to set up a process to control the output of a machine that was manufacturing buttons. The following measurements of the diameter of the button were made. Each hour a sample of four buttons was taken. The measurement shown in the table is the measured ten-thousandths of an inch in excess of 1.000 inches. The engineering tolerance on this part is 1.000 +/- .005. (See image for data values). What is the value for R bar?

Hour	Item 1	Item 2	Item 3	Item 4
1	10	20	17	31
2	22	43	−12	40
3	16	29	36	33
4	05	44	−24	33
5	10	−44	33	42
6	08	33	−44	−23
7	25	27	50	−12
8	33	41	22	10
9	48	−33	31	04
10	−25	28	12	22

(A) 55.1 inches
(B) .00551 inches
(C) 10 inches
(D) .010 inches

27. You are a project manager for a major information systems project when someone from the quality department comes to see you about beginning a quality audit of your project. The team, already under pressure to complete the project as soon as possible, objects to the audit. You should explain to the team that the purpose of a quality audit is:

(A) To check if customer is following its quality process.
(B) Part of an ISO 9000 investigation.
(C) To check accuracy of costs submitted by the team.
(D) To identify lessons learned that can improve performance on project.

28. Quality assurance promotes quality improvement. The quality "gurus" discuss the importance of making annual improvements in quality and annual reductions in quality-related costs. In fact, Joseph Juran states that a "breakthrough" is the accomplishment of any improvement that takes the organization to unprecedented levels of performance. In Deming's terms, a breakthrough attacks:

(A) Common causes of variation
(B) Special causes of variation
(C) Specific tolerances
(D) Inspection over prevention

29. You are a project manager for residential construction. As a project manager, you must be especially concerned with building codes: particularly in the quality planning process. You must ensure that building codes are reflected in your project plans because:

(A) Quality audits serve to ensure there is compliance with regulations
(B) Standards and regulations are an input to quality planning
(C) Compliance with standards is the primary objective of quality control
(D) They are a cost associated with quality initiatives

30. Quality seems to be your company motto. First the company obtained certification under ISO 9000. Now the CEO wants to win the Malcolm Baldrige Award. Each project has a quality statement that is consistent with the organization's vision and mission. Both internal and external quality assurance is provided on all projects to:

(A) Provide confidence that the project will satisfy relevant quality standards
(B) Monitor specific project results to note whether they comply with relevant quality standards
(C) Identify ways to eliminate causes of unsatisfactory results
(D) Use inspection to keep errors out of the process

31. A project manager is identifying the quality standards relevant to the project and determining how to meet them. This activity is:

(A) Quality assurance.
(B) Quality management.
(C) Quality control.
(D) Quality planning.

32. A company uses sampling inspection to inspect parts that are sent to its customers. If a lot of parts are rejected from sampling inspection, it is inspected 100% and the rejected parts are sent back to the manufacturing department for rework or scrap. What happens to the overall outgoing quality level as the number of defective parts increases?

(A) The overall outgoing quality level increases at first and then decreases.
(B) The overall outgoing quality level decreases at first and then increases.
(C) The overall outgoing quality level increases.
(D) The overall outgoing quality level decreases.

33. Identifying ways to eliminate the causes of unsatisfactory performance is part of:

(A) Quality management.
(B) Quality assurance.
(C) Quality planning.
(D) Quality control.

34. A control chart is being used to control a manufacturing process. As part of the control a sample of five parts is taken from the manufacturing process each hour of operation. Each of the five parts is measured and the dimension is recorded on the work sheet. The difference between the highest and lowest measured dimension of the five parts is plotted on the control chart. This is called which of the following values?

(A) R
(B) R bar
(C) X
(D) X bar

35. Evaluating overall project performance regularly is part of:

(A) Quality management.
(B) Quality assurance.
(C) Quality planning.
(D) Quality control.

36. The quality management plan describes all the following except the:

(A) Method for implementing the quality policy
(B) Project quality system
(C) Organizational structure, responsibilities, procedures, processes, and resources needed to implement project quality management
(D) Procedures used to conduct trade-off analyses among cost, schedule, and quality

37. Attribute inspection is performed on a lot of motor shafts. The lot of parts is rejected as the parts are supposed to have a diameter of 2 inches and have an engineering tolerance of .015. What is the average dimension of the parts?

(A) Greater than 0.000
(B) Greater than 2.015 or less than 1.985
(C) The inspector should be fired for not writing a better report.
(D) Parts should not be rejected.

38. A project manager is determining the factors that might influence specific quality variables. He has chosen to analyze the color/size combination that will contribute most to the functionality of the new product. In what part of the quality management process is the project manager involved?

(A) Quality assurance
(B) Quality analysis
(C) Quality planning
(D) Quality control

39. Which of the following statements is true regarding common (random) causes and special causes with respect to statistical quality control?

(A) Common causes are a result of variances that are linked to unusual events.
(B) Special causes are a result of variances that are always present in the process.
(C) Special causes are a result of variances that are linked to unusual events.
(D) Common causes are controllable at the operational level.

40. Project quality assurance:

(A) Includes policing the conformance of the project team to specs.
(B) Provides the project team and stakeholders with standards, by which the project performance is measured.
(C) Is a managerial process that defines the organization, design, resources, and objectives of quality management.
(D) Provides confidence that the project will satisfy relevant quality standards.

41. An early version of one of W. Edward Deming's 14 points encouraged companies to "cease dependence on mass inspection by building quality into the product in the first place." Deming stated that, typically, products are inspected as they come off the line or at major stages. Defective products are either thrown out or reworked. Both options are expensive. This approach, in effect, meant that companies would pay workers to make defects and then correct them. Deming later recognized the value of inspections and revised the point to say that people should "understand the purpose of inspection." He said, "Inspections must be carried out in a professional way, not by lick-and-spit methods." This supports the PMBOK®, which indicates that inspections can be used to determine whether results conform to requirements. Inspections also may be called:

(A) Control tests
(B) Walk-throughs
(C) Statistical sampling
(D) Checklists

42. Recently, your company, a chicken-parts processor, had several health scares with regard to its products. These were isolated incidents that occurred in different geographic locations but over the same 3-week period. The company has had no product safety concerns in the past and believes that there are no problems with its inspection system. However, a new processing system was recently introduced. You were the project manager for this system and now have been asked to lead a team to investigate the situation and implement any needed changes. To help you analyze the new process, you and your team have decided to use which of the following techniques?

    (A) System flowcharts
    (B) Design of experiments
    (C) Pareto analysis
    (D) Control charts

43. If a data point falls outside the upper control limit of a control chart the process is said to be:

    (A) out of control.
    (B) gold plated.
    (C) in control.
    (D) assigned a cause.

44. Constancy of purpose is a core concept for continuous improvement. An organization displaying constancy of purpose must have all the following elements except:

    (A) Documented and well-disseminated statements of purpose and vision
    (B) A set of strategic and tactical plans
    (C) An awareness by all members of the organization of the purpose, vision, goals, and objectives and their roles in achieving them
    (D) Separate quality assurance and control departments reporting to senior management

45. Which of the following is not true about the cost of quality?

    (A) It should be compared to the cost of inspection and re-work using Benefit/Cost analysis in order to finalize the quality management plan.
    (B) It refers to the total cost of all efforts to achieve product/service quality.
    (C) It includes prevention, appraisal and failure costs.
    (D) Includes all work resulting from nonconformance to requirements as well as all work to ensure conformance to requirements.

46. The purpose of the Taguchi method is to:

    (A) Design, group, and manage production operations as self-contained flexible cells capable of start-to-finish processing of a family of items
    (B) Regulate coordination and communication among process stages
    (C) Manage the flow of material for better visibility and control
    (D) Use statistical techniques to compute a "loss function" to determine the cost of producing products that fail to achieve a target value

47. It was decided to set up a process to control the output of a machine that was manufacturing buttons. The following measurements of the diameter of the button were made. Each hour a sample of four buttons was taken. The measurement shown in the table is the measured ten-thousandths of an inch in excess of 1.000 inches. The engineering tolerance on this part is 1.000 +/- .005. (See image for data values). What is the value of X bar for hour number 7?

Hour	Item 1	Item 2	Item 3	Item 4
1	10	20	17	31
2	22	43	−12	40
3	16	29	36	33
4	05	44	−24	33
5	10	−44	33	42
6	08	33	−44	−23
7	25	27	50	−12
8	33	41	22	10
9	48	−33	31	04
10	−25	28	12	22

(A) 22.5 inches
(B) .00900 inches
(C) .00225 inches
(D) 90 inches

48. The project management team should be aware that modern quality management complements modern project management. For example, both disciplines recognize the importance of:

(A) Making a maximum profit.
(B) Completion in the shortest possible time frame.
(C) Customer satisfaction.
(D) Having lower cost than a competitor.

49. Based on quality control measurements on your manufacturing project, management realizes that immediate corrective action is required to the material requirements planning (MRP) system to prevent future problems on other projects and to minimize rework. To implement the necessary changes you should follow:

(A) Established operational definitions and procedures
(B) Procedures for integrated change control
(C) The organization's quality policy
(D) The quality management plan

50. ISO standards are reviewed and reissued every:

(A) Ten years.
(B) One year.
(C) Two years.
(D) Five years.

51. A project manager for the quality department is trying to solve a problem with a machine that makes die cast aluminum parts that are used in automobiles. These parts are frequently made with defects. The project manager has decided to hold a meeting to discuss the process of making the parts. He creates a diagram that has branches that show the possible causes of the problems. Each of the branches breaks the cause down into more and more detail. This diagram is called a:

    (A) Pareto diagram.
    (B) Fishhook diagram.
    (C) Cause and effect diagram.
    (D) Scatter diagram.

52. You are in charge of developing a new product for a bank. Your quality metrics are based on the 65th percentile of each of the last four products developed. This is an example of?

    (A) Metrics.
    (B) Operational definitions.
    (C) Benchmarking.
    (D) Statistical sampling.

53. The three most important aspects of a project to stakeholders are:

    (A) Quality, Cost, Risk
    (B) Cost, Schedule, Quality
    (C) Cost, Schedule, Strategy
    (D) Schedule, Quality, Risk

54. Results of quality control testing and measurement are used:

    (A) As an input to quality planning.
    (B) To prepare an operational definition.
    (C) To prepare a control chart.
    (D) As an input to quality assurance.

55. Which of the following are not assignable causes of variation?

    (A) Differences between employee effectiveness.
    (B) Differences among measurements.
    (C) Differences in raw materials.
    (D) Differences between new and old machines

56. It was decided to set up a process to control the output of a machine that was manufacturing buttons. The following measurements of the diameter of the button were made. Each hour a sample of four buttons was taken. The measurement shown in the table is the measured ten-thousandths of an inch in excess of 1.000 inches. The engineering tolerance on this part is 1.000 +/- .005. (See image for data values). What is the value for R bar?

    (A) 55.1 inches
    (B) .00551 inches
    (C) 10 inches
    (D) .010 inches

Hour	Item 1	Item 2	Item 3	Item 4
1	10	20	17	31
2	22	43	-12	40
3	16	29	36	33
4	05	44	-24	33
5	10	-44	33	42
6	08	33	-44	-23
7	25	27	50	-12
8	33	41	22	10
9	48	-33	31	04
10	-25	28	12	22

57. The principal use of a Pareto diagram is to:

(A) Quantify risks.
(B) Focus attention on the most critical issues.
(C) Improve risk management.
(D) Help predict future problems.

58. Rank ordering of defects should be used to guide corrective action. This is the underlying principle behind
_____.

(A) Inspections
(B) Trend analysis
(C) Pareto charts
(D) Control charts

59. You are in the middle of a major new facility construction project. The structural steel is in place, and the heating conduits are going into place when the project sponsor informs you that he is worried the project will not meet the quality standards. What should you do in this situation?

(A) Assure the sponsor that during planning it was determined the project would meet the quality standards.
(B) Inspect the results so far and use them to determine future results.
(C) Perform a quality audit.
(D) Check the results from the last quality management plan.

60. Senior management does a regular evaluation of project performance in order to be more confident in quality product standards. This is an example of?

(A) Quality control
(B) Quality planning
(C) Quality management
(D) Quality assurance

61. During project execution, a new ISO version of standard 9000 was issued and now the project team is meeting with the quality department to determine how the standard will apply to the project. Which part of the quality process is this?

(A) Quality analysis
(B) Quality assurance
(C) Quality control
(D) Quality planning

62. The quality management plan provides input to and addresses quality control, quality assurance, and quality improvement.

(A) The WBS
(B) The overall project plan
(C) External stakeholders
(D) The project scope

63. A project manager from the quality control area is trying to categorize the number of mistakes that are made in the area that paints the right front fender of the Mercedes 560 SL. She lists all the possible defects on a sheet of paper and asks the inspector to make a mark each time one of the listed defects is found. This is an example of using which of the following quality tools?

(A) Statistical measurements
(B) Scatter diagram
(C) Random sampling
(D) Check sheet

64. What does ''cost of acceptance'' mean?

    (A) The life cycle cost of the project.
    (B) The cost of establishing and maintaining the quality function.
    (C) The cost of meeting project objectives.
    (D) The cost of inspection and re-inspection, quality assurance, quality management, and quality planning.

65. A project manager has discovered a problem and is trying to determine the cause. The process whereby he identifies the variables that have the most influence on the project by holding all the variables constant and changing one at a time is called:

    (A) Design of an experiment.
    (B) Product correlation.
    (C) Output processing.
    (D) System integration.

66. To use statistical quality control effectively, the project team should know the differences between:

    (A) Attribute sampling and statistical sampling
    (B) Control limits and operational definitions
    (C) Prevention and quality control
    (D) Special causes and random causes

67. Conformance to specifications is one description of _____.

    (A) Grade
    (B) Scope
    (C) Quality
    (D) Technical information

68. Continuous improvement in a company's products is known as:

    (A) Ishikawa.
    (B) Life-cycle costing.
    (C) Management by objectives.
    (D) Total quality management.

69. A project manager and team from a firm that designs railroad equipment are tasked to design a machine to load stone onto railroad cars. The design allows for 2% spillage, amounting to over two tons of spilled rock per day. In which of the following does the project manager document quality control, quality assurance, and quality improvements for this project?

    (A) Quality policy.
    (B) Quality management plan.
    (C) Project management plan.
    (D) Control charts.

70. You are the program level manager with several project activities underway. In the execution phase, you begin to become concerned about the accuracy of progress reports from the projects. Which of the following would best support your opinion that there is a problem?

    (A) Quality audits
    (B) Risk quantification reports
    (C) Regression analysis
    (D) Monte Carlo simulation

71. The organization that controls the standards for quality is the _____.

    (A) INA
    (B) ISO
    (C) IIQ
    (D) PMI

72. A control chart helps the project manager:

    (A) Focus on the most critical issues to improve quality.
    (B) Focus on stimulating thinking.
    (C) Explore a desired future outcome.
    (D) Determine if a process is functioning within set limits.

73. Your company, a leading chain manufacturer for snowmobiles and chainsaws, is working to develop an interchangeable chain that can be used on both. To anticipate and help develop approaches to deal with potential quality problems, you want to use a variety of root-cause analysis techniques including all the following approaches except:

    (A) System or process flowcharts
    (B) Checklists
    (C) Fishbone diagrams
    (D) Ishikawa diagrams

74. All of the following are used in the quality control process except?

    (A) Control charts
    (B) Statistical sampling
    (C) Pareto charts
    (D) Gantt charts

75. A quality management plan is created during:

    (A) Execution.
    (B) Quality planning.
    (C) Quality assurance.
    (D) Quality control.

76. After a long and frustrating day, your company CEO found himself circling the attendant's booth at the adjacent parking garage in a futile attempt to find his way out of the building (his limousine driver had taken the day off). He approached the building manager the next day and said he would have his staff design an improved system for vehicle egress and ingress. You are the project manager for this project. You decide to use flowcharting to:

    (A) Show the results of a process
    (B) Forecast future outcomes
    (C) Help analyze how problems occur
    (D) Show dependencies between tasks

77. During project execution, a project team member comes to the project manager to tell her that, based on what he sees of the project, the project cannot meet the quality standards set for the project. The project manager meets with all the relevant parties to analyze the situation. Which step of the quality management process is the project manager in?

    (A) Quality assurance
    (B) Quality planning
    (C) Quality control
    (D) Quality analysis

78. As the manager of the production department where electrical circuits are being made you observe the inspection station where the completed printed circuit assemblies are being inspected. In this operation the inspector takes the printed circuit assembly and puts it into a fixture. The fixture is part of a testing machine that has three digital readouts. The inspector records the readings on the three digital readouts on his inspection report. This is an example of:

    (A) Sampling inspection.
    (B) Process control.
    (C) Attribute inspection.
    (D) Variable inspection.

79. In the image, what does the highlighted area represent?

    (A) In control data points
    (B) Out of control data points
    (C) Standard deviation
    (D) Rule of seven

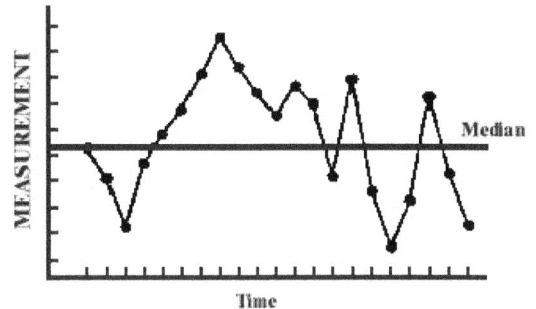

80. Which of the following statements best describes attribute sampling versus variable sampling?

    (A) Attribute sampling is concerned with conformance, whereas variable sampling is concerned with the degree of conformity.
    (B) Attribute sampling is concerned with prevention, whereas variable sampling is concerned with inspection.
    (C) Both are the same concept.
    (D) Attribute sampling is concerned with special causes, whereas variable sampling is concerned with any causes.

81. A control chart indicates the last 12 weights produced were outside the upper control limit. What should the project manager do?

    (A) Stop production
    (B) Work to better meet ISO 9000 standards
    (C) Look for the non-random causes for the variations
    (D) Plan to rework the 12 weights

82. The statistical control chart is a tool used primarily to help:

    (A) Determine whether results conform
    (B) Determine whether results conform to requirements
    (C) Monitor process variation over time
    (D) Measure the degree of conformance

83. A large project is being worked on by a large company. The client is interested in knowing how the company will be able to meet the quality needs of the project. In order to satisfy this request of the client the project manager arranges a meeting between the client and the:

    (A) Quality control manager.
    (B) General manager.
    (C) Chief designer.
    (D) Quality assurance manager.

84. Your quality assurance department recently performed a quality audit of your project and identified a number of findings and recommendations. One recommendation seems critical and should be implemented because it affects successful delivery of the product to your customer. If the recommendation is not implemented, the product will not conform to requirements. Your next step should be to:

    (A) Call a meeting of your project team to see who is responsible for the problem
    (B) Reassign the team member who had responsibility for oversight of the problem
    (C) Perform product rework immediately
    (D) Issue a change request to implement the needed corrective action

85. Which of the following illustrates a chart with upper / lower limits on which values of some statistical measure for a series of samples are plotted using sample variance measurements, where the mean and standard deviation are determined from the samples selected?

    (A) Gantt chart
    (B) Control chart
    (C) Pareto diagram
    (D) Scatter diagram

86. In order to monitor the number of errors or defects that have been identified and the number that remain undetected, you should use or do which of the following?

    (A) Conduct a trend analysis.
    (B) Perform an audit.
    (C) Design an experiment.
    (D) Use a checklist.

87. Six sigma refers to the aim of setting tolerance limits at 6 standard deviations from the mean, whereas the normally expected deviation of a process is:

    (A) 1 standard deviation
    (B) 2 standard deviations
    (C) 3 standard deviations
    (D) Undeterminable because of the unique nature of every process

88. You recognize the importance of quality control on your project. However, you also know that quality control has costs associated with it and that the project has a limited budget. One way to reduce the cost of quality control is to:

    (A) Work to ensure that the overall quality program is ISO compliant
    (B) Use statistical sampling
    (C) Conduct inspections throughout the process
    (D) Use trend analysis

89. Your company is establishing a cost of quality approach to determine the relative importance of its quality problems and to identify major opportunities for cost reduction. Your company believes this approach can help it evaluate its success in achieving quality objectives. When setting up this approach, you were asked to categorize four types of costs: prevention, appraisal, internal failure, and external failure. As you examine the cost of quality, however, you realize that training and its associated costs have become a major factor. Training costs are included in which one of the following areas?

    (A) Prevention costs
    (B) Appraisal costs
    (C) Internal failure costs
    (D) External failure costs

90. According to Deming and Juran most of the quality problems that exist are due to a defect or failure in processes that are controlled by:

(A) Upper management.
(B) Stakeholders.
(C) The project manager.
(D) The procurement manager.

91. The testing results for a new computer modulation project indicate a problem with the on-board computer's sensors. The project manager calls a meeting with the team to analyze the problem. The project manager is involved in:

(A) Quality assurance.
(B) Quality management.
(C) Quality control.
(D) Quality planning.

92. A project manager and his team are trying to determine how various factors might be linked to potential problems using an Ishikawa diagram. The project manager would be involved in which step of the quality management process?

(A) Quality tools
(B) Quality planning
(C) Quality control
(D) Quality assurance

93. What does "cost of acceptance" mean?

(A) The life cycle cost of the project.
(B) The cost of establishing and maintaining the quality function.
(C) The cost of meeting project objectives.
(D) The cost of inspection and re-inspection, quality assurance, quality management, and quality planning.

94. A control chart is being used to control a manufacturing process. As part of the control a sample of five parts is taken from the manufacturing process each hour of operation. Each of the five parts is measured, and the dimension is recorded on the work sheet. The average of the five parts is plotted on the control chart. This is called which of the following values?

(A) X
(B) X bar
(C) Sample average
(D) Control average

95. A company uses sampling inspection to inspect parts that are sent to its customers. If a lot of parts are rejected from sampling inspection, it is inspected 100% and the rejected parts are sent back to the manufacturing department for rework or scrap. What happens to the overall outgoing quality level as the number of defective parts increases?

(A) The overall outgoing quality level increases at first and then decreases.
(B) The overall outgoing quality level decreases at first and then increases.
(C) The overall outgoing quality level increases.
(D) The overall outgoing quality level decreases.

96. Quality Assurance was preceded by:

(A) Quality Control
(B) Inspection
(C) Quality Circles
(D) Employee Empowerment

97. The quality manager of a company wishes to analyze the data that is coming to him in the form of a list of defects that have occurred in the shipping department. The report comes with defects listed chronologically as they occurred, the cost of the repair necessary to correct each defect, the person involved, and a description of the defect. The manager would like to determine which of the defects should be corrected first according to the frequency of the defect occurring. He should use which of the following quality tools?

      (A) Sampling inspection
      (B) Cause and effect diagram
      (C) Quality critical path
      (D) Pareto diagram

98. The diagram that ranks defects in the order of frequency of occurrence and shows the number of defects and the cumulative percentage from the greatest number of defects to the least number of defects is called a:

      (A) Bar chart.
      (B) Critical path.
      (C) Pie chart.
      (D) Pareto diagram.

99. The widget production project is well underway. The requirements are clear that each widget must weigh between .320 and .325 ounces. The first day of test production resulted in 1247 widgets. Of the widgets inspected 47% fell within the acceptable weight range. This is an example of?

      (A) Variable sampling
      (B) Attribute sampling
      (C) Control charting
      (D) Flow charting

100. Your project team is working to design and manufacture a "smart zipper" that never jams. You established a project quality management system and are performing both quality assurance and quality control throughout the project. You recognize that some rework may be necessary. The term rework, however, is not used in your organization. You explain that rework

      (A) Action taken to bring a nonconforming item into compliance
      (B) Not a concern if errors are detected early
      (C) Acceptable under certain circumstances
      (D) An adjustment made that is based on quality control measurements

Sample Answer Sheet

	T F			T F			T F			T F
1	Ⓐ Ⓑ Ⓒ Ⓓ Ⓔ	26	Ⓐ Ⓑ Ⓒ Ⓓ Ⓔ	51	Ⓐ Ⓑ Ⓒ Ⓓ Ⓔ	76	Ⓐ Ⓑ Ⓒ Ⓓ Ⓔ
2	Ⓐ Ⓑ Ⓒ Ⓓ Ⓔ	27	Ⓐ Ⓑ Ⓒ Ⓓ Ⓔ	52	Ⓐ Ⓑ Ⓒ Ⓓ Ⓔ	77	Ⓐ Ⓑ Ⓒ Ⓓ Ⓔ
3	Ⓐ Ⓑ Ⓒ Ⓓ Ⓔ	28	Ⓐ Ⓑ Ⓒ Ⓓ Ⓔ	53	Ⓐ Ⓑ Ⓒ Ⓓ Ⓔ	78	Ⓐ Ⓑ Ⓒ Ⓓ Ⓔ
4	Ⓐ Ⓑ Ⓒ Ⓓ Ⓔ	29	Ⓐ Ⓑ Ⓒ Ⓓ Ⓔ	54	Ⓐ Ⓑ Ⓒ Ⓓ Ⓔ	79	Ⓐ Ⓑ Ⓒ Ⓓ Ⓔ
5	Ⓐ Ⓑ Ⓒ Ⓓ Ⓔ	30	Ⓐ Ⓑ Ⓒ Ⓓ Ⓔ	55	Ⓐ Ⓑ Ⓒ Ⓓ Ⓔ	80	Ⓐ Ⓑ Ⓒ Ⓓ Ⓔ
6	Ⓐ Ⓑ Ⓒ Ⓓ Ⓔ	31	Ⓐ Ⓑ Ⓒ Ⓓ Ⓔ	56	Ⓐ Ⓑ Ⓒ Ⓓ Ⓔ	81	Ⓐ Ⓑ Ⓒ Ⓓ Ⓔ
7	Ⓐ Ⓑ Ⓒ Ⓓ Ⓔ	32	Ⓐ Ⓑ Ⓒ Ⓓ Ⓔ	57	Ⓐ Ⓑ Ⓒ Ⓓ Ⓔ	82	Ⓐ Ⓑ Ⓒ Ⓓ Ⓔ
8	Ⓐ Ⓑ Ⓒ Ⓓ Ⓔ	33	Ⓐ Ⓑ Ⓒ Ⓓ Ⓔ	58	Ⓐ Ⓑ Ⓒ Ⓓ Ⓔ	83	Ⓐ Ⓑ Ⓒ Ⓓ Ⓔ
9	Ⓐ Ⓑ Ⓒ Ⓓ Ⓔ	34	Ⓐ Ⓑ Ⓒ Ⓓ Ⓔ	59	Ⓐ Ⓑ Ⓒ Ⓓ Ⓔ	84	Ⓐ Ⓑ Ⓒ Ⓓ Ⓔ
10	Ⓐ Ⓑ Ⓒ Ⓓ Ⓔ	35	Ⓐ Ⓑ Ⓒ Ⓓ Ⓔ	60	Ⓐ Ⓑ Ⓒ Ⓓ Ⓔ	85	Ⓐ Ⓑ Ⓒ Ⓓ Ⓔ
11	Ⓐ Ⓑ Ⓒ Ⓓ Ⓔ	36	Ⓐ Ⓑ Ⓒ Ⓓ Ⓔ	61	Ⓐ Ⓑ Ⓒ Ⓓ Ⓔ	86	Ⓐ Ⓑ Ⓒ Ⓓ Ⓔ
12	Ⓐ Ⓑ Ⓒ Ⓓ Ⓔ	37	Ⓐ Ⓑ Ⓒ Ⓓ Ⓔ	62	Ⓐ Ⓑ Ⓒ Ⓓ Ⓔ	87	Ⓐ Ⓑ Ⓒ Ⓓ Ⓔ
13	Ⓐ Ⓑ Ⓒ Ⓓ Ⓔ	38	Ⓐ Ⓑ Ⓒ Ⓓ Ⓔ	63	Ⓐ Ⓑ Ⓒ Ⓓ Ⓔ	88	Ⓐ Ⓑ Ⓒ Ⓓ Ⓔ
14	Ⓐ Ⓑ Ⓒ Ⓓ Ⓔ	39	Ⓐ Ⓑ Ⓒ Ⓓ Ⓔ	64	Ⓐ Ⓑ Ⓒ Ⓓ Ⓔ	89	Ⓐ Ⓑ Ⓒ Ⓓ Ⓔ
15	Ⓐ Ⓑ Ⓒ Ⓓ Ⓔ	40	Ⓐ Ⓑ Ⓒ Ⓓ Ⓔ	65	Ⓐ Ⓑ Ⓒ Ⓓ Ⓔ	90	Ⓐ Ⓑ Ⓒ Ⓓ Ⓔ
16	Ⓐ Ⓑ Ⓒ Ⓓ Ⓔ	41	Ⓐ Ⓑ Ⓒ Ⓓ Ⓔ	66	Ⓐ Ⓑ Ⓒ Ⓓ Ⓔ	91	Ⓐ Ⓑ Ⓒ Ⓓ Ⓔ
17	Ⓐ Ⓑ Ⓒ Ⓓ Ⓔ	42	Ⓐ Ⓑ Ⓒ Ⓓ Ⓔ	67	Ⓐ Ⓑ Ⓒ Ⓓ Ⓔ	92	Ⓐ Ⓑ Ⓒ Ⓓ Ⓔ
18	Ⓐ Ⓑ Ⓒ Ⓓ Ⓔ	43	Ⓐ Ⓑ Ⓒ Ⓓ Ⓔ	68	Ⓐ Ⓑ Ⓒ Ⓓ Ⓔ	93	Ⓐ Ⓑ Ⓒ Ⓓ Ⓔ
19	Ⓐ Ⓑ Ⓒ Ⓓ Ⓔ	44	Ⓐ Ⓑ Ⓒ Ⓓ Ⓔ	69	Ⓐ Ⓑ Ⓒ Ⓓ Ⓔ	94	Ⓐ Ⓑ Ⓒ Ⓓ Ⓔ
20	Ⓐ Ⓑ Ⓒ Ⓓ Ⓔ	45	Ⓐ Ⓑ Ⓒ Ⓓ Ⓔ	70	Ⓐ Ⓑ Ⓒ Ⓓ Ⓔ	95	Ⓐ Ⓑ Ⓒ Ⓓ Ⓔ
21	Ⓐ Ⓑ Ⓒ Ⓓ Ⓔ	46	Ⓐ Ⓑ Ⓒ Ⓓ Ⓔ	71	Ⓐ Ⓑ Ⓒ Ⓓ Ⓔ	96	Ⓐ Ⓑ Ⓒ Ⓓ Ⓔ
22	Ⓐ Ⓑ Ⓒ Ⓓ Ⓔ	47	Ⓐ Ⓑ Ⓒ Ⓓ Ⓔ	72	Ⓐ Ⓑ Ⓒ Ⓓ Ⓔ	97	Ⓐ Ⓑ Ⓒ Ⓓ Ⓔ
23	Ⓐ Ⓑ Ⓒ Ⓓ Ⓔ	48	Ⓐ Ⓑ Ⓒ Ⓓ Ⓔ	73	Ⓐ Ⓑ Ⓒ Ⓓ Ⓔ	98	Ⓐ Ⓑ Ⓒ Ⓓ Ⓔ
24	Ⓐ Ⓑ Ⓒ Ⓓ Ⓔ	49	Ⓐ Ⓑ Ⓒ Ⓓ Ⓔ	74	Ⓐ Ⓑ Ⓒ Ⓓ Ⓔ	99	Ⓐ Ⓑ Ⓒ Ⓓ Ⓔ
25	Ⓐ Ⓑ Ⓒ Ⓓ Ⓔ	50	Ⓐ Ⓑ Ⓒ Ⓓ Ⓔ	75	Ⓐ Ⓑ Ⓒ Ⓓ Ⓔ	100	Ⓐ Ⓑ Ⓒ Ⓓ Ⓔ

Project Quality Management - Answers

1. **(D) Reading a project management magazine each month and looking for past projects to help determine quality measures for future projects.** Benchmarking involves comparing actual or planned project practices to those of other projects to generate ideas for improvement and to provide a basis by which to measure performance. These other projects can be within the performing organization or outside of it, and can be within the same or in another application area.

2. **(A) A fishbone diagram.** Cause and effect diagrams, also called Ishikawa diagrams or fishbone diagrams, illustrate how various factors might be linked to potential problems or effects.

3. **(D) quality assurance.** Quality assurance – applying the planned, systematic quality activities to ensure that the project employs all processes needed to meet requirements.

4. **(D) Greater than one.** The benefits should always be greater than the cost of implementing quality management. The benefit-cost ratio should always be greater than one.

5. **(A) Ensure that Quality Assurance steps were followed**. Ensure that Quality Assurance steps were followed.

6. **(A) Should not be adjusted**. Processes may be changed only through established change procedures. An adjustment implies an informal change falling outside those procedures.

7. **(C) Provide better product definition and product development**. Quality function deployment helps a design team to define, design, manufacture, and deliver a product or service to meet or exceed customer needs. Its main features are to capture the customer's requirements, ensure cross-functional teamwork, and link the main phases of product development—product planning, part deployment, process planning, and production planning.

8. **(B) Quality audit**. A quality audit is a structured, independent review to determine whether project activities comply with organizational and project policies, processes, and procedures. The objective of a quality audit is to identify inefficient and ineffective policies, processes, and procedures in use on the project.

9. **(C) Sampling and probability**. Sampling and probability form the basis of statistical process control, which helps the team monitor project results for compliance with relevant quality standards so that methods can be identified to eliminate causes of unsatisfactory results.

10. **(A) quality assurance.** Quality assurance – applying the planned, systematic quality activities to ensure that the project employs all processes needed to meet requirements.

11. **(C) rule of seven.** This rule of thumb (heuristic) states that if seven or more observations in a row occur on the same side of the mean (or if they trend in the same direction), even though they may be within the control limit, they should be investigated as if they had an assignable cause. It is extremely unlikely that seven observations in a row would be on the same side of the mean if the process is operating normally.

12. **(A) The process is not in control and should be adjusted.** The process is not in control. Although the values of X bar are all within the upper and lower control limits of the process, there is a trend showing five values in a row all increasing. There are several observations on the control chart that can indicate that the process is out of control even though the values measured are within the upper and lower control limits.

13. **(D) Inputs to quality control.** Work results, quality checklists, operational definitions, and the management plan are the items listed in the Guide to the PMBOK as the inputs to the quality control function.

14. **(B) Quality control**. Quality Assurance – applying the planned, systematic quality activities to ensure that the project employs all processes needed to meet requirements.

15. **(D) Greater than one.** The benefits should always be greater than the cost of implementing quality management. The benefit-cost ratio should always be greater than one.

16. (D) Upper management. Projects are typically part of an organization larger than the project—corporations, government agencies, health care institutions, international bodies, professional associations, and others. Projects are typically authorized as a result of one or more needs. These stimuli may also be called problems, opportunities, or business requirements. The central theme of all these terms is that management generally must make a decision about how to respond. Projects are authorized by upper management, which is responsible for setting strategic company goals.

17. (A) Inevitable. Traditional thinking on quality held that human beings make mistakes; accordingly, the cost to secure zero defects would be significantly greater than the value of achieving "perfection."

18. (C) Quality planning. Quality planning involves identifying which quality standards are relevant to the project and determining how to satisfy them. It is one of the key processes when doing the Planning Process Group and during development of the project management plan, and should be performed in parallel with the other project planning processes.

19. (D) A Pareto diagram. In the late 1800s, Vilfredo Pareto, an Italian economist, found that typically 80 percent of the wealth in a region was concentrated in less than 20 percent of the population. Later, Dr. Joseph Juran formulated what he called the Pareto Principle of Problems: only a "vital few" elements (20 percent) account for the majority (80 percent) of the problems. For example, in a manufacturing facility, 20 percent of the equipment problems account for 80 percent of the downtime. Because the Pareto Principle has proven to be valid in numerous situations, it is useful to examine data carefully to identify the vital few items that most deserve attention.

20. (B) Quality control. Quality control (QC) involves monitoring specific project results to determine whether they comply with relevant quality standards and identifying ways to eliminate causes of unsatisfactory results. It should be performed throughout the project. Quality standards include project processes and product goals. Project results include deliverables and project management results, such as cost and schedule performance. QC is often performed by a quality control department or similarly titled organizational unit. QC can include taking action to eliminate causes of unsatisfactory project performance.

21. (D) Evaluate failure modes and causes associated with the design and manufacture of a new product. This technique is a method of analyzing design reliability. A list of potential failure modes is developed for each element, and then each mode is given a numeric rating for frequency of occurrence, criticality, and probability of detection. These data are used to assign a risk priority number for prioritizing problems and guiding the design effort.

22. (A) Develop a quality policy for the project. The quality policy includes the overall intentions and direction of the organization with regard to quality, as formally expressed by top management. If the performing organization lacks a formal quality policy or if the project involves multiple performing organizations, as in a joint venture, the project management team must develop a quality policy for the project as an input to its quality planning.

23. (C) Quality planning should be performed regularly throughout the project. Quality planning involves identifying which quality standards are relevant to the project and determining how to satisfy them. It is one of the key processes when doing the Planning Process Group, and during development of the project management plan, and should be performed in parallel with the other project planning processes.

24. (B) Benchmarking. Benchmarking involves comparing actual or planned project practices to those of other projects to generate ideas for improvement and to provide a basis by which to measure performance. These other projects can be within the performing organization or outside of it, and can be within the same or in another application area.

25. (A) Cost and delays are reduced, production improves, market share increases, and profits go up. Cost and delays are reduced, production improves, market share increases, and profits go up. Cost to the customer should not go up when quality management is implemented properly. Capital expenditures should not necessarily go down or up as a result of quality management. Profits should increase.

26. (B) .00551 inches. To calculate the value for R bar, we take the value for R for each hour and find the mean or average value. Value for R for each hour is:

Hour	1	2	3	4	5	6	7	8	9	10
R	21	52	20	68	86	77	62	31	81	53

The sum of the values is 551, which is 55.1 when divided by 10. Since this number is in ten thousandths of an inch, the correct answer is .00551.

27. (D) to identify lessons learned that can improve performance on project. A Quality Audit is a systematic and independent examination to determine whether quality activities and related results comply with planned arrangements and whether these arrangements are implemented effectively and are suitable to achieve objectives.

28. (A) Common causes of variation. Quality improvement includes action taken to increase project effectiveness and efficiency in order to provide added benefits to stakeholders. A breakthrough attacks chronic losses, or in Deming's terminology, common causes of variation.

29. (B) Standards and regulations are an input to quality planning. In quality planning, the project management team must consider any application-area specific standards or regulations that may affect the project. Building codes are an example of regulations.

30. (A) Provide confidence that the project will satisfy relevant quality standards. Quality assurance increases project effectiveness and efficiency and provides added benefits to project stakeholders. It is all the planned and systematic activities implemented within the quality system that provide confidence that the project will satisfy relevant quality standards. It should be performed throughout the project.

31. (D) quality planning. Quality planning involves identifying which quality standards are relevant to the project and determining how to satisfy them. It is one of the key processes when doing the Planning Process Group, and during development of the project management plan, and should be performed in parallel with the other project planning processes.

32. (B) The overall outgoing quality level decreases at first and then increases. When sampling inspection is used, it will discover lots that are above the AQL. These lots are then returned for 100% inspection. When the 100% inspection is done, the defective parts are removed, and the acceptable ones are sent to the customer. As the number of defective parts increases, more lots will have to be inspected 100%. Initially, the quality delivered to the customer will fall, but because of the added work of the 100% inspection, the quality will then improve.

33. (D) quality control. Quality control involves monitoring specific project results to determine whether they comply with relevant quality standards and identifying ways to eliminate causes of unsatisfactory results.

34. (A) R. The averaging of the five parts that are sampled is called the X bar value. In control charts the two values that are normally plotted on the control chart are the X bar value and the R value, the difference between the highest and lowest value of the dimension in the sampled parts.

35. (B) quality assurance. Quality assurance – applying the planned, systematic quality activities to ensure that the project employs all processes needed to meet requirements.

36. (D) Procedures used to conduct trade-off analyses among cost, schedule, and quality. A part of the overall project plan, the quality management plan should address all aspects of how quality management will be implemented on the project rather than focusing on one or two specific areas of continuous improvement. Trade-off analyses are business judgments and, as such, are not procedural steps to be included in the quality management plan.

37. (A) Greater than 0.000. Because the parts are attribute inspected, we do not have data other than the parts failed to pass a Go–No Go gauge. We know only that an unacceptable number of parts were either above or below the allowed dimension. It is possible that the average for the rejected parts is 2.000 inches. The only thing we know for sure is that the part diameters are greater than 0.000, or they would not exist.

38. (C) Quality planning. Quality planning involves identifying which quality standards are relevant to the project and determining how to satisfy them. It is one of the key processes when doing the Planning Process Group and during development of the project management plan, and should be performed in parallel with the other project planning processes.

39. (C) Special causes are a result of variances that are linked to unusual events. Special causes are a result of variances that are linked to unusual events. Special cause variances are generally manageable at the operational level. For example, perhaps a machine needs to be recalibrated after running non-stop for 48 hours. Common causes are a result of variances that are always present in the process. (PMBOK Guide - page 354)

40. (D) Provides confidence that the project will satisfy relevant quality standards. Quality assurance is all the planned and systematic activities implemented within the quality system to provide confidence that the project will satisfy the relevant quality standards.

41. (B) Walk-through. Inspections include those activities undertaken to determine whether results conform to requirements. Additional names for inspections are audits, reviews, or product reviews (in some application areas, these terms may have narrow and specific meanings).

42. (D) Control charts. This function of control charts is achieved through graphical display of results over time to determine whether differences in the results are created by random variations or are unusual events. Although frequently used to track repetitive actions such as manufactured lots, control charts can also be used to monitor project management processes such as cost and schedule variances, volume and frequency of scope changes, and errors in project documents.

43. (A) out of control. The upper and lower control limits (UCL and LCL) must not be confused with specification limits. Control limits describe the natural variation of the process such that points within the limits are generally indicative of normal and expected variation. Points outside the limits signal that something has occurred that requires special attention because it is outside of the built-in systemic causes of variation in the process. Note that the circled point on the X-bar chart means that the process is out of control and should be investigated. These points outside the control limits are referred to as special events having either assignable causes or random causes.

44. (D) Separate quality assurance and control departments reporting to senior management. Top management should provide constancy of purpose so that it can be infused throughout the organization. Constancy of purpose also requires a shared belief among organization members that management's behavior clearly signals its commitment to and support of achievement of the vision. Quality assurance and control are functions that must be performed by everyone, not just those assigned to specific departments.

45. (A) It should be compared to the cost of inspection and re-work using Benefit/Cost analysis in order to finalize the quality management plan. It is axiomatic of the quality management discipline that the benefits of meeting quality requirements rather than correcting errors that are discovered through inspection outweigh the costs. Thus the cost of inspection and re-work, according to PMI, will almost always be less than the cost of avoiding errors in the first place.

46. (D) Use statistical techniques to compute a "loss function" to determine the cost of producing products that fail to achieve a target value. The Taguchi method is used to estimate the loss associated with controlling or failing to control process variability. It is based on the principle that by carefully selecting design parameters to produce robust designs, an organization can produce products that are more forgiving and tolerant. The tool helps determine the value or break-even point of improving a process to reduce variability.

47. (C) .00225 inches. The value of X bar for hour number 7 is the sum of the four observed values for hour 7 divided by 4. 25 27 50 -12. This is 90 / 4 or 22.5. Since this is the number of ten-thousandths of an inch, the correct answer is .00225.

48. (C) Customer satisfaction. Quality management and project management are very concerned about customer satisfaction.

49. (B) Procedures for integrated change control. Process adjustments consist of immediate corrective or preventive action as a result of quality control measurements. In some cases, these process adjustments should be handled according to procedures for integrated change control.

50. (D) Five years. ISO standards are reviewed every five years.

51. (C) Cause and effect diagram. The diagram the manager is using is a cause and effect diagram, also known as a fishbone diagram. These diagrams are often called Ishikawa diagrams as well.

52. (C) Benchmarking. Benchmarking involves comparing actual or planned project practices to those of other projects to generate ideas for improvement and to provide a basis by which to measure performance. These other projects can be within the performing organization or outside of it, and can be within the same or in another application area. (

53. (B) Cost, Schedule, Quality. These are known as the "triple constraints" within a project.

54. (D) As an input to quality assurance. Quality control measurements are records of quality control testing and measurement in a format for comparison and analysis. These measurements serve as an input to quality assurance, which consists of all the planned and systematic activities implemented within the quality system to provide confidence that the project will satisfy the relevant quality standards.

55. (B) Differences among measurements. Measurements reflect the consequence of variation rather than being a cause.

56. (B) .00551 inches. To calculate the value for R bar, we take the value for R for each hour and find the mean or average value. Value for R for each hour is:

Hour	1	2	3	4	5	6	7	8	9	10
R	21	52	20	68	86	77	62	31	81	53

The sum of the values is 551, which is 55.1 when divided by 10. Since this number is in ten thousandths of an inch, the correct answer is .00551.

57. (B) focus attention on the most critical issues. Pareto Diagram - A histogram ordered by frequency of occurrence that shows how many results were generated by each identified cause.

58. (C) Pareto charts. A Pareto chart is a specific type of histogram, ordered by frequency of occurrence, which shows how many defects were generated by type or category of identified cause. The Pareto technique is used primarily to identify and evaluate non-conformities. In Pareto diagrams, rank ordering is used to guide corrective action. The project team should take action to fix the problems that are causing the greatest number of defects first. Pareto diagrams are conceptually related to Pareto's Law, which holds that a relatively small number of causes will typically produce a large majority of the problems or defects. This is commonly referred to as the 80/20 principle, where 80 percent of the problems are due to 20 percent of the causes. Pareto diagrams also can be used to summarize all types of data for 80/20 analyses

59. (C) Perform a quality audit. A quality audit is a structured, independent review to determine whether project activities comply with organizational and project policies, processes, and procedures. The objective of a quality audit is to identify inefficient and ineffective policies, processes, and procedures in use on the project.

60. (D) Quality assurance. Quality Assurance – applying the planned, systematic quality activities to ensure that the project employs all processes needed to meet requirements.

61. (C) Quality control. Quality Control (QC) involves monitoring specific project results to determine whether they comply with relevant quality standards and identifying ways to eliminate causes of unsatisfactory results

62. (B) The overall project plan. The quality plan is part of the overall project plan and is an important input to the project plan.

63. (D) Check sheet. This is a check sheet. Check sheets are simple devices that can be used almost anywhere. On them you make a mark in the appropriate category. After many marks are made, they can be added up to give the number of each defect passing the point.

64. (D) The cost of inspection and re-inspection, quality assurance, quality management, and quality planning. The acceptance costs of quality are the things that must be done to ensure that the quality of the product or service is acceptable. This includes the cost associated with inspection and re-inspection, the cost of the quality plan, quality assurance, and quality management.

65. (A) Design of an experiment. Experiments are used to determine the impact of the different variables. The design of the experiment is a controlled study of the problem. Holding all variables constant and varying one of them is sensitivity analysis. The results will show which variable has the most impact on the process.

66. (D) Special causes and random causes. Special causes are unusual events; random causes are normal process variations. The project team must be able to identify unusual events so that their causes can be identified and corrected.

67. (C) Quality. Quality on a project means that you are conforming to a standard that is set before you begin the project.

68. (D) total quality management. Total quality management is a broader, more ambitious system (philosophy) than Quality Management for identifying what the client really wants, defining the organization's mission, measuring throughout the whole process how well performance meets the required standards, and involving the total organization in the implementation of a deliberate policy of continuous improvement.

69. (B) Quality management plan.   The quality management plan describes how the project management team will implement its quality policy. The quality management plan should describe the project quality system: the organizational structure, responsibilities, procedures, processes, and resources needed to implement quality management. It also provides input to the overall project plan and must address quality control, quality assurance, and quality improvement for the project. The quality management plan may be formal or informal, highly detailed or broadly framed, depending on the requirements of the project.

70. (A) Quality audits. A quality audit is a structured, independent review to determine whether project activities comply with organizational and project policies, processes, and procedures. The objective of a quality audit is to identify inefficient and ineffective policies, processes, and procedures in use on the project.

71. (B) ISO. The ISO is the international organization that controls the standards for quality.

72. (D) determine if a process is functioning within set limits. A control chart is a graph that displays data taken over time and computed variations of those data. Control charts are used to show the variation on a variety of variables including average (X) and range (R) and also the number of defects (PN), percent defective (P), defects per variable unit (U), and defects per fixed unit (C). The control chart allows you to distinguish between measurements that are predictably within the inherent capability of the process (normal causes of variation that are to be expected) and measurements that are unpredictable and produced by special causes.

73. (B) Checklists. Checklists are used to verify that a set of required steps has been performed in the quality control process.

74. (D) Gantt charts. See PMBOK Guide - page 192, for more information on the quality control process.

75. (C) quality assurance. Quality Assurance – applying the planned, systematic quality activities to ensure that the project employs all processes needed to meet requirements.

76. (C) Help analyze how problems occur. By showing how components of a system relate, flowcharts can help the project team anticipate where quality problems might occur and develop approaches for dealing with them.

77. (A) Quality assurance. Quality Assurance – applying the planned, systematic quality activities to ensure that the project employs all processes needed to meet requirements.

78. (D) Variable inspection. This is an example of variable inspection. If the testing machine had a light that showed green when the parts were acceptable, then it would have been attribute inspection. We don't know whether sampling or 100% inspection is taking place. A variable is an actual measurement of some characteristic of a part. An attribute is a yes or no determination of whether the part is good or bad.

79. (D) Rule of seven. The highlighted area shows seven consecutive sampling results all on one side of the mean; this is known as the rule of seven and is an assignable cause.

80. (A) Attribute sampling is concerned with conformance, whereas variable sampling is concerned with the degree of conformity. Attribute sampling determines whether a result does or does not conform. Variable sampling rates a result on a continuous scale to measure the degree of conformity.

81. (A) Stop production. A control chart is a graph that displays data taken over time and computed variations of those data. Control charts are used to show the variation on a variety of variables including average (X) and range (R) and also the number of defects (PN), percent defective (P), defects per variable unit (U), and defects per fixed unit (C). The control chart allows you to distinguish between measurements that are predictably within the inherent capability of the process (normal causes of variation that are to be expected) and measurements that are unpredictable and produced by special causes.

82. (C) Monitor process variation over time. Used to monitor process variation and to detect and correct changes in process performance, the statistical control chart helps people understand and control their processes and work.

83. (D) Quality assurance manager. Quality assurance is all the planned and systematic activities implemented within the quality system to provide confidence that the project will satisfy the relevant quality standards.

84. (D) Issue a change request to implement the needed corrective action. The information obtained from a quality audit can be used to improve quality systems and performance. In most cases, implementing quality improvements requires preparation of change requests.

85. (B) Control chart. A control chart determines whether or not a process is stable or as a predictable performance. Control charts may serve as a data gathering tool to show when a process is subject to special cause variation, which creates an out-of-control condition. Control charts also illustrate how a process behaves over time. They are a graphic display of the interaction of process variables on a process to answer the question: Are the process variables within acceptable limits? Examination of the non-random pattern of data points on a control chart may reveal wildly fluctuating values, sudden process jumps or shifts, or a gradual trend in increased variation. By monitoring the output of a process over time, a control chart can be employed to assess whether the application of process changes resulted in the desired improvements.

86. (A) Conduct a trend analysis. Trend analysis is performed using run charts. Trend analysis involves using mathematical techniques to forecast future outcomes based on historical results. Trend analysis is often used to monitor: (1) technical performance - how many errors or defects have been identified, how many remain uncorrected and (2) cost and schedule performance - how many activities per period were completed with significant variances?

87. (C) 3 standard deviations. When the results of a sample of items measured falls within 3 standard deviations and that sample is representative of the entire population, you can assume that more than 99% of all items fall within that range. This generally accepted range of results has been used by quality control professionals through the years. Six sigma is a program started by Motorola that, from a statistical standpoint, indicates a quality standard of only 3.4 defects per million.

88. (B) Use statistical sampling. Because it involves choosing part of a population of interest for inspection, statistical sampling can significantly reduce the cost of quality control.

89. (A) Prevention costs. Cost of quality refers to the total cost of all efforts to achieve product or service quality. Prevention costs are a category of quality costs. Prevention costs are investments made to keep nonconforming products from occurring and reaching the customer. They include quality planning costs, process control costs, information systems costs, and training and general management costs. (PMBOK Guide - page 181)

90. (A) Upper management. According to Juran and Deming, 85% to 95% of the quality problems that occur in organizations are from processes controlled by upper management.

91. (C) quality control. Quality control involves monitoring specific project results to determine whether they comply with relevant quality standards and identifying ways to eliminate causes of unsatisfactory results.

92. (B) Quality planning. Quality planning involves identifying which quality standards are relevant to the project and determining how to satisfy them. It is one of the key processes when doing the Planning Process Group and during development of the project management plan, and should be performed in parallel with the other project planning processes.

93. (D) The cost of inspection and re-inspection, quality assurance, quality management, and quality planning. The acceptance costs of quality are the things that must be done to ensure that the quality of the product or service is acceptable. This includes the cost associated with inspection and re-inspection, the cost of the quality plan, quality assurance, and quality management.

94. (B) X bar. The averaging of the five parts that are sampled is called the X bar value. In control charts the two values that are normally plotted on the control chart are the X bar value and the R value, the difference between the highest and lowest value of the dimension in the sampled parts.

95. (B) The overall outgoing quality level decreases at first and then increases. When sampling inspection is used, it will discover lots that are above the AQL. These lots are then returned for 100% inspection. When the 100% inspection is done, the defective parts are removed, and the acceptable ones are sent to the customer. As the number of defective parts increases, more lots will have to be inspected 100%. Initially, the quality delivered to the customer will fall, but because of the added work of the 100% inspection, the quality will then improve.

96. (A) Quality Control. This process was in place before the idea of Quality Assurance became important.

97. (D) Pareto diagram. A Pareto diagram is a histogram, ordered by frequency of occurrence, which shows how many results were generated by type or category of identified cause. By using this tool the manager can identify the defects that occurred most often.

98. (D) Pareto diagram. The Pareto diagram shows a histogram where the defect classes are arranged in the order of the highest to lowest frequency of occurrence of the defect. It also shows the cumulative percent of defects from the highest to lowest number of defects.

99. (B) Attribute sampling. Attribute sampling is the examination of one or more attributes in a lot. A limit of acceptability is established for the entire lot. For example, we may consider a "lot" of 10,000 parts. A random sample of 150 parts is selected for examination. For that sample, the acceptance number is 3, meaning that if more than 3 parts are found to be defective; the entire lot of 10,000 will be rejected. You can conduct single-attribute sampling, double-attribute sampling, multiple-attribute sampling, or sequential attribute sampling (single attribute sampling performed sequentially on the same lot for different attributes).

100. (A) Action taken to bring a nonconforming item into compliance. An output of the quality control process, rework is a frequent cause of project overruns in most application areas. The project team must make every reasonable effort to control and minimize rework.

Project Human Resource Management

The Project Human Resource Management section of the PMP® exam focuses heavily on organizational structures, roles and responsibilities of the project manager, team building, and conflict resolution.

In contrast to other areas of the PMBOK® Guide in which commonly known terms are used, much of the terminology developed for Project Human Resource Management seems peculiar to PMI®. In spite of the unfamiliarity of some terminology, most people do find the human resource questions to be difficult.

Project Human Resource Management involves all aspects of people management and personal interaction including leading, coaching, dealing with conflict, and more. Some of the project participants whom you'll get to practice these skills on include stakeholders, team members, and customers. Each requires the use of different communication styles, leadership skills, and team-building skills. A good project manager knows when to enact certain skills and communication styles based on the situation.

The PMP® exam is heavily weighted toward team development (that is, behavioral topics). In the past only a few questions have appeared on administrative issues, and they should be relatively easy to answer, given familiarity with general corporate—personnel policies governing your everyday work life. The questions predominantly focus on forms of organization, project manager roles and responsibilities, types of power, project conflict, conflict management, and team building.

Project Human Resource Management - Questions

1. Which motivational theorist said that people cannot ascend to the next level until the levels below are fulfilled?

     (A) Deming
     (B) Maslow
     (C) Herzberg
     (D) McGregor

2. Your organization has just created and established a reward and recognition system for its project managers. Project cost performance is used as the main criteria to determine rewards. What should you do to ensure that rewards reflect actual performance?

     (A) Prepare a cost baseline.
     (B) Consider overtime work as part of the job.
     (C) Estimate and budget controllable and uncontrollable costs separately.
     (D) Use earned value management to monitor performance.

3. A project manager is concerned about team building on her project. One of the mandatory things that she must have in order to have good team building is:

     (A) Commitment from top level management.
     (B) Co-location of team members.
     (C) Establishment of clear negotiated goals.
     (D) Open discussion of poor individual performance.

4. Team development is based on the:

    (A) Training provided to the project team
    (B) Organizational structure of the project
    (C) Project's organizational climate of cooperation, open communication, and trust
    (D) Individual development of each team member

5. Distance and communication issues between people on the team are managed as a part of the _____ of the team.

    (A) Structure
    (B) Problems
    (C) Logistics
    (D) Tactics

6. When choosing the most appropriate form of project organization, the first step is to:

    (A) Produce an initial project plan and determine the functional areas responsible for each task
    (B) Create the WBS and let it determine the project organizational structure
    (C) Develop a project schedule, including a top-down flowchart, and identify the functional areas to perform each task
    (D) Refer to the project charter developed by top management

7. The organization that is a formalized structure where the project teams and the project managers reside is called:

    (A) Project office.
    (B) Project management office.
    (C) Project team.
    (D) Matrix organization.

8. In a team meeting today two of the managers start a discussion that escalated into an argument. To restore peace to the meeting you point out a solution and using a friendly voice try to defuse the current situation. This is an example of what type of conflict management?

    (A) Problem solving.
    (B) Smoothing.
    (C) Compromising.
    (D) Withdrawal.

9. Your project team is composed of six experts in marine biology and two administrative assistants. One component of your scientific research project involves the development of a complex, real-time programming system that uses commercial-off-the-shelf products. You are outsourcing this portion of the work. No team members have contract administration experience, and no contracts department staff can be assigned to the project. To ensure that you create a successful relationship with the prospective seller, you must provide two team members with project procurement management training. Direct and indirect training costs should be:

    (A) Charged directly to the project budget
    (B) Paid for by your organization
    (C) Considered an input to cost budgeting
    (D) Paid for by the procurement department

10. In which motivation theory do hygiene factors play a part?

    (A) Herzberg's
    (B) McGregor's
    (C) Theory Y
    (D) Maslow's hierarchy

11. Employees who believe their efforts will lead to effective performance and expect to be rewarded for their accomplishments remain productive as rewards meet their expectations. This is called:

    (A) a perquisite.
    (B) a halo effect.
    (C) the expectancy theory.
    (D) a motivational theory.

12. Which of the following represents a constraint on the staff acquisition process?

    (A) Pre-assignment of staff to the project
    (B) Recruitment practices of the organizations involved
    (C) Use of outsourcing
    (D) Team member training requirements

13. In a large organization a project expediter is being used to manage a project for an important client. The position of project expediter would be found in what kind of an organization?

    (A) Weak matrix
    (B) Projectized
    (C) Functional
    (D) Strong matrix

14. Major difficulties arise when multiple projects need to be managed in the functional organizational structure because of:

    (A) The level of authority of the project manager
    (B) Conflicts over the relative priorities of different projects in competition for limited resources
    (C) Project team members who are focused on their functional specialty rather than on the project
    (D) The need for the project manager to use interpersonal skills to resolve conflicts informally

15. Templates and checklists are examples of _____.

    (A) Organizational design
    (B) Organizational culture
    (C) Process assets
    (D) Process tactics

16. A large, complicated software development project is being contemplated by a large company. The project will be done as part of a company strategic plan. The project will be multifunctional and will require many of the project team members to work on multiple other projects during the life of this project. The best kind of organization to support this project is which of the following?

    (A) Strong matrix
    (B) Weak matrix
    (C) Projectized
    (D) Functional

17. The beginning and the end of the project is defined by:

   (A) The team charter.
   (B) The project life cycle.
   (C) The project plan.
   (D) The project charter.

18. You have just found out that a major subcontractor for your project consistently delivers items late. You decide that you have bigger problems to address, so you do nothing. What conflict resolution mode are you using?

   (A) Ignoring
   (B) Compromise
   (C) Withdrawal
   (D) Withdrawal

19. Project A is being administered using a matrix form of organization. The project manager reports to a senior vice president who provides visible support to the project. In this scenario, which of the following statements best describes the relative power of the project manager?

   (A) In this strong matrix, the balance of power is shifted to the functional line managers.
   (B) The project manager will probably not be challenged by project stakeholders.
   (C) In this strong matrix, the balance of power is shifted to the project manager.
   (D) In this tight matrix, the balance of power is shifted to the project manager.

20. Conflict management will be easier if _____ ground rules are set before the project begins.

   (A) Strategic
   (B) Informal
   (C) Formal
   (D) Tactical

21. You have been assigned as project manager on what could be a "bet the company" project. If the project is successful, management will be carrying you around on a sedan chair; if it fails, you will be in the unemployment line. You realize that to be successful you need to exercise maximum control over project resources. Which form of project organization should you establish for this project?

   (A) Projectized
   (B) Weak matrix
   (C) Project coordinator
   (D) Strong matrix

22. In organizing a project, a project manager must deal with conflict. Which statement is true regarding conflict in projects?

   (A) A matrix form of organization can produce a lack of clear role definitions and lead to ambiguous jurisdictions between and among functional leaders and project managers.
   (B) Sources of conflict include project priorities, CPM schedules, contract administrative procedures, and type of contract.
   (C) Conflict is to be avoided whenever possible.
   (D) Strong matrix project managers have few human resource conflicts, because they can dictate their needs to functional managers.

23. The major difference between the project coordinator and project expediter forms of organization is that:

    (A) The project coordinator cannot personally make or enforce decisions
    (B) The project coordinator reports to a higher-level manager in the organization
    (C) The project expediter acts only as an intermediary between management and the project team
    (D) Strong commitment to the project usually does not exist in the project expediter form of organization

24. The management theory that all people can direct their own efforts is:

    (A) Herzberg's theory
    (B) Theory Y
    (C) Theory X
    (D) Maslow's hierarchy

25. On a project team one of the team members has a problem collecting on a medical insurance claim. The team member comes to the project manager and explains the problem. The problem is the responsibility of the:

    (A) Project manager.
    (B) Human Resources Department.
    (C) Executive manager.
    (D) Project team.

26. At a critical design review meeting for a large project, several important issues surfaced. After hearing about a major technical problem, one of the subcontractor's engineers mentions that he experienced a similar situation on another project; he has some ideas on how to solve the current problem. What type of power is the engineer using?

    (A) Experience
    (B) Manipulative
    (C) Referent
    (D) Expert

27. The team members on your project have been complaining that they do not have any sense of identity as a team because they are located in different areas of the building. To remedy this situation, you developed a project logo and had it printed on T-shirts to promote the project, but this action has not worked. Your next step is to:

    (A) Create an air of mystery about the project
    (B) Initiate a newsletter
    (C) Issue guidelines on how team members should interact with other stakeholders
    (D) Establish a "war room"

28. A project manager is responsible for all that goes on in the project. One of the most important duties that the project manager can perform is the function of:

    (A) Risk management.
    (B) Quality management.
    (C) Cost management.
    (D) Integration.

29. Your project management work frustrates you. Although management will reward you if you meet project cost objectives, those objectives are impossible to meet because you cannot control staffing or procurement decisions. You must pressure functional managers to release staff as planned, and you always seem to be arguing with the contracting department about awarding contracts to quality sellers. Because of your complaints, management asked you to lead a team to recommend an equitable reward and recognition system for project managers. Your team has completed its report and will brief the executives. Before detailing the plan, you want to ensure executives understand the basic objective of reward systems. This objective is to:

   (A) Motivate project managers to work toward common objectives and goals as defined by the company
   (B) Attract people to join the organization's project management career path
   (C) Be comparable with the award system established for functional managers to indicate parity and to show the importance of project management to the company
   (D) Make the link between project performance and reward clear, explicit, and achievable

30. As a project manager, you realize that team development is essential for project success. Therefore, you want to review the technical context within which your team operates. This information can be found in the:

   (A) Project plan
   (B) Team charter
   (C) Organizational policies and guidelines
   (D) Staffing management plan

31. Recruitment, regulatory issues, performance appraisal, and labor relations are skills generally used more in which of the following area?

   (A) Managerial
   (B) General management
   (C) Accounting
   (D) Administrative

32. You are managing a virtual team. Your team members all work in different geographic locations and will meet face-to-face only once or twice. The project has been under way for several months, and you have a strong feeling that your team members do not view themselves as a team or unified group. To help rectify this situation, you should:

   (A) Ensure that every member of the project team uses e-mail as a form of communication
   (B) Mandate that the team follow the vision and mission statement of his or her organization
   (C) Create symbols and structures that solidify the unity of the dispersed work group
   (D) Provide team members with the latest in communications technology and mandate its use

33. Your organization is characterized by hierarchical organizational structures with rigid rules and policies and strict supervisory controls. Individual team members are not expected to engage in problem solving or use creative approaches to plan and execute work. But because a lot of company work involves crisis situations, this authoritarian management style has some benefits. Your organization is characterized by which one of the following theories?

   (A) Ouchi's Theory
   (B) McGregor's Theory X
   (C) Maslow's self-esteem level
   (D) Vroom's Expectancy Theory

34. A project manager is selecting team members for her project team. She collects the resumes and past performance reviews for the potential team members and discusses each with their functional manager. Which of the following is not a characteristic that the project manager should use in selecting the team members?

    (A) Personal characteristics
    (B) Salary
    (C) Personal interest
    (D) Previous experience

35. The primary result of effective team development is:

    (A) Improved project performance
    (B) An effective, smoothly running team
    (C) An understanding by project team members that the project manager is ultimately responsible for project performance
    (D) Enhancement of the ability of stakeholders to contribute as individuals and team members

36. The team you have organized for your new project consists of three people who will work full-time and five people who will support the project on a part-time basis. All team members know one another and have worked together in the past. To ensure a successful project start-up, your first step should be to:

    (A) Distribute the project plan and WBS to the team
    (B) Hold a project kickoff meeting
    (C) Meet with each team member individually to discuss assignments
    (D) Prepare a responsibility assignment matrix and distribute it to each team member

37. The people needed for the project team are defined as part of which of the following?

    (A) Human resource planning
    (B) Work breakdown structure
    (C) Tactical planning
    (D) Organizational charts

38. Organization charts, positions, descriptions, ground rules, and useful recognition events are all examples of _____.

    (A) Project behavior
    (B) Lessons learned
    (C) HR control
    (D) Project activity

39. Leading, communicating, and problem solving are examples of what type of management skills.

    (A) General
    (B) Senior
    (C) Project
    (D) Human Resource

40. Which of the following factors contributes the most to team communication?

    (A) Performance appraisals
    (B) External feedback
    (C) Colocation
    (D) Smoothing over of team conflicts by the project manager

41. John is a project manager who gets the job done through salary, promotion, and bonus incentives. He is using which of the following types of interpersonal influence?

   (A) Reward power
   (B) Expert power
   (C) Referent power
   (D) Formal authority

42. Your project has been under way for some time, but indicators show that it is in trouble. You have observed all the following symptoms of bad teamwork in your project team except:

   (A) Excessive meetings
   (B) Unproductive meetings
   (C) Lack of trust or confidence in the project manager
   (D) Frustration

43. Herzberg divided motivation factors into two classes: satisfiers and dissatisfiers. Examples of satisfiers are:

   (A) Vacation time, assignment of a personal staff assistant.
   (B) Work satisfaction, fringe benefits.
   (C) Plush office space, performance-based salary raise.
   (D) Sense of personal achievement, work satisfaction.

44. During a recent status review meeting for your project, one team member was critical of others and seemed to try to diminish their status on the team. This person was assuming which of the following destructive team roles?

   (A) Blocker
   (B) Dominator
   (C) Aggressor
   (D) Recognition seeker

45. Given that you are neighbors, you and the CEO of your company have established a friendly personal relationship. This fact has not gone unnoticed by your peers and associates. Recently, your company appointed you project manager for a new project that is crucial to achieving next year's financial targets. Which type of power available to project managers might you be able to rely on?

   (A) Reward
   (B) Referent
   (C) Expert
   (D) Formal

46. A project manager has just been hired and is trying to gain the cooperation of others. What is the best form of power for gaining cooperation under these circumstances?

   (A) Penalty
   (B) Expert
   (C) Legitimate
   (D) Referent

47. The terms strong matrix, balanced matrix, and weak matrix when applied to the matrix structure in project organization refer to the:

   (A) Physical proximity of project team members to one another and to the project manager
   (B) Ability of the organization to achieve its goals
   (C) Degree to which team members bond together
   (D) Degree of authority the project manager has over team resources

48. What theory proposes that efforts will lead to effective performance and will be rewarded for accomplishments?

    (A) Maslow's hierarchy
    (B) Expectancy
    (C) McGregor's
    (D) Conditional reinforcement

49. The skill of listening involves more than just hearing the sounds. One of the characteristics of a good listener is that he or she:

    (A) Takes good notes.
    (B) Agrees with the speaker.
    (C) Repeats some of the things said.
    (D) Finishes the speaker's sentences.

50. The process of establishing clear and achievable objectives, measuring their achievement, and adjusting performance in accordance with the results of the measurement is called:

    (A) strategic planning.
    (B) alternative objectives inventory.
    (C) management by objectives.
    (D) contingency planning.

51. A project manager is managing a project where there will be a number of persons working together. She wants to enhance the ability of the team to work together and perform as a team. One of the things that she can do to maximize the ability of the team to do this is:

    (A) Co-location.
    (B) Cohabitation.
    (C) Work breakdown structure.
    (D) Staffing plan.

52. Your technical team lead, Ted, proposed an action that would improve overall project quality with a minor cost increase. The project control officer, Sun Ha, recommended an approach that would shorten the project schedule, but reduce product features. Increasing quality and accelerating the schedule are critical from your point of view. Although you believe that Ted and Sun Ha could learn from each other, they typically like to agree to disagree. You need a conflict resolution method that provides a long-term resolution. You decide to use which one of the following approaches:

    (A) Problem solving
    (B) Confronting
    (C) Smoothing
    (D) Collaborating

53. The structure of the organization, collective bargaining agreements, and the overall economic conditions of the organization itself are examples of _____.

    (A) Constraints
    (B) Organizational issues
    (C) Control issues
    (D) Documents

54. You are the project manager at an advertising firm that specializes in marketing and promotional campaigns for athletic shoes. Your company frequently uses sports celebrities as part of the marketing and advertising campaigns. Advertising that uses celebrities to influence consumers' purchasing decisions is an example of what type of power?

(A) Legitimate power
(B) Referent power
(C) Expert power
(D) Coercive power

55. According to the PMBOK Guide, delegating, motivating, coaching, and mentoring skills are used to manage which of the following?

(A) Organization
(B) Project team
(C) Individual
(D) Personal relations

56. A project manager wants to do as much as she can to help in developing her project team. A key barrier to project team development is which of the following?

(A) Strong matrix management structure.
(B) Major problems that delay the project completion date or budget targets.
(C) Team members who are accountable to both functional and project managers.
(D) Formal training plans that cannot be implemented.

57. Which of the following techniques do project managers use most often to resolve conflicts?

(A) Smoothing
(B) Forcing
(C) Compromising
(D) Problem solving

58. You are part of a team that is working to develop a medical implant that would accentuate the biceps of middle-aged men. Numerous articles in prestigious medical journals have discussed this controversial product. Your project manager, a medical doctor by training, is an expert in medical implantation devices and many journal articles have mentioned him by name. Although his knowledge of the subject is vast, he continually seeks opinions from the team about a wide variety of project and product issues. Team members often run project meetings while he sits silently at the head of the table. His most likely response to a question is "What do you think we should do?" Which one of the following best characterizes his leadership style?

(A) Team directed
(B) Laissez-faire
(C) Shared leadership
(D) Collaborative

59. The key way for a project manager to promote optimum team performance in project teams whose members are not colocated is to:

(A) Build trust
(B) Establish a reward and recognition system
(C) Obtain the support of the functional managers in the other locations
(D) Exercise his or her right to control all aspects of the project

60. There are five sources of power that people have: legitimate, coercive, reward, expert and referent. If the team knows that the project manager who is managing the project is reporting straight up to the President, what type of power is most prevalent?

    (A) Referent
    (B) Reward
    (C) Legitimate
    (D) Coercive

61. Team-building activities include management and individual actions taken specifically and primarily to improve team performance. Many of these actions may enhance team performance as a secondary effect. An example of some action that may enhance team performance as a secondary effect is:

    (A) Establishing a team-based reward and recognition system
    (B) Involving non-management-level team members in the planning process
    (C) Establishing team performance goals and holding off-site retreats to review ways of best achieving these goals
    (D) Colocating all teams members in a single physical location

62. Abraham Maslow developed a model to explain the motivational process in relation to the way human needs change throughout an individual's developmental life cycle. This model has five levels. Food, water and shelter are examples of needs at which level?

    (A) Esteem
    (B) Self-actualization
    (C) Social
    (D) Physiological

63. A project manager is in need of a solution to a problem. He decides that the best thing will be to arrange a meeting to solve the problem rather than solve the problem himself or by having one of the project team members solve it individually. Generally, this will result in:

    (A) The solution to the problem being less accurate.
    (B) The group taking more time than one individual.
    (C) It depends on the specific problem.
    (D) The group taking less time than an individual.

64. A project team is worried that the integration of the components of the project will result in uncovering flaws. Instead of continuing their work, they are constantly looking for flaws to try to prevent their system from being the only one found to have flaws during integration. It might be best for the project manager to:

    (A) tell the team to create quality testing plans.
    (B) let management know of the concern.
    (C) smooth the situation.
    (D) compromise the situation.

65. Your organization is adopting a project-based approach to business. The change, however, has been very difficult. Although project teams have been created, they are little more than a collection of functional and technical experts who focus on their specialties. You are managing the company's most important project. This project is so vital to the company's future that the CEO told you she would allow you all the resources you need to complete the job on time. She said, "Money is no object, but time is our enemy." As you begin this project, you must place a high priority on:

    (A) Creating an effective team
    (B) Identifying the resources needed to finish the project on time
    (C) The best way to communicate status to the CEO
    (D) Establishing firm project requirements

66. The chances for successful completion of a multidisciplinary project are increased if project team members are:

(A) Problem oriented
(B) Politically sensitive to top management's needs
(C) Focused on individual project activities
(D) Focused on customer demands

67. The term "requested changes" as it refers to managing the project team deals with _____ changes.

(A) Schedule
(B) Work breakdown structure
(C) Staffing
(D) Computer

68. Actions that are taken to avoid problems in the future are called _____ actions.

(A) Management
(B) Control
(C) Standard
(D) Preventive

69. In both the weak and strong matrix organizational structures, the primary condition leading to conflict is:

(A) Communication barriers
(B) Conflicting interests
(C) Need for consensus
(D) Ambiguous jurisdictions

70. According to PMI®, what type of power is coercive?

(A) Penalty
(B) Expert
(C) Reward
(D) Referent

71. An automotive oil change station was receiving complaints that service took too long. A coffee machine and television were installed in the waiting room and the complaints went down. This is an example of:

(A) Smith-Bayham method.
(B) Creative problem solving.
(C) Analytical problem solving.
(D) Decision analysis.

72. The breakdown structure that shows departments or units of the organization is the _____.

(A) Unit breakdown structure
(B) Work breakdown structure
(C) Department breakdown structure
(D) Organizational breakdown structure

73. As a project manager, you believe in using a "personal touch" to further team development. One approach that has proven effective toward this goal

    (A) Providing flexible work time
    (B) Celebrating special occasions
    (C) Issuing a project charter
    (D) Creating a team name

74. Team members are arguing about the location of specification limits on a control chart. The discussion is becoming heated when the project manager walks in and says, "It seems that the real problem here is that we do not have enough information about the customer's specifications. Let's..." This is an example of:

    (A) problem solving.
    (B) asserting the project manager's authority.
    (C) withdrawal.
    (D) compromising.

75. A project manager wants to have some of the people trained on his project team. The project team is working in a balanced matrix organization. Generally, the approval for this training should come from which of the following managers?

    (A) Project manager
    (B) Executive manager
    (C) Functional manager
    (D) Human resources manager

76. In a team meeting today two of the managers start a discussion that escalated into an argument. To restore peace to the meeting you point out a solution and using a friendly voice try to defuse the current situation. This is an example of what type of conflict management?

    (A) Compromising.
    (B) Withdrawal.
    (C) Problem solving.
    (D) Smoothing.

77. The issues log should be _____.

    (A) Short
    (B) Written
    (C) Interesting
    (D) Informal

78. A management style characterized by little or no information flowing up or down between the project manager and project team is called:

    (A) Egocentric
    (B) Democratic
    (C) Participative
    (D) Laissez-faire

79. As a project manager, you are aware of a number of different conflict resolution methods. Two team members on your current construction project are engaged in a major argument concerning storm window installation. They refuse to listen to each other. Although it is March and hurricane season does not begin until June, a freak storm is expected to hit your area in less than 8 hours. Windows must be installed now or the entire project is in jeopardy. The most appropriate conflict resolution approach for you to use in this situation is:

(A) Compromising
(B) Accommodating
(C) Forcing
(D) Collaborating

80. Each of your 10 stakeholders has a copy of the project plan. In project review meetings, many of which are attended by a majority of the stakeholders, the plan is used as a baseline for performance measurement. It describes project objectives, deliverables, constraints, and assumptions and contains information about stakeholder expectations. Many stakeholders vocalize their concerns at these meetings and constantly emphasize their interests to ensure the project satisfies their requirements. External feedback such as this is:

(A) An input to team development
(B) An output of the organizational planning process
(C) An item in the project's stakeholder management plan
(D) A requirement of the project's team charter

81. The _____ of the team may contract and expand depending on the phase of the project.

(A) Abilities
(B) Capabilities
(C) Size
(D) Concept

82. Your project management work has taught you that you are primarily responsible for implementing the project plan by authorizing the execution of project activities and tasks to produce project deliverables. Because you do not work in a purely projectized organization, however, you do not have direct access to human resource administrative activities. Therefore you need to:

(A) Outsource these functions
(B) Prepare a project team charter that is signed off by a member of the human resources department to delineate responsibilities
(C) Ensure that your team is sufficiently aware of administrative requirements to ensure compliance
(D) Ask the head of human resources to approve your project staffing plan personally

83. You are project manager for a 2-year project, now beginning its second year. Changes have occurred in some project roles and responsibilities since the project began. Some team members have left the project, and others have been added. In addition, several of the completed work packages have not received the required sign-offs. Some team members believe they should be reviewing certain work packages or at least providing input. With the unplanned departure of one key team member, three work packages are 5 weeks behind schedule. You do not seem to know who is responsible for many project activities. To gain control of this project, you need to:

(A) Rebaseline your original staffing management plan with current resource requirements
(B) Change to a projectized organizational structure for maximum control over resource assignments
(C) Work with your team to prepare a responsibility assignment matrix
(D) Create a new division of labor by assigning technical leads to the most critical activities

84. Disciplinary actions should be done in accordance with _____ policy.

    (A) Sponsor
    (B) Organizational
    (C) Government
    (D) Project team

85. A(n) _____ does not generally have complete control over the team.

    (A) Internal project manager
    (B) Contracted project manager
    (C) Internal project lead
    (D) External project lead

86. A project team is worried that the integration of the components of the project will result in uncovering flaws. Instead of continuing their work, they are constantly looking for flaws to try to prevent their system from being the only one found to have flaws during integration. It might be best for the project manager to:

    (A) compromise the situation.
    (B) smooth the situation.
    (C) let management know of the concern.
    (D) tell the team to create quality testing plans.

87. Which of the following is a ground rule for project team building?

    (A) Ensure that each team member reports to his or her functional manager in addition to the project manager.
    (B) Do frequent performance appraisals.
    (C) Try to solve team political problems.
    (D) Start early.

88. A project manager will manage a large complicated project that is located in a remote part of Mexico and the project will last for five years and will have the product of producing a nuclear reactor that will generate 900 megawatts of power at start-up. The best kind of organization for managing this project is:

    (A) Strong matrix management.
    (B) Weak matrix management.
    (C) Projectized organization.
    (D) Functional organization.

89. A constraining factor that may affect the organization of the project team is:

    (A) The organizational structure of the performing organization
    (B) Poor communication among team members
    (C) Ambiguous staffing requirements
    (D) Team morale

90. An architect who is employed by a design firm has been asked by the firm's CEO to explain geodesic dome design considerations to a construction contractor's project management team. Although the construction company has done no work on the architect's current project, the construction company owner is the design firm CEO's brother-in-law. This situation demonstrates that:

    (A) As a project manager, communications should occur according to the chain of command
    (B) Organizational, technical, and interpersonal interfaces on projects often occur simultaneously
    (C) You should always do what the boss requests
    (D) The architect's involvement is a constraint in organizational planning

91. Primary outputs from team development are:

  (A) Input to performance appraisals.
  (B) High project team morale.
  (C) Reduced project cost.
  (D) Greater customer satisfaction.

92. The Organization breakdown structure and the work breakdown structure are all examples of a _____.

  (A) Project standard
  (B) Hierarchical charts
  (C) Tactical controls
  (D) Control chart

93. Team development on a project is often complicated when individual team members are accountable to both a functional manager and the project manager. Effective management of this dual reporting relationship is generally the responsibility of the:

  (A) Team members involved
  (B) Project manager
  (C) Project owner or sponsor
  (D) Functional manager

94. Conflicts in which of the following three areas represent over 50% of all project conflicts?

  (A) Personalities, cost objectives, and schedules
  (B) Cost objectives, administrative procedures, and schedules
  (C) Schedules, project priorities, and personnel resources
  (D) Personalities, project priorities, and cost objectives

95. A project manager who generally makes decisions without considering information provided by team members is using which management style?

  (A) Autocratic
  (B) Judicious
  (C) Bureaucratic
  (D) Laissez-faire

96. The project manager of a new project wants to get things started in a positive way with the project team. The project manager wants the team members to get to know one another, to introduce the project team and the project manager to one another, to discuss the objectives and goals of the project, and to identify some of the potential problem areas. This meeting is called a:

  (A) Goal setting meeting.
  (B) Introduction meeting.
  (C) Project team meeting.
  (D) Project kick-off meeting.

97. When doing a performance appraisal, it is helpful to set _____ for the upcoming period.

  (A) Objectives
  (B) Schedules
  (C) Issues
  (D) Compromises

98. Two of your team members have been arguing for the past several weeks about which accounting package will work best for the project. You are tired of listening to them. So you decide to conduct a meeting to see whether they can reach consensus on the matter by identifying common points of agreement and striving for fair resolution. Which style of conflict resolution will you employ?

     (A) Withdrawal
     (B) Smoothing
     (C) Problem solving
     (D) Compromise

99. The project manager of a project is concerned with managing cost and improving morale and is also concerned about notifying other project managers when individuals from his project team will be available to work on other projects. This is best addressed in the project's:

     (A) Communications plan.
     (B) Work breakdown structure.
     (C) Staffing plan.
     (D) Project schedule.

100. Constant bickering, absenteeism, and substandard performance have characterized the behavior of certain members of your team. You have planned a gathering in the local mountains for the team to engage in a variety of activities, including aromatherapy, wine tasting, meditation, and soaking in sulfur springs hot tubs. Other more strenuous activities, such as croquet and lawn bowling, are also planned. Your primary objective for investing time and money in this event is to improve:

     (A) Morale
     (B) Individual performance
     (C) Quality
     (D) Team performance

Sample Answer Sheet

	T F				T F				T F				T F	
1	Ⓐ Ⓑ Ⓒ Ⓓ Ⓔ		26	Ⓐ Ⓑ Ⓒ Ⓓ Ⓔ		51	Ⓐ Ⓑ Ⓒ Ⓓ Ⓔ		76	Ⓐ Ⓑ Ⓒ Ⓓ Ⓔ					
2	Ⓐ Ⓑ Ⓒ Ⓓ Ⓔ		27	Ⓐ Ⓑ Ⓒ Ⓓ Ⓔ		52	Ⓐ Ⓑ Ⓒ Ⓓ Ⓔ		77	Ⓐ Ⓑ Ⓒ Ⓓ Ⓔ					
3	Ⓐ Ⓑ Ⓒ Ⓓ Ⓔ		28	Ⓐ Ⓑ Ⓒ Ⓓ Ⓔ		53	Ⓐ Ⓑ Ⓒ Ⓓ Ⓔ		78	Ⓐ Ⓑ Ⓒ Ⓓ Ⓔ					
4	Ⓐ Ⓑ Ⓒ Ⓓ Ⓔ		29	Ⓐ Ⓑ Ⓒ Ⓓ Ⓔ		54	Ⓐ Ⓑ Ⓒ Ⓓ Ⓔ		79	Ⓐ Ⓑ Ⓒ Ⓓ Ⓔ					
5	Ⓐ Ⓑ Ⓒ Ⓓ Ⓔ		30	Ⓐ Ⓑ Ⓒ Ⓓ Ⓔ		55	Ⓐ Ⓑ Ⓒ Ⓓ Ⓔ		80	Ⓐ Ⓑ Ⓒ Ⓓ Ⓔ					
6	Ⓐ Ⓑ Ⓒ Ⓓ Ⓔ		31	Ⓐ Ⓑ Ⓒ Ⓓ Ⓔ		56	Ⓐ Ⓑ Ⓒ Ⓓ Ⓔ		81	Ⓐ Ⓑ Ⓒ Ⓓ Ⓔ					
7	Ⓐ Ⓑ Ⓒ Ⓓ Ⓔ		32	Ⓐ Ⓑ Ⓒ Ⓓ Ⓔ		57	Ⓐ Ⓑ Ⓒ Ⓓ Ⓔ		82	Ⓐ Ⓑ Ⓒ Ⓓ Ⓔ					
8	Ⓐ Ⓑ Ⓒ Ⓓ Ⓔ		33	Ⓐ Ⓑ Ⓒ Ⓓ Ⓔ		58	Ⓐ Ⓑ Ⓒ Ⓓ Ⓔ		83	Ⓐ Ⓑ Ⓒ Ⓓ Ⓔ					
9	Ⓐ Ⓑ Ⓒ Ⓓ Ⓔ		34	Ⓐ Ⓑ Ⓒ Ⓓ Ⓔ		59	Ⓐ Ⓑ Ⓒ Ⓓ Ⓔ		84	Ⓐ Ⓑ Ⓒ Ⓓ Ⓔ					
10	Ⓐ Ⓑ Ⓒ Ⓓ Ⓔ		35	Ⓐ Ⓑ Ⓒ Ⓓ Ⓔ		60	Ⓐ Ⓑ Ⓒ Ⓓ Ⓔ		85	Ⓐ Ⓑ Ⓒ Ⓓ Ⓔ					
11	Ⓐ Ⓑ Ⓒ Ⓓ Ⓔ		36	Ⓐ Ⓑ Ⓒ Ⓓ Ⓔ		61	Ⓐ Ⓑ Ⓒ Ⓓ Ⓔ		86	Ⓐ Ⓑ Ⓒ Ⓓ Ⓔ					
12	Ⓐ Ⓑ Ⓒ Ⓓ Ⓔ		37	Ⓐ Ⓑ Ⓒ Ⓓ Ⓔ		62	Ⓐ Ⓑ Ⓒ Ⓓ Ⓔ		87	Ⓐ Ⓑ Ⓒ Ⓓ Ⓔ					
13	Ⓐ Ⓑ Ⓒ Ⓓ Ⓔ		38	Ⓐ Ⓑ Ⓒ Ⓓ Ⓔ		63	Ⓐ Ⓑ Ⓒ Ⓓ Ⓔ		88	Ⓐ Ⓑ Ⓒ Ⓓ Ⓔ					
14	Ⓐ Ⓑ Ⓒ Ⓓ Ⓔ		39	Ⓐ Ⓑ Ⓒ Ⓓ Ⓔ		64	Ⓐ Ⓑ Ⓒ Ⓓ Ⓔ		89	Ⓐ Ⓑ Ⓒ Ⓓ Ⓔ					
15	Ⓐ Ⓑ Ⓒ Ⓓ Ⓔ		40	Ⓐ Ⓑ Ⓒ Ⓓ Ⓔ		65	Ⓐ Ⓑ Ⓒ Ⓓ Ⓔ		90	Ⓐ Ⓑ Ⓒ Ⓓ Ⓔ					
16	Ⓐ Ⓑ Ⓒ Ⓓ Ⓔ		41	Ⓐ Ⓑ Ⓒ Ⓓ Ⓔ		66	Ⓐ Ⓑ Ⓒ Ⓓ Ⓔ		91	Ⓐ Ⓑ Ⓒ Ⓓ Ⓔ					
17	Ⓐ Ⓑ Ⓒ Ⓓ Ⓔ		42	Ⓐ Ⓑ Ⓒ Ⓓ Ⓔ		67	Ⓐ Ⓑ Ⓒ Ⓓ Ⓔ		92	Ⓐ Ⓑ Ⓒ Ⓓ Ⓔ					
18	Ⓐ Ⓑ Ⓒ Ⓓ Ⓔ		43	Ⓐ Ⓑ Ⓒ Ⓓ Ⓔ		68	Ⓐ Ⓑ Ⓒ Ⓓ Ⓔ		93	Ⓐ Ⓑ Ⓒ Ⓓ Ⓔ					
19	Ⓐ Ⓑ Ⓒ Ⓓ Ⓔ		44	Ⓐ Ⓑ Ⓒ Ⓓ Ⓔ		69	Ⓐ Ⓑ Ⓒ Ⓓ Ⓔ		94	Ⓐ Ⓑ Ⓒ Ⓓ Ⓔ					
20	Ⓐ Ⓑ Ⓒ Ⓓ Ⓔ		45	Ⓐ Ⓑ Ⓒ Ⓓ Ⓔ		70	Ⓐ Ⓑ Ⓒ Ⓓ Ⓔ		95	Ⓐ Ⓑ Ⓒ Ⓓ Ⓔ					
21	Ⓐ Ⓑ Ⓒ Ⓓ Ⓔ		46	Ⓐ Ⓑ Ⓒ Ⓓ Ⓔ		71	Ⓐ Ⓑ Ⓒ Ⓓ Ⓔ		96	Ⓐ Ⓑ Ⓒ Ⓓ Ⓔ					
22	Ⓐ Ⓑ Ⓒ Ⓓ Ⓔ		47	Ⓐ Ⓑ Ⓒ Ⓓ Ⓔ		72	Ⓐ Ⓑ Ⓒ Ⓓ Ⓔ		97	Ⓐ Ⓑ Ⓒ Ⓓ Ⓔ					
23	Ⓐ Ⓑ Ⓒ Ⓓ Ⓔ		48	Ⓐ Ⓑ Ⓒ Ⓓ Ⓔ		73	Ⓐ Ⓑ Ⓒ Ⓓ Ⓔ		98	Ⓐ Ⓑ Ⓒ Ⓓ Ⓔ					
24	Ⓐ Ⓑ Ⓒ Ⓓ Ⓔ		49	Ⓐ Ⓑ Ⓒ Ⓓ Ⓔ		74	Ⓐ Ⓑ Ⓒ Ⓓ Ⓔ		99	Ⓐ Ⓑ Ⓒ Ⓓ Ⓔ					
25	Ⓐ Ⓑ Ⓒ Ⓓ Ⓔ		50	Ⓐ Ⓑ Ⓒ Ⓓ Ⓔ		75	Ⓐ Ⓑ Ⓒ Ⓓ Ⓔ		100	Ⓐ Ⓑ Ⓒ Ⓓ Ⓔ					

Project Human Resource Management - Answers

1. (B) Maslow. Maslow theorized that people are driven to satisfy survival needs first, followed by safety needs, and so on. Once these needs are fulfilled, the drive to fulfill them goes away until the needs arise again. The application to human resource management is that certain needs must be met in order for people to function at their peak physical and mental levels, enabling them to fulfill their project responsibilities.

2. (C) Estimate and budget controllable and uncontrollable costs separately. To be effective, reward and recognition systems must make and establish the link between performance and reward clear, explicit, and achievable. For example, if a project manager is to be rewarded for meeting the project's cost objectives, he should have the appropriate control over both staffing and procurement decisions. In addition, a reliable method for estimating, budgeting, and tracking controllable costs must be in place.

3. (A) Commitment from top level management. The project management team must identify the stakeholders, determine what their needs and expectations are, and then manage and influence those expectations to ensure a successful project.

4. (D) Individual development of each team member. Individual development, both managerial and technical, is the cornerstone of team development, which is critical to the project's ability to meet its objectives.

5. (C) Logistics. The logistics can get very complicated if you are using a multinational team with members in various far-flung places.

6. (A) Produce an initial project plan and determine the functional areas responsible for each task. All effort on a project starts from the project plan, which details the work that must be accomplished.

7. (B) Project management office. The project management office is the place where the project teams and the project managers reside. It should not be confused with the project office, which is a support organization for the project teams and the project managers. The manager of the project management office has the project managers report to him or her.

8. (B) Smoothing. Smoothing consists of de-emphasizing the opponents' differences and emphasizing their commonalties over the issues in question. Smoothing keeps the atmosphere friendly, but avoids solving the root causes of the conflict.

9. (B) Paid for by your organization. If project team members lack necessary management or technical skills, such skills must be developed as part of the project, or steps must be taken to find new staff. Direct and indirect training costs generally are paid for by the performing organization.

10. (A) Herzberg's. Frederick Herzberg constructed a two-dimensional paradigm of factors affecting people's attitudes about work. He concluded that such factors as company policy, supervision, interpersonal relations, working conditions, and salary are hygiene factors rather than motivators. According to the theory, the absence of hygiene factors can create job dissatisfaction, but their presence does not motivate or create satisfaction.

11. (C) the expectancy theory. Expectancy theory holds that people will tend to be highly productive and motivated if the following two conditions are satisfied: (1) people believe that their efforts will likely lead to successful results and (2) those people also believe they will be rewarded for their success. Expectancy theory says two things. One, you get what you expect— self-fulfilling prophecy. The other is, if people think that their outcomes are going to be significant, if they think they are going to matter in terms of the organization, then they do better. People like to be involved in something where they think they are making a difference.

12. (B) Recruitment practices of the organizations involved. One or more of the organizations involved in the project may have policies, procedures, or guidelines governing staff assignments. These policies will constrain the project manager's actions in acquiring a project team.

13. (A) Weak matrix. Weak matrices maintain many of the characteristics of a functional organization, and the project manager role is more that of a coordinator or expediter than that of a manager. In similar fashion, strong matrices have many of the characteristics of the projectized organization— full-time project managers with considerable authority and full-time project administrative staff.

14. (B) Conflicts over the relative priorities of different projects in competition for limited resources. When a finite group of resources must be distributed across multiple projects, conflicts in work assignments will occur.

15. (C) Process assets. These two process assets can be used to help reduce the amount of time needed in the planning process if used correctly.

16. (A) Strong matrix. In a projectized organization, team members are often colocated. Most of the organization's resources are involved in project work exclusively for this project, and project managers have a great deal of independence and authority. In functional organizations the project manager may not exist and therefore little attention is paid to individual projects. In the weak matrix organization the project manager is given little authority to get things done and is primarily concerned with communication problems with managers who direct the work of people for the project. In a strong matrix organization the project manager manages the people and usually colocates them at the project's location. This would be the best organization for the situation.

17. (B) The project life cycle. The project life cycle defines the beginning and the end of the project. Depending on the project life cycle definition, the beginning and ending parts of the project may or may not be included in this project. For example, transition at the end of the project to some ongoing effort may be part of the project or the ongoing effort.

18. (D) Withdrawal. Withdrawal is defined as retreating from actual or potential disagreements and conflict situations. It is really a delaying tactic that fails to resolve the conflict but does cool down the situation temporarily.

19. (C) In this strong matrix, the balance of power is shifted to the project manager. The project manager's ability to influence project decisions increases the higher up he or she and the person to whom he or she reports is placed in the organization.

20. (C) Formal. If formal ground rules are set at the beginning of the project, it may be possible to avoid conflicts by referring to the established ground rules.

21. (A) Projectized. In a projectized organizational structure, all project team members report directly and solely to the project manager. He or she has complete control over these resources and, therefore, exercises more authority over them than in any other project organizational structure.

22. (A) A matrix form of organization can produce a lack of clear role definitions and lead to ambiguous jurisdictions between and among functional leaders and project managers. Matrix management is useful but complex, involving difficult communication because of the use of borrowed and often part-time resources who are spread throughout the organization.

23. (B) The project coordinator reports to a higher-level manager in the organization. The relative position of the project coordinator in the organization is thought to lead to an increased level of authority and responsibility.

24. (B) Theory Y. With Theory Y assumptions, management's role is to develop the potential in employees and help them to release that potential toward common goals.

25. (B) Human Resources Department. Human resource administrative activities are seldom a direct responsibility of the project management team. Many organizations have a variety of policies, guidelines, and procedures that can help the project management team with various aspects of organizational planning. For example, an organization that views managers as ''coaches'' is likely to have documentation on how the role of ''coach'' is to be performed.

26. (D) Expert. Expert power can only be exercised by individuals who are held in particular esteem because of their special knowledge or skill. The project manager's ability to use this power derives from reputation, knowledge, and experience.

27. (D) Establish a "war room". Providing a gathering place for team members to relax and get to know each other, as well as talk about project work, can be an excellent way of promoting team building.

28. (D) Integration. Since the project manager is responsible for a temporary multifunctional team of people who are brought together for the purpose of one project it is most important that the project manager perform the function of integration.

29. (D) Make the link between project performance and reward clear, explicit, and achievable. Reward and recognition systems are formal management actions that promote or reinforce desired behavior. As a tool and a technique for team development, these systems can be very effective.

30. (A) Project plan. As an input to team development, the project plan describes the technical context within which the team operates.

31. (D) Administrative. These are generally thought of as administrative skills and often are not done by the project manager if the organization has experts in these skills on staff.

32. (C) Create symbols and structures that solidify the unity of the dispersed work group. Because the dispersed project team does not share the same physical space each day, team members need symbols and structures to identify them as a unified group. As the group works together, symbols should be developed to show accomplishments as a group. These symbols should be visible throughout the organization.

33. (B) McGregor's Theory X. McGregor observed two types of managers and classified them by their perceptions of workers. Theory X managers thought that workers were lazy, needed to be watched and supervised closely, and were irresponsible. Theory Y managers thought that, given the correct conditions, workers could be trusted to seek responsibility and work hard at their jobs.

34. (B) Salary. When the project management team is able to influence or direct staff assignments, it must consider the characteristics of the potentially available staff. Considerations include, but are not limited to:
• Previous experience—have the individuals or groups done similar or related work before? Have they done it well?
• Personal interests—are the individuals or groups interested in working on this project?
• Personal characteristics—are the individuals or groups likely to work well together as a team?
• Availability—will the most desirable individuals or groups be available in the necessary time frames?

35. (A) Improved project performance. Better project performance can result from improvements in individual skills, team behaviors, and team capabilities.

36. (B) Hold a project kickoff meeting. An indispensable tool in project management, the kickoff meeting is held at the outset of the project and is designed to get the project rolling. The meeting provides the opportunity not only to present the project charter and discuss the project's goals and objectives but also to establish rapport among team members.

37. (A) Human resource planning. Human resource planning is the area where required people are identified.

38. (B) Lessons learned. These, and others, are examples of information that may be contained in your lessons learned. Lessons Learned is the capture of what went well as well as past errors of judgment resulting in material failures, wrong timing or other mistakes, all for the purposes of improving future performance.

39. (A) General. These are general skills that managers of any type will need to use in order to perform successfully for the organization.

40. (C) Colocation. Colocation is the placement of team members in the same physical location to enhance their ability to perform as a team, primarily through increased communication.

41. (A) Reward power. Reward power involves positive reinforcement and the ability to award people something of value in exchange for their cooperation. The project manager's ability to use this power derives from his or her position in the organizational hierarchy and degree of control over the project.

42. (A) Excessive meetings. The problem is not too many meetings but unproductive ones. The purpose of project meetings is to focus the skills and resources of the project team on project performance. Meetings that are considered "gripe sessions" or a time for the project manager to "lay down the law" are demoralizing to the team.

43. (D) Sense of personal achievement, work satisfaction. Projects must often have their own reward and recognition systems since the systems of the performing organization may be not appropriate. For example, the willingness to work overtime in order to meet an aggressive schedule objective should be rewarded or recognized; needing to work overtime as the result of poor planning should not be.

44. (C) Aggressor. The aggressor is destructive in that he or she criticizes others and attempts to deflate their status. Other destructive team roles are the blocker, withdrawer, recognition seeker, topic jumper, dominator, and, in some cases, devil's advocate. Destructive behavior, if allowed to continue, can endanger a team-building effort.

45. (B) Referent. Referent power is based on a less powerful person's identification with a more powerful person. This type of power is useful in terms of persuasion and helps the project manager exert influence over individuals from whom he or she needs support.

46. (C) Legitimate. Legitimate power is derived from the person's formal position within the organization. The project manager's ability to use this power derives from his or her position in the organizational hierarchy and his or her degree of control over the project, as modified by the organizational climate. Use of this power should be in conjunction with expert and reward power whenever possible.

47. (D) Degree of authority the project manager has over team resources. In a strong matrix organization, the balance of power shifts toward the project manager. In a weak matrix organization, the balance of power shifts toward the functional or line manager.

48. (B) Expectancy. Expectancy theory holds that people will tend to be highly productive and motivated if the following two conditions are satisfied: (1) people believe that their efforts will likely lead to successful results and (2) those people also believe they will be rewarded for their success. Expectancy theory says two things. One, you get what you expect—self-fulfilling prophecy. The other is, if people think that their outcomes are going to be significant, if they think they are going to matter in terms of the organization, then they do better. People like to be involved in something where they think they are making a difference.

49. (C) Repeats some of the things said. Good listening is an important skill for any manager. One of the ways that you can become a skilled listener is by repeating some of the things that are said. Summarizing gives yourself and others a repeat of important points and makes the speaker feel more relaxed and in a friendly atmosphere.

50. (C) management by objectives. Management by Objectives ("MBO") is a management theory that calls for managing people based on documented work statements mutually agreed to by manager and subordinate. Progress on these work statements is periodically reviewed, and in a proper implementation, compensation is tied to MBO performance.

51. (A) Co-location. Co-location involves placing all, or almost all, of the most active project team members in the same physical location to enhance their ability to perform as a team. Co-location is widely used on larger projects and can also be effective for smaller projects (e.g., with a ''war room'' where the team congregates or leaves in-process work items).

52. (D) Collaborating. Collaborating is an effective technique for managing conflict when a project is too important to be compromised. It involves incorporating multiple ideas and viewpoints from people with different perspectives and offers a good opportunity to learn from others. It provides a long-term resolution.

53. (A) Constraints. All of these are constraints that may affect the project and the project manager. The key for the project manager is to check at the beginning of the project to determine whether any of these constraints will affect the project as it is executed.

54. (B) Referent power. Referent power is based on citing the authority of a more powerful person (for example, one's supervisor or someone's spouse is the CEO) as the basis for one's own authority. The project manager's ability to use this power derives from his or her position in the organizational hierarchy.

55. (C) Individual. These are discussed in the PMBOK Guide as skills that deal with the individual for the most part. However, these skills also can be used in situations with more than one person.

56. (C) Team members who are accountable to both functional and project managers. Team development on a project is often complicated when individual team members are accountable to both a functional manager and to the project manager. Effective management of this dual reporting relationship is often a critical success factor for the project and is generally the responsibility of the project manager.

57. (D) Problem solving. Problem Solving (or Confrontation) - with problem solving, the project manager addresses conflict directly in a problem-solving mode to get the parties working together to define the problem, collect information, develop and analyze alternatives, and select the most appropriate alternative. PMI® recommends problem solving as the conflict resolution method of choice.

58. (C) Shared leadership. Shared leadership is more than participatory management or collaboration; it involves letting the project team take over as much of the leadership role as it will accept.

59. (A) Build trust. Team members who are physically separate from each other tend not to know each other well. They have few opportunities to develop trust in the traditional way, and they tend to communicate poorly with one another. Trust then must become the foundation upon which all team-building activities are built.

60. (A) Referent. Referent power is based on citing the authority of a more powerful person (for example, one's supervisor or someone's spouse is the CEO) as the basis for one's own authority. The project manager's ability to use this power derives from his or her position in the organizational hierarchy.

61. (B) Involving nonmanagement-level team members in the planning process. Team-building activities vary from 5-minute agenda items in regularly scheduled status review meetings to professionally facilitated, extended off-site experiences designed to improve interpersonal relationships among key stakeholders. The purpose of all team-building activities, however, is to improve team performance. Many actions, such as involving nonmanagement-level team members in the planning process or establishing ground rules for surfacing and dealing with conflict, may enhance team performance as a secondary effect.

62. (D) Physiological. According to Maslow's Hierarchy of Needs, people have the following five kinds of needs:
1. Physiological needs, of which the most important are the need for food and other things necessary for survival.
2. The need for safety—from danger, threat, and deprivation.
3. Social needs for association with one's fellows, for friendship, and love.
4. The need for self-respect, self-esteem, the respect of one's fellows, status.
5. The need for self-fulfillment through the development of powers and skills, and a chance to use creativity (self-actualization).

63. (B) The group taking more time than one individual. Groups of people will generally take longer to solve a problem, but the quality of the solution will be superior to the individual solutions that are reached.

64. (C) smooth the situation. Smoothing consists of de-emphasizing the opponents' differences and emphasizing their commonalties over the issues in question. Smoothing keeps the atmosphere friendly, but avoids solving the root causes of the conflict.

65. (A) Creating an effective team. An effective team is critical to project success, but such a team is not born spontaneously. In early project phases, it is vitally important for the project manager to place a high priority on initiating and implementing the team-building process.

66. (A) Problem oriented. Problem-oriented people tend to learn and use whatever problem-solving techniques appear helpful. Although the project manager must be politically sensitive, team members need not have developed this skill to the extent required of the project manager; and rather than focusing on individual activities, team members should take a systems approach focusing on the entire project.

67. (C) Staffing. Requested staffing changes are an output of managing the project team.

68. (D) Preventive. These types of actions should be taken when you have reason to believe that some type of problem may occur in the future. It is always better to anticipate problems and deal with them than it is to react to them after they have occurred.

69. (D) Ambiguous jurisdictions. Ambiguous jurisdictions exist when two or more parties have related responsibilities, but their work boundaries and role definitions are unclear. This situation is found frequently in weak and strong matrix organizations because of the "two-boss" concept.

70. (A) Penalty. Coercive power is predicated on fear (for example, a subordinate fears being deprived of something for failing to do what the supervisor asks). The ability to use this power derives from the project manager's control over the project and project personnel.

71. (B) Creative problem solving. Creative problem solving is when an innovative approach to the problem is used. The problem was solved not by improving service but by making the area where the customers wait more friendly and enjoyable.

72. (D) Organizational breakdown structure. The Organizational Breakdown Structure ("OBS") is a hierarchical structure designed to pinpoint the area of an organization responsible for each part of a project.

73. (B) Celebrating special occasions. Project managers can show interest in their team members by celebrating occasions such as birthdays, anniversaries with the organization, and special achievements. Other approaches are being supportive, being clear, learning some information about each team member, and being accessible.

74. (A) problem solving. Problem Solving (or Confrontation) - With problem solving, the project manager addresses conflict directly in a problem-solving mode to get the parties working together to define the problem, collect information, develop and analyze alternatives, and select the most appropriate alternative. PMI® recommends problem solving as the conflict resolution method of choice.

75. (C) Functional manager. The functional manager in a balanced matrix organization should be the person responsible for the training of the people within his or her organization. It is appropriate for this manager to have this responsibility since this manager knows the skills of the people in the functional department and knows what training is appropriate for them.

76. (D) Smoothing. Smoothing consists of de-emphasizing the opponents' differences and emphasizing their commonalties over the issues in question. Smoothing keeps the atmosphere friendly, but avoids solving the root causes of the conflict.

77. (B) Written. By writing issues down, you create a record of how issues were handled and resolved. The purpose of the issue log is to: (1) allocate a unique number to each project issue; (2) record the type of project issue; and (3) be a summary of all the project issues, their analysis and status.

78. (D) Laissez-faire. With this management style, decision-making authority is diffuse. Because little or no information flows between the project manager and team, team members are left to make decisions for themselves. This style may be effective for strong, self-directed work groups, but it can cause frustration and a sense of isolation in teams that need more direction.

79. (C) Forcing. Forcing, using power or dominance, implies the use of position power to resolve conflict. It involves imposing one viewpoint at the expense of another. Project managers may use it when time is of the essence, an issue is vital to the project's well being, or when they think they are right based on available information. Although this approach is appropriate when quick decisions are required or when unpopular issues are an essential part of the project, it puts project managers at risk.

80. (A) An input to team development. The project team must periodically measure its progress against the expectations of those outside the project. This shows the importance of continually working with all project stakeholders.

81. (C) Size. The size of the team may change as people are added or let go to meet the requirements of certain phases of the project.

82. (C) Ensure that your team is sufficiently aware of administrative requirements to ensure compliance. A purely projectized work environment is unusual because project managers rarely have every function under their control. But compliance with administrative requirements is a consideration in human resource management. The project management team must be aware of this requirement to ensure compliance.

83. (C) Work with your team to prepare a responsibility assignment matrix. The responsibility assignment matrix defines project roles and responsibilities in terms of the project scope definition. It can be used to show who is a participant, who is accountable, who handles review, who provides input, and who must sign off on specific work packages or project phases.

84. (B) Organizational. The organization should set policies concerning disciplinary actions. You should contact the HR department to make sure you are in compliance with the organizational policy.

85. (A) Internal project manager. The various members of the project team that is built within an organization will have reporting lines to their functional managers and will not report directly to the project manager.

86. (B) smooth the situation. Smoothing consists of de-emphasizing the opponents' differences and emphasizing their commonalties over the issues in question. Smoothing keeps the atmosphere friendly, but avoids solving the root causes of the conflict.

87. (D) Start early. Starting the team-building process early in the project is crucial for setting the right tone and preventing bad habits and patterns from developing.

88. (C) Projectized organization. The projectized organization has a very strong project manager because there is little chance for the home company organization to be able to correctly judge and make decisions for the project. The project manager has nearly autonomous authority.

89. (A) The organizational structure of the performing organization. Constraints are factors over which the project team has no control and that limit the team's options. The organizational structure of the performing organization determines whether the project manager's role is a strong one (as in a strong matrix) or a weak one (as in a weak matrix).

90. (B) Organizational, technical, and interpersonal interfaces on projects often occur simultaneously. Project interfaces define formal and informal reporting relationships. These interfaces are often varied and complex and are likely to occur simultaneously.

91. (A) Input to performance appraisals. The outputs from team development are performance improvements and input to performance appraisals.

92. (B) Hierarchical charts. All of them have a graphic, top-down, "family tree" orientation.

93. (B) Project manager. Effective management of this dual reporting relationship is critical to project success and is, therefore, generally the responsibility of the project manager.

94. (C) Schedules, project priorities, and personnel resources. Although all the areas listed contain potential conflicts, over 50% of all conflict in a project environment is caused by schedules, priorities, and personnel resources.

95. (A) Autocratic. Autocratic managers are not concerned with processing information coming from outside themselves. The autocratic style is sometimes appropriate because of time pressure or an emergency situation when decisions must be made quickly. When used in other situations, this style blocks out needed input from the project team.

96. (D) Project kick-off meeting. The project team kick-off meeting is the first meeting of the project team. It should aim to do all of the items mentioned.

97. (A) Objectives. If you set clear objectives, you can use them as discussion points in the next performance appraisal.

98. (B) Smoothing. Smoothing consists of de-emphasizing the opponents' differences and emphasizing their commonalties over the issues in question. Smoothing keeps the atmosphere friendly, but avoids solving the root causes of the conflict.

99. (C) Staffing plan. Particular attention should be paid to how project team members (individuals or groups) will be released when they are no longer needed on the project.

100. (D) Team performance. Team development leads to improved team performance, which ultimately results in improved project performance. Improvements in team performance can come from many sources and can affect many areas of project performance. For example, improved individual skill levels may enable team members to perform their assigned activities more effectively, and improvements in team behaviors, such as dealing with conflict, may give team members more time to direct toward technical activities. In addition, improvements in either individual skills or team capabilities may facilitate identifying and developing better ways of doing project work.

Project Communications Management

The Project Communications Management questions on the PMP® exam are basic and are taken primarily from the PMBOK® Guide and other PMI® published materials. Common sense and your own expertise will play a large role in your ability to answer the questions on this topic.

PMI® considers management style to be an essential component of how a project manager communicates, and thinks of the kickoff meeting as one of the most effective mechanisms in Project Communications Management. The questions on the exam about this focus on formal and informal communication, verbal versus written communication, conflict resolution, and management styles.

The processes that make up the Project Communications Management knowledge area are as follows: Communications Planning, Information Distribution, Performance Reporting, and Manage Stakeholders.

The processes in the Project Communications knowledge area are related to general communication skills but aren't the same thing. Communication skills are considered general management skills that the project manager utilizes on a daily basis. The processes in the Communications knowledge area seek to ensure that all project information including project plans, risk assessments, meeting notes, and more is collected and documented. These processes also ensure information is distributed and shared with appropriate stakeholders and project members. At project closure, the information is archived and used as a reference for future projects. This is referred to as historical information in several project processes.

Communication Skills
The general management skill of communicating is related to, but not the same as, project communications management. Communicating is the broader subject and involves a substantial body of knowledge that is not unique to projects.

Communicating consists of using sender receiver models which includes both feedback loops and barriers to communication. Note that you will want to create internal and external feedback loops to help evaluate the effectiveness of communications. Feedback is considered either positive or negative based on the effect it has, not on its content. Research suggests that, amongst the many reasons why information fails to be communicated, the following are the main barriers:

- Different status of the sender and the receiver - (e.g. a senior manager sends a memo to a production supervisor - who is likely to pay close attention to the message. The same information, conveyed in the opposite direction might not get the attention it deserves).
- Use of jargon - employees who are "specialists" may fall for the trap of using specialist language for a non-specialist audience (e.g. the IT technician who cannot tries to explain how users should log onto a network, in language that sounds foreign to most users of the network).
- Selective reporting - where the reporter gives the recipient incorrect or incomplete information.
- Poor timing - information that is not immediately relevant (e.g. notice of some deadline that seems a long way off) is not always actioned straightaway.
- Conflict - where the communicator and recipient are in conflict; information tends to be ignored or distorted.
- Choice of Media - Choice of media is when to communicate in writing versus orally, when to write an informal memo versus a formal report, and when to communicate face-to-face, or via e-mail. The media chosen for communication activities will depend upon the situation.
- Writing Style - Writing style deals with grammar issues such as voice structure (active versus passive), sentence structure, and proper word selection.
- Presentation Techniques - This area includes both body language and presentation of material. It also includes such things as agenda preparation and dealing with conflict.

The Communications Model
According to PMI®, the communications model consists of four major parts, as indicated below:

- Sender - The originator of the message.
- Message - Thoughts, feelings, or ideas, reduced to "code" that are understandable by both sender and receiver.
- Medium - The vehicle or method used to convey the message. The choice of medium will color and influence the effect of the message. The most common media are visual, audio, and tactile.
- Receiver - The person for whom the message is intended. He or she must accept and understand the message before communication has taken place.

The receiver may filter the information, that is, selectively reduce its quantity or quality. If the receiver is actively listening, he or she is attentive and asks for clarification or repetition of ambiguous messages. The sender should request feedback to ensure the message has been received in its entirety.

Project Communications Management- Questions

1. At the end of each project, the project team should prepare a lessons learned summary that focuses on all the following except:

    (A) Sharing best practices with other project teams in the organization
    (B) Warning others of potential problems
    (C) Suggesting methods to mitigate risks effectively to ensure success
    (D) Sharing only positive aspects of the project for future replication elsewhere in the organization

2. You are the project manager for a manufacturer of children's software. Your project team is in the process of designing a new software program for next year's Christmas season. Your 5-member project team has been working together for the past six months and has become a complete self-directed team, with little, if any management supervision required. All five members of the project team are in constant communication with each other. How many lines of communication are there within your project team?

    (A) 5
    (B) 10
    (C) 15
    (D) 20

3. In person-to-person communication, messages are sent on verbal levels and nonverbal levels simultaneously. As a general rule, what percentage of the message actually is sent through nonverbal cues?

    (A) 25% to 50%
    (B) 5% to 25%
    (C) Greater than 75%
    (D) 50% to 75%

4. What is your SPI if EV = 8 and PV = 6?

    (A) 1.0
    (B) .75
    (C) 1.33
    (D) .66

5. Performance reports are used to provide information to stakeholders on project scope, schedule, cost, and quality. Which statement most accurately describes this process?

(A) Performance reporting includes status reports, which detail where the project is now; progress reports, which describe accomplishments; and forecasts, which predict future status and progress.
(B) Performance reporting includes histograms, flow charts, and bar charts to show network dependencies and relationships.
(C) The configuration control board receives performance reports and generates change requests to modify aspects of the project.
(D) Performance reporting focuses on examining earned value analysis to determine whether cost overruns will require budget revisions.

6. Statements of organizational policies and philosophies, position descriptions, and constraints are examples of:

(A) Lateral communication
(B) Horizontal communication
(C) External communication
(D) Downward communication

7. Which of the following qualifications is the most important for a project manager?

(A) Negotiation skill
(B) Ability to work well with others
(C) Education in a technical field
(D) Supervisory experience

8. Both under communication and over communication can cause problems on a project. You want to ensure that the information you collect showing project progress and status is meaningful to stakeholders. To determine specific metrics, you will conduct a stakeholder analysis, and then determine the level of detail stakeholders require. This is available through the:

(A) Project management methodology
(B) Communications management plan
(C) Project strategy and approach
(D) Performance measurement baseline

9. The major processes of project communications management are:

(A) Communications planning, information distribution, performance reporting, and administrative closure.
(B) Communications planning, information distribution, schedule reporting, and stakeholder analysis.
(C) Communications planning, response planning, progress reporting, and information distribution.
(D) Communication, requirements, information distribution, performance reporting, and administrative procedures.

10. Which type of channel is the best for good communication?

(A) Email
(B) Phone
(C) FAX
(D) All of them

11. You recently were appointed vice president of project management. As such, you will participate in performance reviews for all projects that last more than 1 year, involve major clients, or are estimated to cost more than $1 million. To prepare for these reviews and to ensure they are meaningful and can be used to determine future project direction, you believe project managers must ensure that:

(A) Earned value analysis is used for all projects
(B) Accurate, uniform information about work results is provided
(C) The focus is on cost and schedule variances rather than scope, resources, quality, and risks
(D) All project documents are available to meeting attendees before the meeting

12. The people who get specific types of information from the project manager are _____.

(A) Stakeholders
(B) Project team members
(C) People in the communication plan
(D) Project administrators

13. The three directions of communication listed in the PMBOK are upward, downward, and _____ communication.

(A) Lateral
(B) Outward
(C) Inward
(D) Distant

14. Which of the following is not a process of Project Communications Management?

(A) Conflict Resolution
(B) Communications Planning
(C) Communications Planning
(D) Information Distribution

15. You are the project manager for a manufacturer of children's software. Your project team is in the process of designing a new software program for next year's Christmas season. Your 10-member project team has been working together for the past year and has become a complete self-directed team, with little, if any management supervision required. All ten members of the project team are in constant communication with each other. How many lines of communication are there within your project team?

(A) 45
(B) 40
(C) 55
(D) 50

16. Acceptance of the output of the project by the sponsor or customer should be _____.

(A) Oral
(B) Early
(C) Indexed
(D) Formal

17. Receiving formal confirmation that a project has met or exceeded customer requirements is an essential part of project management. Such confirmation includes all the following except:

(A) Formal customer acceptance of deliverables
(B) Passing a quality control inspection
(C) Formal customer acceptance of project results
(D) Meeting requirements of the delivering organization, such as staff evaluations, budget reports, and lessons learned

18. The best type of communication method for passing information to stakeholders is _____.

(A) Face-to-face
(B) Telephone
(C) Emails
(D) Smoke signals

19. A project team includes five people when the project manager adds two more. How many additional channels of communication are there?

(A) 7
(B) 10
(C) 11
(D) 21

20. Your project team consists of three people, however due to a scope increase you had to add two more members to your team. How many communication channels do you now have?

(A) 3
(B) 2
(C) 10
(D) 5

21. When communicating with an action-oriented person, a project manager should:

(A) Provide options, including the pros and cons
(B) Be as brief as possible and emphasize the practicality of his or her ideas
(C) Speak as quickly as possible to ensure that all the information is conveyed
(D) Remain patient if the other person goes off on tangents

22. Which of the following terms describes the strong pressures within a group to conform to group norms at the expense of critical and innovative thinking?

(A) Group oppression
(B) Group speak
(C) Group think
(D) Group agreement

23. You recently were appointed vice president of project management. As such, you will participate in performance reviews for all projects that last more than 1 year, involve major clients, or are estimated to cost more than $1 million. To prepare for these reviews and to ensure they are meaningful and can be used to determine future project direction, you believe project managers must ensure that:

    (A) Earned value analysis is used for all projects.
    (B) Accurate, uniform information about work performance information is provided.
    (C) The focus is on cost and schedule variances rather than scope, resources, quality, and risks.
    (D) All project documents are available to meeting attendees before the meeting.

24. The _____ is the most important stakeholder to keep current on the project execution.

    (A) Sponsor
    (B) Consultant
    (C) Advisory board
    (D) Project member

25. In the closing phase of your project, a number of administrative issues must be addressed and completed. A principal concern is to assess project effectiveness. One way to accomplish this task is to:

    (A) Hold a performance review
    (B) Conduct a procurement audit
    (C) Prepare a performance report
    (D) Perform an inspection

26. The process of conferring with others to come to terms or reach an agreement is called:

    (A) Negotiation
    (B) Confrontation
    (C) Getting to "yes"
    (D) Win-win

27. The three project situations that require the most negotiation skills are:

    (A) Developing the WBS, determining the master schedule, and managing project changes.
    (B) Working with functional managers to ensure that resources are available to support the project, providing performance appraisals to project team members, and developing the WBS.
    (C) Securing upper management support for the project, working with functional managers, and building the project team.
    (D) Using subcontractors, developing the project scope statement, and managing changes after the project is under way.

28. International activities and diverse stakeholders are a part of more projects than ever. Because the objectives of time, cost, and performance may be interpreted differently for these types of projects, kickoff meetings (even those conducted electronically) are especially important. All the following are objectives of the kickoff meeting except:

    (A) Reviewing project plans
    (B) Discussing specific legal issues regarding the contract
    (C) Establishing individual and group responsibilities and accountabilities
    (D) Establishing working relationships and standard formats for global communication

29. Communication is important to the success of a project. As the project manager, you have four stakeholders you need to communicate with. As such, you have six channels of communication. A new stakeholder has been added that you also need to communicate with. How many total communication channels do you have now?

    (A) 15
    (B) 25
    (C) 20
    (D) 10

30. In person-to-person communication, messages are sent on verbal levels and nonverbal levels simultaneously. As a general rule, what percentage of the message actually is sent through nonverbal cues?

    (A) 40% to 50
    (B) Greater than 50%
    (C) 5% to 15%
    (D) 20% to 30%

31. The Communication Management Plan provides all of the following except:

    (A) A distribution structure for project information.
    (B) Project communication schedules.
    (C) A collection and filing structure for project information.
    (D) Communication barriers.

32. In dealing with the customer, the project manager should:

    (A) Strive to develop a friendly, honest, and open relationship
    (B) Be honest to the extent that the project organization is protected from litigation
    (C) Do whatever it takes to satisfy the customer and win additional business
    (D) Try to maximize profits by encouraging scope creep

33. The 50-50 rule of progress reporting is used to:

    (A) Provide a good statistical approximation of earned value (EV)
    (B) Determine schedule variance in monetary terms
    (C) Determine schedule variance
    (D) Calculate the exact earned value (EV)

34. You have decided to organize a study group of other project managers in your company to help prepare for the PMP exam. Most are motivated to earn the certification because the president has decided to pay a bonus to each person who becomes certified. What type of communication are you employing in your efforts to organize this group?

    (A) External
    (B) Formal
    (C) Vertical
    (D) Horizontal

35. The project manager can enhance project communications and team building by doing all the following except:

    (A) Being a good communication blocker
    (B) Having a "war room"
    (C) Holding effective meetings
    (D) Being a communication expediter

36. You are responsible for a systems integration project in your organization that has multiple internal customers. You have just begun preparing a project plan. Because many people in your organization are interested in this system and its progress, you decide to prepare a project communications management plan. Your first step in preparing this plan is to:

(A) Conduct a communications requirements analysis to assess information needs.
(B) Determine a production schedule to show when each type of communication will be produced.
(C) Describe the information you plan to distribute.
(D) Set up a repository for all project documents so that they will be easily accessible.

37. Of the various tools or techniques for performance reporting, which one integrates scope, cost (or resource), and schedule information as a key element of its approach?

(A) Performance reviews
(B) Variance analysis
(C) Trend analysis
(D) Earned value analysis

38. Project team members often obtain new skills and increase proficiency with existing skills during the course of their project work. When this happens, it is important to update employee skills in the staff pool database. This should be done in which of the following processes:

(A) Team development
(B) Administrative closure
(C) Resource planning
(D) Communications planning

39. The three project situations that require the most negotiation skills are:

(A) Working with functional managers to ensure that resources are available to support the project, providing performance appraisals to project team members, and developing the WBS
(B) Developing the WBS, determining the master schedule, and managing project changes
(C) Using subcontractors, developing the project scope statement, and managing changes after the project is under way
(D) Securing upper management support for the project, working with functional managers, and building the project team

40. Communication is important to the success of a project. As the project manager, you have six stakeholders you need to communicate with. As such, you have fifteen channels of communication. Four new stakeholders have been added that you also need to communicate with. How many total communication channels do you have now?

(A) 50
(B) 55
(C) 40
(D) 45

41. The process of determining who needs what information, when they need it, and how it will be given to them is:

(A) Communications planning.
(B) Communications management.
(C) Information distribution.
(D) Communications requirements.

42. You finally have been appointed project manager for a major company project. In your work for other project and functional managers as a team member, you have been frustrated because the entire team rarely met after the kickoff meeting. As a result, you felt that you did not know how the project was progressing. On some occasions, you did not receive copies of progress reports submitted to upper management. You believe it is important to share information with the team. One of your first activities as project manager has been to set up an information retrieval system. Your information sharing methods will include all the following except:

     (A) Manual filing systems
     (B) Project management software
     (C) Project Intranet
     (D) Electronic databases

43. How do you get the communications requirements for stakeholders?

     (A) Ask them
     (B) Prayer
     (C) Osmosis
     (D) Meetings

44. Project records must be _____.

     (A) Detailed
     (B) Lengthy
     (C) Tactical
     (D) Permanent

45. Which of the following best describes project archives?

     (A) Lessons learned on the project.
     (B) Documentation of the project's product.
     (C) Maintained only on an organization's most significant and complex projects.
     (D) A complete set of indexed project records.

46. Based on the image in the exhibit, how many total communication channels do you have?

     (A) 10
     (B) 15
     (C) 13
     (D) 8

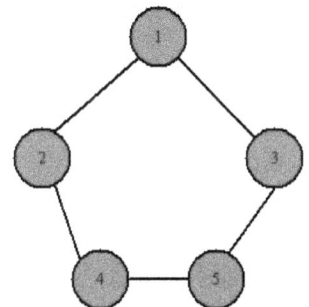

47. A project manager uses manual filing systems, electronic text databases, and project management software to manage his project. These are examples of:

     (A) Information retrieval systems.
     (B) Communications technology.
     (C) Information distribution systems.
     (D) Project records.

48. One purpose of the communications management plan is to provide information about the:

     (A) Methods that will be used to gather and store information
     (B) Methods that will be used for releasing team members from the project when they are no longer needed
     (C) Project organization and stakeholder responsibility relationships
     (D) Experience and skill levels of each team member

49. Your company CEO just sent you an e-mail asking you to make a presentation on your project, which has been in progress for 18 months, to all identified internal and external stakeholders. He scheduled the presentation for next Monday. You expect more than 50 people to attend. The first step in preparing the presentation is to:

    (A) Define the audience
    (B) Determine the objective
    (C) Decide on the general form of the presentation
    (D) Plan a presentation strategy

50. The three main types of communication are:

    (A) Written, oral, and visual.
    (B) Written, oral, and graphic.
    (C) Verbal, formal documentation, and informal documentation.
    (D) Verbal, written, and electronic.

51. The performance measurement baseline is the:

    (A) Earned Value (EV)
    (B) Actual Cost of Work Performed (ACWP)
    (C) Actual Cost (AC)
    (D) Planned Value (PV)

52. The most common communication problem that occurs during negotiation is that:

    (A) One side may try to confuse the other side
    (B) One side may be too busy thinking about what to say next to hear what is being said
    (C) Each side may misinterpret what the other side has said
    (D) Each side may give up on the other side

53. Your project team consists of three people, however due to a scope increase you had to add two more members to your team. How many communication channels do you now have?

    (A) 3
    (B) 2
    (C) 10
    (D) 5

54. In addition to the stakeholder needs, who else's needs should also be considered in communication requirements?

    (A) The advisory board
    (B) The project manager
    (C) The customer
    (D) The sponsor

55. It is important to control the _____ of the software just as much as the hardware technologies.

    (A) Version
    (B) Amount
    (C) Brand
    (D) Concept

56. Currency fluctuations, political instability, and competition from national and regional governments and special interest groups can interfere with project management of international projects. Project managers for international projects should recognize the primary factors in cross-cultural settings and place special emphasis on:

(A) Developing a system to manage communications
(B) Using translation services for formal, written project reports
(C) Establishing and following a production schedule for information distribution to avoid responding to requests for information between scheduled communications
(D) Establishing a performance reporting system

57. The process of collecting and disseminating information in order to provide the stakeholders with information about the project and how the projects resources are being used to reach the project objectives is called:

(A) Performance reporting.
(B) Status reports.
(C) Project reports.
(D) Activity reporting.

58. As a project manager, you try to use empathic listening skills to help understand another person's frame of reference. In following this approach, you should:

(A) Probe, then evaluate the content
(B) Mimic the content of the message
(C) Rephrase the content and reflect the feeling
(D) Evaluate the content, then advise

59. A project manager has many different ways of communicating. Which of the following is a good communication tool for the project manager to use?

(A) Sending a videotape of the project progress to the client
(B) Inputting a task into the project manager's personal computer
(C) Writing notes on a handheld computer
(D) Putting the project budget into a spreadsheet

60. A cumulative SPI of less than one most likely indicates:

(A) The project is ahead of schedule.
(B) Time for a team celebration.
(C) The project is neither behind or ahead of schedule.
(D) The project is behind schedule.

61. What is your SPI if PV=8 and EV = 6?

(A) .75
(B) 1.0
(C) 2.0
(D) 1.33

62. Five people are involved on a project that requires significant communication between all project participants. How many lines of communication exist on this project?

(A) 5
(B) 6
(C) 8
(D) 10

63. If the performance reporting shows a completion percentage, you are doing _____.

    (A) Forecasting
    (B) Scheduling
    (C) Progress reporting
    (D) Status reporting

64. You have just received formal acceptance of the project from your customer. Your next step should be to:

    (A) Distribute the acceptance documentation to other stakeholders as appropriate
    (B) File the acceptance documentation in the project archives
    (C) Document lessons learned with your staff
    (D) Conduct a project audit

65. Which of the following media can a communicator use to present information?

    (A) Tactile
    (B) Visual, audio, and tactile
    (C) Visual
    (D) Audio and visual

66. N (N-1)/2 is the formula for:

    (A) Industrial estimation
    (B) Channels of communication
    (C) Risk assessment
    (D) Quality levels

67. The three principal interests in maintaining good document control are:

    (A) Effective communication, ability to reconstruct why decisions were made, and historical value.
    (B) Security, change management, and procedural documentation.
    (C) Timely communication, collection of performance appraisal data, and assuring proper disposal of sensitive documents.
    (D) Timely communication, maintaining proper approvals, and communication cost control.

68. You are a program manager responsible for five projects in your company. One of your projects is coming to an end, and most of its team members have been reassigned. Today, the project manager asked you if she could leave the project before it is formally closed out so that she can take a new assignment to which she must report in 3 days or it will be offered to someone else. You know that many administrative details remain to be done on this project. Your best course of action is to:

    (A) Make the project manager stay with the project because she is in the best position to close certain administrative matters.
    (B) Appoint another person as the closeout manager and release the project manager to her new assignment, inquiring if she might be available for final customer meetings.
    (C) Have the project manager report to her new assignment but have her do the closeout tasks in her spare time, including nights and weekends.
    (D) Close out the project yourself, notwithstanding your multiple other duties.

69. The report that explains the current condition of the project is _____.

    (A) Status reporting
    (B) Progress reporting
    (C) Schedule analysis
    (D) Forecasting

70. You are responsible for a new email application project within your company that has multiple internal and external users. You have just begun preparing a project management plan. Because many people in your organization are interested in this system and its progress, you decide to prepare a communications management plan. Your first step in preparing this plan is to do which of the following?

(A) Describe the information you plan to distribute.
(B) Set up a repository for all project documents so that they will be easily accessible.
(C) Conduct a stakeholder analysis to assess information needs.
(D) Determine a production schedule to show when each type of communication will be produced.

71. Project archives are best described as:

(A) Lessons learned on the project
(B) Documentation of the project's product
(C) Maintained only on an organization's most significant and complex projects
(D) A complete set of indexed project records

72. Project archives need to be _____ to be most useful.

(A) Written
(B) Oral
(C) Controlled
(D) Indexed

73. Administrative closure should not be delayed until project completion because:

(A) Project team members may be reassigned by that time
(B) Sellers are anxious for payments
(C) Useful information may be lost
(D) The project manager may be reassigned

74. Performance reports usually discuss _____ between estimated and actual performance on the project.

(A) Differences
(B) Variances
(C) Connections
(D) Relationships

75. You are responsible for a systems integration project in your organization that has multiple internal customers. You have just begun preparing a project plan. Because many people in your organization are interested in this system and its progress, you decide to prepare a project communications management plan. Your first step in preparing this plan is to:

(A) Determine a production schedule to show when each type of communication will be produced
(B) Set up a repository for all project documents so that they will be easily accessible
(C) Describe the information you plan to distribute
(D) Conduct a stakeholder analysis to assess information needs

76. In person-to-person communication, messages are sent on verbal levels and nonverbal levels simultaneously. As a general rule, what percentage of the message actually is sent through nonverbal cues?

(A) 40% to 50%
(B) Greater than 50%
(C) 5% to 15%
(D) 20% to 30%

77. The part of performance reporting that is an estimate of the future is _____.

   (A) Schedule
   (B) Progress reporting
   (C) Forecasting
   (D) WBS

78. During closeout, many project managers tend to delay personnel reassignment as long as possible because:

   (A) They believe that no one will want to leave the project
   (B) They are reluctant to confront any interpersonal conflicts that may occur in the process
   (C) The team members do not want to move on to new assignments
   (D) The functional managers do not want the team members to return

79. You are a program manager responsible for five projects in your company. One of your projects is coming to an end, and most of its team members have been reassigned. Today, the project manager asked you if she could leave the project before it is formally closed out so that she can take a new assignment to which she must report in 3 days or it will be offered to someone else. You know that many administrative details remain to be done on this project. Your best course of action is to:

   (A) Make the project manager stay with the project because she is in the best position to close certain administrative matters
   (B) Have the project manager report to her new assignment but have her do the closeout tasks in her spare time, including nights and weekends
   (C) Close out the project yourself, notwithstanding your multiple other duties
   (D) Appoint another person as the closeout manager and release the project manager to her new assignment, inquiring if she might be available for final customer meetings

80. Information is not useful to the receiver if it is not _____.

   (A) Timely
   (B) Interesting
   (C) Complex
   (D) Scarce

81. You are working to close out your project. During these hectic final days of the project, most conflict arises from:

   (A) Technical problems
   (B) Lack of customer acceptance
   (C) Schedule problems
   (D) Cost overruns

82. Both under communication and over communication can cause problems on a project. You want to ensure that the information you collect showing project progress and status is meaningful to stakeholders. To determine specific metrics, you will conduct a stakeholder analysis, and then determine the level of detail stakeholders require. This is available through the:

   (A) Performance measurement baseline.
   (B) Project management methodology.
   (C) Project strategy and approach.
   (D) Communications management plan.

83. One organizational option for improving communications and teamwork is using a tight matrix. This approach also serves to facilitate:

(A) Concurrent engineering
(B) Work on geographically dispersed or virtual teams
(C) Resource leveling
(D) Fast-tracking

84. Performance reports are used to provide information to stakeholders on project scope, schedule, cost, and quality. Which statement most accurately describes this process?

(A) Performance reporting includes status reports, which detail where the project is now; progress reports, which describe accomplishments; and forecasts, which predict future status and progress.
(B) Performance reporting includes histograms, flow charts, and bar charts to show network dependencies and relationships.
(C) The configuration control board receives performance reports and generates change requests to modify aspects of the project.
(D) Performance reporting focuses on examining earned value analysis to determine whether cost overruns will require budget revisions.

85. What is your CPI if EV = 5 and AC = 4?

(A) 1.25
(B) 2.0
(C) .80
(D) 1.0

86. A project's culture can affect its success significantly during several life cycle phases. As manager of an international project with a team of people representing diverse cultures, you should create an environment that maximizes team efforts as the project progresses. Although most people view the values of other cultures in terms of their own culture, a project's cultural emphasis will change during different life cycle phases. During the closing phase, the emphasis basically is:

(A) Competitive
(B) Participative
(C) Cooperative
(D) Focused on information transfer

87. What is your CPI if EV = 20 and AC = 20?

(A) 2.0
(B) 1.25
(C) 4.0
(D) 1.0

88. Communication is important to the success of a project. As the project manager, you have four stakeholders you need to communicate with. As such, you have six channels of communication. Two new stakeholders were just added that you also need to communicate with. How many total communication channels do you have now?

(A) 15
(B) 10
(C) 25
(D) 20

89. You have decided to organize a study group of other project managers in your organization to help prepare for the PMP® exam. Everyone is highly motivated to earn the credential because the CEO has decided to pay a $5,000 bonus to each person who becomes certified. What type of communication are you employing in your efforts to organize this group?

(A) Horizontal
(B) Vertical
(C) Formal
(D) External

90. Which of the following is true regarding communication within a project environment?

(A) If a project consists of 12 people, 48 potential channels of communication exist.
(B) Most project managers spend 30% of their working hours engaged in communication.
(C) The project manager must assume the primary burden of responsibility to ensure that messages sent have been received.
(D) Effective meetings, a "war room," and a tight matrix promote effective communication.

91. A project manager hears a rumor through the project team that the client for the project is supposed to visit the project team office and present the project manager with a purchase order for a large change in the project. The change will authorize a new budget for $50,000. This is an example of what type of communications?

(A) Formal
(B) Informal
(C) Verbal
(D) Nonwritten

92. The key factor in closing issues is the person to whom you will _____ the issue in order to resolve it.

(A) Send
(B) Escalate
(C) Communicate
(D) Write

93. Your project team is a good group of developers who work long hard hours. They have just completed the forming stage of communication. All nine members communicate with each other frequently usually via e-mail. How many different communication channels are there?

(A) 18
(B) 36
(C) 27
(D) 9

94. The process of conferring with others to come to terms or reach an agreement is called:

(A) Motivation
(B) Confrontation
(C) Win-win
(D) Negotiation

95. What is your CPI if AC = 10 and EV = 8?

(A) 1.25
(B) 2.0
(C) .80
(D) 80

96. The SPI, which is used to forecast project completion date, is calculated by using which formula?

    (A) PV/EV
    (B) EV/AC
    (C) EV/PV
    (D) ACWS/PV

97. Effective communication is vital for project success. Scope changes, constraints, assumptions, integration and interface requirements, overlapping roles and responsibilities, and many other factors all pose communications challenges. The presence of communication barriers is most likely to lead to:

    (A) Low morale
    (B) Increased conflict
    (C) Reduced productivity
    (D) Increased hostility

98. A project team includes seven people when the project manager adds two more. How many additional channels of communication are there?

    (A) 21
    (B) 15
    (C) 42
    (D) 36

99. A project manager wants to handle communications well in his project. In order to do this he has chosen to write a communications plan. Of the items listed below, which one is not part of the communications plan?

    (A) Distribution plan
    (B) Collection and filing structure
    (C) Project organizational structure
    (D) Method for accessing information

100. Your project is roughly two months behind schedule due to conflict between several key team members. After resolving the conflict by reassigning several of the members of your project, you should consider _____ to try and bring the project up to schedule.

    (A) Leveling the resources
    (B) Reducing resource loads
    (C) Reassigning resources
    (D) Crashing the schedule

Sample Answer Sheet

T F	T F	T F	T F
1 Ⓐ Ⓑ Ⓒ Ⓓ Ⓔ	26 Ⓐ Ⓑ Ⓒ Ⓓ Ⓔ	51 Ⓐ Ⓑ Ⓒ Ⓓ Ⓔ	76 Ⓐ Ⓑ Ⓒ Ⓓ Ⓔ
2 Ⓐ Ⓑ Ⓒ Ⓓ Ⓔ	27 Ⓐ Ⓑ Ⓒ Ⓓ Ⓔ	52 Ⓐ Ⓑ Ⓒ Ⓓ Ⓔ	77 Ⓐ Ⓑ Ⓒ Ⓓ Ⓔ
3 Ⓐ Ⓑ Ⓒ Ⓓ Ⓔ	28 Ⓐ Ⓑ Ⓒ Ⓓ Ⓔ	53 Ⓐ Ⓑ Ⓒ Ⓓ Ⓔ	78 Ⓐ Ⓑ Ⓒ Ⓓ Ⓔ
4 Ⓐ Ⓑ Ⓒ Ⓓ Ⓔ	29 Ⓐ Ⓑ Ⓒ Ⓓ Ⓔ	54 Ⓐ Ⓑ Ⓒ Ⓓ Ⓔ	79 Ⓐ Ⓑ Ⓒ Ⓓ Ⓔ
5 Ⓐ Ⓑ Ⓒ Ⓓ Ⓔ	30 Ⓐ Ⓑ Ⓒ Ⓓ Ⓔ	55 Ⓐ Ⓑ Ⓒ Ⓓ Ⓔ	80 Ⓐ Ⓑ Ⓒ Ⓓ Ⓔ
6 Ⓐ Ⓑ Ⓒ Ⓓ Ⓔ	31 Ⓐ Ⓑ Ⓒ Ⓓ Ⓔ	56 Ⓐ Ⓑ Ⓒ Ⓓ Ⓔ	81 Ⓐ Ⓑ Ⓒ Ⓓ Ⓔ
7 Ⓐ Ⓑ Ⓒ Ⓓ Ⓔ	32 Ⓐ Ⓑ Ⓒ Ⓓ Ⓔ	57 Ⓐ Ⓑ Ⓒ Ⓓ Ⓔ	82 Ⓐ Ⓑ Ⓒ Ⓓ Ⓔ
8 Ⓐ Ⓑ Ⓒ Ⓓ Ⓔ	33 Ⓐ Ⓑ Ⓒ Ⓓ Ⓔ	58 Ⓐ Ⓑ Ⓒ Ⓓ Ⓔ	83 Ⓐ Ⓑ Ⓒ Ⓓ Ⓔ
9 Ⓐ Ⓑ Ⓒ Ⓓ Ⓔ	34 Ⓐ Ⓑ Ⓒ Ⓓ Ⓔ	59 Ⓐ Ⓑ Ⓒ Ⓓ Ⓔ	84 Ⓐ Ⓑ Ⓒ Ⓓ Ⓔ
10 Ⓐ Ⓑ Ⓒ Ⓓ Ⓔ	35 Ⓐ Ⓑ Ⓒ Ⓓ Ⓔ	60 Ⓐ Ⓑ Ⓒ Ⓓ Ⓔ	85 Ⓐ Ⓑ Ⓒ Ⓓ Ⓔ
11 Ⓐ Ⓑ Ⓒ Ⓓ Ⓔ	36 Ⓐ Ⓑ Ⓒ Ⓓ Ⓔ	61 Ⓐ Ⓑ Ⓒ Ⓓ Ⓔ	86 Ⓐ Ⓑ Ⓒ Ⓓ Ⓔ
12 Ⓐ Ⓑ Ⓒ Ⓓ Ⓔ	37 Ⓐ Ⓑ Ⓒ Ⓓ Ⓔ	62 Ⓐ Ⓑ Ⓒ Ⓓ Ⓔ	87 Ⓐ Ⓑ Ⓒ Ⓓ Ⓔ
13 Ⓐ Ⓑ Ⓒ Ⓓ Ⓔ	38 Ⓐ Ⓑ Ⓒ Ⓓ Ⓔ	63 Ⓐ Ⓑ Ⓒ Ⓓ Ⓔ	88 Ⓐ Ⓑ Ⓒ Ⓓ Ⓔ
14 Ⓐ Ⓑ Ⓒ Ⓓ Ⓔ	39 Ⓐ Ⓑ Ⓒ Ⓓ Ⓔ	64 Ⓐ Ⓑ Ⓒ Ⓓ Ⓔ	89 Ⓐ Ⓑ Ⓒ Ⓓ Ⓔ
15 Ⓐ Ⓑ Ⓒ Ⓓ Ⓔ	40 Ⓐ Ⓑ Ⓒ Ⓓ Ⓔ	65 Ⓐ Ⓑ Ⓒ Ⓓ Ⓔ	90 Ⓐ Ⓑ Ⓒ Ⓓ Ⓔ
16 Ⓐ Ⓑ Ⓒ Ⓓ Ⓔ	41 Ⓐ Ⓑ Ⓒ Ⓓ Ⓔ	66 Ⓐ Ⓑ Ⓒ Ⓓ Ⓔ	91 Ⓐ Ⓑ Ⓒ Ⓓ Ⓔ
17 Ⓐ Ⓑ Ⓒ Ⓓ Ⓔ	42 Ⓐ Ⓑ Ⓒ Ⓓ Ⓔ	67 Ⓐ Ⓑ Ⓒ Ⓓ Ⓔ	92 Ⓐ Ⓑ Ⓒ Ⓓ Ⓔ
18 Ⓐ Ⓑ Ⓒ Ⓓ Ⓔ	43 Ⓐ Ⓑ Ⓒ Ⓓ Ⓔ	68 Ⓐ Ⓑ Ⓒ Ⓓ Ⓔ	93 Ⓐ Ⓑ Ⓒ Ⓓ Ⓔ
19 Ⓐ Ⓑ Ⓒ Ⓓ Ⓔ	44 Ⓐ Ⓑ Ⓒ Ⓓ Ⓔ	69 Ⓐ Ⓑ Ⓒ Ⓓ Ⓔ	94 Ⓐ Ⓑ Ⓒ Ⓓ Ⓔ
20 Ⓐ Ⓑ Ⓒ Ⓓ Ⓔ	45 Ⓐ Ⓑ Ⓒ Ⓓ Ⓔ	70 Ⓐ Ⓑ Ⓒ Ⓓ Ⓔ	95 Ⓐ Ⓑ Ⓒ Ⓓ Ⓔ
21 Ⓐ Ⓑ Ⓒ Ⓓ Ⓔ	46 Ⓐ Ⓑ Ⓒ Ⓓ Ⓔ	71 Ⓐ Ⓑ Ⓒ Ⓓ Ⓔ	96 Ⓐ Ⓑ Ⓒ Ⓓ Ⓔ
22 Ⓐ Ⓑ Ⓒ Ⓓ Ⓔ	47 Ⓐ Ⓑ Ⓒ Ⓓ Ⓔ	72 Ⓐ Ⓑ Ⓒ Ⓓ Ⓔ	97 Ⓐ Ⓑ Ⓒ Ⓓ Ⓔ
23 Ⓐ Ⓑ Ⓒ Ⓓ Ⓔ	48 Ⓐ Ⓑ Ⓒ Ⓓ Ⓔ	73 Ⓐ Ⓑ Ⓒ Ⓓ Ⓔ	98 Ⓐ Ⓑ Ⓒ Ⓓ Ⓔ
24 Ⓐ Ⓑ Ⓒ Ⓓ Ⓔ	49 Ⓐ Ⓑ Ⓒ Ⓓ Ⓔ	74 Ⓐ Ⓑ Ⓒ Ⓓ Ⓔ	99 Ⓐ Ⓑ Ⓒ Ⓓ Ⓔ
25 Ⓐ Ⓑ Ⓒ Ⓓ Ⓔ	50 Ⓐ Ⓑ Ⓒ Ⓓ Ⓔ	75 Ⓐ Ⓑ Ⓒ Ⓓ Ⓔ	100 Ⓐ Ⓑ Ⓒ Ⓓ Ⓔ

1. (D) Sharing only positive aspects of the project for future replication elsewhere in the organization. The lessons learned summary should document the major positive and negative aspects of the project so that future projects can benefit from the team's successes and failures, by replicating the good things about the project and avoiding the mistakes.

2. (B) 10. The formula to calculate the number of lines of communication is: $(n * (n-1)) / 2$ --> where n = number of team members = $5 * 4 / 2 = 10$.

3. (C) Greater than 75%. Nonverbal cues can be divided into four categories: physical, aesthetic, signs, and symbols. Many studies have demonstrated that most messages are conveyed through such nonverbal cues as facial expression, touch, and body motion, rather than through the words spoken.

4. (C) 1.33. EV = 8 and PV = 6, and the formula reads SPI=8/6, which is 1.33.

5. (A) Performance reporting includes status reports, which detail where the project is now; progress reports, which describe accomplishments; and forecasts, which predict future status and progress. Information from these reports is valuable only to the extent that the project manager, customer, and other key stakeholders use them to make decisions regarding present and future actions. In the decision-making process, the project manager needs to know the current situation (status reports); the past performance capability that led to the current status (progress reports); and a best estimate of future progress, using past performance as a predictor (forecasts).

6. (D) Downward communication. Downward communication provides direction and control for project team members and other employees. It contains job-related information, such as actions required, standards, the time activities should be performed, activities to be completed, and progress measurement.

7. (B) Ability to work well with others. Project management requires getting things done through people who generally do not report directly to the project manager. The ability to influence project team members, as well as other key stakeholders, is crucial for success.

8. (A) Project management methodology. Performance reports organize and summarize the information gathered and present any analysis results. These reports should provide the information and detail that stakeholders require, as documented in the communications management plan.

9. (A) Communications planning, information distribution, performance reporting, and administrative closure. Communications planning—determining the information and communications needs of the stakeholders; who needs what information, when they will need it, and how it will be given to them. Information distribution—making needed information available to project stakeholders in a timely manner. Performance reporting—collecting and disseminating performance information. This includes status reporting, progress measurement, and forecasting. Administrative closure—generating, gathering, and disseminating information to formalize phase or project completion.

10. (D) All of them. There is no one best channel of communication. Each channel has specific properties that make it unique. The best communication comes from a combination of channels. Using only one channel all the time will result in bad communication some of the time. Choose the channel to fit the communication need.

11. (B) Accurate, uniform information about work results is provided. Work results are an output of project plan execution and an input to performance reporting (for example, what deliverables have been fully or partially completed, and what costs and resources have been incurred or committed). Work results should be reported within the framework of the project communications management plan. Accurate, uniform information about work results is essential to performance reporting.

12. (C) People in the communication plan. Although all of the other people may get communication at some time, the people in the communication plan are the ones who will get specific types of information. This is why the planning of your communication process is done early in the process of managing a project. If the list of people who need to get information changes, then change your communication plan.

13. (A) Lateral. Lateral communication occurs between team members and all stakeholders who are peers.

14. (A) Conflict Resolution. Project communication management processes include: communication planning, information distribution, performance reporting and managing stakeholders.

15. (A) 45. The formula to calculate the number of lines of communication is: (n * (n-1)) / 2 --> where n = number of team members = 10 * 9 / 2 = 45.

16. (D) Formal. It's extremely important to have formal acceptance when the project is being brought to Administrative Closure. If the acceptance is formal, you will have a record of it. You can refer to this record at any later time, and it forestalls any arguments about whether the project was done correctly.

17. (B) Passing a quality control inspection. Project closure is a key output of administrative closure. For project closure, confirmation that the project has met all customer requirements for the product of the project must be received.

18. (A) Face-to-face. Although this type of communication is not always possible or practical, it remains the best possible way to communicate to stakeholders.

19. (C) 11. n (n-1) / 2 = 5 (5-1) / 2 = 5 (4) / 2 = 20 / 2 = 10; n (n-1) / 2 = 7 (7-1) / 2 = 7 (6) / 2 = 42 / 2 = 21; 21 total - 10 previous = 11 additional channels.

20. (C) 10. PMBOK Guide - page 226.

21. (B) Be as brief as possible and emphasize the practicality of his or her ideas. Action-oriented people tend to be pragmatic and do not like to belabor an issue. Therefore, the best approach is to present ideas succinctly along with the benefits associated with their application.

22. (C) Group think. Irving Janis invented this term in 1971 to alert people to a serious disadvantage that can arise when a team becomes too cohesive and too amiable.

23. (B) Accurate, uniform information about work performance information is provided. Work performance information are an output of direct and manage project execution process and an input to performance reporting (for example, what deliverables have been fully or partially completed, and what costs and resources have been incurred or committed). Work performance information should be reported within the framework of the project communications management plan. Accurate, uniform information about Work performance information is essential to performance reporting.

24. (A) Sponsor. Because the sponsor started the entire process and is ultimately responsible for the outcome of the project, he or she is the single most important stakeholder to keep informed.

25. (A) Hold a performance review. The performance review is a useful tool for evaluating the successes and failures of the project.

26. (A) Negotiation. Negotiation involves compromise so that each party feels it has received something of value, even though it has had to make certain sacrifices.

27. (D) Using subcontractors, developing the project scope statement, and managing changes after the project is under way. The use of subcontractors accounts for more litigation than all other aspects of the project combined, and project managers report that developing the scope statement and managing changes are the most common and troublesome issues they face. Thus, having the ability to negotiate an approach that satisfies all stakeholders is important.

28. (B) Discussing specific legal issues regarding the contract. Conducted after contract award or approval of the project, the kickoff meeting provides an opportunity for project participants to get to know each other and review information about the project. It is not a forum to discuss detailed project issues.

29. (D) 10. n (n-1) / 2 = 5 (6-1) / 2 - 5 (4) / 2 = 20 / 2 = 10.

30. (B) Greater than 50%. Nonverbal cues can be divided into four categories: physical, aesthetic, signs, and symbols. Many studies have demonstrated that most messages are conveyed through such nonverbal cues as facial expression, touch, and body motion, rather than through the words spoken.

31. (D) Communication barriers. Communication Management Plan - describes the communications needs and expectations for the project; how and in what format information will be communicated; when and where each communication will be made; and who is responsible for providing each type of communication. A communication management plan can be formal or informal, highly detailed or broadly framed, based on the requirements of the project stakeholders. The communication management plan is contained in, or is a subsidiary plan of, the project management plan.

32. (A) Strive to develop a friendly, honest, and open relationship. Relationships built on honesty can withstand adversity. Therefore, the best approach for a project manager is to be honest in his or her dealings. When a customer has faith in the credibility of the project manager, additional revenue-generating work will likely follow.

33. (A) Provide a good statistical approximation of earned value (EV). Calculating the EV requires knowing what percentage of a task has been completed. The 50-50 rule is used for this purpose. As soon as a task has started, half the effort is assumed to be completed and half the PV associated with the task is entered into the project accounts book. Only after the task is completed is the remaining half of the PV value entered. When many tasks are being considered, this approach provides a good statistical approximation of EV.

34. (D) Horizontal. Lateral communication (horizontally) - information exchange between the project manager and his/her peers: functional managers, staff personnel, contractors, other project managers, etc. Involves negotiating resources, schedules, and budgets; coordinating activities between groups, as well as developing plans for future operating periods. Is vital to the success of a project and is also the most important factor for survival and growth in a highly competitive and turbulent environment. Requires diplomacy and experience. If managed properly, it creates a harmonious, cooperative environment based on trust and respect for one another. If poorly managed, it may lead to conflict, blame, and failure to meet project objectives.

35. (A) Being a good communication blocker. In addition to the other items listed, the project manager can also enhance communication by eliminating communication blocks and serving as an example of an effective communicator.

36. (A) Conduct a communications requirements analysis to assess information needs. Communications requirements analysis is used to analyze the information needs of the stakeholders and determine the sources to meet those needs. The analysis should include consideration of appropriate methods and technologies for providing the information needed.

37. (D) Earned value analysis. Earned value analysis integrates cost and schedule using EV, PV, and AC to measure and assess project performance.

38. (B) Administrative closure. Administrative closure includes collecting project records; ensuring that they reflect final specifications; analyzing project success, effectiveness, and lessons learned; and archiving such information for future use. Each project phase should be closed properly to ensure that useful information is not lost.

39. (C) Using subcontractors, developing the project scope statement, and managing changes after the project is under way. The use of subcontractors accounts for more litigation than all other aspects of the project combined, and project managers report that developing the scope statement and managing changes are the most common and troublesome issues they face. Thus, having the ability to negotiate an approach that satisfies all stakeholders is important.

40. (D) 45. n (n-1) / 2 = 10 (10-1) / 2 = 10 (9) / 2 = 90 / 2 = 45.

41. (A) Communications planning. Communications Planning - the process of determining the information and communications needs of the project stakeholders: who they are, what is their level of interest and influence on the project, who needs what information, when will they need it, and how it will be given to them

42. (C) Project Intranet. Information retrieval systems and information distribution systems are tools and techniques for information distribution. Project meetings, hard-copy document distribution, shared access to networked electronic databases, fax, e-mail, voice mail, videoconferencing, and project Intranet are examples of information distribution methods.

43. (A) Ask them. Questioning people about their communication requirements for the project is the first step in getting these requirements.

44. (D) Permanent. The records must be permanent so that they can be referred to after they have been sent and received. This means that you will not use verbal communications as project records unless someone writes down the conversation. In that case, the notes of the conversation or meeting should be circulated to get agreement that what is captured is what was actually said.

45. (D) A complete set of indexed project records. The project archives should include all the documents, communications, and other data pertaining to the project. When projects are conducted under contract or when they involve significant procurement, particular attention should be paid to archiving financial records.

46. (A) 10. PMBOK Guide - page 226.

47. (A) Information retrieval systems. Project data is put into a variety of retrieval systems. These are not necessarily distribution systems but are storage and retrieval systems.

48. (A) Methods that will be used to gather and store information. The plan should also contain a distribution structure that shows the methods that will be used to distribute various types of information and the individuals or organizations to whom the information will be distributed, production schedules showing when each type of communication will be produced, and methods to access information between scheduled communications. Also included should be a discussion of how the plan will be updated and revised as needs change. The communication plan is a component of the project plan and may be formal or informal, highly detailed or broadly framed, based on the needs of the project.

49. (B) Determine the objective. Only after the objective is determined can the other issues listed be addressed effectively. The information must be relevant to audience needs.

50. (D) Verbal, written, and electronic. The technologies or methods used to transfer information back and forth among project elements can vary significantly: from brief conversations to extended meetings, from simple written documents to immediately accessible online schedules and databases. Information can be shared by team members through a variety of methods, including manual filing systems, electronic text databases, project management software, and systems that allow access to technical documentation such as engineering drawings. Project information may be distributed using a variety of methods including project meetings, hard copy document distribution, shared access to networked electronic databases, fax, electronic mail, voice mail, and video conferencing.

51. (D) Planned Value (PV). The PV is the performance measurement baseline, or the originally scheduled project cost. The PV, EV, and AC are used to determine the EAC and the cost and schedule variances. Project overruns and slippage at any given point in time can be determined using these data.

52. (C) Each side may misinterpret what the other side has said. Effective communication is the key to successful negotiation. Misunderstanding is the most common communication problem. A project manager should listen actively, acknowledge what is being said, and speak for a purpose.

53. (C) 10. The total number of communication channels is n(n-1)/2, where n = number of stakeholders. Thus, a project with 5 stakeholders has 10 potential communication.

54. (B) The project manager. The project manager should consider what information he or she believes will be important to the stakeholders and be sure to include that information in the communication requirements.

55. (A) Version. If people use different versions of the software, this is certain to delay communication and frustrate project team members.

56. (A) Developing a system to manage communications. Project stakeholders must receive information in a timely fashion. Global communications that use standard formats through a communications management system may reduce the impact of cultural differences.

57. (A) Performance reporting. Performance reporting involves collecting and disseminating information in order to provide stakeholders with information about how resources are being used to achieve project objectives. This process includes status reporting and progress reporting and forecasting.

58. (C) Rephrase the content and reflect the feeling. Empathic listening requires seeing the world the way the other person sees it, with the goal of understanding that person's views and feelings. Unlike sympathetic listening, empathic listening contains no element of value judgment.

59. (A) Sending a videotape of the project progress to the client. The act of communicating involves an exchange of information between two parties. The definition of communications is: An exchange of information between two parties with understanding.

60. (D) The project is behind schedule. SPI = EV/PV. An SPI < 1 would indicate that planned value is greater than earned value which would be an indicator that the project is behind schedule. The schedule efficiency ratio of earned value accomplished against the planned value. The SPI describes what portion of the planned schedule was actually accomplished. The SPI = EV/PV.

61. (A) .75. EV = 6 and PV = 8, and the formula reads SPI=6/8, which is .75.

62. (D) 10. The formula used to compute the total number of communications channels between N persons is: N(N-1))/2. In this case the answer is 10.

63. (C) Progress reporting. When percentage of completion is used in performance reporting, you are doing progress reporting.

64. (A) Distribute the acceptance documentation to other stakeholders as appropriate. Formal acceptance of the project requires documentation showing that the customer has accepted the product of the project. Before other administrative closure activities are initiated, the acceptance documentation should be distributed to stakeholders.

65. (B) Visual, audio, and tactile. A communicator can use all three media to communicate.

66. (B) Channels of communication. Communication Channels - The path along which the exchange of information takes place or is supposed to take place. Typically refers to the sequence of individuals in a chain of command.

67. (A) Effective communication, ability to reconstruct why decisions were made, and historical value. The project manager has three main reasons for or interests in having good document control: effective communications, making sure that all necessary information is distributed and received by all those who need it; ability to reconstruct why certain decisions were made and the conditions under which they were made; historical value, so that lessons learned can be used in the future on other projects.

68. (B) Appoint another person as the closeout manager and release the project manager to her new assignment, inquiring if she might be available for final customer meetings. Although the new closeout manager may lack technical knowledge about the project, he or she can obtain it by contacting the project manager or a member of the project team. Having the project manager available for customer meetings can help ensure that formal acceptance of the project is obtained and working relationships continue with the customer.

69. (A) Status reporting. Status reporting shows the current condition of the project, usually using at least the schedule conformance and the budget conformance as two main pieces of information.

70. (C) Conduct a stakeholder analysis to assess information needs. Communication Management Plan - a document that describes: the communications needs and expectations for the project; how and in what format information will be communicated; when and where each communication will be made; and who is responsible for providing each type of communication. A communication management plan can be formal or informal, highly detailed or broadly framed, based on the requirements of the project stakeholders. The communication management plan is contained in, or is a subsidiary plan of, the project management plan.

71. (D) A complete set of indexed project records. The project archives should include all the documents, communications, and other data pertaining to the project. When projects are conducted under contract or when they involve significant procurement, particular attention should be paid to archiving financial records.

72. (D) Indexed. In order to search for materials after Administrative Closure has occurred and the project is finished, indexing archives helps make searching for information much faster and simpler.

73. (C) Useful information may be lost. Closure includes collecting project records, ensuring that the records accurately reflect final specifications, analyzing project or phase success and effectiveness, and archiving such information for future use. Each phase of the project should be properly closed while important project information is still available.

74. (B) Variances. Variance management consists of comparing the actual performance of the project to the baseline. The project manager manages variances and looks for the reasons the variances occurred.

75. (D) Conduct a stakeholder analysis to assess information needs. Stakeholder analysis is used to analyze the information needs of the stakeholders and determine the sources to meet those needs. The analysis should include consideration of appropriate methods and technologies for providing the information needed.

76. (B) Greater than 50%. Nonverbal cues can be divided into four categories: physical, aesthetic, signs, and symbols. Many studies have demonstrated that most messages are conveyed through such nonverbal cues as facial expression, touch, and body motion, rather than through the words spoken.

77. (C) Forecasting. Forecasting is a form of estimate that describes the potential needs of a project.

78. (B) They are reluctant to confront any interpersonal conflicts that may occur in the process. Project managers recognize that interpersonal conflicts may arise when new assignments or layoffs are announced and may worry that team members will lose interest in the project and stop working as hard once they know that they are being reassigned.

79. (D) Appoint another person as the closeout manager and release the project manager to her new assignment, inquiring if she might be available for final customer meetings. Although the new closeout manager may lack technical knowledge about the project, he or she can obtain it by contacting the project manager or a member of the project team. Having the project manager available for customer meetings can help ensure that formal acceptance of the project is obtained and working relationships continue with the customer.

80. (A) Timely. In order for information to be useful, it must come at the correct time.

81. (C) Schedule problems. Any schedule slippage during project execution will become apparent in the final phase of the project. During closeout, projects with firm deadlines often become hectic, with activity focused on completing the project on time and to specification.

82. (D) Communications management plan. Performance reports organize and summarize the information gathered and present any analysis results. These reports should provide the information and detail that stakeholders require, as documented in the communications management plan.

83. (A) Concurrent engineering. The term tight matrix means that all team members are working in one location or in close proximity to each other. This concept has been used effectively for construction projects, new product development, public works projects, and so on. A tight matrix facilitates concurrent engineering because the design engineers work in the same location as the manufacturing engineers. This ensures that the project is designed to be cost effective to manufacture.

84. (A) Performance reporting includes status reports, which detail where the project is now; progress reports, which describe accomplishments; and forecasts, which predict future status and progress. Performance reports organize and summarize the information gathered, and present the results of any analysis as compared to the performance measurement baseline. Reports should provide the status and progress information, and the level of detail required by various stakeholders, as documented in the communications management plan.

85. (A) 1.25. $EV = 5$, $AC = 4$, and the formula reads $CPI = 5/4$, which is 1.25.

86. (D) Focused on information transfer. Projects wind down during the closing phase, and team members start leaving the project. Project managers must show leadership during this phase and maintain the same efficiency and performance standards as in other phases. The closing phase emphasizes information transfer, and this advances the project management profession.

87. (A) 2.0. $C = 20$, $EV = 20$, and the formula reads $CPI = 20/20$, which is 1.

88. (A) 15. $n(n-1) / 2 = 6(6-1) / 2 = 6(5) / 2 = 30 / 2 = 15$.

89. (A) Horizontal. Communication skills are used to exchange information between the sender and the receiver. Horizontal communication occurs between or among peers, that is, across, rather than up and down, the organization.

90. (D) Effective meetings, a "war room," and a tight matrix promote effective communication. Effective meetings start and end on time, follow an agenda, and result in action items for people to complete. A "war room" provides team identity and a place to conduct project business. A tight matrix indicates that project team members are located within close physical proximity, which fosters informal communication and team building.

91. (B) Informal. This is an example of informal communications. Informal communications are unplanned written or verbal communications. Frequently these communications can bring valuable information to the project manager, but they can also be a source of erroneous information, and care should be taken when using them.

92. (B) Escalate. You must have a person who can resolve the issue between two laterals. That person must have the authority to make a decision, and in order to get that decision, you escalate the issue to him or her.

93. (B) 36. The total number of communication channels is $n(n-1)/2$, where n = number of stakeholders. Thus, a project with 9 stakeholders has 36 potential communication channels.

94. (D) Negotiation. Negotiation and Conflict Management - Conferring with others in order to come to terms or reach an agreement; may focus on any or all of the following: scope, cost, and schedule objectives; changes; contract terms and conditions; assignments; or resources.

95. (C) .80. $EV = 8$, $AC = 4$, and the formula reads $CPI = 8/10$, which is .80.

96. (C) EV/PV. The SPI is calculated by taking the earned value, or EV, and dividing it by the PV, the portion of the approved cost estimate planned to be spent on the activity during a given period.

97. (B) Increased conflict. Barriers to communication lead to a poor flow of information. Accordingly, messages are misinterpreted by recipients, thereby creating different perceptions, understanding, and frames of reference. Left unchecked, poor communication increases conflict among project stakeholders, which causes the other problems listed to arise.

98. (B) 15. $n(n-1) / 2 = 7(7-1) / 2 = 7(6) / 2 = 42 / 2 = 21$; $n(n-1) / 2 = 9(9-1) / 2 = 9(8) / 2 = 72 / 2 = 36$; 36 total - 21 previous = 15 additional channels.

99. (C) Project organizational structure. The Communication Management Plan is a document that describes: the communications needs and expectations for the project; how and in what format information will be communicated; when and where each communication will be made; and who is responsible for providing each type of communication. A communication management plan can be formal or informal, highly detailed or broadly framed, based on the requirements of the project stakeholders. The communication management plan is contained in, or is a subsidiary plan of, the project management plan.

100. (D) Crashing the schedule. In project planning, an activity can be conducted at a normal pace or at an accelerated pace, known as crashing the activity of the project. Crashing is completed at a greater cost than a normal-paced project.

Project Risk Management

On past exams many people find the project risk management questions demanding because they address many concepts that some project managers have not been exposed to in their work or education. However, the questions correspond closely to the PMBOK® Guide material so you should not have much difficulty if you study the concepts and terminology found in the PMBOK® Guide. Although the questions included do not contain mathematically complex work problems, they do require you to know certain theories, such as expected monetary value (EMV) and decision-tree analysis. Additionally, you are likely to encounter questions related to levels of risk faced by both buyer and seller based on various types of contacts.

Project Risk Management contains six processes: Risk Management Planning, Risk Identification, Qualitative Risk Analysis, Quantitative Risk Analysis, Risk Response Planning, and Risk Monitoring and Control.

As the name of this knowledge area implies, these processes are concerned with identifying and planning for potential risks that may impact the project. Organizations will often combine several of these processes into one step. The important thing about this process is that you should strive to identify all the risks and develop responses for those with the greatest consequences to the project objectives.

In order to manage project risk, you must first understand what constitutes risk. First, risks are generally associated with uncertain outcomes or a lack of knowledge of future events. Second, risks are measured according to the probability of their occurrence and the consequences of not achieving project goals. Finally, project risk compares actual project and product results to the project's quality standards. Know the concept of risk versus reward.

A risk is any factor that may potentially interfere with successful completion of the project. A risk is not a problem—a problem has already occurred; a risk is the recognition that a problem or opportunity might occur. By recognizing potential problems, the project manager can attempt to avoid or minimize a problem through proper actions.

The procedure that the team will use to manage project risks is defined in the Planning Phase, documented in the Project Plan, and then executed throughout the Execution Phase of the project.

The Risk Management Plan, documents the parameters used to manage risk throughout the project. In addition to documenting the results of the risk identification and analysis steps, it must cover who is responsible for managing various areas of risk, how risks will be tracked throughout the project, how contingency plans will be implemented, and how project contingency reserves will be allocated to handle risk.

Project reserves are resources (people, dollars, and commodities) that are available to the project if needed. Reserves can come in two types -- contingency reserves (known unknowns) and management reserves (unknown unknowns). Contingency reserves are developed based on the results of risk planning, and are usually available for release at the project manager's discretion to address risks that materialize, and to ensure the project succeeds even if the risk occurs. Management reserves are developed at the discretion of management, and are put in place when the ability to obtain additional budget may compromise the success of the project. Management reserves are typically part of project budgeting, and not part of risk planning.

Project risks are identified, monitored and carefully managed throughout the life of the project. It is particularly important in the Planning Phase to document risks and identify contingency reserves that have been applied to the risks.

There are various areas that can affect a project's risk level:

- The technology used on the project
- The environment in which the project is executed
- The relationships between team members
- How well the project fits the business area or strategic objectives of the organization
- How great of a change will result from the project

Risks are documented so that contingency measures can be taken to mitigate their effects. Risks to both the internal and external aspects of the project should be tracked. Internal risks are those items that the project team can directly control (e.g., staffing), and external risks are those events that happen outside the direct influence of the project team.

As stated before, risk identification begins early in the Planning Phase of the project. A Risk Management Plan is started during the Planning Phase. Then, as scheduling, budgeting, and resource planning occur, the plan is updated to reflect further risks identified throughout the Planning Phase.

Project Risk Management - Questions

1. A project manager is looking at the risk associated with the project schedule. Realizing that if the risks occur the project will be delivered to the stakeholders late, the project manager decides to consider the risk and promise delivery later than the most likely project completion date. He then takes the time between the promise date and the most likely completion date and distributes it among the activities of the project schedule. This creates float in the schedule. This process is called:

    (A) Schedule delay.
    (B) Critical chain scheduling.
    (C) Buffering.
    (D) Contingency scheduling.

2. The project is one with many hazards that could easily injure one or more persons and there is no method of avoiding potential for damages. The project manager should consider _____ as a means of deflecting the risk.

    (A) buying insurance for personal bodily injury
    (B) abandoning the project
    (C) establishing a management reserve
    (D) establishing a contingency fund

3. In the Monte Carlo technique, what is the criticality index?

    (A) The percent of time a given activity will be on the critical path.
    (B) The sum of the duration of the critical path activities divided by the project expected value for duration.
    (C) The percent of time an activity will be late.
    (D) The number of days the project will be late divided by the project duration.

4. You are the project manager for the construction building a chemical depository and the local residents have produced reams of data showing the risk to the community of the storage facility is built. They have threatened to take your company to court. You find you are spending most of your time trying to work with these groups to alleviate their concerns. After much time and effort you persuade management to move this project to a different location outside of this town. This is an example of which of the following risk responses?

    (A) Active acceptance
    (B) Passive acceptance
    (C) Avoidance
    (D) Mitigation

5. A risk probability or impact scale that uses rank-ordered values such as very low, low, moderate, high, and very high is called:

    (A) A nonlinear scale
    (B) A linear scale
    (C) An ordinal scale
    (D) A cardinal scale

6. Risks are accepted when:

(A) The project team reduces the probability and consequences of an adverse risk event to an acceptable threshold.
(B) Risks are never accepted.
(C) The project team decides to transfer the risk to a third party.
(D) The project team decides not to change the project plan to deal with a risk or is unable to identify any other suitable response strategy.

7. The development of response plans for project risks could be considered a form of risk?

(A) Quantification.
(B) Identification.
(C) Control.
(D) Mitigation.

8. Contingency planning is a means to _____ risks to the project through a formal process and provide the resources to meet the risk events.

(A) resolve
(B) eliminate
(C) address
(D) classify

9. A problem occurs in the design of a grocery cart. In this case it is determined that the wheels will wear out much quicker in areas of heavy snow and ice because the salt will corrode the wheel bearings. Using sealed bearing wheels will significantly increase cost, and it is determined that the carts themselves will be rusty and damaged at about the same time the wheel bearings begin to fail. By injecting the wheel bearings with a high temperature grease the life of the wheel bearings is increased considerably. The project recommends using the high temperature grease. This is called:

(A) Risk avoidance.
(B) Risk acceptance.
(C) Risk deflection.
(D) Risk mitigation.

10. As the project manager, you have the option of proposing one of three computer systems to a client: a full feature system that satisfies the minimum requirements but also offers numerous special functions (computer option 1); a system that meets the client's minimum requirements (computer option 3); and a system that satisfies the minimum requirements plus has a few extra features (computer option 2). The on-time records and associated profits and losses are depicted on the decision tree (see image). What is the expected monetary value of computer option 1?

    (A) $15,000
    (B) $27,500
    (C) $25,000
    (D) $10,000

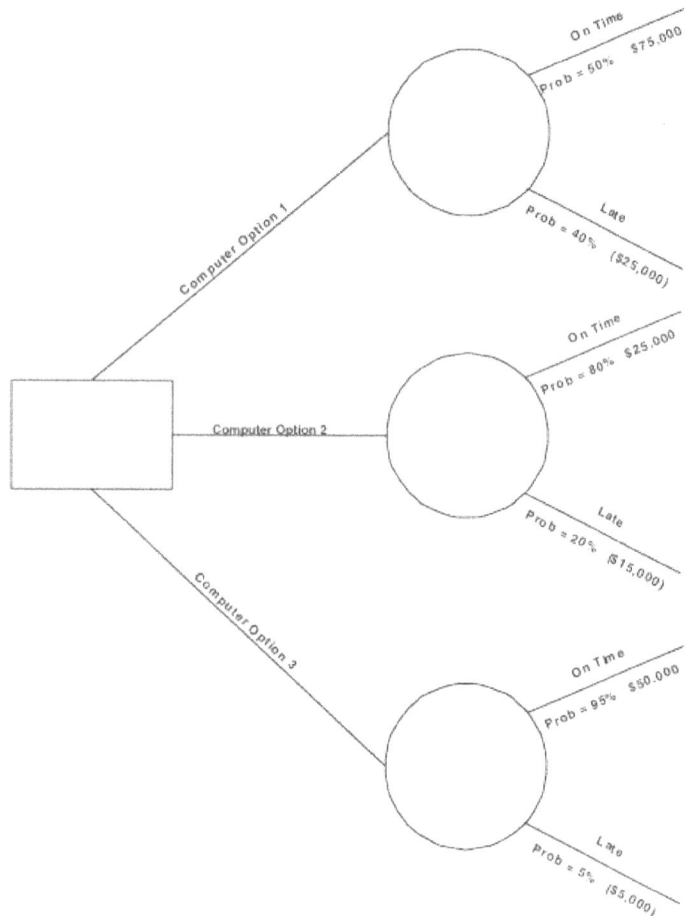

11. Goldratt's critical chain theory says that in order to reduce risk in schedules we should:

    (A) Start activities in the feeder chains as late as possible.
    (B) Start activities in the feeder chains as early as possible.
    (C) Add buffer to the critical chains.
    (D) Start activities in the critical chains as early as possible.

12. The primary characteristic that distinguishes between external and internal risk areas is the?

    (A) use of more or less contractors.
    (B) project manager's ability to influence the risk.
    (C) project manager's perception of risk.
    (D) technical nature of the project.

13. Which of the following is the output from Risk Identification?

    (A) Risk events
    (B) Risk register
    (C) Decision trees
    (D) Risk triggers

14. Workarounds are mentioned as an output of the Risk Monitoring and Control process. Which of the following best describes what is a workaround?

    (A) Workarounds are used for monitoring overall project performance against a baseline plan.
    (B) Workarounds are unplanned responses to risks that were previously unidentified or accepted.
    (C) Workarounds are ways to mitigate risk using avoidance, transfer, or risk mitigation responses.
    (D) Workarounds are a result of implementing a risk response.

15. Risk Management is the systematic process of identifying, analyzing and responding to project risks. It includes which of the following?

   (A) maximizing the probability and consequence of positive events.
   (B) maximizing the probability and consequence of negative events.
   (C) maximizing the consequence of negative events.
   (D) minimizing the probability of positive events.

16. A risk response which involves eliminating a threat is called:

   (A) Deflection
   (B) Transfer
   (C) Avoidance
   (D) Mitigation

17. The management reserve for the project contains:

   (A) Money to offset missing schedule objectives.
   (B) Money to handle the effects of known risks in the project.
   (C) Money to offset missing cost or schedule objectives.
   (D) Money to offset missing cost objectives.

18. According to what you know as a project manager, risk mitigation could involve which of the following?

   (A) A policy response system
   (B) Corrective action
   (C) Eliminating risk through quality assurance
   (D) Purchasing insurance

19. A particular process produces parts with a standard deviation of 6 units. Every 3 hours a sample of 3 items is taken and its mean is plotted. The standard deviation of the sample mean is:

   (A) 2
   (B) 3
   (C) 4
   (D) 5

20. As the project manager, you have the option of proposing one of three computer systems to a client: a full feature system that satisfies the minimum requirements but also offers numerous special functions (computer option 1); a system that meets the client's minimum requirements (computer option 3); and a system that satisfies the minimum requirements plus has a few extra features (computer option 2). The on-time records and associated profits and losses are depicted on the decision tree (see image). What is the expected monetary value of computer option 1?

   (A) $15,000
   (B) $10,000
   (C) $27,500
   (D) $25,000

21. The project team has put together a project plan for a project, and the plan has been approved by the stakeholders. The customer asks the project manager if the project can be delivered seven weeks sooner. The customer offers sufficient monetary incentive for the project manager. The project manager decides to fast track the project. This decision will:

    (A) Increase risk.
    (B) Decrease risk.
    (C) Not affect risk.
    (D) Risk change cannot be determined.

22. Using a contractor to perform a high-risk task is which form of risk response?

    (A) Insurance
    (B) Assumption
    (C) Transference
    (D) Mediation

23. A project manager holds the first risk meeting of the project team. The client is present at the meeting. At the meeting several risks are identified and assigned to members of the project team for evaluation and quantification. The result of the meeting is:

    (A) Strategies for the risk events.
    (B) General statements about risks for the project.
    (C) A list of potential risk events.
    (D) Expected value of the risk events.

24. Project risk management is typically defined as a function that consists of reducing:

    (A) Uncertainty and damage
    (B) Staffing and time
    (C) Time and cost
    (D) Cost and staffing

25. Risk event is the precise description of what might happen to the _____ of the project.

    (A) manager
    (B) detriment
    (C) budget
    (D) length

26. Future events or outcomes that are unfavorable are called?

    (A) Risks
    (B) Opportunities
    (C) Surprises
    (D) Contingencies

27. Warning signs that indicate a risk has occurred or is about to occur are called:

    (A) Triggers
    (B) Risks
    (C) Stop gaps
    (D) Sign posts

28. A project manager and her project team are analyzing risk in their project. One of the things that they might do to help identify potential risks or opportunities would be to review:

(A) The project budget.
(B) The goals and objectives of the project.
(C) Lessons learned from other similar projects.
(D) The monetary value of changes for similar projects.

29. Which of the following is true concerning the Monte Carlo Analysis?

(A) The basis for most schedule simulations.
(B) Difficult to perform and bring about clear results.
(C) Very informative, but requires a Cray supercomputer.
(D) Useful for figuring the odds of the occurrence of an unanticipated problem.

30. Decreasing the probability of a risk is an example of risk:

(A) mitigation.
(B) transference.
(C) analysis.
(D) quantification.

31. The independence of two events in which the occurrence of one is not related to the occurrence of the other is called:

(A) Independent probability
(B) Event phenomenon
(C) Statistical probability
(D) Statistical independence

32. A risk event has a very high probability of occurring and the consequences, should the event occur, are catastrophic. Which strategy would most project managers not take if all were available?

(A) Avoidance
(B) Transference
(C) Acceptance
(D) Mitigation

33. The amount of money or time needed above the estimate to reduce the risk of overruns of project objectives to a level acceptable to the organization is usually called the:

(A) Project manager slush fund
(B) Mitigation buffer
(C) Contingency reserve
(D) Executive reserve

34. Examples of probability distributions used in quantitative risk analysis are:

(A) Six-sigma distributions
(B) Probability-impact matrix distributions
(C) Delphi distributions
(D) Beta and triangular distributions

35. In probability theory, what is the probability that if you roll two dice (cubes with consecutive numbers 1 to 6 on each of the six faces) you will have at least one 6?

    (A) 11/36
    (B) 1/6
    (C) 1/36
    (D) 1/3

36. In the path convergence example (see image), if the odds of completing activities 1, 2, and 3 on time are 40%, 50%, and 60%, what are the chances of stating activity 4 on day 4?

    (A) 12%
    (B) 11%
    (C) 10%
    (D) 15%

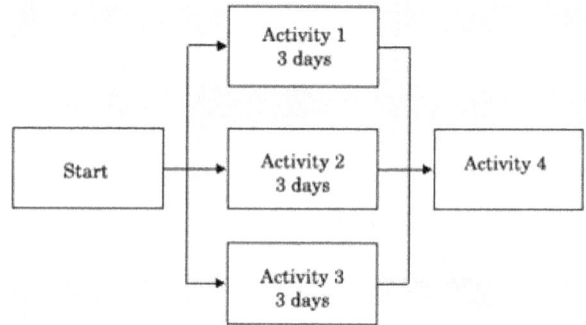

37. In managing the risk of the project schedule we are managing the risk that the project will not be delivered or completed on time. If we assume that the project's possible completion dates are normally distributed and we promise the client the most likely of the project's possible completion dates, what is the probability that the project will be delivered late?

    (A) 50%
    (B) 77%
    (C) 5%
    (D) 10%

38. Which of the following processes is used in risk management to determine which risks might affect the project and documenting their characteristics?

    (A) Risk qualitative analysis
    (B) Risk identification
    (C) Risk response planning
    (D) Risk management planning

39. In the path convergence example (see image), if the odds of completing activities 1, 2, and 3 on time are 50%, 50%, and 50%, what are the chances of stating activity 4 on day 5?

    (A) 13
    (B) 10
    (C) 50
    (D) 40

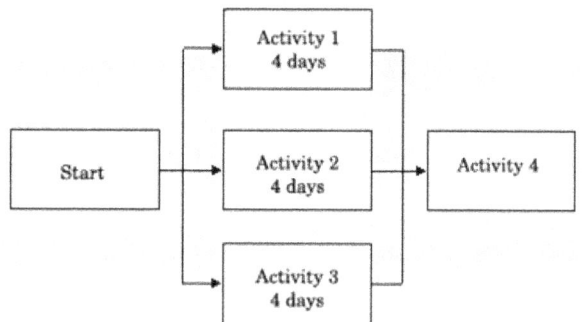

40. An analysis has identified four different options for reducing project costs. Given the following decision tree, which option should be selected?

(A) Option B
(B) Option A
(C) Option D
(D) Option C

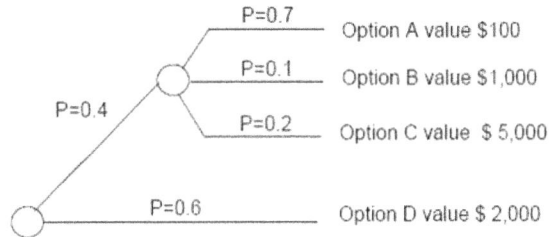

```
                                          P=0.7
                                          ───────  Option A value $100
                                   ◯      P=0.1
                           P=0.4          ───────  Option B value $1,000
                                          P=0.2
                                          ───────  Option C value $ 5,000

          ◯        P=0.6
                   ────────────────────            Option D value $ 2,000
```

41. A project manager is faced with making a decision about a risk that the team has identified. The risk involves the design of a bicycle. It has been found that the neck of the bicycle, where the steering bearing is located and the two supporting bars of the frame come together, will corrode in a high salt environment. If this takes place the neck may fail and injure the rider. The project team decides that the design of the bicycle should be modified by using corrosion resistant materials in the design of the neck. This will eliminate the risk from consideration. This technique is called:

(A) Risk acceptance.
(B) Risk avoidance.
(C) Risk deflection.
(D) Risk rejection.

42. Which of the following is not a technique for reducing or controlling risk?

(A) Avoidance
(B) Mitigation
(C) Acceptance
(D) Prevarication

43. Risk management is defined as the art and science of _____ risk factors throughout the life cycle of a project.

(A) reviewing, monitoring and managing
(B) identifying, reviewing and avoiding
(C) researching, reviewing and acting on
(D) identifying, analyzing and responding to

44. Deflection or transfer of a risk to another party is part of which of the following risk response categories?

(A) Accept
(B) Mitigate
(C) Transfer
(D) Avoid

45. A project manager wants to give some guidelines to the project team as to how risk events should be described. Which of the following items would not be appropriate in describing a risk event?

(A) The cost of the risk should it occur
(B) The client's outsourcing method
(C) Expected timing of the risk when it is expected to occur
(D) Probability that the risk will occur

46. In the path convergence example (see image), if the odds of completing activities 1, 2, and 3 on time are 40%, 50%, and 60%, what are the chances of stating activity 4 on day 4?

(A) 10%
(B) 11%
(C) 15%
(D) 12%

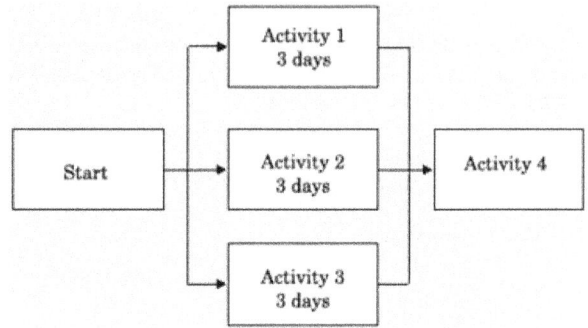

47. The inherent chances for both profit or loss associated with a particular endeavor is called:

(A) Pure risk
(B) Business risk
(C) Favorable risk
(D) Opportunity risk

48. Which of the following processes involves ensuring that risk plans are properly executed?

(A) Risk management planning
(B) Risk identification
(C) Risk response planning
(D) Risk monitoring and control

49. When there is uncertainty associated with one or more aspects of the project, one of the first steps to take is to?

(A) Conduct a risk-benefit analysis.
(B) Increase the estimated cost of the project.
(C) Conduct a needs analysis.
(D) Revise project plan.

50. The project has done its risk analysis. In the process of risk identification the project team has determined that there are risks that will probably happen that have not been identified or evaluated except by noting that other projects of this type have historically had a certain amount of risk discussed in the lessons learned of the project. This project team should set aside money to handle these risks in which financial category?

(A) Contingency budget
(B) Risk management fund
(C) Emergency fund
(D) Management reserve

51. Organizations that desire very much to avoid high-impact risks may use which of the following techniques during qualitative risk analysis? Choose the best answer.

(A) Avoidance.
(B) Data precision ranking with low precision.
(C) A probability-impact risk rating matrix using nonlinear scales.
(D) The organization would not use any techniques.

52. A project manager is dealing with risk analysis on a software development project. There is a risk that the module that creates the most important report that the system will create will not work properly and will require 200 person-hours to correct. The project manager decides to do nothing about this risk. Which of the following risk strategies is the project manager employing?

     (A) Mitigation
     (B) Deflection
     (C) Acceptance
     (D) Avoidance

53. A contingency allowance established to cover unforeseen costs on your project has been set at 8% of the total project cost. The total dollars in the contingency allowances are _____ as the project nears completion.

     (A) decreased to reduce the accounting work
     (B) increased to meet the unidentified surprises
     (C) reduced to reflect a percentage of the remaining work
     (D) spent to ensure there is no extra money shown in the budget

54. Risk management planning involves which of the following?

     (A) deciding how to approach and plan risk management activities for the project.
     (B) maximizing the probability and consequence of negative events.
     (C) measuring the probability and consequences of risks and estimating their implications on project objectives.
     (D) developing procedures and techniques to enhance opportunities and reduce threats to project objectives.

55. If the probability of event 1 is 20%, event 2 is 75%, and event 3 is 57%, and they are independent events, how likely is it that all events will occur?

     (A) 55%
     (B) 68%
     (C) 30%
     (D) 47%

56. During the project life cycle, in which part of the life cycle will risk be the lowest?

     (A) Planning
     (B) Closeout
     (C) Execution
     (D) Initiation

57. A project manager managing any project should perform risk analysis with his or her project team:

     (A) On a regular basis throughout the project.
     (B) Just before any major meeting with the client.
     (C) When preparing the project plan.
     (D) Only when justified by the awareness of new risks becoming a possibility.

58. A risk event in a project is something that can have an effect on the project:

     (A) For the better only, a positive effect.
     (B) For the worse, a negative effect.
     (C) Both better or worse, a positive or negative effect.
     (D) Neither better nor worse, neither a positive nor a negative effect.

59. Which of the following best describes project risk?

    (A) an uncertain event or condition that if occurs, has a positive or a negative effect on a project objective.
    (B) is a known unknown event.
    (C) is an unknown unknown event.
    (D) a certain event or condition with a probability and impact and when it occurs has a positive or a negative effect on a project objective.

60. The four types of risk response plans are:

    (A) Avoidance, Contingency Planning, Insurance and Mitigation
    (B) Acceptance, Mitigation, Contingency Planning, and Transfer
    (C) Avoidance, Acceptance, Mitigation and Transfer
    (D) Acceptance, Insurance, Mitigation and Transfer

61. What is a trigger in project risk management?

    (A) A warning sign that an identified risk event has occurred.
    (B) An unexpected situation causing an unidentified risk event to occur.
    (C) An unexpected situation causing an identified risk event to occur.
    (D) An expected situation causing an unidentified risk event to occur.

62. A risk event is defined as:

    (A) How likely the event is to occur.
    (B) The severity of the consequences of a loss.
    (C) A symptom of a risk.
    (D) A discrete occurrence that may affect the project for better or worse.

63. Which of the following best describes active risk acceptance?

    (A) Developing a plan to minimize probability.
    (B) Making additional resources available.
    (C) Creating contingency reserves in money and time.
    (D) Developing a plan to minimize potential impact.

64. Since risk is associated with most projects, the best course of action is to?

    (A) Eliminate all known risks prior to the execution phase of the project.
    (B) Identify various risks and implement actions to mitigate their potential impact.
    (C) Cover all project risks by buying appropriate insurance.
    (D) Ignore the risks, since nothing can be done about them and move forward with the project in an expeditious manner.

65. You are managing the construction of sophisticated data center in Florida. The data center will house more than 500 servers for one of the world's largest retailers who has decided to launch an e-business program in North America. Although this location offers significant economic advantages, the threat of hurricanes has caused you to create a backup plan to operate out of Arizona in case the center is flooded. What type of risk response is this?

    (A) Mitigation
    (B) Passive avoidance
    (C) Deflection
    (D) Active acceptance

66. The process of examining a situation and identifying and classifying areas of potential risk is known as?

    (A) Risk assessment
    (B) Risk handling
    (C) Lessons learned
    (D) Risk analysis

67. If a business venture has a 65% chance to earn $ 4 million and a 25%, chance to lose $2 million, what is the expected monetary value of the venture?

    (A) $2,100,000
    (B) $2,400,000
    (C) $1,100,000
    (D) $1,600,000

68. Which of the following processes involves determining and documenting which risks are likely to affect the project?

    (A) Risk Identification
    (B) Risk Monitoring and Control
    (C) Risk Management Planning
    (D) Risk Response Planning

69. Which of the following is not an information gathering technique for identification of risks:

    (A) Interviewing
    (B) Pareto charts
    (C) Brainstorming
    (D) Delphi

70. A project manager must make a decision about a risk in his project. He examines the extent to which the uncertainty of each of the elements of the project affects the objective being examined when all other uncertain elements are held at their baseline values. This technique is called which of the following?

    (A) Sensitivity analysis
    (B) Simulation
    (C) Decision tree analysis
    (D) Expected value analysis

71. What is the S-curve in project management?

    (A) A graph that is to be integrated to generate a normal curve.
    (B) The graph that describes the typical growth of earned value during the course of the project.
    (C) A metaphoric description of the short term uncertainties that are present in every project.
    (D) A graph that is generated if a normal curve is integrated.

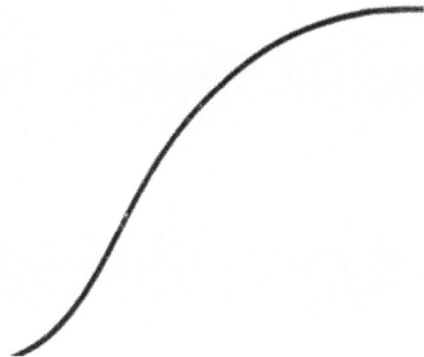

72. A project manager is reviewing the risks of her project. One of the risks she is reviewing has an impact of $25,000 and an associated probability of 10%. The risk is associated with an activity that is the predecessor to seven other activities in the schedule. All eight activities are on the critical path. The seven other activities have a budget of $75,000. What is the expected value of this risk?

    (A) $100,000
    (B) $2,500
    (C) $25,000
    (D) $10,000

73. Project risk is characterized by three factors:

    (A) identification, type of risk category and probability of impact.
    (B) severity of impact, duration of impact and cost of impact.
    (C) risk event, risk probability and the amount at stake.
    (D) occurrence, frequency and cost.

74. The project manager has critical parts that are needed for the project. If the first order of parts is delivered late, the project will be late delivering a critical deliverable to the customer. The seller that has been selected to make these parts for the project has been used in the past and historically has failed to deliver on time 10% of the time. Another vendor can be found that has the same delivery record. The project manager decides to divide the order between the two vendors in hopes that at least one of them will deliver on time. What is the probability that at least one of the vendors will deliver on time?

    (A) 1.8
    (B) 1.0
    (C) .99
    (D) .81

75. What is the Delphi technique as it relates to the risk identification process?

    (A) An information-gathering technique where experts are briefed about the project and then interviewed for their opinions.
    (B) An information-gathering technique where experts perform a Strengths, Weaknesses, Opportunities, Threats (SWOT) analysis.
    (C) An information-gathering technique where experts participate anonymously and ideas about project risk are gathered via a circulated questionnaire.
    (D) An information-gathering technique where experts meet and generate ideas about project risk.

76. There may be implied warranties associated with a contract which are not specifically detailed. These represent future costs for failure to meet the contract requirements, and are a risk to the contractor. Implied warranties are usually those associated with _____, as required in common law and legislation.

    (A) operability and durability
    (B) lawful use of the product and safety of use
    (C) regulatory agency requirements and environmental pollution
    (D) merchantability and fitness for purpose

77. One of the risks your team has discovered is a high probability that the equipment you are developing will not perform under the pressure it needs to in the workplace. In order to handle this risk, you have chosen to prototype the equipment. This is an example of risk:

(A) avoidance.
(B) mitigation.
(C) acceptance.
(D) transference.

78. A project manager discovers that there is a part of the project that contains some risk. His strategy with this risk is to subcontract the work to an outside supplier by using a firm fixed-price contract. Which of the following must the project manager do?

(A) The project manager should make every effort to make sure that the supplier is made aware of the risk after the contract is signed.
(B) The project manager should make certain that the project team does not reveal the risk to the supplier until the contract is signed.
(C) The project manager should assign a member of the project team to monitor the activity of the supplier to make sure that the supplier deals with the risk properly if it occurs.
(D) The project manager should make sure that the supplier understands the risk before the contract is signed.

79. If the probability of event 1 is 60%, event 2 is 90%, and they are independent events, how likely is it that both events will occur?

(A) 50%
(B) 54%
(C) 67%
(D) 75%

80. A project manager uses the breakeven point to justify his project. He presents this as a justification for buying a new machine. What risk does the project manager run by using this technique to justify buying a new machine for his company?

(A) Breakeven point will favor buying a cheap, low-quality machine.
(B) Breakeven point will favor buying a machine that is too expensive for the work required.
(C) The company may not have the funds to buy the machine in spite of the justification.
(D) The machine may not be available because the justification method takes a long time to calculate.

81. If the probability of event 1 is 20%, event 2 is 45%, and they are independent events, how likely is it that both events will occur?

(A) 17%
(B) 9%
(C) 32%
(D) 27%

82. What is risk event probability?

(A) The value used in mitigation and deflection.
(B) An estimate of the risk value at loss.
(C) The probability of the risk not occurring at this time.
(D) An estimate of the probability that a given risk will occur.

83. When developing a risk response plan, which risks should you focus on first? Choose the best answer.

(A) Risks with a low risk score.
(B) Easily identifiable risks.
(C) Near term risks with a high probability of occurrence.
(D) High impact risks with a low probability of occurrence.

84. Future events or outcomes that are favorable are called:

(A) Opportunities
(B) Risks
(C) Contingencies
(D) Surprises

85. Risk avoidance involves:

(A) Accepting the consequences.
(B) Developing a contingency plan.
(C) Eliminating a specific threat, usually by eliminating the cause.
(D) Reducing the effect of the risk event by reducing the probability of the occurrence.

86. Contingency planning involves which of the following?

(A) Establishing a management reserve to cover unplanned scope changes.
(B) Defining the steps to be taken if an identified risk event should occur.
(C) Determining adjustments that will be needed during the implementation phase.
(D) Preparing a separate document that will detail an alternate project plan.

87. A project manager chooses a computerized laser cutting machine to cut metal rods for his project. The process has a standard deviation of 0.005 inches. The project manager must have the rods cut 10 inches long +/-0.05 inches. What is the process capability index of this process in this situation?

(A) 2
(B) 5
(C) 3.33
(D) 0.1

88. The project manager of a large project meets several times with the client for the project. During the meeting the project manager judges that the client has a very low risk tolerance. This means that the client will probably:

(A) Understand when risks happen on the project.
(B) Not understand when risks happen on the project.
(C) Be willing to take large risks to make large profits.
(D) Be unwilling to take large risks to make large profits.

89. A project manager is doing risk analysis with the project team members. They are concerned about evaluating the risks in such a way that the risks will be ranked according to their severity in relation to the project. What method should be used to rank the risks in the order of importance?

(A) Determine the cost of the impact
(B) Determine the expected value
(C) Use subjective analysis
(D) Determine the probability

90. To achieve an unbiased risk analysis:

(A) the project sponsor should do the final iteration of risk identification process.
(B) the project manager should do the final iteration of risk identification process.
(C) the entire project team and stake holders should do the final iteration of risk identification process.
(D) a subject matter experts (SME) who are not involved in the project should do the final iteration of risk identification process.

91. You have just been assigned a project manager on a highly risky project and have decided to use a contractor to perform a high-risk task. What form of risk response have you opted for?

(A) Assumption
(B) Insurance
(C) Mediation
(D) Transference

92. If a business venture has a 75% chance to earn $ 3 million and a 25%, chance to lose $1 million, what is the expected monetary value of the venture?

(A) $1,000,000
(B) $2,000,000
(C) $250,000
(D) $750,000

93. A project manager states, "I know the risk exists and am aware of the possible consequences. I am willing to wait and see what happens. I accept the consequences should they occur." He or she is exercising the _____ method of risk control.

(A) Mitigation
(B) Acceptance
(C) Transference
(D) Avoidance

94. Bankruptcy of a major supplier was initially judged to be a low probability risk and no risk containment strategy was planned. The supplier did, in fact, go bankrupt. The team must now re-examine their risk plan. Which of the following tool and techniques are most relevant?

(A) Technical performance measurement.
(B) Variance and trend analysis.
(C) Risk reassessment.
(D) Risk audits.

95. As the project manager, you have the option of proposing one of three computer systems to a client: a full feature system that satisfies the minimum requirements but also offers numerous special functions (computer option 1); a system that meets the client's minimum requirements (computer option 3); and a system that satisfies the minimum requirements plus has a few extra features (computer option 2). The on-time records and associated profits and losses are depicted on the decision tree (see image). What is the expected monetary value of computer option 2?

    (A) $20,000
    (B) $35,000
    (C) $3,000
    (D) $17,000

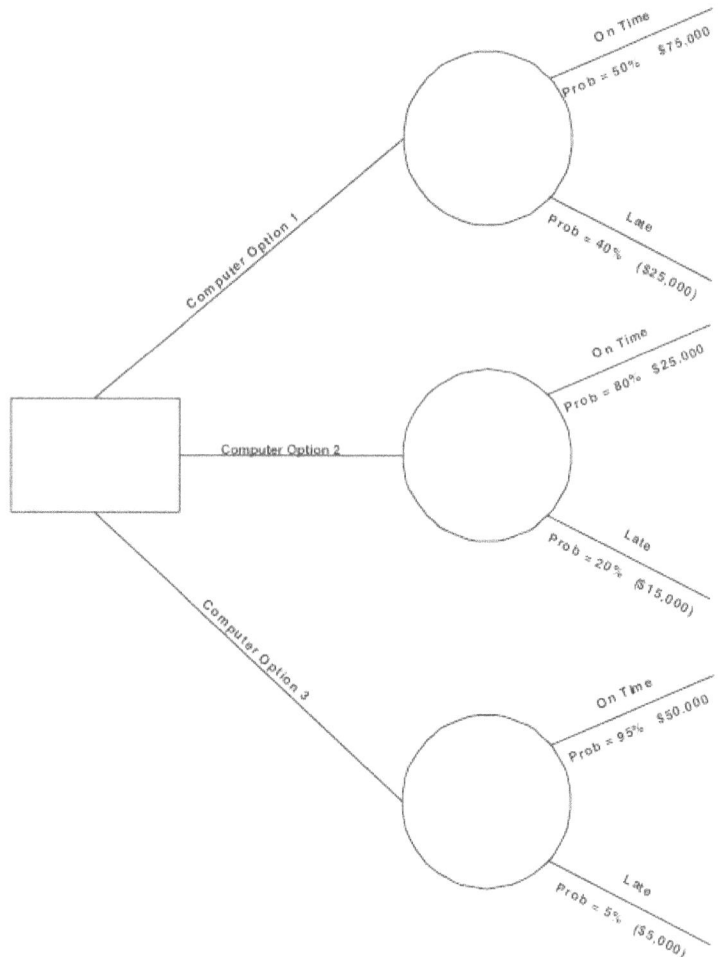

Computer Option 1
- On Time — Prob = 50% — $75,000
- Late — Prob = 40% — ($25,000)

Computer Option 2
- On Time — Prob = 80% — $25,000
- Late — Prob = 20% — ($15,000)

Computer Option 3
- On Time — Prob = 95% — $50,000
- Late — Prob = 5% — ($5,000)

96. The project manager of a project evaluates the risks of the project by assessing the probability of the risk by categorizing the risks as likely or not likely and assesses their impact as high impact, medium impact, or low impact. This would be which type of risk assessment?

    (A) Qualitative
    (B) Quantitative
    (C) Characteristic
    (D) General

97. A project of $1.5 million has an adverse event that has a probability of 0.07 of occurring and a potential loss of $15,000. This represents an expected negative monetary value of how much?

    (A) $100,500
    (B) $105
    (C) $1,050
    (D) $15,000

98. The contingency budget will:

    (A) Reduce the probability of scope changes.
    (B) Reduce the probability of cost overruns.
    (C) Increase the probability of a cost overrun.
    (D) Increase the probability of scope changes.

99. A project team evaluates risk in the project. As an outcome there are some positive and negative risks that are identified and evaluated. To evaluate the worst case for the project the project team should evaluate and summarize:

   (A) Only the negative risks.
   (B) The positive risks minus the negative risks.
   (C) The negative risks minus the positive risks.
   (D) All of the risks affecting the project.

100. You are driving across town and estimate that it will most likely take 1 hour. On further thought, you estimate that the trip could take as little as 45 minutes, best case, or as long as 1 hour and 45 minutes, worst case. What is the standard deviation?

   (A) 10 minutes
   (B) 15 minutes
   (C) 20 minutes
   (D) 30 minutes

Sample Answer Sheet

	T F		T F		T F		T F
1	(A) (B) (C) (D) (E)	26	(A) (B) (C) (D) (E)	51	(A) (B) (C) (D) (E)	76	(A) (B) (C) (D) (E)
2	(A) (B) (C) (D) (E)	27	(A) (B) (C) (D) (E)	52	(A) (B) (C) (D) (E)	77	(A) (B) (C) (D) (E)
3	(A) (B) (C) (D) (E)	28	(A) (B) (C) (D) (E)	53	(A) (B) (C) (D) (E)	78	(A) (B) (C) (D) (E)
4	(A) (B) (C) (D) (E)	29	(A) (B) (C) (D) (E)	54	(A) (B) (C) (D) (E)	79	(A) (B) (C) (D) (E)
5	(A) (B) (C) (D) (E)	30	(A) (B) (C) (D) (E)	55	(A) (B) (C) (D) (E)	80	(A) (B) (C) (D) (E)
6	(A) (B) (C) (D) (E)	31	(A) (B) (C) (D) (E)	56	(A) (B) (C) (D) (E)	81	(A) (B) (C) (D) (E)
7	(A) (B) (C) (D) (E)	32	(A) (B) (C) (D) (E)	57	(A) (B) (C) (D) (E)	82	(A) (B) (C) (D) (E)
8	(A) (B) (C) (D) (E)	33	(A) (B) (C) (D) (E)	58	(A) (B) (C) (D) (E)	83	(A) (B) (C) (D) (E)
9	(A) (B) (C) (D) (E)	34	(A) (B) (C) (D) (E)	59	(A) (B) (C) (D) (E)	84	(A) (B) (C) (D) (E)
10	(A) (B) (C) (D) (E)	35	(A) (B) (C) (D) (E)	60	(A) (B) (C) (D) (E)	85	(A) (B) (C) (D) (E)
11	(A) (B) (C) (D) (E)	36	(A) (B) (C) (D) (E)	61	(A) (B) (C) (D) (E)	86	(A) (B) (C) (D) (E)
12	(A) (B) (C) (D) (E)	37	(A) (B) (C) (D) (E)	62	(A) (B) (C) (D) (E)	87	(A) (B) (C) (D) (E)
13	(A) (B) (C) (D) (E)	38	(A) (B) (C) (D) (E)	63	(A) (B) (C) (D) (E)	88	(A) (B) (C) (D) (E)
14	(A) (B) (C) (D) (E)	39	(A) (B) (C) (D) (E)	64	(A) (B) (C) (D) (E)	89	(A) (B) (C) (D) (E)
15	(A) (B) (C) (D) (E)	40	(A) (B) (C) (D) (E)	65	(A) (B) (C) (D) (E)	90	(A) (B) (C) (D) (E)
16	(A) (B) (C) (D) (E)	41	(A) (B) (C) (D) (E)	66	(A) (B) (C) (D) (E)	91	(A) (B) (C) (D) (E)
17	(A) (B) (C) (D) (E)	42	(A) (B) (C) (D) (E)	67	(A) (B) (C) (D) (E)	92	(A) (B) (C) (D) (E)
18	(A) (B) (C) (D) (E)	43	(A) (B) (C) (D) (E)	68	(A) (B) (C) (D) (E)	93	(A) (B) (C) (D) (E)
19	(A) (B) (C) (D) (E)	44	(A) (B) (C) (D) (E)	69	(A) (B) (C) (D) (E)	94	(A) (B) (C) (D) (E)
20	(A) (B) (C) (D) (E)	45	(A) (B) (C) (D) (E)	70	(A) (B) (C) (D) (E)	95	(A) (B) (C) (D) (E)
21	(A) (B) (C) (D) (E)	46	(A) (B) (C) (D) (E)	71	(A) (B) (C) (D) (E)	96	(A) (B) (C) (D) (E)
22	(A) (B) (C) (D) (E)	47	(A) (B) (C) (D) (E)	72	(A) (B) (C) (D) (E)	97	(A) (B) (C) (D) (E)
23	(A) (B) (C) (D) (E)	48	(A) (B) (C) (D) (E)	73	(A) (B) (C) (D) (E)	98	(A) (B) (C) (D) (E)
24	(A) (B) (C) (D) (E)	49	(A) (B) (C) (D) (E)	74	(A) (B) (C) (D) (E)	99	(A) (B) (C) (D) (E)
25	(A) (B) (C) (D) (E)	50	(A) (B) (C) (D) (E)	75	(A) (B) (C) (D) (E)	100	(A) (B) (C) (D) (E)

Project Risk Management - Answers

1. (C) Buffering. A buffered schedule is one where float is deliberately created in the schedule. Buffers are deliberately created between tasks on the critical path, and the activities are rescheduled to more closely approximate the schedule to the new promise date.

2. (A) buying insurance for personal bodily injury. Risk transference requires shifting the negative impact of a threat, along with ownership of the response, to a third party. Transferring the risk simply gives another party responsibility for its management; it does not eliminate it. Transferring liability for risk is most effective in dealing with financial risk exposure. Risk transference nearly always involves payment of a risk premium to the party taking on the risk. Transference tools can be quite diverse and include, but are not limited to, the use of insurance, performance bonds, warranties, guarantees, etc. Contracts may be used to transfer liability for specified risks to another party.

3. (A) The percent of time a given activity will be on the critical path. The Monte Carlo technique allows for shifts that may occur in the critical path during possible values of the durations of the activities of the project. It is a simulation technique that produces a value called the criticality index, which is the percent of simulations that a particular activity is on the critical path. That is, criticality index is the percent of the number of simulations that an activity is on the critical path.

4. (C) Avoidance. Avoidance. Risk avoidance involves changing the project management plan to eliminate the threat posed by an adverse risk, to isolate the project objectives from the risk's impact, or to relax the objective that is in jeopardy, such as extending the schedule or reducing scope. Some risks that arise early in the project can be avoided by clarifying requirements, obtaining information, improving communication, or acquiring expertise.

5. (C) An ordinal scale. Risk probability assessment may be difficult because of dependence on expert judgment. It should be noted that risk impact assessment can be done using ordinal scales (very high to very low) or cardinal scales (either linear or non-linear). Risk rating matrix can be prepared by combining the probability and impact scales. Risks with high probability and high impact require either further analysis by quantification or aggressive risk management.

6. (D) The project team decides not to change the project plan to deal with a risk or is unable to identify any other suitable response strategy. Acceptance: A strategy that is adopted because it is seldom possible to eliminate all risk from a project. This strategy indicates that the project team has decided not to change the project management plan to deal with a risk, or is unable to identify any other suitable response strategy. It may be adopted for either threats or opportunities. This strategy can be either passive or active. Passive acceptance requires no action, leaving the project team to deal with the threats or opportunities as they occur. The most common active acceptance strategy is to establish a contingency reserve, including amounts of time, money, or resources to handle known—or even sometimes potential, unknown—threats or opportunities.

7. (D) Mitigation. Risk mitigation implies a reduction in the probability and/or impact of an adverse risk event to an acceptable threshold. Taking early action to reduce the probability and/or impact of a risk occurring on the project is often more effective than trying to repair the damage after the risk has occurred.

8. (C) address. Contingency Planning - The development of a management plan that identifies alternative strategies to be used to ensure project success if specified risk events occur.

9. (D) Risk mitigation. Risk Mitigation is a risk response planning technique associated with threats that seeks to reduce the probability of occurrence or impact of a risk to below an acceptable threshold.

10. (B) $27,500. EMV = ($75,000 X 50%) + (-$25,000 X 40%) = $37,500 + (-$10,000) = $27,500

11. (C) Add buffer to the critical chains. In critical chain theory the feeder chains are activities that are not on the critical path. These tasks are scheduled to be done as late as possible and then buffered so that they start earlier than the late schedule dates. Buffer is also added to the critical path of the schedule to improve the probability that the project will finish on time. Feeder chain activities as well as critical chain activities are not started as early as possible or as late as possible. They are started as late as possible minus their buffer.

12. (B) project manager's ability to influence the risk. Internal risks are those items that the project team can directly control (e.g., staffing), and external risks are those events that happen outside the direct influence of the project team.

13. (B) Risk register. The primary outputs from Risk Identification are the initial entries into the risk register, which becomes a component of the project management plan. The risk register ultimately contains the outcomes of the other risk management processes as they are conducted.

14. (B) Workarounds are unplanned responses to risks that were previously unidentified or accepted. According to PMI, workarounds are responses that were not initially planned, but are required to deal with emerging risks that were previously unidentified or accepted passively.

15. (A) maximizing the probability and consequence of positive events. Project Risk Management includes the processes concerned with conducting risk management planning, identification, analysis, responses, and monitoring and control on a project; most of these processes are updated throughout the project. The objectives of Project Risk Management are to increase the probability and impact of positive events, and decrease the probability and impact of events adverse to the project.

16. (C) Avoidance.
Risk avoidance involves changing the project management plan to eliminate the threat posed by an adverse risk, to isolate the project objectives from the risk's impact, or to relax the objective that is in jeopardy, such as extending the schedule or reducing scope. Some risks that arise early in the project can be avoided by clarifying requirements, obtaining information, improving communication, or acquiring expertise.

17. (C) Money to offset missing cost or schedule objectives. The management reserve is time and money used to offset the effect of unknown risks affecting cost and schedule. These risks can only be approximated since none of them are specifically identified. PMI refers to these risks as the known-unknown risks and the identified risks as the known-known risks.

18. (D) Purchasing insurance. Risk mitigation implies a reduction in the probability and/or impact of an adverse risk event to an acceptable threshold. Taking early action to reduce the probability and/or impact of a risk occurring on the project is often more effective than trying to repair the damage after the risk has occurred. Adopting less complex processes, conducting more tests, or choosing a more stable supplier are examples of mitigation actions. Mitigation may require prototype development to reduce the risk of scaling up from a bench-scale model of a process or product. Where it is not possible to reduce probability, a mitigation response might address the risk impact by targeting linkages that determine the severity. For example, designing redundancy into a subsystem may reduce the impact from a failure of the original component.

19. (B) 3. Process SD = 6 units; Sample size = 3 units; Sample SD = Process SD / (Sample size – 1) = 6/(3-1) = 3

20. (C) $27,500. EMV = ($75,000 X 50%) + (-$25,000 X 40%) = $37,500 + (-$10,000) $27,500

21. (A) Increase risk. Fast tracking is changing the project plan to schedule activities that were planned to be done in sequence so that they can be done completely or partially in parallel. This will increase risk, because more work will be done if a problem is discovered.

22. (C) Transference. Risk transference requires shifting the negative impact of a threat, along with ownership of the response, to a third party. Transferring the risk simply gives another party responsibility for its management; it does not eliminate it. Transferring liability for risk is most effective in dealing with financial risk exposure. Risk transference nearly always involves payment of a risk premium to the party taking on the risk. Transference tools can be quite diverse and include, but are not limited to, the use of insurance, performance bonds, warranties, guarantees, etc. Contracts may be used to transfer liability for specified risks to another party. In many cases, use of a cost-type contract may transfer the cost risk to the buyer, while a fixed-price contract may transfer risk to the seller, if the project's design is stable.

23. (C) A list of potential risk events. The result of the first risk meeting of a project team is to identify as many risks as possible in the time allowed.

24. (A) Uncertainty and damage. Project risk management is the systematic process of identifying, analyzing, and responding to project risk. It includes maximizing the probability and consequences of positive events and minimizing the probability and consequences of adverse events to project objectives.

25. (B) detriment. Risk Event - A discrete occurrence that may affect the project for better or worse.

26. (A) Risks. Risk. An uncertain event or condition that, if it occurs, has a positive or negative effect on a project's objectives.

27. (A) Triggers. Triggers - indications that a risk has occurred or is about to occur. Triggers may be discovered in the risk identification process and watched in the risk monitoring and control process. Triggers are sometimes called risk symptoms or warning signs.

28. (C) Lessons learned from other similar projects. The lessons learned document from other similar projects can be a great help in determining the new risks associated with this project. Many times risks repeat themselves from one project to another. This makes the lessons learned document very important for all projects.

29. (A) The basis for most schedule simulations. Monte Carlo Analysis - A technique that performs a project simulation many times to calculate a distribution of likely results.

30. (A) mitigation. Risk mitigation implies a reduction in the probability and/or impact of an adverse risk event to an acceptable threshold. Taking early action to reduce the probability and/or impact of a risk occurring on the project is often more effective than trying to repair the damage after the risk has occurred. Adopting less complex processes, conducting more tests, or choosing a more stable supplier are examples of mitigation actions. Mitigation may require prototype development to reduce the risk of scaling up from a bench-scale model of a process or product. Where it is not possible to reduce probability, a mitigation response might address the risk impact by targeting linkages that determine the severity.

31. (D) Statistical independence. Statistical Independence - the concept of statistical independence is a necessary condition for the use of tools such as expected value and decision-tree analysis. A practical definition of statistical independence is that two events are said to be independent if the occurrence of one is not related to the occurrence of the other. If events are occurring at random, they are independent; if events are not occurring at random, they are not independent. A set or group of possible events are said to be mutually exclusive and collectively exhaustive if they are all independent, and the sum of their probabilities of occurrence is 1.0. This is the basic notion behind expected value.

32. (C) Acceptance. Acceptance: A strategy that is adopted because it is seldom possible to eliminate all risk from a project. This strategy indicates that the project team has decided not to change the project management plan to deal with a risk, or is unable to identify any other suitable response strategy. It may be adopted for either threats or opportunities. This strategy can be either passive or active. Passive acceptance requires no action, leaving the project team to deal with the threats or opportunities as they occur. The most common active acceptance strategy is to establish a contingency reserve, including amounts of time, money, or resources to handle known—or even sometimes potential, unknown—threats or opportunities.

33. (C) Contingency reserve. Contingency Reserve - the amount of funds, budget, or time needed above the estimate to reduce the risk of overruns of project objectives to a level acceptable to the organization.

34. (D) Beta and triangular distributions. (PMBOK Guide - page 256)

35. (A) 11/36. This is a matter of applying the probability rule of addition. This rule says that the probability of either one of two events is equal to the probability of one event plus the probability of the second event minus the probability of both of the events occurring.

P(6 or 6) = P(6) + P(6) - P(6 and 6)
P(6 and 6) = P(6) X P(6)
P(6 and 6) = 1/6 X 1/6 = 1/36
P(6 or 6) = 1/6 + 1/6 - 1/36 = 11/36

36. (A) 12%. Probability (starting activity 4 on day 5) = .4 X .5 X .5 = .12 or 12%

37. (A) 50%. In the normal probability distribution or any symmetric probability distribution, the most likely value of the distribution is the peak of the distribution curve. This is the value that has the highest probability of occurring. In a symmetric probability distribution this will be the center of the curve as well. There is a 50% probability that the project will finish past the most likely date and a 50% chance that the project will finish earlier than that date.

38. (B) Risk identification. Risk Identification. The process of determining which risks might affect the project and documenting their characteristics.

39. (A) 13. Probability (starting activity 4 on day 5) = .5 X .5 X .5 = .125 or 13%

40. (C) Option D.
Option A Expected value of Opportunity = (.4)(.7)($100) = $28.
Option B Expected value of Opportunity = (.4)(.1)($1000) = $40.
Option C Expected value of Opportunity = (.4)(.2)($5000) = $400.
Option D Expected value of Opportunity = (.6)($2000) = $1200.

41. (B) Risk avoidance. Risk Avoidance is a risk response planning technique for a threat that creates changes to the project management plan that are meant to either eliminate the risk or to protect the project objectives from its impact. Generally, risk avoidance involves relaxing the time, cost, scope, or quality objectives.

42. (D) Prevarication. Three strategies typically deal with threats or risks that may have negative impacts on project objectives if they occur. These strategies are to avoid, transfer, or mitigate.

43. (D) identifying, analyzing and responding to. Risk Management includes the processes concerned with conducting risk management planning, identification, analysis, responses, and monitoring and control on a project. The objectives of Risk Management are to increase the probability and impact of positive events and decrease the probability and impact of events adverse to project objectives.

44. (C) Transfer. Risk transference requires shifting the negative impact of a threat, along with ownership of the response, to a third party. Transferring the risk simply gives another party responsibility for its management; it does not eliminate it. Transferring liability for risk is most effective in dealing with financial risk exposure. Risk transference nearly always involves payment of a risk premium to the party taking on the risk. Transference tools can be quite diverse and include, but are not limited to, the use of insurance, performance bonds, warranties, guarantees, etc. Contracts may be used to transfer liability for specified risks to another party. In many cases, use of a cost-type contract may transfer the cost risk to the buyer, while a fixed-price contract may transfer risk to the seller, if the project's design is stable.

45. (B) The client's outsourcing method. The client's outsourcing method has nothing to do with risk management; all the other choices are items that should be included in the risk description.

46. (D) 12%. Probability (starting activity 4 on day 5) = .4 X .5 X .5 = .12 or 12%

47. (B) Business risk. Know the difference between a pure and a business risk. Using the analogy of an auto accident, the risk for you, as the driver, is generally a pure risk; you only have the opportunity for loss. However, the risk for your insurance company is a business risk. It is part of that company's opportunity for gain or loss whenever they do business.
48. (D) Risk monitoring and control. Risk Monitoring and Control is the process where risks are monitored and any new risks are identified. Furthermore, this process involves ensuring that risk plans are properly executed.

49. (A) Conduct a risk-benefit analysis. Conduct a risk benefit analysis, because the first thing you want to do is understand the nature of the risk. How you respond this analysis may result in any of the other three actions.

50. (D) Management reserve. Management reserve is funds set aside to manage unidentified risks. PMI refers to these as the "unknown unknowns." When the management reserve is used, it is moved from the management reserve to the cost or schedule baseline.

51. (C) A probability-impact risk rating matrix using nonlinear scales. A nonlinear scale can provide a greater risk score for risks with high impacts and probabilities. This allows the organization with high-impact risk aversion to better rank and focus on these risks. The use of data with low precision as suggested may lead to qualitative risk analysis of little use to the project manager.

52. (C) Acceptance. Risk acceptance is doing nothing about the risk until it happens. This is done with risks that are below the risk tolerance level.

53. (C) reduced to reflect a percentage of the remaining work. Reserve. A provision in the project management plan to mitigate cost and/or schedule risk. Often used with a modifier (e.g., management reserve, contingency reserve) to provide further detail on what types of risk are meant to be mitigated. The specific meaning of the modified term varies by application area.

54. (A) deciding how to approach and plan risk management activities for the project. Risk Management Planning is the process of deciding how to approach, plan, and execute risk management activities for a project.

55. (C) 30%. The likelihood is determined by multiplying the probability of event 1 by the probability of event 2 and the probability of event 3. .50 X .75 X .80 = .30 or 30%

56. (B) Closeout. During project closeout much of the project work has been completed and many of the risks have passed the time in which they can occur. The total risk of the project is therefore lowest during closeout.

57. (A) On a regular basis throughout the project. Risk analysis should be done frequently throughout the project.

58. (C) Both better or worse, a positive or negative effect. Risks are events that affect a project for better or worse. Positive risks increase the positive cash flow or benefits to the project, and negative risks increase the negative cash flow or effects of the project.

59. (A) an uncertain event or condition that if occurs, has a positive or a negative effect on a project objective. Project risk is an uncertain event or condition that, if it occurs, has a positive or a negative effect on at least one project objective, such as time, cost, scope, or quality (i.e., where the project time objective is to deliver in accordance with the agreed-upon schedule; where the project cost objective is to deliver within the agreed-upon cost; etc.).

60. (C) Avoidance, Acceptance, Mitigation and Transfer. The four types of risk responses are 1) Avoidance (change the plan to eliminate the risk), 2) Transference (shift the consequences to a third party), 3) Mitigation (reduce the probability and/or consequences to an acceptable threshold, and 4) Acceptance (acknowledge the risk but take no specific action at this time).

61. (A) A warning sign that an identified risk event has occurred. Triggers. Indications that a risk has occurred or is about to occur. Triggers may be discovered in the risk identification process and watched in the risk monitoring and control process. Triggers are sometimes called risk symptoms or warning signs.

62. (D) A discrete occurrence that may affect the project for better or worse. Risk Event - a discrete occurrence that may affect the project for better or worse.

63. (C) Creating contingency reserves in money and time. Risk Acceptance. A risk response planning technique that indicates that the project team has decided not to change the project management plan to deal with a risk, or is unable to identify any other suitable response strategy.

64. (B) Identify various risks and implement actions to mitigate their potential impact.

65. (D) Active acceptance. Acceptance means accepting the consequences of a risk. Acceptance can be active, such as developing a contingency plan to execute should the risk occur, or passive, such as accepting a lower profit should some activities overrun.

66. (A) Risk assessment. Risk Acceptance. A risk response planning technique that indicates that the project team has decided not to change the project management plan to deal with a risk, or is unable to identify any other suitable response strategy.

67. (A) $2,100,000. EMV = (4,000,000 X 65%) + (-$2,000,000 X 25%) $2,600,000 + (-$500,000) = $2,100,000

68. (A) Risk Identification. Risk Identification determines which risks might affect the project and documents their characteristics. Participants in risk identification activities can include the following, where appropriate: project manager, project team members, risk management team (if assigned), subject matter experts from outside the project team, customers, end users, other project managers, stakeholders, and risk management experts. While these personnel are often key participants for risk identification, all project personnel should be encouraged to identify risks.

69. (B) Pareto charts. Examples of information gathering techniques used in identifying risk can include: brainstorming, Delphi technique, interviewing, root cause identification and SWOT analysis.

70. (A) Sensitivity analysis. Sensitivity Analysis is a quantitative risk analysis and modeling technique used to help determine which risks have the most potential impact on the project. It examines the extent to which the uncertainty of each project element affects the objective being examined when all other uncertain elements are held at their baseline values. The typical display of results is in the form of a tornado diagram.

71. (B) The graph that describes the typical growth of earned value during the course of the project. A graphic display of cumulative costs, labor hours, percentage of work, plotted against time. The name derives from the S-like curve of a project that starts slowly, accelerates, then tails off. Also a term for the cumulative likelihood distribution that is a result of simulation.

72. (B) $2,500. The expected value is found by multiplying the probability of the risk by the cost of the impact of the risk should it occur. EV = 25,000 X 10%

73. (C) risk event, risk probability and the amount at stake. Project risk is an uncertain event or condition that, if it occurs, has a positive or a negative effect on at least one project objective, such as time, cost, scope, or quality (i.e., where the project time objective is to deliver in accordance with the agreed-upon schedule; where the project cost objective is to deliver within the agreed-upon cost; etc.).

74. (C) .99. The probability is that at least one of the sellers will deliver the parts on time. This is the same as saying either vendor A or B must deliver. This is the addition rule in probability. The probability that the first seller will deliver is .9. The probability that the second seller will deliver is also .9, but the second seller delivering on time is only of consequence if the first seller fails to deliver on time, or .1. The calculation is then .9 + (.1 X .9) = .99.

75. (C) An information-gathering technique where experts participate anonymously and ideas about project risk are gathered via a circulated questionnaire. Delphi Technique - an information gathering technique used as a way to reach a consensus of experts on a subject. Experts on the subject participate in this technique anonymously. A facilitator uses a questionnaire to solicit ideas about the important project points related to the subject. The responses are summarized and are then recirculated to the experts for further comment. Consensus may be reached in a few rounds of this process. The Delphi technique helps reduce bias in the data and keeps any one person from having undue influence on the outcome.

76. (D) merchantability and fitness for purpose. Implied warranties are created by state law, and all states have them. Almost every purchase you make is covered by an implied warranty. The most common type of implied warranty—a "warranty of merchantability," means that the seller promises that the product will do what it is supposed to do. For example, a car will run and a toaster will toast. Another type of implied warranty is the "warranty of fitness for a particular purpose." This applies when you buy a product on the seller's advice that it is suitable for a particular use. For example, a person who suggests that you buy a certain sleeping bag for zero-degree weather warrants that the sleeping bag will be suitable for zero degrees.

77. (B) Mitigation. Risk mitigation implies a reduction in the probability and/or impact of an adverse risk event to an acceptable threshold. Taking early action to reduce the probability and/or impact of a risk occurring on the project is often more effective than trying to repair the damage after the risk has occurred. Adopting less complex processes, conducting more tests, or choosing a more stable supplier are examples of mitigation actions. Mitigation may require prototype development to reduce the risk of scaling up from a bench-scale model of a process or product. Where it is not possible to reduce probability, a mitigation response might address the risk impact by targeting linkages that determine the severity.

78. (D) The project manager should make sure that the supplier understands the risk before the contract is signed. In a fixed-price contract the supplier is obligated to deliver the contracted-for item at a fixed price. The supplier is aware of the risk and will put an allowance for the risk in the contracted price. This often means that the project team will pay the supplier for the cost of the risk regardless of whether the risk occurs.

79. (B) 54%. The likelihood is determined by multiplying the probability of event 1 by the probability of event 2. .60 X .90 = .54 or 54%

80. (A) Breakeven point will favor buying a cheap, low-quality machine. The breakeven-point justification technique predicts a point in time where the benefits offset the costs involved. It is a simple justification technique that takes into consideration a lot of assumptions. Since it predicts the point in time where the benefits exceed the cost, given the choice of an expensive and a cheap machine, the cheap machine will usually have high short-term benefits, and the expensive machine will have higher long-term benefits.

81. (B) 9%. The likelihood is determined by multiplying the probability of event 1 by the probability of event 2. .20 X .45 = .09 or 9%

82. (D) An estimate of the probability that a given risk will occur. Risk event probability—an estimate of the probability that a given risk event will occur.

83. (C) Near term risks with a high probability of occurrence. Risk Response Planning – developing options and actions to enhance opportunities, and to reduce threats to project objectives.

84. (A) Opportunities. Opportunity. A condition or situation favorable to the project, a positive set of circumstances, a positive set of events, a risk that will have a positive impact on project objectives, or a possibility for positive changes.

85. (C) Eliminating a specific threat, usually by eliminating the cause. Risk avoidance involves changing the project management plan to eliminate the threat posed by an adverse risk, to isolate the project objectives from the risk's impact, or to relax the objective that is in jeopardy, such as extending the schedule or reducing scope. Some risks that arise early in the project can be avoided by clarifying requirements, obtaining information, improving communication, or acquiring expertise.

86. (B) Defining the steps to be taken if an identified risk event should occur. Contingency plans are developed as a result of a risk being identified. Contingency plans are predefined action plans that can be implemented if identified risks actually occur. If a risk event actually occurs, the contingency plan may need to be implemented and contingency reserves allocated, depending on the risk's impact.

87. (C) 3.33. Process capability Index (Cp) = (USL – LSL)/6 sigma; Cp = (10+0.05) – (10-0.05)/6 x (0.005) = 0.1/0.03 = 3.33

88. (D) Be unwilling to take large risks to make large profits. Risk tolerance is the measure of the client's likelihood to take risks. A client with a low risk tolerance will not be willing to take very many or large risks even though they may produce considerable opportunities to make large profits.

89. (B) Determine the expected value. The expected value of the risk is the probability of the risk multiplied by its cost. This is one method of ranking risks. Risks can also be ranked qualitatively by assigning them qualitative values like ''very risky'' and ''not too risky'' and ranking them in groups.

90. (D) a subject matter experts (SME) who are not involved in the project should do the final iteration of risk identification process. Risk Analysis - A technique designed to quantify the impact of uncertainty. Usually, but not necessarily, associated with the Monte Carlo Simulation.

91. (D) Transference. Risk transference requires shifting the negative impact of a threat, along with ownership of the response, to a third party. Transferring the risk simply gives another party responsibility for its management; it does not eliminate it. Transferring liability for risk is most effective in dealing with financial risk exposure. Risk transference nearly always involves payment of a risk premium to the party taking on the risk. Transference tools can be quite diverse and include, but are not limited to, the use of insurance, performance bonds, warranties, guarantees, etc. Contracts may be used to transfer liability for specified risks to another party. In many cases, use of a cost-type contract may transfer the cost risk to the buyer, while a fixed-price contract may transfer risk to the seller, if the project's design is stable.

92. (B) $2,000,000. EMV = (3,000,000 X 75%) + (-$1,000,000 X 25%) = $2,250,000 + (-$250,000) = $2,000,000

93. (B) Acceptance. Acceptance: A strategy that is adopted because it is seldom possible to eliminate all risk from a project. This strategy indicates that the project team has decided not to change the project management plan to deal with a risk, or is unable to identify any other suitable response strategy. It may be adopted for either threats or opportunities. This strategy can be either passive or active. Passive acceptance requires no action, leaving the project team to deal with the threats or opportunities as they occur. The most common active acceptance strategy is to establish a contingency reserve, including amounts of time, money, or resources to handle known—or even sometimes potential, unknown—threats or opportunities.

94. (C) Risk reassessment. If a risk emerges that was not anticipated in the risk register … the planned response may not be adequate. It will then be necessary to perform additional response planning to control the risk."

95. (D) $17,000. EMV = ($25,000 X 80%) + (-$15,000 X 20%) = $20,000 + (-$3,000) = $17,000

96. (A) Qualitative. Qualitative assessment of risks is often appropriate. When there is little impact from a risk or when little is known about the risk parameters it may only be practical to evaluate risks in a qualitative way.

97. (C) $1,050. $15,000 x .07 = $1,050

98. (B) Reduce the probability of cost overruns. Including a contingency budget will set aside money for known, identified risks. This will give more control to the project and reduce the problem of known risks using budget that was set aside for the work of the project and causing a cost overrun in the project.

99. (A) Only the negative risks. In determining the worst-case situation, all of the negative risks are included and none of the positive risks are included in the total. This makes the assumption of the worst case as being that all of the bad things happen and none of the good things happen.

100. (A) 10 minutes. SD = b - a / 6 = 105 min - 45 / 6 = 60 / 6 = 10 minutes

Project Procurement Management

The Project Procurement Management questions on the PMP® exam tend to be more process oriented than legally focused. The exam requires you to know the differences between the two categories of contracts (fixed-price and cost-reimbursement) and the risks inherent in each category for both the buyer and seller. Several questions will also test your knowledge of the various types of contracts within each category.

The processes in the Project Procurement Management knowledge area are as follows: Plan Purchases and Acquisitions, Plan Contracting, Request Seller Responses, Select Sellers, Contract Administration, and Contract Closure.

Project procurement management is the process required to acquire the goods and services necessary to attain project scope. Goods and services typically are referred to as a product and are obtained from outside the performing organization.

PMI® discusses Project Procurement Management from the perspective of the buyer in the buyer-seller relationship but notes that the buyer-seller relationship can exist at many levels on one project. On the exam the seller may be called a subcontractor, vendor, or supplier. The seller generally manages work as a project in and of itself. The buyer may also be referred to as the customer. The terms and conditions of the contract are a major input to the seller's processes. The terms and conditions may actually contain the input as it may describe key milestones, deliverables, or objectives, or they may serve as a constraint since they may limit the project team's options (for example, requiring buyer approval of staffing decisions or staffing changes).

PMI® further discusses project procurement management from the perspective of the seller being external to the organization but notes that the discussion is also applicable to formal agreements entered into with other units in the performing organization. If informal agreements are used, then processes in Human Resource Management and Communications Management are more likely to apply. Apply extra caution when answering questions in this area: make sure you know whom the question refers to when you see the words buyer and seller. In most cases, the buyer is the project manager.

Procurement planning is the process in which the project manager identifies those needs of the project that can be met by purchasing products or services from outside the organization. Procurement planning deals with the following:

- What to procure
- When to procure
- How to procure
- How much to procure

It is very uncommon for an organization to be able to create or supply all the products necessary to complete a project internally. In those circumstances where it is necessary to go outside the organization, the response is to purchase the product or service from an external source or enter into a contract with an outside vendor to perform a service or develop the product for the organization. Whatever choice is made, there is definitely a considerable amount of forethought and planning that needs to go into such a decision.

Project Procurement Management - Questions

1. Debbie is the project manager for a large company project. She has created a Statement of Work (SOW) for a vendor. For Mary's SOW to be a legal contract, what must be included?

(A) Signatures of both parties agreeing to SOW
(B) Affidavit of agreement
(C) Signature of Mary
(D) Signature of vendor

2. Payment bonds are often required by the contract and require specific actions under the stated conditions. Payment bonds are specifically designed to ensure payment of _____ by the prime contractor.

    (A) Insurance premiums.
    (B) Subcontractors, laborers, and materials.
    (C) Damages for accidents caused.
    (D) Incremental earned value charges.

3. In what process group does source selection happen?

    (A) Initiating
    (B) Planning
    (C) Executing
    (D) Closing

4. Because you are working under a firm-fixed-price contract, management wants you to submit the final invoice and close out the contract as soon as possible. Before final payment on the contract can be authorized, you must:

    (A) Audit the procurement process.
    (B) Prepare a contract completion statement.
    (C) Settle subcontracts.
    (D) Update and archive contract records.

5. A customer after explaining performance needs for a prospective purchase, accepts the seller's recommendation. This is an example of:

    (A) Guarantee
    (B) Buyer's warranty
    (C) Implied warranty
    (D) Implied guarantee

6. Buyers use a variety of methods to provide incentives to a seller to complete work early or within certain contractually specified time frames. One such incentive is the use of liquidated damages. From the seller's perspective, liquidated damages are what form of incentive?

    (A) Positive
    (B) Negative
    (C) Nominal
    (D) Not an incentive

7. Which type of bilateral contract is used for high dollar, standard items?

    (A) Request for proposal (RFP).
    (B) Purchase order.
    (C) Request for quotation (RFQ).
    (D) Invitation for bid (IFB).

8. A legally binding document offered unilaterally is a:

    (A) Purchase order
    (B) Scope of work
    (C) Express warranty
    (D) Work breakdown structure

9. A contract is a promise to do or not do something in exchange for some form of consideration. A negotiated contract is one where both participants agree on the basis for principal considerations: _____.

     (A) the period of performance and the specifications for the project.
     (B) how the work will be performed, at what time, and for what price.
     (C) the services to be rendered by one party and the price to be paid by the other party.
     (D) who will perform the work and who will pay for the work.

10. A contractual action that authorizes commencement of work prior to the establishment of a final definitive price but less than the "not to exceed' price is known as a(n):

     (A) Letter contract/Letter of Intent (LOI)
     (B) Undefined contractual action
     (C) Request for Bid
     (D) Constructive change

11. Which of the following is considered during the plan purchases and acquisitions process?

     (A) Whether to procure.
     (B) How to procure and how much to procure.
     (C) What and when to procure.
     (D) All of the above.

12. A no-cost settlement sometimes is used:

     (A) In lieu of formal termination procedures.
     (B) To close out a successful contract.
     (C) When such an arrangement is acceptable to one of the parties involved.
     (D) When buyer property has been furnished under the contract.

13. Requirements for formal contract acceptance and closeout usually are defined in the:

     (A) Statement of work
     (B) Proposal
     (C) Procurement audit report
     (D) Contract terms and conditions

14. A fixed-price contract represents:

     (A) more risk for the buyer.
     (B) more risk for the seller.
     (C) a reasonable balance of risk for both buyer and seller.
     (D) an uncertain balance of risk for both buyer and seller.

15. You are the project manager for a large company project. You have created a contract for your customer. The contract must have what two things?

     (A) Offer and consideration
     (B) Signatures and the stamp of a notary public
     (C) Value and worth of the procured item
     (D) Start date and acceptance of start date

16. Contract administration is the process of:

(A) Obtaining information from prospective sellers.
(B) Product verification and administrative close-out.
(C) Monitoring contract performance, making payments, and awarding contract modifications.
(D) Clarification and mutual agreement on the structure and requirements of the contract.

17. Neil is the project manager for a large company project. He needs to purchase a piece of equipment for his project. The Accounting department has informed Neil he needs a unilateral form of contract. Accounting is referring to which of the following?

(A) SOW
(B) Legal binding contract
(C) Purchase Order
(D) Invoice from the vendor

18. Requirements for inspection and acceptance are defined in the:

(A) Contract documentation
(B) Procurement management plan
(C) Project management plan
(D) Specifications

19. Contract closeout is a process that involves:

(A) Customer satisfaction analysis and final payment.
(B) Administrative closure and archiving records.
(C) Final contractor payment and lessons learned.
(D) Product verification and administrative closure.

20. As you prepare to close out contracts on your project, you should review all the following types of documentation except the:

(A) Procurement audit.
(B) Contract document for the contract being closed out.
(C) Seller performance reports.
(D) Invoice and payment records.

21. The language of contracts sometimes causes misunderstandings and creates situations that adversely affect project completion. Therefore, a relatively fast and informal method for removing the obstacles to progress should always be available. One such method is to submit the issue in question to an impartial third party for resolution. This process is known as:

(A) Problem processing
(B) Alternative dispute resolution
(C) Mediation litigation
(D) Steering resolution

22. In which stage of the negotiation meeting are points of concession identified?

(A) Agreement
(B) Scratch bargaining
(C) Probing
(D) Closure

23. A project manager may issue a "waiver" on items received from a vendor because the items are less than the purchase order specified. If the project manager knowingly accepts faulty material, the vendor is usually _____ any damages that the material may cause.

      (A) made to pay a percentage of
      (B) relieved of responsibility for
      (C) not paid in the amount of
      (D) willing to repair / correct

24. You have decided to award a contract to a seller that has provided its services to your company frequently in the past. This seller has a good record in terms of schedule and cost performance, and your working relationship with this seller is excellent. Your current project, although somewhat different from previous projects, is similar to other work the seller has performed. In this situation, to minimize your risk you should award what type of contract?

      (A) Fixed-price incentive
      (B) Fixed-price with economic price adjustment
      (C) Cost-plus-award fee
      (D) Firm-fixed-price

25. You are working on a contract for a Canadian province. The contract requires you to be on site at the government affairs office on a daily basis. You were unable to get to the office for 3 days last month because of severe blizzard conditions. Your failure to appear at the office was excused because of a clause in the contract entitled:

      (A) Non compos mentis
      (B) Holus-bolus
      (C) Force majeure
      (D) Alter idem

26. A project is engaged in making electronic devices. It is necessary for the company to purchase materials to make the printed circuit boards. All of the parts are common parts that are available from several vendors. The most likely contract that should be issued for these parts is:

      (A) Unit price contract.
      (B) Firm fixed-price contract.
      (C) Cost-reimbursable contract.
      (D) Award fee contract.

27. Which of the following are characteristics of a purchase order?

      (A) A bilateral contract used for low dollar items.
      (B) A unilateral contract used when routine, standard cost items are required.
      (C) A bilateral contract used for high dollar, standard items.
      (D) A unilateral contract used for high dollar, standard items.

28. In negotiations, what is a fait accompli tactic?

      (A) Completing a phase of work before the other side is ready.
      (B) Pretending to accept the other side's offer.
      (C) Claiming an issue has already been decided and therefore cannot be changed.
      (D) Promising that a requirement will be completed before it is due.

29. A single source seller means what?

    (A) There is only one seller the company wants to do business with.
    (B) There is only one qualified seller.
    (C) There is only one seller in the market.
    (D) There is a seller that can provide all aspects of the project procurement needs.

30. Your company, a leading provider of project management services through outsourcing, is facing a cash-flow shortage. In an effort to obtain a steady stream of revenue, it bid on an IFB and won a contract issued by the city for trash pickup services. Although management was pleased to win the contract, the garbage trucks your company was planning to buy were sold to someone else. The landfill your company was planning to use was closed, and project managers objected to the new company slogan, "We don't talk trash, we haul it!" Today is Thursday, and work begins next Monday. The CEO recognizes that this is not an opportunity for a successful project and is meeting with the mayor to end the contract because the company cannot perform the work. This is called:

    (A) Expiration
    (B) Formal acceptance
    (C) Cessation
    (D) Termination

31. A cost-plus-percentage-cost (CPPC) contract has an estimated cost of $120,000 with an agreed profit of 10% of the costs. The actual cost of the project is $130,000. What is the total reimbursement to the seller?

    (A) $142,000
    (B) $143,000
    (C) $132,000
    (D) $140,000

32. Breach of contract is best described as:

    (A) Failure by the buyer to perform part or all of the duties of a contract.
    (B) Failure by either the buyer or seller to perform part or all of the duties of a contract.
    (C) Failure by the seller to perform part or all of the duties of a contract.
    (D) None of the above.

33. Which of the following may be used as a risk mitigation tool?

    (A) Contract
    (B) Vendor proposal
    (C) Project requirements
    (D) Quotation

34. The product description of a project can help a project manager create procurement details. Which one of the following best describes this process?

    (A) The product description defines the contracted work.
    (B) The product description defines the requirements for the contract work.
    (C) The product description defines the contracted work, which must support the requirements of the project customer.
    (D) Both parties must have and retain their own copy of the product description.

35. Steve has sent the ABC Contracting Company a letter of intent. This means which one of the following?

(A) Steve intends to buy from the ABC Contracting Company.
(B) Steve intends to sue the ABC Contracting Company.
(C) Steve intends to fire the ABC Contracting Company.
(D) Steve intends to bid on a job from the ABC Contracting Company.

36. Josh is the project manager for a large company project. He is considering proposals and contracts presented by vendors for a portion of the project work. Of the following, which contract is least dangerous to the DSA Project?

(A) Cost plus percentage of cost
(B) Cost plus fixed fee
(C) Fixed-price
(D) Cost plus incentive fee

37. The United States backs all contracts through which of the following?

(A) Federal law
(B) State law
(C) Court system
(D) Lawyers

38. What doctrine causes a party to relinquish rights under a contract because it knowingly fails to execute those rights?

(A) Waiver
(B) Warranties
(C) Assignment of claims
(D) Material breach

39. Generally speaking, compensation to a contractor in a cost-reimbursement contract is based on:

(A) Delivery of the goods and services stipulated in the contract.
(B) Actual costs incurred based on the contractor's best efforts.
(C) Actual costs incurred minus profit if the cost ceiling was exceeded.
(D) The number of resources used.

40. In an effort to reduce project team members' increasing stress levels, you decided to conduct power yoga sessions during every project status meeting. You need to hire someone to conduct these sessions. Citing the organization's project management methodology, your subcontracts department informed you that the following document must be prepared before starting the procurement:

(A) Procurement management plan
(B) Statement of work
(C) Contract terms and conditions
(D) Evaluation methodology

41. Randi is the project manager for a large company project. She has contracted a portion of the project to the ABC Construction Company. Randi has offered a bonus to ABC if they complete their portion of the work by August 30. This is an example of which one of the following?

(A) Project goal
(B) Fixed-price contract
(C) Project requirement
(D) Project incentive

42. A purchase order is a good example of which form of contracting?

    (A) Bilateral
    (B) Unilateral
    (C) Severable
    (D) Multilateral

43. A unilateral contract under which the seller is paid a preset amount per unit of service is called:

    (A) A cost reimbursable contract
    (B) A lump sum contract
    (C) A unit price contract
    (D) A fixed price contract

44. Fixed-price contracts place more risk on which of the following?

    (A) Buyer
    (B) Owner
    (C) Everyone equal
    (D) Seller

45. After conducting a make-or-buy analysis and reviewing its results, your company decided to award a contract for project management services on a pharmaceutical research project. Because your company is new to project management and does not understand the full scope of services that may be needed under the contract, it is most appropriate to award a:

    (A) Cost-pius-a-percentage-of-cost contract
    (B) Time-and-materials contract
    (C) Lump-sum contract
    (D) Fixed-price incentive contract

46. A project has subcontracted part of the work of the project to an outside vendor. The work involves writing modules of software for the project. The first delivery of the subcontracted software has been made, and it is found that the software will not perform the functions that were specified in the contract. The vendor says that the software cannot do what was specified in the contract and refuses to do the work. What should the project team do?

    (A) Hold additional meetings with the vendor to determine the problem and the solution to the problem.
    (B) Cancel the contract and find another vendor.
    (C) Offer the vendor an additional incentive to finish the contract.
    (D) Seek legal advice from the company's attorney.

47. As the senior project manager you have decided to make an immediate decision and award a contract to a contractor that has provided its services to your company occasionally in the past few years. This particular contractor has a great record and your relationship is excellent. Your current project, although somewhat different from previous projects, is somewhat similar to other work he has performed. In this situation, to minimize your risk you should award what type of contract?

    (A) Firm fixed price.
    (B) Cost plus award fee.
    (C) Fixed price with economic price adjustment.
    (D) Fixed price incentive.

48. All the following elements must be evident in a written contract for it to be legally enforceable except:

    (A) Mutual assent
    (B) Pricing structure
    (C) Appropriate form
    (D) Legal capacity

49. Contract type selection is dependent on the degree of risk or uncertainty facing the project manager. From the perspective of the buyer, the preferred contract type in a low-risk situation is:

    (A) Fixed-price incentive
    (B) Cost-pius-a-percentage-of-cost
    (C) Cost-plus-fixed fee
    (D) Firm-fixed-price

50. You are a contractor for the XYZ Company. Your company recently completed a water resource management project for the state and received payment on its final invoice today. A procurement audit has been conducted. Formal notification that the contract has been closed should be provided to your company by the:

    (A) State's project manager
    (B) Person responsible for contract administration
    (C) Project control officer
    (D) Project sponsor or owner

51. Which one of the following is not a valid evaluation criterion for source selection?

    (A) Contract requirements
    (B) Price
    (C) Age of the contact person at the seller
    (D) Technical ability of the seller

52. Recent data indicate that more than 10,000 airline passengers are injured each year from baggage that falls from overhead bins. More than 90% of these accidents result in head injuries to passengers sitting in aisle seats. You recently were assigned to manage a project to make it safer to sit in an aisle seat on planes. You performed a make-or-buy analysis and decided to outsource an improved bin design and manufacture. Your airline, however, does not have a qualified seller list for you to use for the procurement. You do not want to sole source this important effort. Therefore, the project team needs to develop a list of qualified sources. As a general rule, which method would the project team not find especially helpful?

    (A) Advertising
    (B) Internet
    (C) Trade catalogs
    (D) Relevant local associations

53. Which one of the following is true about procurement documents?

    (A) They offer no room for bidders to suggest changes.
    (B) They ensure receipt of complete proposals.
    (C) They inform the performing organization why the bid is being created.
    (D) The project manager creates and selects the bid.

54. You have an emergency on your project. You have hired a vendor that is to start work immediately. What contract is needed now?

    (A) Time and materials
    (B) Fixed fee
    (C) Letter contract
    (D) Incentive contract

55. The principal function of a warranty is to:

    (A) Provide a way to assert claims for late payment.
    (B) Ensure that goods purchased fit the purposes for which they are to be used.
    (C) Provide a way to allow additional time following acceptance to correct deficiencies, without additional costs.
    (D) Provide assurance of the level of quality to be provided.

56. Martha is the project manager for a large company project. She wants a vendor to offer her one price to do all of the detailed work. Martha is looking for which type of document?

    (A) RFP
    (B) RFI
    (C) Proposal
    (D) IFB

57. Which term describes those costs in a contract that are associated with two or more projects but are not traceable to either of them individually?

    (A) Variable
    (B) Direct
    (C) Indirect
    (D) Managerial

58. You are working on a new project in your organization. Your company's existing staff can easily meet some of the proposed project requirements; however, there are other aspects of the project that are new to your company. You are aware of some sellers who specialize in this type of product, and they probably could meet many of, if not all, your requirements. You are preparing your project plan and deciding how best to staff the project and handle all its resource requirements. Your first step should be to:

    (A) Conduct a make-or-buy analysis.
    (B) Conduct a market survey.
    (C) Solicit proposals from sellers via an RFP to determine whether you should outsource the project.
    (D) Review your procurement department's qualified seller lists and send an RFP to selected sellers.

59. You plan to award a contract to provide project management training for your company. You decide it is important that any prospective contractor have an association with a major university that awards master's certificates in project management. This is an example of:

    (A) Preparing requirements for your statement of work.
    (B) Setting up an independent evaluation.
    (C) Establishing a screening system.
    (D) Establishing a weighting system.

60. You are the project manager for a seller. You are managing another company's project. Things have gone well on the project, and the work is nearly complete. There is still a significant amount of funds in the project budget. The buyer's representative approaches you and asks that you complete some optional requirements to use up the remaining budget. You should do which one of the following?

(A) Gain the approval of the project stakeholder for the requested work.
(B) Deny the change because it was not in the original contract.
(C) Negotiate a change in the contract to take on the additional work.
(D) Complete a contract change for the additional work.

61. Which type of contract provides the highest risk to the owner (buyer)?

(A) Cost-plus Incentive Fee
(B) Cost-plus Percentage of Costs
(C) Cost-plus Fixed Fee
(D) Fixed-Price Plus Incentive Fee

62. In the following contract types, which one requires the seller to assume the risk of cost overruns?

(A) Cost plus incentive fee
(B) Time and materials
(C) Lump sum
(D) Cost plus fixed fee

63. In some cases, contract termination refers to:

(A) Contract closeout by mutual agreement.
(B) Contract closeout by delivery of goods or services.
(C) Contract closeout by successful performance.
(D) Certification of receipt of final payment.

64. Nate is the project manager for a large company project. He has hired an independent contractor for a portion of the project work. The contractor is billing the project $120 per hour, plus materials. This is an example of which one of the following?

(A) Time and materials
(B) Cost plus fixed fee
(C) Lump sum
(D) Unit-price

65. The purpose of a contract is to distribute between the buyer and seller a reasonable amount of which of the following:

(A) Reward
(B) Accountability
(C) Responsibility
(D) Risk

66. During the project you realize you need a consultant immediately to begin working on a project. What is the most appropriate contract type in this situation?

(A) Start work order.
(B) Cost plus fixed fee.
(C) Time and material.
(D) Fixed-price.

67. Payment bonds are often required by the contract and require specific actions under the stated conditions. Payment bonds are specifically designed to ensure that the prime contractor provides payment of:

    (A) Insurance premiums
    (B) Weekly payrolls
    (C) Subcontractors, laborers, and sellers of material
    (D) Damages for accidents caused

68. Which type of warranty is enacted if a service or product does not meet the level of quality specified in the contract?

    (A) Express warranty.
    (B) Simplified warranty.
    (C) Implied warranty of merchantability.
    (D) Implied warranty of specified quality.

69. A project manager is confronted with significant risk in one or more aspects of a project. She convinces the project stakeholders that the project risk can be reduced if this portion of the project is contracted out to a different organization. In considering what type of contract to negotiate, she may examine the following differences between a firm-fixed price (FFP) and a cost-plus fixed fee (CPFF) contract.

    (A) The FFP contract is used where probability of deliver is high; CPFF is used when the client pays for most of the risk.
    (B) The FFP contract is used where risk of deliver is low; CPFF is used in situations where the client has little say over changes.
    (C) The FFP contract shifts all of the risk on the seller, where the CPFF contract is used where the scope objectives are well known.
    (D) The FFP contract is used where risk is assumed by the client; CPFF is used where the client has significant say over changes.

70. Which term describes the failure by either the buyer or seller to perform part or all of the duties of a contract?

    (A) Termination of contract
    (B) Partial performance
    (C) Breach of contract
    (D) Contract waiver

71. A contract is a stand-alone legal document and must be individually managed to ensure the proper performance. Many projects have several contracts to be initiated and executed throughout the life of the project. Therefore, it is best to have a _____ that anticipates and describes the types of contracts required for the project.

    (A) listing of contracts
    (B) responsibility matrix
    (C) project contract management plan
    (D) contracting manual

72. A project manager is about to request bids on a large part of the work that must be done on the project. This work amounts to over $1 million. The best reason that the bid should be advertised is:

    (A) It is a legal requirement to do so.
    (B) Advertising will notify more companies that you are interested in contracting the work.
    (C) It will avoid criticism from other potential vendors.
    (D) It avoids having pressure from the public.

73. Jake has outsourced a portion of the project to a vendor. The vendor has discovered some issues that will influence the cost and schedule of its portion of the project. How must the vendor update the agreement?

(A) As a new contract signed by Jake and the vendor.
(B) As a contract addendum signed by Jake and the vendor.
(C) As a memo and SOW signed by Jake and the vendor.
(D) Project Management contracts have clauses that allow vendors to adjust their work according to unknowns.

74. You are the project manager for a consulting firm specializing in web-based UI development. Your company designs and develops custom web-sites and provides backwards integration with legacy systems. Your company is in the process of bidding on a project to develop an online student registration website for a major university. As a potential bidder for this project, you worked on the RFP response and submitted the proposal. The university's selection committee received the RFP responses from all the vendors, and applied a weighted system in order to make a selection. Which of the following process just took place?

(A) Contract administration
(B) Select sellers
(C) Request seller responses
(D) Plan purchases and acquisitions

75. You are completing the closeout of a project to design a warehouse in San Francisco, California. The contract is a Cost Plus Incentive Fee contract. The target costs are $300,000, with a 10 percent target profit. However, the project came in at $275,000. The incentive split is 80/20. How much is the total contract cost?

(A) $275,000
(B) $300,000
(C) $330,000
(D) $310,000

76. A project is coming to a close, and the project manager is listing the things that must be done to close out the project. One of the things that must be done by the person responsible for contract administration is:

(A) Issue a formal written notice of project completion to the contractors.
(B) Issue letters of recommendation for the project team.
(C) Request final inspection reports for all vendor-supplied materials.
(D) Put a legal notice in the newspapers indicating that all invoices must be submitted.

77. A guarantee imposed by law in a sale even though the seller may not make any explicit promises is?

(A) Guarantee
(B) Express warranty
(C) Buyer's warranty
(D) Implied warranty

78. Which term is not a common name for a procurement document that solicits an offer from prospective sellers?

(A) Contractor initial response
(B) Request for information
(C) Request for quotation
(D) Invitation for negotiation

79. Which of the following contract types places the greatest risk on the seller?

    (A) Cost-plus-fixed-fee contract.
    (B) Cost plus-incentive-fee contract.
    (C) Firm-fixed-price contract.
    (D) Fixed-price-incentive contract.

80. During the plan contracting phase, the project team is responsible for:

    (A) Determining the make-or-buy decision.
    (B) Developing the procurement documents.
    (C) Specifying schedule parameters in the form of delivery dates.
    (D) Developing the specifications and drawings to accompany the solicitation.

81. A project is being managed by a project manager. A large portion of the work of the project is being subcontracted to an outside vendor. During the project it is found that a significant change in the design of the project is necessary. The project manager should:

    (A) Issue a change notice to the contractor immediately.
    (B) Issue a purchase order to investigate the change.
    (C) Notify the contractor of the design change possibility.
    (D) Rebid the contract.

82. A buyer has negotiated a fixed-price incentive contract with the seller. The contract has a target cost of $200,000, a target profit of $30,000, and a target price of $230,000. The buyer has also negotiated a ceiling price of $270,000 and a share ratio of 70/30. If the seller completes the contract with actual costs of $170,000, how much profit will the buyer pay the seller?

    (A) $21,000
    (B) $35,000
    (C) $39,000
    (D) $51,000

83. From a buyer's standpoint, which of the following is true?

    (A) Procurement planning should include consideration of potential subcontracts.
    (B) Procurement planning does not include consideration of potential subcontracts since this is the duty of the contractor.
    (C) Subcontractors are first considered during the plan purchases and acquisitions.
    (D) None of the above.

84. A contract between an organization and a vendor may include a clause that penalizes the vendor if the project is late. The lateness of a project has a monetary penalty; penalty should be enforced or waived based on which one of the following?

    (A) If the project manager knew the delay was likely.
    (B) If the project manager could have anticipated the delay.
    (C) Who caused the delay and the reason why.
    (D) Whether the delay was because of an unseen risk.

85. Which of the following contract types does not encourage the seller to control costs and, as a result, places the greatest risk on the buyer?

    (A) Cost-plus-fixed fee
    (B) Cost-plus-award fee
    (C) Cost-plus-a-percentage-of-cost
    (D) Cost-plus-incentive fee

86. Which term describes contract costs that are traceable to or caused by a specific project work effort?

    (A) Variable
    (B) Fixed
    (C) Indirect
    (D) Direct

87. What is the main purpose of the procurement audit?

    (A) To improve the procurement management process within the performing organization.
    (B) To ensure each participant in the procurement process is abiding by the organization's vendor management policies.
    (C) To gather evidence of vendor mistakes to use during final payment negotiations.
    (D) To ensure the vendor is performing to quality standards.

88. Which of the following processes involves obtaining information (bids and proposals) from prospective sellers?

    (A) Plan Purchases and Acquisitions.
    (B) Plan Contracting.
    (C) Request Seller Responses.
    (D) Select Seller.

89. A contract cannot have provisions for which one of the following?

    (A) Illegal activities
    (B) Penalties and fines for disclosure of intellectual rights
    (C) Subcontracting the work
    (D) A deadline for the completion of the work

90. You are the project manager for a software development project for an accounting system that will operate over the Internet. Based on your research, you have discovered it will cost you $25,000 to write your own code. Once the code is written you estimate you'll spend $3,000 per month updating the software with client information, government regulations, and maintenance. A vendor has proposed to write the code for your company and charge a fee based on the number of clients using the program every month. The vendor will charge you $5 per month per user of the web-based accounting system. You will have roughly 1,200 clients using the system per month. However, you'll need an in-house accountant to manage the time and billing of the system, so this will cost you an extra $1,200 per month. How many months will you have to use the system before it is better to write your own code than to hire the vendor?

    (A) 4 months
    (B) 15 months
    (C) 6 month
    (D) 3 months

91. Which of the following statements is not true with regard to cost-reimbursement contracts?

    (A) Payment is based solely on the delivery of goods and services.
    (B) The seller's interest in cost control diminishes.
    (C) The buyer bears the greater financial risk.
    (D) The buyer's concern about the seller's performance increases.

92. When a seller breaches a contract, the buyer cannot receive:

   (A) Punitive damages
   (B) Compensatory damages
   (C) Consequential damages
   (D) Liquidated damages

93. You are working on a project at your software development company. Your company's existing staff can easily meet some of the proposed project requirements; however, there are other aspects of the project that are new to your company. You are aware of some sellers who specialize in this product, and they probably could meet many of, if not all, your requirements. You are preparing your project plan and deciding how best to staff the project and handle all its resource requirements. Your first step should be which of the following?

   (A) Conduct a market survey.
   (B) Conduct a make-or-buy analysis.
   (C) Review your procurement department's qualified seller lists and send an RFP to selected sellers.
   (D) Solicit proposals from sellers via an RFP to determine whether you should outsource the project.

94. You are working on a complex procurement. You must reach agreement with the seller about numerous items including responsibilities and authorities, applicable terms and conditions, contract financing, technical and business management approaches, and price before signing the contract. You scheduled a negotiation session. The seller will have eight representatives at the session; you will have ten. Because this procurement is so complex, contract negotiation should be handled:

   (A) By an outside facilitator.
   (B) Through alternative dispute resolution procedures.
   (C) As an independent process with specific input and output.
   (D) By establishing a partnering agreement with the seller.

95. Your company, a leading software developer is facing a cash-flow shortage. In an effort to obtain a steady stream of revenue, it bid on an IFR and won a contract issued by a government agency for document retrieval, processing and storage. Although management was pleased to win the contract, the document equipment your company was planning to buy were sold to someone else. The building your company was planning to use was recently condemned. Today is Monday, and work is scheduled to begin in one week. The CEO recognizes that this is not an opportunity for a successful project and is meeting with the government agency to end the contract because the company cannot perform the work. This is called:

   (A) Formal acceptance
   (B) Expiration
   (C) Termination
   (D) Cessation

96. The buyer has negotiated a cost-plus-incentive fee contract with the seller. The contract has a target cost of $300,000, a target fee of $40,000, a share ratio of 80/20, a maximum fee of $60,000, and a minimum fee of $10,000. If the seller has actual costs of $380,000, how much fee will the buyer pay?

   (A) $30,000
   (B) $24,000
   (C) $104,000
   (D) $56,000

97. You are managing a project that has five subcontractors. You must monitor contract performance, make payments, and manage provider interface. One subcontractor submitted a change request to expand the scope of its work. You decided to award a contract modification based on a review of this request. All these activities are part of:

     (A) Contract execution
     (B) Contract administration
     (C) Contract resolution
     (D) Contract formation

98. Which of the following best describes privity?

     (A) Relationship between the project manager and an unknown vendor.
     (B) Professional information regarding the sale between customer and vendor.
     (C) Contractual, confidential information between customer and vendor.
     (D) Relationship between the project manager and a known vendor.

99. Which of the following is a method for quantifying qualitative data in order to minimize the effect of personal prejudice on source selection?

     (A) Selecting system.
     (B) Delphi system.
     (C) Weighting system.
     (D) Screening system.

100. You are responsible for ensuring that your seller's performance meets contractual requirements. For effective contract administration, you should:

     (A) Hold a bidders' conference.
     (B) Establish the appropriate contract type.
     (C) Implement the contract change control system.
     (D) Develop a statement of work.

Sample Answer Sheet

	T F				
1	Ⓐ Ⓑ Ⓒ Ⓓ Ⓔ	26	Ⓐ Ⓑ Ⓒ Ⓓ Ⓔ	51	Ⓐ Ⓑ Ⓒ Ⓓ Ⓔ	76	Ⓐ Ⓑ Ⓒ Ⓓ Ⓔ

1 Ⓐ Ⓑ Ⓒ Ⓓ Ⓔ   26 Ⓐ Ⓑ Ⓒ Ⓓ Ⓔ   51 Ⓐ Ⓑ Ⓒ Ⓓ Ⓔ   76 Ⓐ Ⓑ Ⓒ Ⓓ Ⓔ

2 Ⓐ Ⓑ Ⓒ Ⓓ Ⓔ   27 Ⓐ Ⓑ Ⓒ Ⓓ Ⓔ   52 Ⓐ Ⓑ Ⓒ Ⓓ Ⓔ   77 Ⓐ Ⓑ Ⓒ Ⓓ Ⓔ

3 Ⓐ Ⓑ Ⓒ Ⓓ Ⓔ   28 Ⓐ Ⓑ Ⓒ Ⓓ Ⓔ   53 Ⓐ Ⓑ Ⓒ Ⓓ Ⓔ   78 Ⓐ Ⓑ Ⓒ Ⓓ Ⓔ

4 Ⓐ Ⓑ Ⓒ Ⓓ Ⓔ   29 Ⓐ Ⓑ Ⓒ Ⓓ Ⓔ   54 Ⓐ Ⓑ Ⓒ Ⓓ Ⓔ   79 Ⓐ Ⓑ Ⓒ Ⓓ Ⓔ

5 Ⓐ Ⓑ Ⓒ Ⓓ Ⓔ   30 Ⓐ Ⓑ Ⓒ Ⓓ Ⓔ   55 Ⓐ Ⓑ Ⓒ Ⓓ Ⓔ   80 Ⓐ Ⓑ Ⓒ Ⓓ Ⓔ

6 Ⓐ Ⓑ Ⓒ Ⓓ Ⓔ   31 Ⓐ Ⓑ Ⓒ Ⓓ Ⓔ   56 Ⓐ Ⓑ Ⓒ Ⓓ Ⓔ   81 Ⓐ Ⓑ Ⓒ Ⓓ Ⓔ

7 Ⓐ Ⓑ Ⓒ Ⓓ Ⓔ   32 Ⓐ Ⓑ Ⓒ Ⓓ Ⓔ   57 Ⓐ Ⓑ Ⓒ Ⓓ Ⓔ   82 Ⓐ Ⓑ Ⓒ Ⓓ Ⓔ

8 Ⓐ Ⓑ Ⓒ Ⓓ Ⓔ   33 Ⓐ Ⓑ Ⓒ Ⓓ Ⓔ   58 Ⓐ Ⓑ Ⓒ Ⓓ Ⓔ   83 Ⓐ Ⓑ Ⓒ Ⓓ Ⓔ

9 Ⓐ Ⓑ Ⓒ Ⓓ Ⓔ   34 Ⓐ Ⓑ Ⓒ Ⓓ Ⓔ   59 Ⓐ Ⓑ Ⓒ Ⓓ Ⓔ   84 Ⓐ Ⓑ Ⓒ Ⓓ Ⓔ

10 Ⓐ Ⓑ Ⓒ Ⓓ Ⓔ   35 Ⓐ Ⓑ Ⓒ Ⓓ Ⓔ   60 Ⓐ Ⓑ Ⓒ Ⓓ Ⓔ   85 Ⓐ Ⓑ Ⓒ Ⓓ Ⓔ

11 Ⓐ Ⓑ Ⓒ Ⓓ Ⓔ   36 Ⓐ Ⓑ Ⓒ Ⓓ Ⓔ   61 Ⓐ Ⓑ Ⓒ Ⓓ Ⓔ   86 Ⓐ Ⓑ Ⓒ Ⓓ Ⓔ

12 Ⓐ Ⓑ Ⓒ Ⓓ Ⓔ   37 Ⓐ Ⓑ Ⓒ Ⓓ Ⓔ   62 Ⓐ Ⓑ Ⓒ Ⓓ Ⓔ   87 Ⓐ Ⓑ Ⓒ Ⓓ Ⓔ

13 Ⓐ Ⓑ Ⓒ Ⓓ Ⓔ   38 Ⓐ Ⓑ Ⓒ Ⓓ Ⓔ   63 Ⓐ Ⓑ Ⓒ Ⓓ Ⓔ   88 Ⓐ Ⓑ Ⓒ Ⓓ Ⓔ

14 Ⓐ Ⓑ Ⓒ Ⓓ Ⓔ   39 Ⓐ Ⓑ Ⓒ Ⓓ Ⓔ   64 Ⓐ Ⓑ Ⓒ Ⓓ Ⓔ   89 Ⓐ Ⓑ Ⓒ Ⓓ Ⓔ

15 Ⓐ Ⓑ Ⓒ Ⓓ Ⓔ   40 Ⓐ Ⓑ Ⓒ Ⓓ Ⓔ   65 Ⓐ Ⓑ Ⓒ Ⓓ Ⓔ   90 Ⓐ Ⓑ Ⓒ Ⓓ Ⓔ

16 Ⓐ Ⓑ Ⓒ Ⓓ Ⓔ   41 Ⓐ Ⓑ Ⓒ Ⓓ Ⓔ   66 Ⓐ Ⓑ Ⓒ Ⓓ Ⓔ   91 Ⓐ Ⓑ Ⓒ Ⓓ Ⓔ

17 Ⓐ Ⓑ Ⓒ Ⓓ Ⓔ   42 Ⓐ Ⓑ Ⓒ Ⓓ Ⓔ   67 Ⓐ Ⓑ Ⓒ Ⓓ Ⓔ   92 Ⓐ Ⓑ Ⓒ Ⓓ Ⓔ

18 Ⓐ Ⓑ Ⓒ Ⓓ Ⓔ   43 Ⓐ Ⓑ Ⓒ Ⓓ Ⓔ   68 Ⓐ Ⓑ Ⓒ Ⓓ Ⓔ   93 Ⓐ Ⓑ Ⓒ Ⓓ Ⓔ

19 Ⓐ Ⓑ Ⓒ Ⓓ Ⓔ   44 Ⓐ Ⓑ Ⓒ Ⓓ Ⓔ   69 Ⓐ Ⓑ Ⓒ Ⓓ Ⓔ   94 Ⓐ Ⓑ Ⓒ Ⓓ Ⓔ

20 Ⓐ Ⓑ Ⓒ Ⓓ Ⓔ   45 Ⓐ Ⓑ Ⓒ Ⓓ Ⓔ   70 Ⓐ Ⓑ Ⓒ Ⓓ Ⓔ   95 Ⓐ Ⓑ Ⓒ Ⓓ Ⓔ

21 Ⓐ Ⓑ Ⓒ Ⓓ Ⓔ   46 Ⓐ Ⓑ Ⓒ Ⓓ Ⓔ   71 Ⓐ Ⓑ Ⓒ Ⓓ Ⓔ   96 Ⓐ Ⓑ Ⓒ Ⓓ Ⓔ

22 Ⓐ Ⓑ Ⓒ Ⓓ Ⓔ   47 Ⓐ Ⓑ Ⓒ Ⓓ Ⓔ   72 Ⓐ Ⓑ Ⓒ Ⓓ Ⓔ   97 Ⓐ Ⓑ Ⓒ Ⓓ Ⓔ

23 Ⓐ Ⓑ Ⓒ Ⓓ Ⓔ   48 Ⓐ Ⓑ Ⓒ Ⓓ Ⓔ   73 Ⓐ Ⓑ Ⓒ Ⓓ Ⓔ   98 Ⓐ Ⓑ Ⓒ Ⓓ Ⓔ

24 Ⓐ Ⓑ Ⓒ Ⓓ Ⓔ   49 Ⓐ Ⓑ Ⓒ Ⓓ Ⓔ   74 Ⓐ Ⓑ Ⓒ Ⓓ Ⓔ   99 Ⓐ Ⓑ Ⓒ Ⓓ Ⓔ

25 Ⓐ Ⓑ Ⓒ Ⓓ Ⓔ   50 Ⓐ Ⓑ Ⓒ Ⓓ Ⓔ   75 Ⓐ Ⓑ Ⓒ Ⓓ Ⓔ   100 Ⓐ Ⓑ Ⓒ Ⓓ Ⓔ

Project Procurement Management – Answers

1. (A) Signatures of both parties agreeing to SOW. An SOW can be a contract if both parties agree to the SOW and sign the document as a contract.

2. (B) Subcontractors, laborers, and materials. Payment bond: Guaranteed payment to subcontractors and laborers by the prime or the guarantor.

3. (C) Executing. Source selection happens during the Execution process group.

4. (C) Settle subcontracts. All payments due must be settled by the seller before the contract can be closed out. The other items listed are activities performed by the buyer.

5. (C) Implied warranty. Implied Warranty - The legal theory that when an owner requires a contractor to execute a project in accordance with plans and specifications supplied by the owner, there is an implied warranty that those plans and specifications are adequate to accomplish the work.

6. (B) Negative. Liquidated damages are considered negative incentives because they result in a loss of revenue for the seller if it fails to perform rather than a gain in revenue if it performs well.

7. (D) Invitation for bid (IFB). PMBOK® equates this with Request for Proposal and recognizes that it may have a more specific meaning in certain application areas. (appropriate for high dollar, standard items.)

8. (B) Scope of work. Depending upon the application area, contracts can also be called an agreement, subcontract, or purchase order. Most organizations have documented policies and procedures specifically defining who can sign and administer such agreements on behalf of the organization.

9. (C) the services to be rendered by one party and the price to be paid by the other party. Negotiated Contract - The process of buyer and seller discussion and position modification until mutual agreement is reached on contract content.

10. (A) Letter contract/Letter of Intent (LOI). Letter of Intent - A type of letter sometimes issued to a contractor to confirm the award of a contract and pending the signing of formal contract documents. It is a commitment document. It allows the contractor to prepare for mobilization. Permitting work to start on site before the contract is signed is not recommended as the Owner is without full protection at that point until the construction contract is signed.

11. (D) All of the above. The Plan Purchases and Acquisitions process identifies which project needs can best be met by purchasing or acquiring products, services, or results outside the project organization, and which project needs can be accomplished by the project team during project execution. This process involves consideration of whether, how, what, how much, and when to acquire.

12. (A) In lieu of formal termination procedures. A no-cost settlement can be used in lieu of formal termination procedures when the seller has indicated that such an arrangement is acceptable, no buyer property has been furnished under the contract, no payments are due the seller, no other obligations are outstanding, and the product or service can be readily obtained elsewhere.

13. (D) Contract terms and conditions. The contract terms and conditions typically prescribe specific procedures for contract closeout.

14. (D) an uncertain balance of risk for both buyer and seller. Be careful with these sorts of questions! A fixed-price contract certainly represents more cost risk for the buyer, but to the extent that the product is not well defined, both the buyer and seller are at risk.

15. (A) Offer and consideration Of all choices presented contracts have an offer and a consideration.

16. (C) Monitoring contract performance, making payments, and awarding contract modifications. Contract Administration – managing the contract and relationship between the buyer and seller, reviewing and documenting how a seller is performing or has performed to establish required corrective actions and provide a basis for future relationships with the seller, managing contract-related changes and, when appropriate, managing the contractual relationship with the outside buyer of the project.

17. (C) Purchase Order. A unilateral form of a contract is simply a purchase order.

18. (A) Contract documentation. Inspections and audits, required by the buyer and supported by the seller as specified in the contract documentation, can be conducted during execution of the project to identify any weaknesses in the seller's work processes or deliverables. If authorized by contract, some inspection and audit teams can include buyer procurement personnel.

19. (D) Product verification and administrative closure. The Contract Closure process supports the Close Project process, since it involves verification that all work and deliverables were acceptable. The Contract Closure process also involves administrative activities, such as updating records to reflect final results and archiving such information for future use.

20. (A) Procurement audit. Documentation that should be reviewed includes the contract itself, seller-developed technical documentation, seller performance reports, financial documents, and the results of contract-related inspections. Procurement audits are tools used in the closeout process.

21. (B) Alternative dispute resolution. Alternative dispute resolution, or dispute resolution, is a relatively informal way to address differences of opinion on contracts. Its purpose is to address such issues without having to seek formal legal redress through the courts.

22. (B) Scratch bargaining. Scratch Bargaining this is the essence of the meeting. Actual bargaining occurs and concessions are made. Points of concession are identified.

23. (B) relieved of responsibility for. Waiver - buyer action that grants contract relief from achieving specified performance. Usually applied when the required performance is not worth the cost and/or schedule to achieve full compliance.

24. (D) Firm-fixed-price. In a firm-fixed-price contract, the seller receives a fixed sum of money for the work performed regardless of costs. This arrangement places the greatest financial risk on the seller and encourages it to control costs.

25. (C) Force majeure. Force Majeure literally means "greater force." These clauses excuse a party from liability if some unforeseen event beyond the control of that party prevents it from performing its obligations under the contract. Typically, force majeure clauses cover natural disasters or other "Acts of God," war, or the failure of third parties—such as suppliers and subcontractors—to perform their obligations to the contracting party. It is important to remember that force majeure clauses are intended to excuse a party only if the failure to perform could not be avoided by the exercise of due care by that party.

26. (B) Firm fixed-price contract. Fixed-price or lump sum contracts—this category of contract involves a fixed total price for a well-defined product. To the extent that the product is not well-defined, both the buyer and seller are at risk—the buyer may not receive the desired product or the seller may need to incur additional costs in order to provide it. Fixed-price contracts may also include incentives for meeting or exceeding selected project objectives such as schedule targets.

27. (B) A unilateral contract used when routine, standard cost items are required. A unilateral contract takes the form of a purchase order—a standardized form listing routine items at standard (for example, vendor catalog) prices. The seller usually accepts the purchase order automatically. Unilateral contracts issued in this way normally do not involve any negotiation and contain relatively low monetary amounts.

28. (C) Claiming an issue has already been decided and therefore cannot be changed. Fait accompli - Claiming that a topic of dispute has already been decided or accomplished and cannot be changed.

29. (A) There is only one seller the company wants to do business with. A single source seller means there is only one seller the company wants to do business with.

30. (D) Termination. Contracts typically end in one of three ways: successful performance, mutual agreement, or breach. Termination is a word used to define a contract ending through mutual agreement or breach. It is a special case of contract closeout.

31. (B) $143,000. A type of cost reimbursable contract where the buyer reimburses the seller for seller's allowable costs for performing the contract work and seller also receives a fee calculated as an agreed upon percentage of the costs. The fee varies with the actual cost. Actual cost = $130,000 + 10% profit ($13,000) = $143,000.

32. (B) Failure by either the buyer or seller to perform part or all of the duties of a contract. Breach of contract: failure to perform a contractual obligation. The measure of the damages for a breach is the amount of loss the injured party has sustained.

33. (A) Contract. Contracts can be used as a risk mitigation tool. Procurement of risky activities is known as transference; the risk does not disappear, but the responsibility for the risk is transferred to the vendor.

34. (C) The product description defines the contracted work, which must support the requirements of the project customer. The product description defines the details and requirements for acceptance of the project. This information also serves as a valuable input to the process of determining what needs to be procured. The product description defines what the end result of the project will be. When dealing with vendors to procure a portion of the project, the work to be procured must support the requirements of the project's customer.

35. (A) Steve intends to buy from the ABC Contracting Company. He intends to buy from the ABC Contracting Company.

36. (C) Fixed-price. A Fixed-Price contract contains the least amount of risk for a project. The seller assumes all of the risk.

37. (C) Court system. All contracts in the United States are backed by the US court systems.

38. (A) Waiver. Under the doctrine of waiver, a party can relinquish rights that it otherwise has under the contract. If the seller offers incomplete, defective, or late performance and the buyer's project manager knowingly accepts that performance, the buyer has waived its right to strict performance. In some circumstances, the party at fault may remain liable for provable damages, but the waiver will prevent the buyer from claiming a material breach and, thus, from terminating the contract.

39. (B) Actual costs incurred based on the contractor's best efforts. A buyer is generally procuring a level of effort (that is, labor) in a cost-reimbursement contract and not a product or other tangible item. As long as the seller provides his or her "best efforts" in the performance of the contract, payment is guaranteed based on actual costs incurred.

40. (A) Procurement management plan. The procurement management plan describes how the procurement processes, from solicitation planning through closing will be managed. This includes the type contracts to be used, preparation of independent estimates, actions to be taken by the procurement department and the project management team, location of standardized procurement documents, management of multiple providers, and coordination of the procurement with other aspects of the project.

41. (D) Project incentive. A bonus to complete the work by August 30 is an incentive.

42. (B) Unilateral. A unilateral contract takes the form of a purchase order—a standardized form listing routine items at standard (for example, vendor catalog) prices. The seller usually accepts the purchase order automatically. Unilateral contracts issued in this way normally do not involve any negotiation and contain relatively low monetary amounts.

43. (C) A unit price contract. A unilateral contract takes the form of a purchase order—a standardized form listing routine items at standard (for example, vendor catalog) prices. The seller usually accepts the purchase order automatically. Unilateral contracts issued in this way normally do not involve any negotiation and contain relatively low monetary amounts.

44. (D) Seller. Fixed-price or Lump-sum - These contracts set a specific, firm price for the goods and/or services rendered. The buyer and seller agree on a well-defined deliverable for a set price. In this kind of contract, the biggest risk is borne by the seller. Fixed price contracts are usually used for projects that will take a long time to complete and have a high value to the company. This is the most common contract type, because it is best suited for situations with reasonably definite specifications and relatively certain costs.

45. (B) Time-and-materials contract. Time and Material (T&M) contracts - are a hybrid type of contractual arrangement that contains aspects of both cost-reimbursable and fixed-price type arrangements. These types of contracts resemble costreimbursable type arrangements in that they are open ended. The full value of the agreement and the exact quantity of items to be delivered are not defined by the buyer at the time of the contract award. Thus, T&M contracts can grow in contract value as if they were cost-reimbursable type arrangements. Conversely, T&M arrangements can also resemble fixed-price arrangements. For example, unit rates can be preset by the buyer and seller when both parties agree on the rates for a specific resource category.

46. (A) Hold additional meetings with the vendor to determine the problem and the solution to the problem. It is better to try to save a contract that is nearly completed than to start all over with another vendor. There are problems in this work, and it seems likely that the work is not clearly defined.

47. (A) Firm fixed price. Firm-Fixed-Price (FFP) Contract - a type of fixed price contract where the buyer pays the seller a set amount (as defined by the contract), regardless of the seller's costs.

48. (B) Pricing structure. The following elements must be present for a contract to be legally enforceable: legal capacity, mutual assent, consideration, legality, and an appropriate contract form that follows applicable laws governing businesses.

49. (D) Firm-fixed-price. Buyers prefer the firm-fixed-price contract because it places more risk on the seller. Although the seller bears the greatest degree of risk, it also has the maximum potential for profit. Because the seller receives an agreed-upon amount regardless of its costs, it is motivated to decrease costs by efficient production.

50. (B) Person responsible for contract administration. Formal notification that the contract has been completed should be provided to the seller in writing by the person responsible for managing the contract. Requirements for formal acceptance and closeout are usually defined in the contract.

51. (C) Age of the contact person at the seller. The age of the contact at the seller should not influence the source selection. The experience of the person doing the work, however, can.

52. (A) Advertising. Existing lists of potential sellers can often be expanded by placing advertisements in general circulation publications such as newspapers or in specialty publications such as professional journals. Some government jurisdictions require public advertising of certain types of procurement items; most government jurisdictions require public advertising of pending government contracts.

53. (B) They ensure receipt of complete proposals. Procurement documents detail the requirements for the work to ensure complete proposals from sellers.

54. (C) Letter contract. For immediate work, a letter contract may suffice. The intent of the letter contract is to allow the vendor to get to work immediately to solve the project problem.

55. (D) Provide assurance of the level of quality to be provided. A warranty is one party's assurance to the other that goods will meet certain standards of quality, including condition, reliability, description, function, or performance. This assurance may be express or implied.

56. (D) IFB. An IFB is typically a request for a sealed document that lists the seller's firm price to complete the detailed work.

57. (C) Indirect. The nature of an indirect cost is such that it is neither possible nor practical to measure how much of the cost is attributable to a single project. These costs are allocated to the project by the performing organization as a cost of doing business.

58. (A) Conduct a make-or-buy analysis. A make-or-buy analysis is a procurement planning tool used to determine whether a particular product can be produced cost effectively by the performing organization or should be contracted out. The analysis includes both direct and indirect costs.

59. (C) Establishing a screening system. A screening system involves establishing minimum requirements of performance for one or more of the evaluation criteria, and can employ a weighting system and independent estimates. For example, a prospective seller might be required to propose a project manager who has specific qualifications before the remainder of the proposal would be considered. These screening systems are used to provide a weighted ranking from best to worst for all sellers who submitted a proposal.

60. (A) Gain the approval of the project stakeholder for the requested work. Any additional work is a change in the project scope. Changes to project scope should be approved by the mechanisms in the change control system. The stakeholder needs to approve the changes to the project scope.

61. (B) Cost-plus Percentage of Costs. Cost-plus-percentage-of-cost (CPPC) - A CPPC contract provides for the reimbursement of allowable costs of services performed plus an agreed-upon percentage of the estimated cost as profit. The seller is only obligated to make its best effort to fulfill the contract within the estimated amount; the buyer funds all overruns. This contract type is prohibited in U.S. federal contracting and is only rarely used in the commercial sector.

62. (C) Lump sum. A Lump Sum is a fixed fee to complete the contract; the seller absorbs any cost overruns.

63. (A) Contract closeout by mutual agreement. A contract can end in successful performance, mutual agreement, or breach of contract. Contract closeout by mutual agreement or breach of contract is called contract termination.

64. (A) Time and materials. The contractor's rate of $120 per hour plus the cost of the materials is an example of a Time and Materials contract.

65. (D) Risk. A fair contract shares a reasonable amount of risk between the buyer and the seller.

66. (C) Time and material. Time and materials contracts are a cross between the fixed price and cost reimbursable contract. The full amount of the material costs is not known at the time the contract is awarded. This resembles a cost reimbursable contract, as the cost will continue to grow during the contract's life. The buyer assumes most of the risk in time and material contracts.

67. (C) Subcontractors, laborers, and sellers of material. Payment bonds, which are required by the buyer, are issued by guarantors to prime contractors. The buyer wants to ensure that subcontractors of the prime contractor receive payment so that work is not disrupted.

68. (A) Express warranty. Express warranty - contract explicitly states what the level of quality is.

69. (A) The FFP contract is used where probability of deliver is high; CPFF is used when the client pays for most of the risk. A Firm-Fixed-Price (FFP) Contract is a type of fixed price contract where the buyer pays the seller a set amount (as defined by the contract), regardless of the seller's costs. A Cost-Plus-Fixed-Fee (CPFF) Contract is a type of cost-reimbursable contract where the buyer reimburses the seller for the seller's allowable costs (allowable costs are defined by the contract) plus a fixed amount of profit (fee).

70. (C) Breach of contract. A breach of contract is a failure to perform either express or implied duties of the contract. Either the buyer or the seller can be responsible for a breach of contract.

71. (C) project contract management plan. For significant purchases or acquisitions, a plan to administer the contract is prepared based upon the specific buyer-specified items within the contract such as documentation, and delivery and performance requirements that the buyer and seller must meet. The plan covers the contract administration activities throughout the life of the contact. Each contract management plan is a subset of the project management plan.

72. (B) Advertising will notify more companies that you are interested in contracting the work. Existing lists of potential sellers can often be expanded by placing advertisements in general circulation publications such as newspapers or in specialty publications such as professional journals. Some government jurisdictions require public advertising of certain types of procurement items; most government jurisdictions require public advertising of subcontracts on a government contract.

73. (B) As a contract addendum signed by Jake and the vendor. As a contract addendum signed by Jake and the vendor is the best answer of all the choices presented. Because the question is asking for the vendor to update the agreement, as a contract addendum signed by Jake and the vendor is the best choice.

74. (B) Select sellers. Select sellers is the process of reviewing offers, choosing from among potential sellers, and negotiating a written contract with a seller.

75. (D) $310,000. The total contract cost is $310,000. Here's how the answer is calculated: target cost is $300,000. The ten percent profit is $30,000. The finished cost was $275,000, a difference of $25,000 between the target and the actual. The contract calls for an 80/20 split if the contract comes in under budget. The formula reads finished costs + profit margin + (.20 X under budget amount).

76. (A) Issue a formal written notice of project completion to the contractors. The person or organization responsible for contract administration should provide the seller with formal written notice that the contract has been completed. Requirements for formal acceptance and closure are usually defined in the contract.

77. (D) Implied warranty. Implied Warranty - The legal theory that when an owner requires a contractor to execute a project in accordance with plans and specifications supplied by the owner, there is an implied warranty that those plans and specifications are adequate to accomplish the work.

78. (B) Request for information. A type of procurement document whereby the buyer requests a potential seller to provide various pieces of information related to a product or service or seller capability.

79. (C) Firm-fixed-price contract. The seller takes the greatest risk in firm-fixed-price contracts. By contrast, the buyer is taking the lowest risk in a firm-fixed-price contract.

80. (B) Developing the procurement documents. Procurement documents - those documents utilized in bid and proposal activities, which include buyer's Invitation for Bid, Invitation for Negotiations, Request for Information, Request for Quotation, Request for Proposal and seller's responses.

81. (B) Issue a purchase order to investigate the change. The first thing that should be done is to issue a purchase order to the contractor and find out how much the change is going to cost. It is important in managing changes that work on changes does not take place until the cost of doing the change is clearly understood.

82. (C) $39,000. To calculate the fee that the buyer must pay, actual costs are compared with the target cost. If actual costs are less than the target cost, the seller will earn profit that is additional to the target profit. If actual costs are more than the target cost, the seller will lose profit from the target profit. The amount of profit is determined by the share ratio (with the buyer's share listed first). In this example, the seller is under target cost by $30,000. That amount will be split 70/30. So the buyer keeps $21,000, and the seller receives an additional $9,000 added to the target profit, which is the incentive. Total fee is $39,000.

83. (A) Procurement planning should include consideration of potential subcontracts. A complex project can involve managing multiple contracts or subcontracts simultaneously or in sequence. In such cases, each contract life cycle can end during any phase of the project life cycle. Project Procurement Management is discussed within the perspective of the buyer-seller relationship.

84. (C) Who caused the delay and the reason why. The party that caused the delay is typically the party responsible for the delay. It would not be acceptable for the project manager to willingly cause a delay and then penalize the contractor because the project was late.

85. (C) Cost-plus-a-percentage-of-cost. The cost-plus-a-percentage-of-cost contract is the most undesirable type of contract from the standpoint of the buyer. As the seller's costs grow, so do its profits.

86. (D) Direct. Direct costs are always identified with the cost objectives of a specific project. They are costs incurred for the exclusive benefit of the project, such as full-time project staff salaries.

87. (A) To improve the procurement management process within the performing organization. The procurement audit is a structured review of each process step within the procurement management activity with the key objective of improving this process for future procurement initiatives.

88. (C) Request Seller Responses. The Request Seller Responses process obtains responses, such as bids and proposals, from prospective sellers on how project requirements can be met. The prospective sellers, normally at no direct cost to the project or buyer, expend most of the actual effort in this process.

89. (A) Illegal activities. A contract cannot contain illegal activities.

90. (C) 6 month. The monies invested in the vendor's solution would have paid for your own code in six months. This is calculated by finding your cash outlay for the two solutions: $25,000 for your own code creation, and zero cash outlay for the vendor's solution. The monthly cost to maintain your own code is $3,000. The monthly cost of the vendor's solution is $7,200. Subtract your cost of $3,000 from the vendor's cost of $7,200 and this equals $4,200. Divide this number into the cash outlay of $25,000 to create your own code and you'll come up with 5.95 months.

91. (A) Payment is based solely on the delivery of goods and services. Cost-reimbursement contracts shift the financial risk from the seller to the buyer. Because all allowable and allocable costs are reimbursed, the seller has little financial risk. Therefore, the seller becomes less concerned about controlling costs and the buyer becomes more concerned about seller performance. However, payment is based on the contractor's best efforts and not on the delivery of goods and services.

92. (A) Punitive damages. Punitive damages are designed to punish a guilty party and, as such, are considered penalties. Because a breach of contract is not unlawful, punitive damages are not awarded. The other remedies listed are available to compensate the buyer's loss.

93. (B) Conduct a make-or-buy analysis. The make-or-buy analysis is a general management technique and a part of the project Plan Purchases and Acquisition process that can be used to determine whether a particular product or service can be produced by the project team or can be purchased. Any project budget constraints are factored in the make-or-buy decisions. If a buy decision is to be made, then a further decision of whether to purchase or rent is also made. The analysis includes both indirect as well as direct costs. For example, the buy-side of the analysis includes both the actual out-of pocket costs to purchase the product as well as the indirect costs of managing the purchasing process.

94. (C) As an independent process with specific input and output. To the extent possible, final contract language should reflect all agreements reached. For complex procurement items, contract negotiation should be considered an independent process with input (for example, issues or open-items list) and output (for example, memorandum of understanding).

95. (C) Termination. Contracts typically end in one of three ways: successful performance, mutual agreement, or breach. Termination is a word used to define a contract ending through mutual agreement or breach. It is a special case of contract closeout.

96. (B) $24,000. Comparing actual costs with the target cost shows an $80,000 overrun. The overrun is shared 80/20 (with the buyer's share always listed first). In this case 20% of $80,000 is $16,000, the seller's share, which is deducted from the $40,000 target fee. The remaining $24,000 is the fee paid to the seller.

97. (B) Contract administration. The purpose of contract administration is to ensure that the seller's performance meets contractual requirements. This objective is accomplished by monitoring contract performance and performing associated activities.

98. (C) Contractual, confidential information between customer and vendor. Privity is a confidential agreement between the buyer and seller.

99. Weighting system. A weighting system is a method for quantifying qualitative data to minimize the effect of personal prejudice on seller selection. Most such systems involve assigning a numerical weight to each of the evaluation criteria, rating the prospective sellers on each criterion, multiplying the weight by the rating, and totaling the resultant products to compute an overall score.

100. (C) Implement the contract change control system. A contract change control system defines the process by which the contract can be modified. It includes the paperwork, tracking systems, dispute resolution procedures, and approval levels necessary for authorizing changes. The contract change control system is integrated with the integrated change control system.

Professional Responsibility

Professional Responsibility will focus on the following tasks:

- Ensuring integrity and professionalism
- Contributing to the project management knowledge base
- Enhancing individual competence
- Balancing stakeholders' interests
- Interacting with team and stakeholders in a professional and cooperative manner
- Specific knowledge areas and skills have been identified in the Role Delineation Study for each of these tasks.

These questions will be based on situations or scenarios that require an understanding of the Project Management Professional Code of Conduct and the importance of professional ethics, awareness of legal issues, cultural sensitivity, and managing conflict of interest.

Professional Responsibility - Questions

1. What is the project manager's key role during negotiations?

    (A) Ensure that all project risks are thoroughly delineated.
    (B) Ensure that an effective communication plan is established.
    (C) Protect the relationship between buyer and seller.
    (D) Negotiate a price under the seller's estimate.

2. A PMP has been assigned to manage a project in a foreign country. The disorientation the PMP will likely experience as he gets acclimated to the country is known as:

    (A) Ethnocentrism
    (B) Culture shock
    (C) The Sapir-Whorf Hypotheses
    (D) Time dimension

3. During construction of a new manufacturing facility in another country, one of your team members complains to you that the wage paid to the workers is below the acceptable wage in your home country. In this situation it is best to:

    (A) pay the workers at the new facility a little less than the same wage as your country.
    (B) pay the workers at the new facility the same wage as your country.
    (C) ignore the issue as you have not heard the workers complain.
    (D) pay the workers an appropriate wage for the country within which they work.

4. You are the project manager for a new international project, and your project team includes people from four countries. Most of the team members have not worked on similar projects before, but the project has strong support from senior management. What is the best thing to do to ensure that cultural differences do not interfere with the project?

    (A) As the project manager, make sure you choose your words carefully whenever you communicate.
    (B) Spend a little more time creating the work breakdown structure and making sure it is complete.
    (C) Carefully encode all the project manager's communications.
    (D) Ask one person at each team meeting to describe something unique about their culture.

5. Another project manager has a family emergency and must leave. He has asked you to fill in for him during a team meeting to discuss a minor problem with the project. He has already distributed a detailed agenda and provided you with a copy. When you attend the meeting, several members of the team are laughing about the absent project manager's habits. Your company does not have a formal diversity policy. What should you do?

      (A) Hold the meeting as if nothing happened.
      (B) Begin the meeting with a discussion of diversity and professional behavior.
      (C) Because your company does not have a written diversity policy, there is nothing you can do.
      (D) Report the incident to the other project manager.

6. While preparing your risk responses, you realize that you have not planned for unknown risk events. You need to make adjustments to the project to compensate for unknown risk events. These adjustments are based on your past project experience when unknown risk events occurred and knocked the project off track. What should you do?

      (A) Document the unknown risk items and calculate the expected monetary value based on probability and impact that result from the occurrence.
      (B) Apply a general contingency to try to compensate.
      (C) Add a 10% contingency.
      (D) Determine the unknown risk events and the associated cost, and then add the cost to the project budget as reserves.

7. You are working on a very difficult construction project. You have been away from your home country for several months and are weary of consuming the favorite drink of the local workers: coconut milk. All you want is a glass of wine. Finally, you ask someone why the local people do not drink wine, as do the people in your country. The person turns to you and says, "How ethnocentric of you." He is accusing you of which one of the following:

      (A) Attributing behavior to a cause.
      (B) Believing in the inherent superiority and naturalness of your own culture.
      (C) Using a stereotype as you think about his group.
      (D) Focusing on control versus harmony.

8. You are managing a project and the customer's engineers visit your facility on an inspection and general getting acquainted tour. During the tour they make the comment that the parts that are being designed should be in stainless steel instead of plain steel with enamel. What should you do?

      (A) Continue with the present design.
      (B) Authorize the change in design to your engineers.
      (C) Ask the visiting engineers to submit a change proposal to the change system.
      (D) Speak to the visiting engineers and discuss having an informal meeting between your engineers and the visiting engineers.

9. The project has a critical deliverable that requires certain expertise to complete. The person who was going to complete the task has left the company and there is no one who can complete the work within the company. For this reason, the project manager needs to acquire the services of a consultant as soon as possible. To do this, the project manager should:

      (A) Follow the legal requirements set up by the company for using outside services.
      (B) Bypass the company procedures as they are not relevant to the situation.
      (C) Expedite and go directly to your preferred consultant.
      (D) Ask his/her manager what to do.

10. You have always been asked by your management to cut your project estimate by 10% after you have given it to them. The scope of your new project is unclear and there are over 30 stakeholders. Management expects a 25% reduction in downtime as a result of the project. Which of the following is the best course of action in this situation?

(A) Reduce the estimates and note the changes in the risk management plan.
(B) Re-plan to achieve a 35% improvement.
(C) Meet with the team to identify where you can find 10% savings.
(D) Provide an accurate estimate of the actual costs and be able to support it.

11. The customer on a project tells the project manager he has run out of money to pay for the project. Which of the following should the project manager do first?

(A) Stop work.
(B) Release part of the project team.
(C) Shift more of the work to later in the schedule to allow time for the customer to get the funds.
(D) Reduce the scope of work and enter closure.

12. The sponsor and others in your organization are repeatedly requesting changes. When you try to implement some of the changes, you discover the current contract does not include a budget for evaluating changes. What should you do?

(A) Ask senior management for more money from the company's reserve.
(B) Tell the sponsor there is no budget for changes in the project.
(C) Negotiate with the sponsor to decide how to remedy this problem.
(D) Take the matter directly to your contracting/legal department.

13. You have designed an improved system for a consumer product that could decrease repair cost for the consumer. Management has been impressed with your idea but has decided to wait until next year to implement it. What is your best option?

(A) Advise government officials that there is a better alternative that could save the public money.
(B) Wait until next year.
(C) Go to one of your competitors with the idea in order to save consumers cost.
(D) Tell everyone you come in contact with that you have a better design.

14. Under which of the following circumstances could a project manager incur a fine and be jailed?

(A) For failing to file the necessary permits in their own country.
(B) For using people from outside the project manager's country to work on the project.
(C) For not using minority workers on the project.
(D) For paying a bribe to a foreign official.

15. During planning a project manager discovers that part of the scope of work is undefined. What should the project manager do?

(A) Continue to plan for the project until the scope of work is defined.
(B) Remove the scope of work from the project and include it in the upgrade to the project.
(C) Issue a change to the project when the scope is defined.
(D) Ask management to help get the work defined.

16. While staffing a project in another country, the project leader from that country comes to you with a suggested team consisting of members of the project leader's family. Your first course of action should be to:

(A) Review the resumes of the individuals to see if they are qualified.
(B) Inquire if hiring only through family lines is common practice for the project leader's country.
(C) Use a different project leader to prevent problems later in the project.
(D) Ask the project leader to provide additional names of people unrelated to him/her.

17. All of the following are the responsibility of a project manager except which of the following?

(A) Determine the legality of company procedures.
(B) Provide accurate and truthful representations in cost estimates.
(C) Ensure that a legal conflict of interest does not compromise the legitimate interest of the customer.
(D) Maintain the confidentiality of customer confidential information.

18. As a project manager success factors for doing business internationally include all of the following except?

(A) Cross-cultural journeys
(B) Speaking the language of the host country
(C) Cultural understanding
(D) Global management

19. Which of the following statements is not true?

(A) Cultural differences will always be an obstacle to be overcome.
(B) Culture is a critical lever for competitive advantage.
(C) Only those who realize that cultural differences are a resource to be fully utilized will survive.
(D) There is a common ground for people from different cultures on which they can interact without unsolvable conflicts.

20. Which of the following statements concerning cross-cultural differences is true?

(A) There is no one "best way" for project organization.
(B) Some cultures have values, some not.
(C) Cultural dilemmas should be denied to not allow them to disrupt project work.
(D) Communicating across cultures should only be done using language. The nonverbal dimension bears too many risks.

21. You are working on the new oil purification project in a foreign country. A person informs you that you will have to pay him a "transfer fee" for the permit to move heavy equipment through the city. What is the first thing you should do?

(A) Do not pay the fee.
(B) Pay the fee but only to the city.
(C) Negotiate openly with the city officials.
(D) Make sure the person is really a government official.

22. You are doing business in a foreign country and you are advised by your local contact that it will be necessary to make payments to certain officials in order to get the contract. Such payments are expected in the other country, but are illegal for people from your country. What should you do?

(A) Refuse to make the payment and hope to get the contract solely based on your company's abilities.
(B) Have the local contact make payments.
(C) Amend your price increasing the cost to reflect the payments to be made to local officials.
(D) Call your government officials and ask for direction.

23. You are building a water treatment facility. Routine tests reveal that there are contaminants in the water but that they have an extremely low risk for causing any sickness. As the project manager, you should?

    (A) Do nothing because there is extremely low risk for sickness except for some effects on small children and the elderly.
    (B) Inform the public that a detailed examination has been ordered to determine the extent to which the problem exists.
    (C) Educate the public about the advances on water treatment technology and the industry efficiency and safety record.
    (D) Tell the public there is no problem, except for small children and the elderly who need to boil the water before drinking.

24. A project has a tight budget when you begin negotiating with a seller for a piece of equipment. The seller has told you that the equipment price is fixed. Your manager has told you to negotiate the cost with the seller. What is your best course of action?

    (A) Make a good faith effort to find a way to decrease the cost.
    (B) Postpone negotiations until you can convince your manager to change their mind.
    (C) Hold the negotiations but only negotiate other aspects of the project.
    (D) Cancel the negotiations.

25. Which of the following types of payments on an international project are unacceptable?

    (A) Offering to pay the country officials for not awarding the project to a particular company.
    (B) Payment for mail service.
    (C) Payment for a "foreign workers application license" required in the country.
    (D) Payment for policy protection.

26. Your company wants to assign a resource that is not within the project scope to your project and asks you to bill that resource to the customer. This concerns you because you get a bonus for maximizing billings to the customer. Which of the following is the best course to follow?

    (A) Maximize customer billings in any ethical manner possible.
    (B) Ask for the customer's approval before adding the resource to the project scope.
    (C) Ask for clarification of the intent of adding the resource.
    (D) Remind the appropriate members of the billing organization that monetary compensation is not worth compromising the integrity of the individual or the organization.

27. A family member has a copy of a software program. He offers it to you at no cost because it will solve a business problem you have discussed with him. What should you do?

    (A) Do not accept the software and advise the family member that such activity is in violation of copyright law.
    (B) Refuse the software and notify the owner of the software.
    (C) Accept the software and use it until you're able to buy the software yourself.
    (D) Accept the software with thanks since the software creator will not find out.

28. There are over 30 stakeholders on your project. The project is being done in another country with people from three countries as team members. Which of the following is the most important thing to keep in mind?

    (A) Many competing needs and objectives must be satisfied.
    (B) The communication channels will be narrow.
    (C) Conflicts of interest must be disclosed.
    (D) There must be one sponsor from each country.

29. A team member comes to you (the project manager) privately and informs you that an employee of your customer is making unwelcome advances. The team member has repeatedly requested that this person stop, but the advances continue. What is the best course of action?

(A) Suggest that the team member avoid contact with the customer employee.
(B) Facilitate a meeting with the team member, the customer employee, and yourself, to allow the two to work it out amicably.
(C) Contact the employee's manager to arrange a meeting to discuss the matter.
(D) Privately confront the customer employee and threaten legal action if the advances do not stop.

30. As a senior project manager, you know that the most important activity to ensure customer satisfaction is which of the following?

(A) Reporting project activity in a timely matter
(B) Updating project documents in a timely matter
(C) Documenting the requirements
(D) Documenting the scope updates

31. Under which of the following circumstances could a project manager incur a fine and be jailed?

(A) For failing to file the necessary permits in their own country.
(B) For using people from outside the project manager's country to work on the project.
(C) For not using minority workers on the project.
(D) For paying a bribe to a foreign official.

32. You are in the middle of a project when you discover that a software seller for your project is having major difficulty keeping employees due to a labor dispute. Many other projects in your company are using the company's services. What should you do?

(A) Tell the other project managers in your company about the labor problem.
(B) Attempt to keep the required people on your project.
(C) Cease doing business with the company.
(D) Contact the company and advise it that you will cancel its work on the project unless it settles its labor dispute.

33. You are asked by the PMI to provide information concerning the violation of the PMP Code of Professional Conduct by your best friend. To save the friendship, you refuse to provide any information: You are in violation of the responsibility to:

(A) Comply with laws governing professional practice.
(B) Report violations to PMI.
(C) Provide accurate information.
(D) Cooperate with the PMI concerning ethics violations.

34. Your company wants to open a plant in a country where the law stipulates that women can earn only 50% of what men earn. Under these circumstances, what should you recommend to your company?

(A) Do not open the plant.
(B) Your company should meet with government officials and try to get a waiver that equalizes the rate between men and women.
(C) Do not hire women.
(D) Provide the women you hire with extra work to increase their salary.

35. Which of the following is not a measure that determines whether a business practice used by another country is an unfair business practice?

    (A) It does not supply a decent wage for the country and the type of work.
    (B) It discriminates against women.
    (C) It hurts the right to physical movement.
    (D) It is a common practice in the other country.

36. The customer responsible for overseeing your project asks you to provide a written cost estimate that is 30% higher than your estimate of the project's cost. He explains that the budgeting process requires managers to estimate pessimistically to ensure enough money is allocated for projects. What is the best way to handle this?

    (A) Add the 30% as a lump sum contingency fund to handle project risks.
    (B) Add the 30% to your cost estimate by spreading it evenly across all project tasks.
    (C) Create one cost baseline for budget allocation and a second one for the actual project plan.
    (D) Ask for information on risks that would cause your estimate to be too small.

37. Suppose the project manager is called to an informal meeting with the customer and a problem is raised. This problem has major implications for the project manager's company, but the customer wants to pursue a solution at the meeting. The project manager should?

    (A) Give the customer an interim solution that must be approved by his boss.
    (B) Give the customer a range of solutions that might be acceptable to his company
    (C) Tell the customer that he will not address any problems because this is only an information exchange meeting.
    (D) Collect as much information on the problem without committing his company to a solution.

38. Maximizing one's influence facilitates communication. This involves building and sustaining credibility. Which of the following is now a behavior that can help in this regard?

    (A) Exhibiting expertise by the answers you give.
    (B) Being reliable and committed.
    (C) Being flexible and open to differences.
    (D) Being respectful.

39. An employee approaches you and asks if he can tell you something in confidence. He advises you that he has been performing illegal activities within the company for the last year. He is feeling guilty about it and is telling you to receive advice as to what he should do. What should you do?

    (A) Ask for full details.
    (B) Confirm that the activity is really illegal.
    (C) Inform your manager of the illegal activity.
    (D) Tell the employee to inform their boss.

40. What is the ethical code you'll be required to adhere to as a PMP?

    (A) Project Management Professional Standards
    (B) Project Management Professional Code of Professional Conduct
    (C) Project Management Code of Professional Ethics & Standards
    (D) Project Management Policy of Ethics

41. You are a new project manager for company B. You previously worked for company A that had an extensive project management practice. Company B has its own procedures, but you are more familiar with those from company A. Which of the following are you more adapt to do"

    (A) Use the practices from company A but include any forms from company B.
    (B) Use the forms from company B and begin to instruct them on ways to upgrade their own.
    (C) Talk about changes to the change control board of company B.
    (D) Interact with others in an ethical way by sharing the good aspects of company A's procedures.

42. During execution, a major problem occurred that was not included in the risk response plan. Which of the following options should you do first?

    (A) Create a workaround.
    (B) Reevaluate the risk identification process.
    (C) Look for any unexpected effects of the problem.
    (D) Tell management.

43. What is the project manager's key role during negotiations?

    (A) Protect the relationship between buyer and seller.
    (B) Negotiate a price under the seller's estimate.
    (C) Ensure that all project risks are thoroughly delineated.
    (D) Ensure that an effective communication plan is established.

44. You receive a contract to perform testing for a client. After contract award, the customer provides you with the test matrix to use for your 10 tests. A vice president says that the customer's test matrix is wrong, and he wants to use a different test matrix, which should give better results. This is a violation to the SOW. Suppose your sponsor is also the vice president for engineering. You should do which of the following?

    (A) Use the engineering test matrix and inform the customer
    (B) Tell your sponsor that you want to set up a meeting with the customer to resolve the conflict
    (C) Use the customer's test matrix
    (D) Use the engineering test matrix without telling the customer

45. You are managing a project with an estimated BAC of $5 million. About two-thirds through the project, you estimate that the project will be concluded early and just about 35% under budget. The contract is structured so that you will actually make less profit if you finish early. What should you do?

    (A) Direct your project team to increase the quality of their work so it takes the planned amount of time.
    (B) Do nothing and deliver the final project at the planned time and within the allowed budget.
    (C) Have a team meeting and gather input from the team on how to make the project last longer.
    (D) Inform the project stakeholder/sponsor about your budget projections.

46. During project execution, one of the electrical engineers informs the project manager that the life-cycle cost of the new heating and air conditioning system is higher than the life-cycle cost of another heating and air conditioning system. What should the project manager do?

    (A) Determine if there is room in the project budget for the additional cost.
    (B) Select the product with the lower life-cycle cost.
    (C) Select the product with the best life-cycle cost to earned value ratio.
    (D) Select the product with the lowest maintenance cost to life-cycle cost ratio.

47. You are managing a project team with several highly trained professionals. A couple of your team members have requested to work from home one day a week. What should you do?

(A) In the team members are good workers, approve the request.
(B) Issue a statement saying no one can work from home.
(C) Consult with human resources and found out about existing company policies.
(D) Be fair; issue a policy that all team members can work from home.

48. In the course of completing work on the project, the project manager needs to complete a task she has never done before. During this time, the project manager attends a discussion at a professional association where the presenter discusses how he completed a difficult task on his project that is similar to the project manager's task. He provides a handout describing his process. The project manager should do which of the following?

(A) Ignore the information.
(B) Ask your manager for guidance.
(C) Use the process to complete the task.
(D) Ask the speaker for permission to use the information.

49. A project manager discovers a defect in a deliverable due to the customer under contract today. The project manager knows the customer does not have the technical understanding to notice the defect. The deliverable technically meets the contract requirements, but it does not meet the project manager's fitness of use standard. What should the project manager do in this situation?

(A) Issue the deliverable and get formal acceptance from the customer.
(B) Note the problem in the lessons learned so future projects do not encounter the same problem.
(C) Discuss the issue with the customer.
(D) Inform the customer that the deliverable will be late.

50. Making the most of one's influence facilitates communications. When done properly this influence will involve building and sustaining credibility. Which of the following is not a behavior that can help in this regard?

(A) Being flexible and open to differences.
(B) Being respectful.
(C) Exhibiting expertise by the answers you give.
(D) Being reliable and committed.

51. While testing the strength of concrete poured on your project, you discover that over 35% of the concrete does not meet your company's quality standards. You feel certain the concrete will function as it is, and you don't think the concrete needs to meet the quality level specified. What should you do?

(A) List in your reports that the concrete simply "meets our quality needs"
(B) Report the lesser quality level and try to find a solution
(C) Ensure the remaining concrete meets the standard
(D) Change the quality standards to meet the level achieved

52. You are managing procurement for a project and have arranged a bid conference with the potential proposers. All of the following are appropriate for a bid conference except?

(A) Explanation of why particular terms and conditions are in the contract.
(B) A walk through of the project scope.
(C) Working with the bidders to determine alternative solutions for the project.
(D) A request for bidders to offer their thoughts on problems with the scope of the work.

53. You download information from a presentation authored by a colleague and use it in your presentation without crediting her. You are in violation of the responsibility to:

(A) Offer true information to the PMI.
(B) Disclose conflict of interest.
(C) Provide accurate information.
(D) Recognize and respect intellectual property of others.

54. You are the project manager of a project in Asia. You discover that the project leader has hired family members for several lucrative contracts on the project. What should you consider?

(A) Ethical issues
(B) Cultural issues
(C) Political issues
(D) Organizational issues

55. Although your company is not the lowest bidder for a project, the client has come to expect good performance from your company and wants to award the contract to you. To win the contract the client asks you to eliminate your project management costs. The client says that your company has good project processes, and project controls unnecessarily inflate your costs. What should you do under these circumstances?

(A) Remove costs associated with project team communications, meetings, and customer reviews.
(B) Describe the costs incurred on past projects that did not use project management.
(C) Remove meeting costs but not the project manager's salary.
(D) Eliminate your project management costs and rely on experience.

56. You are the project manager for a large project under contract with the government. The contract for this two year, multi-million dollar project was signed six months ago. You were not involved in contract negotiations or setting up procedures for managing changes, but now you are swamped with changes from the sponsor and from people inside your organization. Who is normally responsible for formally reviewing major changes to the project/contract?

(A) The change control board.
(B) The contracting/legal department.
(C) The project manager.
(D) Senior management.

57. You are working on a project that has been assigned to determine the number of highway deaths caused by drunken drives over the last 3 years. Your company received a grant of $700,000 from the U.S. Department of Commerce for this project. The final report is due in 3 weeks. You have prepared an algorithm to calculate the total number killed based on a representative sample of fatalities in 5 states from 2000 to 2005. You were supposed to obtain these data as part of the research project, but your management used $425,000 of the money for other purposes. The deadline is rapidly approaching, and your project manager has asked you to complete the project with incomplete data. You have to formally present your results to your CEO next week and the final report must be submitted to the Commerce Department to receive the monies due. In this situation, you should:

(A) Prepare a rough estimate based on your knowledge of the subject, and complete the project.
(B) Explain in writing and in your oral presentation that you cannot complete the project because of the incomplete data.
(C) Use the results of research prepared by another organization as the basis for your effort, even though you do not have access to the raw data.
(D) Inform management that you need additional time, and ask for a formal extension.

58. You are managing a project that is in process. A large and unexpected problem occurs that will cause a delay in the schedule in excess of the contingency schedule for the project. What should you do?

(A) Reduce testing on the completed tasks.
(B) Speak to the stakeholders about getting additional time and budget for the project.
(C) Require mandatory overtime for the project team.
(D) Look at other tasks in the schedule and see which ones should be reduced to allow time for this problem to be worked.

59. During construction of a new manufacturing facility in another country, one of your team members complains to you that the wage paid to the workers is below the acceptable wage in your home country. In this situation it is best to:

(A) Pay the workers an appropriate wage for the country within which they work.
(B) Ignore the issue as you have not heard the workers complain.
(C) Pay the workers at the new facility the same wage as your country.
(D) Pay the workers at the new facility a little less than the same wage as your country.

60. You are a project manager on an international project of great importance to the client. The client is from another country and is so excited by how well the project is going that he presents you with a company automobile for your personal use. Which of the following is your best option?

(A) Thank him and offer a gift in exchange.
(B) Politely turn down the gift.
(C) Ask that the gift be changed to something that can be shared by the team.
(D) Ask for a gift that can be used up before you return home.

61. You've been assigned to take over managing a project that should be half-complete according to the schedule. You discover that the project is running far behind schedule, and that the project will probably take double the time originally estimated by the previous project manager. However, upper management has been told that the project is on schedule. Which of the following is the best option in this situation?

(A) Try to restructure the schedule to meet the project deadline.
(B) Report your assessment to upper management.
(C) Turn the project back to the previous project manager.
(D) Move forward with the schedule as planned by the previous project manager and report at the first missed milestone.

62. You are the project manager for a large company project. You have completed the project according to the design documents and have met the project scope. The customer agrees that the design document requirements have been met; however, the customer is not pleased with the project deliverables and is demanding additional adjustments be made to complete the project. What is the best way to continue?

(A) Complete the work as the customer has requested.
(B) Complete the work at 1.5 times the billable rate.
(C) Do nothing. The project scope is completed.
(D) Do nothing. Management from the performing organization and the customer's organization will need to determine why the project failed before adding work.

63. Your movie theater business has exploded ever since you introduced a "single night". Accordingly, you need to build another facility and have assembled an invitation for bid (IFB) package with all the necessary descriptions of the required supplies, equipment, and services. You are convinced that the IFB will result in equal and fair competition among all sellers. You want to avoid any confusion regarding the work to be performed because you probably will not conduct negotiations with the sellers; however, you may or may not award the contract to the lowest-bidding seller, and you have made this clear in the IFB. In this situation, you should be prepared to:

(A) Inform the seller who won the bid and indicate to the others that no further discussion will take place on this issue.
(B) Limit the sellers who will receive the IFB to reduce conflict.
(C) Prohibit sellers from attending the bid opening because you will need time to decide to whom to award the contract.
(D) Document your award decision as completely as possible to all sellers.

64. You've been engaged to manage a project. The estimated cost of the project is $1,000,000. The project sponsor has approved this amount. Your earned value calculations indicate that the project will be completed on time and under budget by $200,000. Based on this calculation, your personal profit will decrease by $2,000. Given the estimated decrease in personal profit, what action should you take?

(A) Inform the end-user that you can add features to the project in order to use the entire budget.
(B) Communicate the projected financial outcome to the project sponsor.
(C) Invoice for the full $1,000,000 based on the contract.
(D) Add tasks to improve the outcome and increase the actual project cost.

65. As the leader of a project team, the project manager may be required to assess the competencies of his or her team members. Occasionally, some weaknesses or areas for improvement will be identified. The project manager should:

(A) Hire additional resources to compensate for weak areas
(B) Wait for the team members to fail in an assignment to justify termination
(C) Remove any team members who have demonstrated weaknesses in critical knowledge areas
(D) Communicate those weaknesses and establish a performance improvement program

66. While completing a project, a project manager realizes he needs to decrease project costs. After researching his options, he comes up with the following choices. Which of the following choices would decrease project costs?

(A) Change to component A from component B. Component A costs more to purchase but has a lower life-cycle cost than B.
(B) Change task A to be completed by resource B instead of resource C. Resource B is a more experienced worker.
(C) Move tasks B and H to occur concurrently, and take the risk of a 30% increase in the need for five more resources later.
(D) Delete an acceptance test from the project plan.

67. You have a project team member who is sabotaging your project because he does not agree with it. Which of the following should you do?

(A) Fire the project team member.
(B) Present the problem to management.
(C) Present the problem to management with a solution to remove the team member from the project.
(D) Present the problem to management with a demand to fire the project team member.

68. You are reviewing the expense reports for one of your team members when you notice a payment he made in another country. You think the payment is a bribe. What is your FIRST course of action?

    (A) Seek legal advice.
    (B) Contact the payee in the other country and ask if the payment was a bribe.
    (C) Ignore the problem; it is in the past.
    (D) File a permit authorizing the team to make such payments.

69. One of the engineers on your team performs a presentation to a perspective client about a proposed design. In answering questions, the engineer reveals that she does not agree with the way in which this system is engineered during the presentation. What are your options as the project manager of the engineer, listening to the presentation?

    (A) Ask the engineer to explain the discrepancy and what recommendations she can offer.
    (B) Rephrase the problem to ensure that everyone understands the various major points and solicit input from everyone.
    (C) Communicate an openness to the problem and lead a discussion to resolve the issues.
    (D) Immediately stop the engineer and do damage control.

70. Your organization is having a difficult time managing all of its projects. You have been asked to help senior management get a better understanding of the problems. What is the first thing you should do?

    (A) Meet with individual project managers to get a better sense of what is happening.
    (B) Send a formal memo to all project managers requesting their project plans.
    (C) Meet with senior managers to help them develop a new tracking system for managing projects.
    (D) Review the project charters and Gantt charts for all projects.

71. You are the project manager of a large company project. Your organization is a functional environment and you do not get along well with the functional manager leading the project. You are in disagreement with the manager on how the project should proceed, the timings of the activities, the suggested schedule, and the expected quality of the work. The manager has requested that you get to work on several of the activities on the critical path even though you and she have not solved the issues concerning the project. Which of the following should you do?

    (A) Complete the activities as requested.
    (B) Go to senior management and voice your concerns.
    (C) Refuse to begin activities on the project until the issues are resolved.
    (D) Ask to be taken off of the project.

72. You are the project manager for a high visibility project. The margin on this project is low, and it is extremely important that the cost estimates for the work on the project be accurate. While reviewing the cost estimates for this project you notice that one of the cost estimates for an element in the WBS is 10% higher than two previous projects for very similar work. What should you do?

    (A) Accept the estimate because you trust all of the people on your project team, and they are responsible for estimates.
    (B) Reduce the estimate and add the additional budget to the management reserve.
    (C) Ask the person responsible for the estimate to explain the difference and bring supporting information to you.
    (D) Reduce the estimate and add the additional budget to the contingency reserve.

73. You are in the process of reviewing bids from various vendors for work on your project. One of the bidding vendors has a history of delivering on time within budget, and you have personally worked with this company successfully on previous engagements. You receive a call from the manager submitting the bid inquiring about how the process is going. He asks to have lunch with you to discuss the bid. Which of the following is the best response?

(A) Do not mention the other bidders but simply inform him that based on past experience, he has a good chance of winning the business.
(B) Inform him that it would be inappropriate to discuss the matter at all and inform the customer or a team member of the conversation.
(C) Inform him that it would not be appropriate to discuss the matter over the phone during business hours, but that an informal lunch discussion would be more appropriate.
(D) Politely avoid continuing the conversation and disregard the bid.

74. A major negotiation with a potential subcontractor is scheduled for tomorrow when you discover there is a good chance the project will be canceled. What should you do?

(A) Do not spend too much time preparing for the negotiations
(B) Cut the negotiations short
(C) Only negotiate major items
(D) Postpone the negotiations

75. You are in the middle of a new product development project for your publicly traded company when you discover that the previous project manager made a US $3,000,000 payment that was not approved in accordance with your company policies. Luckily, the project CPI is 1.2. What should you do?

(A) Put the payment in an escrow account.
(B) Contact your manager.
(C) Ignore the payment.
(D) Bury the cost in the largest cost center available.

76. A manager has been given responsibility for a project that has the support of senior management. From the beginning, you have disagreed with the manager as to how the project should proceed and what the deliverables should be. You and she have disagreed over many issues in the past. Your department has been tasked with providing some key tasks for the project. What should you do?

(A) Inform your manager of your concerns to get their support.
(B) Ask to be removed from the project.
(C) Sit down with the manager at the beginning of the project and attempt to describe why you object to the project and discover a way to solve the problem.
(D) Provide the manager with what she needs.

77. You recently completed a major environmental remediation project involving the disposal of hazardous waste from a local power plant. Your client accepted the work, and your company has been paid. The project has been closed officially for more than 6 weeks. Now you are working on a new project that happens to be located at the same local power plant. While working on the new project, you discovered a possible flaw in the disposal system that was delivered for the earlier project. You reviewed drawings for that project and discovered that they are incomplete. No one else has confirmed your concerns. You do not believe any problems will be apparent for about 5 years, if ever. In this situation, you should:

(A) Contact the customer directly and inform it of the potential problem so that it can modify your contract to correct the problem.
(B) Enhance your quality assurance and project review system immediately for future projects.
(C) Do nothing because the project is complete and the customer accepted the work based on its own independent inspection.
(D) Alert your management to the situation, both orally and in writing, and request that someone else confirm your findings.

78. You have been working on a nine-month project for six months. The project is ahead of schedule when one of the functional managers tells you the resources committed to the project are no longer available. After checking further, you discover the company has another project that just started and is using the resources committed to your project. You believe the new project is not critical, but the project manager is the son of a board member. What is the best course of action in this situation?

(A) Determine when resources will become available.
(B) Ask upper management to formally prioritize the projects.
(C) Use the reserve to hire contractors to complete the work.
(D) Negotiate a new schedule with the other project manager.

79. As project manager you are managing a project with a BAC of $ 5 million. About halfway through the project, you estimate that the project will be completed early and roughly 30% under budget. The contract is structured so that you actually make less profit if you finish early. You decide that you should?

(A) Hold a team meeting and let them decide what to do.
(B) Tell the project sponsor about your budget and schedule projections.
(C) Continue working on the project and complete early.
(D) Direct your team to increase work time and quality of work in order to get back on schedule.

80. You are managing a two-year project involving staff from several departments. The project is on schedule and within budget. A key team member leaves for a four-week vacation without completing a highly technical and specialized task assigned to him (task A). The project team cannot begin task B and task E (a critical path task) until task A is completed. Task A has three days slack and is not on the critical path. A team member, a vendor, and a non-team member work overtime to complete task A within its slack time. You need to reimburse the non-team member's department and pay the vendor at an overtime rate. What action should you take?

(A) Re-evaluate your communications management plan.
(B) Send a complaint letter to the team member's boss, and ask him to fund the extra cost expended.
(C) Pay the cost out of your project reserves.
(D) Thank the others for filling in but tell them not to waste time on non-critical path tasks.

81. Your executives, in appreciation for the success of your project, have given you a $10,000 bonus to be disbursed among your five-team members. One of the five, who is a substandard worker and accomplished very little on your project, is in your car pool. You should:

(A) Provide everyone with an equal share
(B) Provide everyone a share based upon their performance
(C) Ask the sponsor to make the decision
(D) Ask the workers to decide among themselves how the bonus should be subdivided

82. You are a newly appointed project manager for a building remodel at your firm. The project is currently in the bidding phase to select the contractors that will do the construction week opened. While shopping at the mall, you run into someone that works for one of the bidders. You decide to have lunch together but do not discuss the project. At the end of the lunch, the person offers to pay for your meal. What do you do?

(A) Let the person pay for your lunch and later on, tell upper management.
(B) A. Let the person pay for your lunch.
(C) Pay for both lunches.
(D) Do not let the person pay for your lunch.

83. A key activity for achieving customer satisfaction is to define:

(A) The business use.
(B) Requirements.
(C) Product specificity.
(D) Change control.

84. You are the project manager for an information technology project. It has come to your attention that a technical problem has stopped the project work. How should the project manager proceed?

(A) Rebaseline the project performance to account for the technical problem.
(B) Measure the project performance to date and account for the cost of the technical problem.
(C) Outsource the technical problem to a vendor.
(D) Work with the project team to develop alternative solutions to the technical problem.

85. You are the project manager at a large automaker in Detroit. Your project involves designing the next generation 4-wheel drive Sports Utility Vehicle for the US market. A new fuel-efficient engine design is required as part of your project. Unfortunately, your project team doesn't have the expertise to design and manufacture a new fuel-efficient engine. Hence, your company subcontracted all the engine design to an outside manufacturer in Japan. During your initial visit to your Japanese partners, you were presented with an expensive gift. You were told that it is local custom to give such gifts to business partners during their visits. What should you do?

(A) Explain that the gift may be construed as a conflict of interest, and hence you cannot accept the gift.
(B) Since the gift will not influence your future decisions, you can accept the gift as there is no conflict or interest.
(C) Since accepting the gift may give the appearance of impropriety, you should decline the gift outright.
(D) Accept the gift so as not to offend anyone. However, report the gift to the appropriate parties at your company so that you do not give the appearance of impropriety.

86. Negotiating across international cultures involves mutual interdependence between parties. The negotiating must be conducted in an atmosphere of?

(A) Generalities and vagueness
(B) Mutual trust and cooperation
(C) Uncertainty and caution
(D) Sincerity and compassion

87. Your project is being completed in another country. It is going reasonably well and is ahead of the cost projections when one of the local officials informs you he will make sure the project work stops unless you pay him $10,000. What is the best thing to do?

(A) Make the payment.
(B) Offer to pay more than the requested amount to get more support from the official in the future.
(C) Offer to pay a smaller amount to discourage future requests for larger amounts.
(D) Do not make the payment.

88. What is the most effective process to ensure that cultural and ethical differences do not impede success of your multi-national project?

(A) Training
(B) Collocating
(C) Teaming
(D) Forming

89. Your company has a policy that only a certain hotel chain may be used for business travel. You discover that a more expensive hotel is offering a discount on the days you need to be in town. What should you do?

(A) Use the company's hotel chain.
(B) Provide justification on your expense report for using the other hotel chain.
(C) Ask your manager for permission to use the other hotel chain.
(D) Contact the hotel chain to negotiate a better rate.

90. A car company that improves their engines so their cars get higher than the legally required minimum standard for miles per gallon is practicing?

(A) The classical view
(B) Social responsibility
(C) Issue intensity
(D) Social responsiveness

91. You are the project manager for a large project. Some members of the project team have come to you and asked that they be permitted to work on a flexible schedule. Some of the other team members feel that it is important that all team members be on site at all times unless they are absent for business reasons. What should you do?

(A) Accept the request for flexible time schedules.
(B) Turn down the request for flexible time schedules.
(C) Discuss this problem with your manager and act on the results of the meeting.
(D) Arrange a meeting of the project team members and allow them to decide.

92. While visiting the country where a new branch office is being built, you are told that you must pay a US $5,000 fee to the government permit officer to obtain the facility permit required by law to start construction. The construction company tells you this is standard practice and is required by law. What should you do?

(A) Refuse to pay the fee.
(B) Have the construction company pay the fee.
(C) Have the customer pay the fee
(D) Pay the fee.

93. On one of your company's medical research projects, you object to how the research is being handled. However, you signed a confidentiality agreement with the company that prohibits you from talking about your research. Which of the following is your best option?

(A) Quit and do not talk about what you know.
(B) Quit and begin talking to the community.
(C) Continue working and begin to talk about your objections to the research to newspapers in other cities.
(D) Destroy the research.

94. While constructing a new drug manufacturing plant, you discover a leak in a pipe that has released chemicals into the ground. It had been difficult to acquire the necessary government approval and community support for the plant, and management has told you to be particularly careful to not upset the community. You are uncertain if the chemicals could leak into the ground water or cause any damage. What should you do?

(A) Follow the instructions to avoid upsetting the community and do nothing.
(B) Start to write articles in the local paper about how poorly treated the local drinking water is.
(C) Wherever possible, communicate all the great benefits of the plant to the community.
(D) Inform local officials and ask for their help.

95. Project Managers can contribute to their organization's knowledge base and to the profession of project management most effectively by:

(A) Promote the use of ad hoc project management
(B) Ensuring that all project plans are developed before the project team is formed
(C) Developing and implementing a project review and lessons learned process
(D) Establishing strict guidelines for protecting intellectual property

96. In order for the project manager to fully and effectively understand a stake holder's personal concerns or grievances it may necessary to:

(A) Schedule a project review session with the entire project team
(B) Ask for a written description of the problem and submit it through the project office
(C) Attempt to empathize with the stakeholder
(D) Involve the project sponsor as an arbitrator

97. You have just been assigned project manager for a new telecommunications project. There appear to be many risks on this project, but no one has evaluated them to assess the range of possible project outcomes. What needs to be done?

(A) Risk quantification
(B) Risk monitoring and control
(C) Risk response planning
(D) Risk identification

98. You are four months into a three year project when your project team makes significant discoveries on your project. What is the best course of action?

(A) Make certain the discoveries are in the monthly status report.
(B) Make certain the discoveries are included in the project lessons learned.
(C) Make certain you tell the other project managers involved in this program at the weekly meeting.
(D) Make certain you mention them at the senior management meeting in two months.

99. You are assigned to a project that senior management has already decided to outsource. As a project manager, you need to work with the contracts department to select the vendor and then oversee the vendor through project completion. Company policy requires that a project of this size go through a formal bid process. A vice president in your company tells you that his friend owns one of the companies that might bid on the project, and it would be an excellent choice as a vendor. This vice president has a reputation for making or breaking careers. What is generally the best course of action?

(A) Obtain written permission to bypass the formal bid process.
(B) Follow the bid process and show the vice president why the favored vendor is or is not the best choice.
(C) Let the contracts department handle the situation.
(D) Let the evaluation team know that management has a favorite vendor.

100. Your client wants you to do some work for him that is not specified in your company's contract with him. To establish good will with the customer, you decide to go forward with the work, and not inform your company about it. Would this action be considered to be:

(A) Failure to satisfy the scope of professional services
(B) An act of impropriety
(C) Conflict of interest
(D) Dishonest representation of information

Sample Answer Sheet

	T F		T F		T F		T F
1	Ⓐ Ⓑ Ⓒ Ⓓ Ⓔ	26	Ⓐ Ⓑ Ⓒ Ⓓ Ⓔ	51	Ⓐ Ⓑ Ⓒ Ⓓ Ⓔ	76	Ⓐ Ⓑ Ⓒ Ⓓ Ⓕ
2	Ⓐ Ⓑ Ⓒ Ⓓ Ⓔ	27	Ⓐ Ⓑ Ⓒ Ⓓ Ⓔ	52	Ⓐ Ⓑ Ⓒ Ⓓ Ⓔ	77	Ⓐ Ⓑ Ⓒ Ⓓ Ⓔ
3	Ⓐ Ⓑ Ⓒ Ⓓ Ⓔ	28	Ⓐ Ⓑ Ⓒ Ⓓ Ⓔ	53	Ⓐ Ⓑ Ⓒ Ⓓ Ⓔ	78	Ⓐ Ⓑ Ⓒ Ⓓ Ⓔ
4	Ⓐ Ⓑ Ⓒ Ⓓ Ⓔ	29	Ⓐ Ⓑ Ⓒ Ⓓ Ⓔ	54	Ⓐ Ⓑ Ⓒ Ⓓ Ⓔ	79	Ⓐ Ⓑ Ⓒ Ⓓ Ⓔ
5	Ⓐ Ⓑ Ⓒ Ⓓ Ⓔ	30	Ⓐ Ⓑ Ⓒ Ⓓ Ⓔ	55	Ⓐ Ⓑ Ⓒ Ⓓ Ⓔ	80	Ⓐ Ⓑ Ⓒ Ⓓ Ⓔ
6	Ⓐ Ⓑ Ⓒ Ⓓ Ⓔ	31	Ⓐ Ⓑ Ⓒ Ⓓ Ⓔ	56	Ⓐ Ⓑ Ⓒ Ⓓ Ⓔ	81	Ⓐ Ⓑ Ⓒ Ⓓ Ⓔ
7	Ⓐ Ⓑ Ⓒ Ⓓ Ⓔ	32	Ⓐ Ⓑ Ⓒ Ⓓ Ⓔ	57	Ⓐ Ⓑ Ⓒ Ⓓ Ⓔ	82	Ⓐ Ⓑ Ⓒ Ⓓ Ⓔ
8	Ⓐ Ⓑ Ⓒ Ⓓ Ⓔ	33	Ⓐ Ⓑ Ⓒ Ⓓ Ⓔ	58	Ⓐ Ⓑ Ⓒ Ⓓ Ⓔ	83	Ⓐ Ⓑ Ⓒ Ⓓ Ⓔ
9	Ⓐ Ⓑ Ⓒ Ⓓ Ⓔ	34	Ⓐ Ⓑ Ⓒ Ⓓ Ⓔ	59	Ⓐ Ⓑ Ⓒ Ⓓ Ⓔ	84	Ⓐ Ⓑ Ⓒ Ⓓ Ⓔ
10	Ⓐ Ⓑ Ⓒ Ⓓ Ⓔ	35	Ⓐ Ⓑ Ⓒ Ⓓ Ⓔ	60	Ⓐ Ⓑ Ⓒ Ⓓ Ⓔ	85	Ⓐ Ⓑ Ⓒ Ⓓ Ⓔ
11	Ⓐ Ⓑ Ⓒ Ⓓ Ⓔ	36	Ⓐ Ⓑ Ⓒ Ⓓ Ⓔ	61	Ⓐ Ⓑ Ⓒ Ⓓ Ⓔ	86	Ⓐ Ⓑ Ⓒ Ⓓ Ⓔ
12	Ⓐ Ⓑ Ⓒ Ⓓ Ⓔ	37	Ⓐ Ⓑ Ⓒ Ⓓ Ⓔ	62	Ⓐ Ⓑ Ⓒ Ⓓ Ⓔ	87	Ⓐ Ⓑ Ⓒ Ⓓ Ⓔ
13	Ⓐ Ⓑ Ⓒ Ⓓ Ⓕ	38	Ⓐ Ⓑ Ⓒ Ⓓ Ⓔ	63	Ⓐ Ⓑ Ⓒ Ⓓ Ⓔ	88	Ⓐ Ⓑ Ⓒ Ⓓ Ⓔ
14	Ⓐ Ⓑ Ⓒ Ⓓ Ⓔ	39	Ⓐ Ⓑ Ⓒ Ⓓ Ⓔ	64	Ⓐ Ⓑ Ⓒ Ⓓ Ⓔ	89	Ⓐ Ⓑ Ⓒ Ⓓ Ⓔ
15	Ⓐ Ⓑ Ⓒ Ⓓ Ⓔ	40	Ⓐ Ⓑ Ⓒ Ⓓ Ⓔ	65	Ⓐ Ⓑ Ⓒ Ⓓ Ⓔ	90	Ⓐ Ⓑ Ⓒ Ⓓ Ⓔ
16	Ⓐ Ⓑ Ⓒ Ⓓ Ⓔ	41	Ⓐ Ⓑ Ⓒ Ⓓ Ⓔ	66	Ⓐ Ⓑ Ⓒ Ⓓ Ⓔ	91	Ⓐ Ⓑ Ⓒ Ⓓ Ⓔ
17	Ⓐ Ⓑ Ⓒ Ⓓ Ⓔ	42	Ⓐ Ⓑ Ⓒ Ⓓ Ⓔ	67	Ⓐ Ⓑ Ⓒ Ⓓ Ⓔ	92	Ⓐ Ⓑ Ⓒ Ⓓ Ⓔ
18	Ⓐ Ⓑ Ⓒ Ⓓ Ⓔ	43	Ⓐ Ⓑ Ⓒ Ⓓ Ⓔ	68	Ⓐ Ⓑ Ⓒ Ⓓ Ⓔ	93	Ⓐ Ⓑ Ⓒ Ⓓ Ⓔ
19	Ⓐ Ⓑ Ⓒ Ⓓ Ⓔ	44	Ⓐ Ⓑ Ⓒ Ⓓ Ⓔ	69	Ⓐ Ⓑ Ⓒ Ⓓ Ⓔ	94	Ⓐ Ⓑ Ⓒ Ⓓ Ⓔ
20	Ⓐ Ⓑ Ⓒ Ⓓ Ⓔ	45	Ⓐ Ⓑ Ⓒ Ⓓ Ⓔ	70	Ⓐ Ⓑ Ⓒ Ⓓ Ⓔ	95	Ⓐ Ⓑ Ⓒ Ⓓ Ⓔ
21	Ⓐ Ⓑ Ⓒ Ⓓ Ⓔ	46	Ⓐ Ⓑ Ⓒ Ⓓ Ⓔ	71	Ⓐ Ⓑ Ⓒ Ⓓ Ⓔ	96	Ⓐ Ⓑ Ⓒ Ⓓ Ⓔ
22	Ⓐ Ⓑ Ⓒ Ⓓ Ⓔ	47	Ⓐ Ⓑ Ⓒ Ⓓ Ⓔ	72	Ⓐ Ⓑ Ⓒ Ⓓ Ⓔ	97	Ⓐ Ⓑ Ⓒ Ⓓ Ⓔ
23	Ⓐ Ⓑ Ⓒ Ⓓ Ⓔ	48	Ⓐ Ⓑ Ⓒ Ⓓ Ⓔ	73	Ⓐ Ⓑ Ⓒ Ⓓ Ⓔ	98	Ⓐ Ⓑ Ⓒ Ⓓ Ⓔ
24	Ⓐ Ⓑ Ⓒ Ⓓ Ⓔ	49	Ⓐ Ⓑ Ⓒ Ⓓ Ⓔ	74	Ⓐ Ⓑ Ⓒ Ⓓ Ⓔ	99	Ⓐ Ⓑ Ⓒ Ⓓ Ⓔ
25	Ⓐ Ⓑ Ⓒ Ⓓ Ⓔ	50	Ⓐ Ⓑ Ⓒ Ⓓ Ⓔ	75	Ⓐ Ⓑ Ⓒ Ⓓ Ⓔ	100	Ⓐ Ⓑ Ⓒ Ⓓ Ⓔ

Professional Responsibility – Answers

1. **(C) Protect the relationship between buyer and seller.**

2. **(B) Culture shock**. Culture shock is the typical disorientation a person feels when visiting a foreign country.

3. **(D) pay the workers an appropriate wage for the country within which they work.**

4. **(D) Ask one person at each team meeting to describe something unique about their culture.**

5. **(B) Begin the meeting with a discussion of diversity and professional behavior.**

6. **(B) Apply a general contingency to try to compensate.**

7. **(B) Believing in the inherent superiority and naturalness of your own culture.** Ethnocentrism is a basic human response, and through it, we rate others according to our standards and ways of doing things. It can be highly destructive because it closes off our ability to relate to others and leads to hasty evaluations and derogatory remarks. It is important to recognize this tendency and try to avoid it.

8. **(D) Speak to the visiting engineers and discuss having an informal meeting between your engineers and the visiting engineers.** This type of problem occurs frequently. Many times there is a misunderstanding on the part of the customer's engineers, and it can be resolved simply by having an informal meeting and discussing the problem. Later, if the disagreement persists, the customer should submit a request for a change, and a formal investigation can be completed.

9. **(A) Follow the legal requirements set up by the company for using outside services.**

10. **(D) Provide an accurate estimate of the actual costs and be able to support it.**

11. **(D) Reduce the scope of work and enter closure.**

12. **(C) Negotiate with the sponsor to decide how to remedy this problem.**

13. **(B) Wait until next year.**

14. **(D) For paying a bribe to a foreign official.**

15. **(A) Continue to plan for the project until the scope of work is defined.**

16. **(B) Inquire if hiring only through family lines is common practice for the project leader's country.**

17. **(A) Determine the legality of company procedures.**

18. **(B) Speaking the language of the host country**

19. **(A) Cultural differences will always be an obstacle to be overcome.**

20. **(A) There is no one "best way" for project organization.**

21. **(D) Make sure the person is really a government official.**

22. **(A) Refuse to make the payment and hope to get the contract solely based on your company's abilities.**

23. **(B) Inform the public that a detailed examination has been ordered to determine the extent to which the problem exists.**

24. **(A) Make a good faith effort to find a way to decrease the cost.**

25. **(A) Offering to pay the country officials for not awarding the project to a particular company**

26. **(C) Ask for clarification of the intent of adding the resource.**

27. **(A) Do not accept the software and advise the family member that such activity is in violation of copyright law.**

28. **(A) Many competing needs and objectives must be satisfied.**

29. **(C) Contact the employee's manager to arrange a meeting to discuss the matter.**

30. **(C) Documenting the requirements**

31. **(A) For failing to file the necessary permits in their own country.**

32. **(A) Tell the other project managers in your company about the labor problem.**

33. **(D) Cooperate with the PMI concerning ethics violations.** PMP Professional Code of Conduct I.A.3

34. **(A) Do not open the plant.**

35. **(D) It is a common practice in the other country.**

36. **(D) Ask for information on risks that would cause your estimate to be too small.**

37. **(D) Collect as much information on the problem without committing his company to a solution.**

38. **(A) Exhibiting expertise by the answers you give.**

39. **(C) Inform your manager of the illegal activity.**

40. **(B) Project Management Professional Code of Professional Conduct**

41. **(B) Use the forms from company B and begin to instruct them on ways to upgrade their own.**

42. **(A) Create a workaround.**

43. **(A) Protect the relationship between buyer and seller.**

44. **(B) Tell your sponsor that you want to set up a meeting with the customer to resolve the conflict**

45. **(D) Inform the project stakeholder/sponsor about your budget projections.** PMP® Professional Code of Conduct.

46. **(B) Select the product with the lower life-cycle cost.**

47. **(C) Consult with human resources and found out about existing company policies.**

48. **(D) Ask the speaker for permission to use the information.**

49. **(C) Discuss the issue with the customer.**

50. **(C) Exhibiting expertise by the answers you give.**

51. **(B) Report the lesser quality level and try to find a solution**

52. (C) Working with the bidders to determine alternative solutions for the project.

53. (D) Recognize and respect intellectual property of others. PMP® Professional Code of Conduct I.C.1

54. (B) Cultural issues. The project manager should first determine what the country's customs and culture call for when hiring relatives. It may be a preferred practice in the country to work with qualified relatives first before hiring other individuals to complete the project work.

55. (B) Describe the costs incurred on past projects that did not use project management.

56. (A) The change control board.

57. (B) Explain in writing and in your oral presentation that you cannot complete the project because of the incomplete data. PMP® Professional Code of Conduct.

58. (D) Look at other tasks in the schedule and see which ones should be reduced to allow time for this problem to be worked. The first thing that should be done is to look for tasks in the project where there is an ability to reschedule to free resources for this problem. If the problem is severe and additional budget and time is needed, it may be necessary to speak to the stakeholders, but the project impacts and plan for the correction should come first.

59. (A) Pay the workers an appropriate wage for the country within which they work.

60. (B) Politely turn down the gift.

61. (B) Report your assessment to upper management.

62. (C) Do nothing. The project scope is completed. When the project scope has been completed, the project is completed. Any additional work, without a contract change or new contract, would be dishonest and would betray the customer or the project manager's company.

63. (D) Document your award decision as completely as possible to all sellers. In an IFB, all bids are open at a specific time, and sellers are allowed to attend the bid opening. Most of the time bids are open and read aloud for those who are present. Usually the contract award goes to the lowest-bidding seller that also is financially responsible and capable of doing the work. On occasion, however, the buyer also will consider quality and time when selecting a seller. Professional judgment is critical. If the contract is not awarded to the lowest seller, it is important to document the reasons carefully. This type of contracting method is open to fraud, collusion, and other dishonest conduct. Therefore, project managers and contracting personnel must practice carefully defined, ethical business procedures.

64. (B) Communicate the projected financial outcome to the project sponsor.

65. (D) Communicate those weaknesses and establish a performance improvement program

66. (D) Delete an acceptance test from the project plan.

67. (C) Present the problem to management with a solution to remove the team member from the project. The project team member that is causing the problems should be presented to management with a solution to remove the project team member from the project. Remember, whenever the project manager must present a problem to management, he should also present a solution to the problem.

68. (A) Seek legal advice.

69. (D) Immediately stop the engineer and do damage control. Presumably, any design issues will be hashed out before this presentation is made. As the PM, you should know why the design choices were made and should be able to answer the engineer's concerns directly to the client as part of your damage control. If there are pending design issues, these should be noted in the presentation, and the engineer's comments can be placed in the context of these noted issues.

70. (A) Meet with individual project managers to get a better sense of what is happening.

71. (A) Complete the activities as requested. The project manager must respect the delegation of the Functional Manager.

72. (C) Ask the person responsible for the estimate to explain the difference and bring supporting information to you. Estimating is just that, an estimating process. Perhaps it would have been better for the project manager to have given all the information to the person responsible for the estimate. At this point the best thing to do is to use all of the information available to create the most accurate estimate that is practical.

73. (B) Inform him that it would be inappropriate to discuss the matter at all and inform the customer or a team member of the conversation.

74. (D) Postpone the negotiations

75. (B) Contact your manager.

76. (D) Provide the manager with what she needs.

77. (D) Alert your management to the situation, both orally and in writing, and request that someone else confirm your findings. PMP® Professional Code of Conduct. In this situation, there is a potential, yet unconfirmed, problem with a deliverable that has been completed and accepted by the customer. The project is closed; however, further action is required. Personal and professional conduct, work-related conduct, community responsibility, and client relations are issues that must be considered when working as a professional in the project management business.

78. (B) Ask upper management to formally prioritize the projects.

79. (B) Tell the project sponsor about your budget and schedule projections. PMP Code of Conduct.

80. (A) Re-evaluate your communications management plan.

81. (D) Ask the workers to decide among themselves how the bonus should be subdivided

82. (D) Do not let the person pay for your lunch.

83. (C) Product specificity.

84. (D) Work with the project team to develop alternative solutions to the technical problem. When problems arise that stop project tasks, the project manager should work with the team to uncover viable alternative solutions.

85. (D) Accept the gift so as not to offend anyone. However, report the gift to the appropriate parties at your company so that you do not give the appearance of impropriety. The best answer in this situation is to accept the gift initially, so as not to offend anyone. However, the acceptance of the gift should be reported to the appropriate parties at your company so that you do not give the appearance of impropriety. (PMP® Professional Code of Conduct)

86. (B) Mutual trust and cooperation

87. (D) Do not make the payment. PMP® Professional Code of Conduct.

88. (A) Training

89. (A) Use the company's hotel chain.

90. (B) Social responsibility

91. (D) Arrange a meeting of the project team members and allow them to decide. It is usually in the best interest of the project if the project team decides matters of personal time themselves unless there are significant reasons for the project team to be on site at certain hours or because they are necessary to interact with other people on the team.

92. (D) Pay the fee.

93. (A) Quit and do not talk about what you know.

94. (D) Inform local officials and ask for their help.

95. (C) Developing and implementing a project review and lessons learned process

96. (C) Attempt to empathize with the stakeholder

97. (D) Risk identification.

98. (C) Make certain you tell the other project managers involved in this program at the weekly meeting.

99. (B) Follow the bid process and show the vice president why the favored vendor is or is not the best choice.

100. (A) Failure to satisfy the scope of professional services. PMP® Professional Code of Conduct II.A.2

PMP Sample Exam – Questions (4 Hours)

1. Your company wants to assign a resource that is not within the project scope to your project and asks you to bill that resource to the customer. This concerns you because you get a bonus for maximizing billings to the customer. Which of the following is the best course to follow?

    (A) Ask for clarification of the intent of adding the resource.
    (B) Remind the appropriate members of the billing organization that monetary compensation is not worth compromising the integrity of the individual or the organization.
    (C) Maximize customer billings in any ethical manner possible.
    (D) Ask for the customer's approval before adding the resource to the project scope.

2. Which of the following represents information presented in its order of priority and helps focus on the most difficult issues?

    (A) A fishbone diagram
    (B) Flow charts
    (C) A Pareto diagram
    (D) A control chart

3. What is the most effective process to ensure that cultural and ethical differences do not impede success of your multi-national project?

    (A) Training
    (B) Collocating
    (C) Teaming
    (D) Forming

4. Your project team is working on a sensitive satellite system for which your company is developing the software for the application; you have just been informed that you will need to procure the hardware components from external sources. The senior project manager has informed you to prepare a product description, which in this case is also called a?

    (A) Statement of work
    (B) Invitation for bid
    (C) Project charter
    (D) Request for bid

5. All of the following statements concerning project stakeholders are true except which of the following?

    (A) Managing stakeholder expectations may be difficult because stakeholders often have very different objectives, which may come into conflict.
    (B) Differences between or among stakeholders should be resolved in favor of the customer.
    (C) Differences between or among stakeholders should be resolved in the most cost efficient manner consistent with project objectives.
    (D) Project stakeholders may influence the course of the project and its results.

6. Which of the following may be employed to shorten a schedule without changing the scope of the task?

    (A) Crashing
    (B) Alter the task priorities
    (C) Releasing resources earlier from tasks which were scheduled with a late start
    (D) Fast tracking

7. Another project manager in your organization is going around talking about how the project charter is a collection of formal, documented procedures that defines how project performance will be monitored and evaluated. You realize he is wrong from your own work experience. You want to correct him and tell him which of the following is actually what he should be referring to?

(A) Change control system
(B) Configuration management
(C) Concurrent engineering
(D) Lessons learned

8. A project manager is monitoring specific project results to determine if they comply with relevant standards and eliminate causes of unsatisfactory results. This activity is a part of:

(A) Performing quality work results.
(B) Performing quality control.
(C) Performing quality planning.
(D) Performing quality assurance.

9. Payment for routine government action by a foreign official is:

(A) A bribe.
(B) Allowed.
(C) Not payable upon violation of government law.
(D) Allowed only if they process the project schedule.

10. The process of establishing clear and achievable objectives, measuring their achievement, and adjusting performance in accordance with the results of the measurement is called:

(A) Strategic planning.
(B) Alternative objectives inventory.
(C) Management by objectives.
(D) Contingency planning.

11. In person-to-person communication, messages are sent on verbal levels and nonverbal levels simultaneously. As a general rule, what percentage of the message actually is sent through nonverbal cues?

(A) 25% to 50%
(B) 5% to 25%
(C) Greater than 75%
(D) 50% to 75%

12. Receiving formal confirmation that a project has met or exceeded customer requirements is an essential part of project management. Such confirmation includes all the following except:

(A) Formal customer acceptance of project results.
(B) Meeting requirements of the delivering organization, such as staff evaluations, budget reports, and lessons learned.
(C) Formal customer acceptance of deliverables.
(D) Passing a quality control inspection.

13. The key way for a project manager to promote optimum team performance in project teams whose members are not colocated is to:

    (A) Establish a reward and recognition system
    (B) Build trust
    (C) Exercise his or her right to control all aspects of the project
    (D) Obtain the support of the functional managers in the other locations

14. A team member comes to you (the project manager) privately and informs you that an employee of your customer is making unwelcome advances. The team member has repeatedly requested that this person stop, but the advances continue. What is the best course of action?

    (A) Suggest that the team member avoid contact with the customer employee.
    (B) Privately confront the customer employee and threaten legal action if the advances do not stop.
    (C) Facilitate a meeting with the team member, the customer employee, and yourself, to allow the two to work it out amicably.
    (D) Contact the employee's manager to arrange a meeting to discuss the matter.

15. Which of the following statements is not true?

    (A) Only those who realize that cultural differences are a resource to be fully utilized will survive.
    (B) There is a common ground for people from different cultures on which they can interact without unsolvable conflicts.
    (C) Cultural differences will always be an obstacle to be overcome.
    (D) Culture is a critical lever for competitive advantage.

16. A project manager is identifying the quality standards relevant to the project and determining how to meet them. This activity is:

    (A) Quality management.
    (B) Quality assurance.
    (C) Quality planning.
    (D) Quality control.

17. The buyer is impressed with the seller's interest and enthusiasm but concerned that the seller has no experience in this market area. If the seller can claim that the buyer is one of their customers, they might have many more sales opportunities. An appropriate contract type might be:

    (A) Cost sharing.
    (B) Cost reimbursement.
    (C) Cost plus an incentive fee.
    (D) Cost plus a percentage of cost.

18. Your technical team lead, Ted, proposed an action that would improve overall project quality with a minor cost increase. The project control officer, Sun Ha, recommended an approach that would shorten the project schedule, but reduce product features. Increasing quality and accelerating the schedule are critical from your point of view. Although you believe that Ted and Sun Ha could learn from each other, they typically like to agree to disagree. You need a conflict resolution method that provides a long-term resolution. You decide to use which one of the following approaches:

    (A) Confronting
    (B) Problem solving
    (C) Collaborating
    (D) Smoothing

19. In the Shewhart and Deming cycle, the letters P D C A stands for:

    (A) Purchase, deliver, cost, and acquisition.
    (B) Prevent defects caused by anyone.
    (C) Plan, do, check, and act.
    (D) Please don't cause accidents.

20. You are managing a large project with 20 stakeholders in three continents. Sixteen different contractors are involved and all their work must be coordinated. With a project this size in scope you realize that you must devote a lot of attention to effective integrated change control. This means you are concerned primarily with

    (A) Establishing a change control board that oversees the overall project changes
    (B) Integrating deliverables from different functional specialties on the project
    (C) Maintaining baseline integrity, integrating product and project scope, and coordinating change across knowledge areas
    (D) Influencing factors that cause change, determining that change has occurred, and managing actual changes as they occur

21. The ISO 9001: 2000 standard is used to:

    (A) Set international standards for quality conformance in organizations.
    (B) Develop standards of excellence for manufacturing facilities.
    (C) Set USA national standards for quality conformance in organizations.
    (D) Formalize the tools of quality management.

22. Analogous estimating is also known as _____ estimating.

    (A) Top-down
    (B) Top-to-bottom
    (C) Bottom-up
    (D) Parametric

23. Deflection or transfer of a risk to another party is part of which of the following risk response categories?

    (A) Mitigate
    (B) Accept
    (C) Avoid
    (D) Transfer

24. What is your SPI if EV = 8 and PV = 6?

    (A) .66
    (B) 1.33
    (C) .75
    (D) 1.0

25. The "rule of seven" as applied to statistical process control charts means that:

    (A) Seven consecutive measurements are ascending, descending, or the same
    (B) A process is not out of control even though seven measurements fall outside the lower and upper control limits
    (C) At least seven inspectors should be in place for every thousand employees
    (D) Seven rejects typically occur per thousand inspections

26. A control chart shows the last eight pipes produced were all less than average weight. You need to tell management there is a problem because the situation violates which of the following?

(A) 50/50 rule.
(B) 6-sigma rule.
(C) Rule of seven.
(D) Rule of eight.

27. You are assigned to a project that senior management has already decided to outsource. As a project manager, you need to work with the contracts department to select the vendor and then oversee the vendor through project completion. Company policy requires that a project of this size go through a formal bid process. A vice president in your company tells you that his friend owns one of the companies that might bid on the project, and it would be an excellent choice as a vendor. This vice president has a reputation for making or breaking careers. What is generally the best course of action?

(A) Obtain written permission to bypass the formal bid process.
(B) Follow the bid process and show the vice president why the favored vendor is or is not the best choice.
(C) Let the contracts department handle the situation.
(D) Let the evaluation team know that management has a favorite vendor.

28. Communication is important to the success of a project. As the project manager, you have four stakeholders you need to communicate with. As such, you have six channels of communication. A new stakeholder has been added that you also need to communicate with. How many total communication channels do you have now?

(A) 15
(B) 25
(C) 20
(D) 10

29. Senior management does a regular evaluation of project performance in order to be more confident in quality product standards. This is an example of?

(A) Quality control
(B) Quality assurance
(C) Quality planning
(D) Quality management

30. The team you have organized for your new project consists of three people who will work full-time and five people who will support the project on a part-time basis. All team members know one another and have worked together in the past. To ensure a successful project start-up, your first step should be to:

(A) Prepare a responsibility assignment matrix and distribute it to each team member
(B) Meet with each team member individually to discuss assignments
(C) Hold a project kickoff meeting
(D) Distribute the project plan and WBS to the team

31. Generally, the largest unit that you can mange in the WBS is _____ hours.

(A) 20
(B) 10
(C) 40
(D) 50

32. Risk management planning involves which of the following?

(A) Deciding how to approach and plan risk management activities for the project.
(B) Maximizing the probability and consequence of negative events.
(C) Measuring the probability and consequences of risks and estimating their implications on project objectives.
(D) Developing procedures and techniques to enhance opportunities and reduce threats to project objectives.

33. Project records must be _____.

(A) Detailed
(B) Tactical
(C) Permanent
(D) Lengthy

34. You find out that a fellow PMP lied about his years of experience on his application for PMP certification. You decide to overlook it because he is a friend of yours. You are in violation of the responsibility to:

(A) Cooperate with PMI concerning ethics violations.
(B) Report possible violations of the code of conduct to PMI.
(C) Support and disseminate the PMP Code of Professional Conduct to other PMPs.
(D) Comply with ethical standards governing professional practice.

35. You signed an agreement with your client that the integration plan and other documents they provided would remain confidential. You needed these documents to complete the project. Another company contacts you because you're an expert in the field. They ask you for samples of integration plans, which they want to include in a book they are writing. They promise you a "thank you" and a payment of $500, but they need the information today. What should you do?
(A) Use the material provided by the customer, but remove all company specific references.
(B) Say no.
(C) Try to get permission from the customer.
(D) Create new material based on the confidential material.

36. Developing an approximation of the costs of the resources needed to complete project activity is _____.

(A) Cost control
(B) Accounting
(C) Budgeting
(D) Cost estimating

37. You are the salesperson and project manager for a product that you are attempting to introduce in another country. Prior to traveling to this country you discover it is customary to bring a gift of wine to the company president. Your company has a strict policy not to give or receive gifts. What should you do?

(A) Follow the customs of the country and bring the gift of wine.
(B) Follow your company policy and do not bring a gift.
(C) Call someone that works in this country and ask his or her advice.
(D) Bring a smaller, less expensive gift.

38. The terms strong matrix, balanced matrix, and weak matrix when applied to the matrix structure in project organization refer to the:

(A) Ability of the organization to achieve its goals
(B) Physical proximity of project team members to one another and to the project manager
(C) Degree of authority the project manager has over team resources
(D) Degree to which team members bond together

39. Function analysis is best done by:

    (A) Professional engineers
    (B) The project manager
    (C) The project team
    (D) The project sponsor

40. Work results, product documentation, Work breakdown structure, Scope Statement, and the project plan are all _____ of scope verification.

    (A) Techniques
    (B) Inputs
    (C) Outputs
    (D) Tools

41. Your company operates a large chemical processing plant, has been convicted of illegally dumping toxic substances into a local town lake causing most fish to die. The court has mandated that the required cleanup activities be completed by within 45 days. Such a constraint is an example of:

    (A) A major milestone.
    (B) A key event.
    (C) An external dependency.
    (D) An imposed date.

42. A project manager states, "I know the risk exists and am aware of the possible consequences. I am willing to wait and see what happens. I accept the consequences should they occur." He or she is exercising the _____ method of risk control.

    (A) Avoidance
    (B) Transference
    (C) Acceptance
    (D) Mitigation

43. Value analysis and value management are other names for:

    (A) Life cycle costing
    (B) Value engineering
    (C) Profitability
    (D) Life cycle management

44. Under which of the following circumstances could a project manager incur a fine and be jailed?

    (A) For failing to file the necessary permits in their own country.
    (B) For using people from outside the project manager's country to work on the project.
    (C) For not using minority workers on the project.
    (D) For paying a bribe to a foreign official.

45. Cost control is easiest to do _____ the project.

    (A) Late in
    (B) Early in
    (C) After
    (D) In the middle of

46. Which of the following is not considered to be one of the fundamental patterns of personal value expression?

    (A) Leadership
    (B) Analytical
    (C) Relationship
    (D) Inclusion

47. You are working in the pharmaceutical industry. Your project has been defined as clinical trials for the drug Fantastica, which improves human memory and stimulates hair growth. As the project proceeds, the product is described more explicitly as four Phase I trials, five Phase II trials, and six Phase III trials. This situation provides an example of:

    (A) Close alignment of project activities with the work breakdown structure
    (B) Progressive elaboration of the product description
    (C) Value analysis
    (D) Quality function deployment

48. The U.S. Bureau of Indian Affairs awarded your firm a contract to renovate an elementary school on a Navajo reservation. One contractual term, Indian preference, requires you to hire Native American laborers and subcontractors from the reservation. This is an example of which type of the following constraints?

    (A) Economical
    (B) Social
    (C) Legal
    (D) Environmental

49. The term activity resource estimating refers to?

    (A) Labor
    (B) Capital equipment
    (C) Materials
    (D) All of the above

50. In order to complete work on your projects, you have been provided confidential information from all of your clients. A university contacts you to help it in its research. Such assistance would require you to provide it with some of the client data from your files. What should you do?

    (A) Release the information, but remove all references to the client's name.
    (B) Provide high level information only.
    (C) Contact your clients and seek permission to disclose the information.
    (D) Disclose the information.

51. The scope statement that is created in the develop preliminary project scope statement process should include which of the following:

    (A) Project and project objectives
    (B) Project boundaries
    (C) Product assumptions
    (D) All of the above

52. You are responsible for a systems integration project in your organization that has multiple internal customers. You have just begun preparing a project plan. Because many people in your organization are interested in this system and its progress, you decide to prepare a project communications management plan. Your first step in preparing this plan is to:

(A) Describe the information you plan to distribute
(B) Set up a repository for all project documents so that they will be easily accessible
(C) Conduct a stakeholder analysis to assess information needs
(D) Determine a production schedule to show when each type of communication will be produced

53. Your company is in competition to win a major project for the government of a country. Your contacts in that country inform you that you must make a large payment to the foreign minister to be considered for the project. What should you do?

(A) Do not make the payment.
(B) Inform your management and ask for direction.
(C) Make the payment.
(D) Have the local contact make the payment.

54. You are preparing your project schedule on a sheet of paper. You abandoned the use of project scheduling software long ago, deciding that it is too feature rich, convoluted, and complex. To keep your life simple, you decided to calculate a single, deterministic early and late start date and an early and late finish date for each activity. Accordingly, you decide to use:

(A) Schedule analysis (SA)
(B) Gantt charts (GC)
(C) Monte Carlo analysis (MCA)
(D) Critical path method (CPM)

55. John is a project manager who gets the job done through salary, promotion, and bonus incentives. He is using which of the following types of interpersonal influence?

(A) Formal authority
(B) Referent power
(C) Expert power
(D) Reward power

56. The project has had a major defect, and the project manager has involved the project team and process engineers in analyzing the situation. One in the group says that the real fault is the age of the equipment. Another says it is the lack of a material for the correct quality. To address the root of the problem, the project manager decides to use an Ishikawa diagram. Which of the following best describes the step of the quality management process in which the group is involved in this situation?

(A) Quality assurance
(B) Quality planning
(C) Quality control
(D) Quality analysis

57. The subdivision of major project deliverables, as identified in the scope statement, into smaller, more manageable components is called:

(A) Parametric estimation.
(B) Scope definition.
(C) Feasibility analysis.
(D) Cost benefits analysis.

58. A floor in one of the office buildings your company owns is now available for rent and management needs this space rented within one month. The only offer received is from a company that is a competitor. What is the best choice in this situation?

    (A) Offer the space to the customer under a short-term lease agreement.
    (B) Report the issue to management and inform the customer of their decision.
    (C) As part of the lease agreement, include a non-competitive agreement.
    (D) Tell the customer that your company has decided to use the space.

59. You have just been assigned project manager for a new telecommunications project. There appear to be many risks on this project, but no one has evaluated them to assess the range of possible project outcomes. What needs to be done?

    (A) Risk response planning
    (B) Risk monitoring and control
    (C) Risk identification
    (D) Risk quantification

60. A risk response which involves eliminating a threat is called:

    (A) Avoidance
    (B) Transfer
    (C) Mitigation
    (D) Deflection

61. In working with triangular distribution, the low, likely and high values are 15, 20 and 40, respectively. The mean is _____.

    (A) 22.5
    (B) 27.5
    (C) 25.0
    (D) 20.0

62. When using either associations or industry groups, it is always important to know what _____ went into the final numbers.

    (A) Thinking
    (B) Data
    (C) Tactics
    (D) Skills

63. The cost estimate of a proposed project has an expected value of $1,000,000 and a standard deviation of $50,000. The project is budgeted for $1,100,000 so as to include a management reserve. Assuming that the cost estimates are normally distributed, what is the probability of completing this project over budget?

    (A) 5%
    (B) 50%
    (C) 2.5%
    (D) 10%

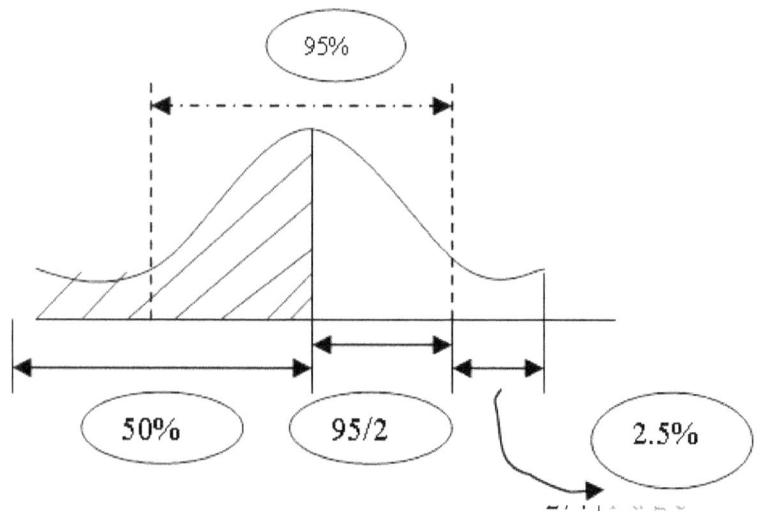

64. Which of the following best describes the meaning of design of experiments?

    (A) Identifies which variables have the least influence on a quality outcome.
    (B) Determines the methods to be used for research and development.
    (C) Determines what a quality outcome is.
    (D) Identifies which variables have the most influence on a quality outcome.

65. In person-to-person communication, messages are sent on verbal levels and nonverbal levels simultaneously. As a general rule, what percentage of the message actually is sent through nonverbal cues?

    (A) 5% to 15%
    (B) 20% to 30%
    (C) 40% to 50
    (D) Greater than 50%

66. The structure of the organization, collective bargaining agreements, and the overall economic conditions of the organization itself are examples of _____.

    (A) Documents
    (B) Constraints
    (C) Control issues
    (D) Organizational issues

67. Project archives need to be _____ to be most useful.

    (A) Oral
    (B) Written
    (C) Indexed
    (D) Controlled

68. During the concept phase of your project, management indicated that it wants the expected benefit of each new product to outweigh its development costs. This is an example of:

    (A) An assumption
    (B) A constraint
    (C) Use of the constrained-optimization method of project selection
    (D) A technical requirement

69. Results of quality control testing and measurement are used:

    (A) As an input to quality planning.
    (B) To prepare an operational definition.
    (C) To prepare a control chart.
    (D) As an input to quality assurance.

70. Acceptance of the output of the project by the sponsor or customer should be _____.

    (A) Early
    (B) Oral
    (C) Formal
    (D) Indexed

71. Your organization has just created and established a reward and recognition system for its project managers. Project cost performance is used as the main criteria to determine rewards. What should you do to ensure that rewards reflect actual performance?

    (A) Consider overtime work as part of the job.
    (B) Prepare a cost baseline.
    (C) Use earned value management to monitor performance.
    (D) Estimate and budget controllable and uncontrollable costs separately.

72. In the initiation phase of your project, it is apparent that factions within the client's company have significantly different views on how the project should be structured and how the deliverables should be defined. Which of the following is the best thing to do?

    (A) Make sure the terms and conditions of the contract are clear
    (B) List the consequences of changes in the contract's requirements section
    (C) Ask the client when they will be in agreement on the project requirements
    (D) Work with leadership from each area to collaboratively engineer a mutually acceptable solution

73. Developing a Risk Management Plan involves all of the following, except:

    (A) Determining the budget for risk management.
    (B) Determining the responses to individual risks.
    (C) Determining roles and responsibilities.
    (D) Setting threshold criteria.

74. Communication is important to the success of a project. As the project manager, you have four stakeholders you need to communicate with. As such, you have six channels of communication. Two new stakeholders were just added that you also need to communicate with. How many total communication channels do you have now?

    (A) 10
    (B) 15
    (C) 20
    (D) 25

75. During execution, a major problem occurred that was not included in the risk response plan. Which of the following options should you do first?

    (A) Look for any unexpected effects of the problem.
    (B) Tell management.
    (C) Create a workaround.
    (D) Reevaluate the risk identification process.

76. Using a contractor to perform a high-risk task is which form of risk response?

    (A) Assumption
    (B) Insurance
    (C) Mediation
    (D) Transference

77. A no-cost settlement sometimes is used:

    (A) In lieu of formal termination procedures.
    (B) To close out a successful contract.
    (C) When such an arrangement is acceptable to one of the parties involved.
    (D) When buyer property has been furnished under the contract.

78. What does "resource leveling" mean in project management?

(A) Hiring contractors to fill in during peak times on the project schedule.
(B) Reducing the project costs.
(C) Shortening the time it takes to complete the project.
(D) Making the most efficient use of the available resources.

79. If the probability of event 1 is 20%, event 2 is 75%, and event 3 is 57%, and they are independent events, how likely is it that all events will occur?

(A) 30%
(B) 47%
(C) 55%
(D) 68%

80. As project manager you are creating a project plan and you and a co-worker are discussing what should be done to limit changes to the project. You both decide that all of the following are acceptable ways by which project documents may be changed except?

(A) Approval from authorized management
(B) Oral communication from key stakeholders
(C) Written scope detail changes
(D) Tracking systems

81. In an effort to reduce project team members' increasing stress levels, you decided to conduct power yoga sessions during every project status meeting. You need to hire someone to conduct these sessions. Citing the organization's project management methodology, your subcontracts department informed you that the following document must be prepared before starting the procurement:

(A) Statement of work
(B) Procurement management plan
(C) Evaluation methodology
(D) Contract terms and conditions

82. An activity has an early start date of the 10th and a late start date of the 19th. The activity has a duration of 4 days. There are no non-workdays. From the information given, what can be concluded about the activity?

(A) The late finish date is the 25th.
(B) The activity can be completed in 2 days if the resources devoted to it are doubled.
(C) Total float for the activity is 9 days.
(D) The early finish date of the activity is the end of the day on the 14th.

83. A project manager discovers a defect in a deliverable due to the customer under contract today. The project manager knows the customer does not have the technical understanding to notice the defect. The deliverable technically meets the contract requirements, but it does not meet the project manager's fitness of use standard. What should the project manager do in this situation?

(A) Issue the deliverable and get formal acceptance from the customer.
(B) Note the problem in the lessons learned so future projects do not encounter the same problem.
(C) Discuss the issue with the customer.
(D) Inform the customer that the deliverable will be late.

84. A unilateral contract under which the seller is paid a preset amount per unit of service is called:

    (A) A lump sum contract
    (B) A fixed price contract
    (C) A unit price contract
    (D) A cost reimbursable contract

85. When it appears that a design error will interfere with meeting technical performance objectives, the PREFERRED response is to:

    (A) Decrease the performance value to equal the assessed value.
    (B) Develop alternative solutions to the problem.
    (C) Increase the specified value to set a new performance goal.
    (D) Reduce the overall technical complexity of the project.

86. If a business venture has a 45% chance to earn $ 3 million and a 65%, chance to lose $1 million, what is the expected monetary value of the venture?

    (A) $700,000
    (B) $650,000
    (C) $2,000,000
    (D) $1,350,000

87. You are the project manager of a large company project. The project customer has requested that you inflate your cost estimates by 25 percent. He reports that his Management always reduces the cost of the estimates so this is the only method to get the monies needed to complete the project. Which of the following is the best response to this situation?

    (A) Do as the customer asked to ensure the project requirements can be met by adding the increase across each task.
    (B) Do as the customer asked to ensure the project requirements can be met by adding the increase as a contingency reserve.
    (C) Complete an accurate estimate of the project. In addition, create a risk assessment on why the project budget would be inadequate.
    (D) Do as the customer asked by creating an estimate for the customer's management and another for the actual project implementation.

88. Integrated change control requires all of the following except?

    (A) Maintaining the integrity of the baseline
    (B) Ensuring that changes to the product scope are reflected in the project scope
    (C) Coordinating changes across knowledge areas
    (D) Making process adjustments as a result of deficiencies

89. You are the project manager for a project with the following network diagram (see image). Studying the diagram, which path is the critical path?

    (A) A B C D
    (B) E B C D
    (C) E F H
    (D) E G H

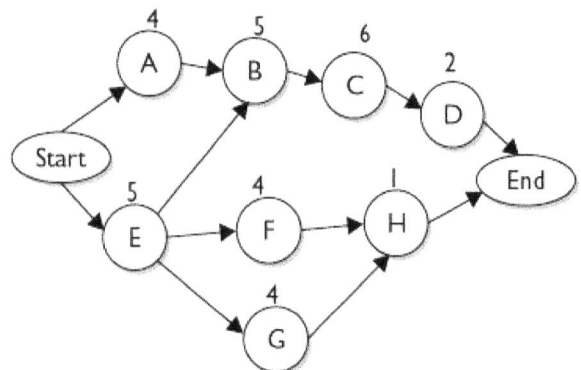

90. Scope verification deals with _____ of the scope while quality control deals with the _____ of the scope.

     (A) Correctness, acceptance
     (B) Acceptance, correctness
     (C) Quality, correctness
     (D) Acceptance, quality

91. You are using earned value progress reporting for your current project in an effort to teach your software developers the benefits of earned value. You plan to display project results so that the team knows how the project is progressing.

$PV = \$5,300$
$EV = \$4,700$
$AC = \$5,900$
$BAC = \$10,000$

What is the EAC for this project?

     (A) $12,500
     (B) $4,100
     (C) $10,600
     (D) $10,000

92. You are the project manager for the Log Cabin Project. One of your vendors is completing a large portion of the project. You have heard a rumor that the vendor is losing many of its workers due to labor issues. In light of this information, what should you do?

     (A) Communicate with the vendor in regard to the rumor.
     (B) Stop work with the vendor until the labor issues are resolved.
     (C) Negotiate with the labor union to secure the workers on your project.
     (D) Look to secure another vendor to replace the current vendor.

93. You have just been hired as a project manager and you want to review your organization's informal and formal policies. A team member has suggested a list items to possible review. Four items are on the list. Which one of the following is not an organizational policy whose effects on the project must be considered?

     (A) Resource assignment matrix
     (B) Continuous improvement targets
     (C) Time reporting
     (D) Employee performance reviews

94. Recently your company introduced a new set of "metal woods" to its established line of golfing equipment. The "metal woods" are made from a combination of titanium, uranium, and manganese. Your company claims the clubs will add 80 yards to any drive. The product launch was spectacular. Every major money-winner on the PGA tour bought a set. However, in the past weeks things have gone horribly wrong. The clubs are causing golfers to hook, slice, and hit the ball "fat." One golfer even claims they have given him the "yips." You decide to conduct a failure mode and criticality analysis to:

     (A) Analyze the product development cycle after product release to determine strengths and weaknesses
     (B) Evaluate failure modes and causes associated with the design and manufacture of an existing product
     (C) Evaluate failure modes and causes associated with the design and manufacture of a new product
     (D) Help management set priorities in its existing manufacturing processes to avoid failures

95. You have a cost plus fixed fee contract with the customer and an arrangement with your manager whereby you will receive 10 percent of the contract fee as your payment for services. While completing the project, you discover that the actual cost will be lower than expected, thus decreasing your fee. What should you do?

   (A) Expand more of the critical path tasks so they cost more.
   (B) Find ways to add tasks to the project that provide more customer benefits and increase costs.
   (C) Notify your manager of the probable decreased cost.
   (D) Purchase more expensive equipment.

96. You are the project manager for a large company project. This project has 32 stakeholders and will require implementation activities in North and South America. You have been requested to provide a duration estimate for the project. Of the following, which will offer the best level of detail in your estimate?

   (A) Order of Magnitude
   (B) Work Breakdown Structure
   (C) Stakeholder Analysis
   (D) Requirements Document

97. ROI and payback period are examples of _____ project analysis.

   (A) Professional
   (B) Quantitative
   (C) Financial
   (D) Management

98. Your project needs to have a major change in the equipment used on it. You know of a product that meets your needs, but you are worried that your brother owns the company that produces the product. What should you do?

   (A) Let the customer know of the issue.
   (B) Negotiate a good deal for the project with your brother.
   (C) Eliminate your brother from bidding.
   (D) Submit the bid and allow your brother to negotiate with the contracting office.

99. Which of the following charts is based on the 80/20 rule?

   (A) A fishbone chart.
   (B) A Pareto diagram.
   (C) A control chart.
   (D) The 50/50 rule.

100. You are the project manager of a large company project. Your organization is a functional environment and you do not get along well with the functional manager leading the project. You are in disagreement with the manager on how the project should precede the timings of the activities, the suggested schedule, and the expected quality of the work. The manager has requested that you get to work on several of the activities on the critical path even though you and she have not solved the issues concerning the project. Which of the following should you do?

   (A) Complete the activities as requested.
   (B) Go to senior management and voice your concerns.
   (C) Refuse to begin activities on the project until the issues are resolved.
   (D) Ask to be taken off of the project.

101. A project manager has just been hired and is trying to gain the cooperation of others. What is the best form of power for gaining cooperation under these circumstances?

    (A) Legitimate
    (B) Referent
    (C) Penalty
    (D) Expert

102. You should do Administrative Closure at the end of each _____ of the project.

    (A) Deliverable
    (B) Month
    (C) Phase
    (D) Week

103. There are over 30 stakeholders on your project. The project is being done in another country with people from three countries as team members. Which of the following is the most important thing to keep in mind?

    (A) Many competing needs and objectives must be satisfied.
    (B) The communication channels will be narrow.
    (C) Conflicts of interest must be disclosed.
    (D) There must be one sponsor from each country.

104. Questions such as "What products are available in the marketplace" and "What is the current balance between supply and demand" are related to what input to procurement planning?

    (A) Cost/benefit analysis.
    (B) Availability assessment.
    (C) Competitive fit analysis.
    (D) Market conditions.

105. All of the following are inputs to the close project process except?

    (A) Project management plan
    (B) Contract documentation
    (C) Deliverables
    (D) Project management methodology

106. The Communication Management Plan provides all of the following except:

    (A) Project communication schedules.
    (B) Communication barriers.
    (C) A collection and filing structure for project information.
    (D) A distribution structure for project information.

107. A task was scheduled to use two persons, full time, and take two weeks to complete. Instead, the project manager was only able to assign one person to this task. At the end of two weeks, the person assigned to the task was 75% complete. What is the cost performance index?

    (A) .75
    (B) 1.5
    (C) 1.33
    (D) .5

108. If the performance reporting shows a completion percentage, you are doing _____.

    (A) Scheduling
    (B) Forecasting
    (C) Status reporting
    (D) Progress reporting

109. You are a new project manager for company B. You previously worked for company A that had an extensive project management practice. Company B has its own procedures, but you are more familiar with those from company A. You should:

    (A) Use the forms from company B and begin to instruct them on ways to upgrade their own.
    (B) Use the practices from company A but include any forms from company B.
    (C) Interact with others in an ethical way by sharing the good aspects of company A's procedures.
    (D) Talk about changes to the change control board of company B.

110. What is risk event probability?

    (A) The value used in mitigation and deflection.
    (B) An estimate of the risk value at loss.
    (C) The probability of the risk not occurring at this time.
    (D) An estimate of the probability that a given risk will occur.

111. Your company is purchasing the services of a consultant. You notice you own stock in one of the consulting companies interested in the work. What should you do?

    (A) Work hard to get the consulting company selected for the project.
    (B) Tell your manager and remove yourself from the selection committee.
    (C) Tell the people from the consulting company that you hope they get the work.
    (D) Keep the information to yourself.

112. Which of the following statements is true regarding scoring models, benefit contribution and economic models?

    (A) These are constrained optimization methods.
    (B) These are inputs to the project charter.
    (C) These are benefit measurement methods.
    (D) These are tools used when applying mathematical models.

113. Statements of organizational policies and philosophies, position descriptions, and constraints are examples of:

    (A) Downward communication
    (B) Lateral communication
    (C) External communication
    (D) Horizontal communication

114. In the following network, all three tasks, A, B and C, each have a duration of 5 days. The value 'p' indicates the probability of each task finishing on schedule. If all 3 tasks start on day 1, what is the probability that all tasks will finish in days?

    (A) P = .003
    (B) P = .4
    (C) Probability cannot be determined from the data given.
    (D) P = .014

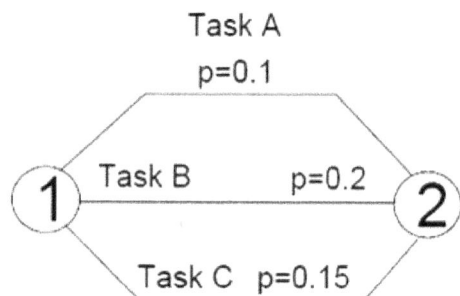

Task A
p=0.1

1 Task B p=0.2 2

Task C p=0.15

115. While reviewing the estimates from the functional managers assigned to your project you discover that one cost estimate is clearly higher than those submitted for previous projects. You should:

(A) Request the supporting details for the estimate to ensure it has been properly prepared.
(B) Question each functional manager for information about this estimate.
(C) Accept the estimate and plan to use the additional funding as a reserve.
(D) Reject the estimate and remove the functional manager from the project.

116. Which of the following is done during scope verification?

(A) Create work breakdown structure.
(B) Performance measurement.
(C) Inspection.
(D) Verify product correctness.

117. You are managing procurement for a project and have arranged a bid conference with the potential proposers. All of the following are appropriate for a bid conference except?

(A) Explanation of why particular terms and conditions are in the contract.
(B) Working with the bidders to determine alternative solutions for the project.
(C) A request for bidders to offer their thoughts on problems with the scope of the work.
(D) A walk through of the project scope.

118. You are in charge of developing a new product for a bank. Your quality metrics are based on the 65th percentile of each of the last four products developed. This is an example of?

(A) Statistical sampling.
(B) Metrics.
(C) Benchmarking.
(D) Operational definitions.

119. The construction phase of a new software product is near completion. The next phase is testing and implementation. The project is two weeks ahead of schedule. What should the project manager be most concerned with before moving onto the final phase?

(A) Quality control
(B) Scope verification
(C) Cost control
(D) Performance reports

120. Future events or outcomes that are favorable are called:

(A) Risks
(B) Opportunities
(C) Surprises
(D) Contingencies

121. Your project needs to have a major change in the equipment used on it. You know of a product that meets your needs, but you are worried that your brother owns the company that produces the product. What should you do?

(A) Let the customer know of the issue.
(B) Eliminate your brother from bidding.
(C) Submit the bid and allow your brother to negotiate with the contracting office.
(D) Negotiate a good deal for the project with your brother.

122. The project manager of a project must buy a large piece of equipment costing $1,543,256. He meets with the accounting department representative to the project team and reviews the different depreciation methods that can be used to depreciate the equipment over the useful life of the equipment. Which of the following is an accelerated depreciation method?

(A) Straight line
(B) Multiplication of the years' digits
(C) Average deflation
(D) Sum of the years' digits

123. Activity A has a duration of 3 days and begins on the morning of Monday the 4th. The successor activity, B, has a finish-to-start relationship with A. The finish-to-start relationship has 3 days of lag, and activity B has a duration of 4 days. Sunday is a non-workday. What can be determined from these data?

(A) Calendar time between the start of A to the finish of B is 11 days.
(B) The total duration of both activities is 8 days.
(C) Calendar time between the start of A to the finish of B is 14 days.
(D) The finish date of B is Wednesday the 13th.

124. Sometimes called risk symptoms or warning signs, are indications that a risk has occurred or is about to occur.

(A) Issues
(B) Events
(C) Predictions
(D) Triggers

125. You work for one of the leading manufacturers of country and western apparel. You are managing a project to redesign retail store layout to improve customer throughput and efficiency. Much of the project work must be done on site and will require the active participation of store employees. Many of these employees are lifelong members of a powerful union that has a reputation for labor unrest. One important component of your schedule must be:

(A) A resource capabilities matrix
(B) Buffers and reserves
(C) A resource calendar
(D) A resource histogram

126. You are the project manager for a large project that is completed on time and on budget. The customer and all of the stakeholders are pleased with the results. As a direct result of the successful completion of the project, your manager approves a bonus of $15,000 to you. There are fifteen members of the project team. One of the people on the project team has been a very low contributor to the project; the other fourteen have all been above standard. What should you do with the money?

(A) Ask the team members how they would divide the money.
(B) Divide the money equally among the team members except for the substandard team member.
(C) Keep the money yourself; you deserve it, and the manager gave it to you.
(D) Divide the money equally among all the team members.

127. A major negotiation with a potential subcontractor is scheduled for tomorrow when you discover there is a good chance the project will be canceled. What should you do?

(A) Cut the negotiations short
(B) Do not spend too much time preparing for the negotiations
(C) Postpone the negotiations
(D) Only negotiate major items

128. Your project team has been informally meeting with sellers to discuss the seller's "best practices" relative to upcoming potential work from your company. During one of these sessions, a seller offers to give you tickets to a sporting event if you will tell him the names of other companies you have been meeting with. What is the best response?

(A) Answer the question, but respectfully refuse the offer.
(B) Ignore the question and refuse to meet with him again.
(C) Refuse to answer the question and remove the company from consideration for future work.
(D) Ask him why he needs to know.

129. One purpose of the communications management plan is to provide information about the:

(A) Methods that will be used for releasing team members from the project when they are no longer needed
(B) Methods that will be used to gather and store information
(C) Experience and skill levels of each team member
(D) Project organization and stakeholder responsibility relationships

130. The completion of a local government study resides on your critical path. This would most likely be referred to as?

(A) Soft logic
(B) Hard logic
(C) An external dependency
(D) A mandatory dependency

131. A client has told you that his company is in extreme financial difficulties, but tells you to keep it under your hat. You decide to tell your sales manager. You are in violation of the responsibility to:

(A) Disclose conflict of interest.
(B) Provide accurate information.
(C) Protect intellectual property of others.
(D) Respect confidentiality of sensitive information.

132. A project manager is considering applying learning curve theory to his project. The project involves designing a number of software modules that are very similar. According to the cost figures that have been collected the first unit required 100 person hours to design and test. The second unit required 90 person-hours to design and test. How many person-hours will the eighth module take to design and test?

(A) 100
(B) 90
(C) 172
(D) 73

133. You have prepared the scope statement and the WBS for your project. You also have an approved project plan. Your project is now under way, but you recognize that, given the nature of project work, scope change is inevitable. You also are aware of the danger of scope creep, having suffered the consequences of it recently. To avoid a similar experience, you meet with your team and decide to establish a project scope change control system. This is:

(A) A documented process used to apply technical and administrative direction and surveillance to identify and document functional and physical characteristics of items, record and report change, control change, and audit the items and system to verify conformance to requirements.
(B) Mandatory for use on projects so that the scope management plan cannot be changed without prior review and sign-off.
(C) A set of procedures by which project scope may be changed, including the paperwork, tracking systems, and approval levels necessary for authorizing change.
(D) A collection of formal, documented procedures to define the steps by which official project documents may be changed.

134. Where is the bulk of the project budget spent?

    (A) Scope management
    (B) Production
    (C) Labor and materials
    (D) Project plan execution

135. An example of a conflict of interest would be:

    (A) As a public official you make a decision about a contract award that will benefit you personally
    (B) You and a functional manager disagree with a task cost estimate
    (C) Your sponsor decides to cancel your project because it no longer supports the company strategy
    (D) Your personality conflicts with that of a key member of your project team

136. You are the project manager for the construction building a chemical depository and the local residents have produced reams of data showing the risk to the community of the storage facility is built. They have threatened to take your company to court. You find you are spending most of your time trying to work with these groups to alleviate their concerns. After much time and effort you persuade management to move this project to a different location outside of this town. This is an example of which of the following risk responses?

    (A) Active acceptance
    (B) Passive acceptance
    (C) Avoidance
    (D) Mitigation

137. Which term describes those costs in a contract that are associated with two or more projects but are not traceable to either of them individually?

    (A) Variable
    (B) Direct
    (C) Indirect
    (D) Managerial

138. What is the major aspect of scope verification?

    (A) It makes sure the project is on track by ensuring the customer's acceptance of the deliverable.
    (B) It ensures the project deliverable is completed on time.
    (C) It provides a chance for differences of opinion to come to light.
    (D) It shows the deliverable meets specifications.

139. Benefit measurement and constrained optimization are examples of:

    (A) Variable costs.
    (B) Benefit cost ratios.
    (C) Project selection methods.
    (D) Types of depreciation.

140. A category or rank given to products that have the same functional use but different technical characteristics is called the products:

    (A) Functional characteristics.
    (B) Technical characteristics.
    (C) Grade.
    (D) Quality.

141. You receive a contract to perform testing for a client. After contract award, the customer provides you with the test matrix to use for your 10 tests. A vice president says that the customer's test matrix is wrong, and he wants to use a different test matrix, which should give better results. This is a violation to the SOW. Suppose your sponsor is also the vice president for engineering. You should do which of the following?

(A) Use the engineering test matrix without telling the customer
(B) Use the customer's test matrix
(C) Tell your sponsor that you want to set up a meeting with the customer to resolve the conflict
(D) Use the engineering test matrix and inform the customer

142. You are trying to implement a project management methodology for your company based on upon recommendations from the PMBOK. This methodology recommends that your company establish a change control board. Based on that recommendation which one of the following statements best describes a change control board?

(A) Recommended for use on large projects lasting more than 18 months
(B) Managed by the project manager
(C) Composed of key stakeholders
(D) Used as required to approve or reject change requests

143. Estimating cost by looking at previous projects is known as _____ estimating.

(A) Analogous
(B) Analytical
(C) Bid
(D) Strategic

144. There are over 30 stakeholders on your project. The project is being done in another country with people from three countries as team members. Which of the following is the most important thing to keep in mind?

(A) There must be one sponsor from each country.
(B) Conflicts of interest must be disclosed.
(C) The communication channels will be narrow.
(D) Many competing needs and objectives must be satisfied.

145. During a team meeting, the team adds a specific area of extra work to the project because they have determined it would benefit the customer. What is wrong in this situation?

(A) Nothing. This is how to meet or exceed customer expectations.
(B) Nothing. The project manager is in control of the situation.
(C) The team is gold plating.
(D) These efforts shouldn't be done in meetings.

146. In performance reports related to schedule performance, which of the following items are unique to activities in progress?

(A) Forecast remaining time.
(B) Actual start date.
(C) Baseline start date.
(D) Baseline finish date.

147. You are managing the construction of sophisticated data center in Florida. The data center will house more than 500 servers for one of the world's largest retailers who have decided to launch an e-business program in North America. Although this location offers significant economic advantages, the threat of hurricanes has caused you to create a backup plan to operate out of Arizona in case the center is flooded. What type of risk response is this?

    (A) Mitigation
    (B) Deflection
    (C) Active acceptance
    (D) Passive avoidance

148. You are managing a project and the customer's engineers visit your facility on an inspection and general getting acquainted tour. During the tour they make the comment that the parts that are being designed should be in stainless steel instead of plain steel with enamel. What should you do?

    (A) Continue with the present design.
    (B) Authorize the change in design to your engineers.
    (C) Ask the visiting engineers to submit a change proposal to the change system.
    (D) Speak to the visiting engineers and discuss having an informal meeting between your engineers and the visiting engineers.

149. Life Cycle Costing is the concept of:

    (A) Considering both development and operating costs when evaluating project alternatives.
    (B) Minimizing project costs through value engineering.
    (C) Predicting the total cost of a project based on the expected cost of each phase in the Project Life Cycle.
    (D) Forecasting the final cost of a project.

150. Written change orders should be required on:

    (A) All projects, large and small
    (B) Only large projects
    (C) Projects with a formal configuration management system in place
    (D) Projects for which the cost of a change control system can be justified

151. One of your employees is up for promotion. If the promotion is granted, the employee will be reassigned elsewhere causing a problem for you on your project. You can delay the promotion until your project is completed. You should:

    (A) Ask the employee to refuse the promotion until your project is completed
    (B) Support the promotion but work with the employee and the employee's new management to develop a good transition plan
    (C) Tell the employee that it is his responsibility to find a suitable replacement so that the project will not suffer
    (D) Arrange to delay the promotion until the project is completed

152. Your project management work frustrates you. Although management will reward you if you meet project cost objectives, those objectives are impossible to meet because you cannot control staffing or procurement decisions. You must pressure functional managers to release staff as planned, and you always seem to be arguing with the contracting department about awarding contracts to quality sellers. Because of your complaints, management asked you to lead a team to recommend an equitable reward and recognition system for project managers. Your team has completed its report and will brief the executives. Before detailing the plan, you want to ensure executives understand the basic objective of reward systems. This objective is to:

    (A) Be comparable with the award system established for functional managers to indicate parity and to show the importance of project management to the company
    (B) Make the link between project performance and reward clear, explicit, and achievable
    (C) Motivate project managers to work toward common objectives and goals as defined by the company
    (D) Attract people to join the organization's project management career path

153. The quality management plan provides input to and addresses quality control, quality assurance, and quality improvement.

(A) The WBS
(B) The overall project plan
(C) External stakeholders
(D) The project scope

154. As project manager you are managing a project with a BAC of $ 5 million. About halfway through the project, you estimate that the project will be completed early and roughly 30% under budget. The contract is structured so that you actually make less profit if you finish early. You decide that you should?

(A) Hold a team meeting and let them decide what to do.
(B) Continue working on the project and complete early.
(C) Direct your team to increase work time and quality of work in order to get back on schedule.
(D) Tell the project sponsor about your budget and schedule projections.

155. The organization that controls the standards for quality is the _____.

(A) INA
(B) IIQ
(C) PMI
(D) ISO

156. You are the project manager for a major company project. You recently assigned a scope of work to a subcontractor. The subcontractor needs to plan and manage that specific scope of work in a more detailed manner. Your friend Michele is the new project manager for the subcontractor. She also is new to the project management profession. You suggest that she first:

(A) Follow the work breakdown structure that you developed for the project and use the work packages you identified
(B) Develop a subproject work breakdown structure for the work package that is her company's responsibility
(C) Establish a similar coding structure to facilitate use of a common project management information system
(D) Develop a work breakdown structure dictionary to show specific staff assignments

157. If the probability of event 1 is 20%, event 2 is 45%, and they are independent events, how likely is it that both events will occur?

(A) 9%
(B) 17%
(C) 27%
(D) 32%

158. Your company is establishing a cost-of-quality approach to determine the relative importance of its quality problems and to identify major opportunities for cost reduction. Your company believes this approach can help it evaluate its success in achieving quality objectives. When setting up this approach, you were asked to categorize four types of costs: prevention, appraisal, internal failure, and external failure. As you examine the cost of quality, however, you realize that training and its associated costs have become a major factor. Training costs are included in which one of the following areas?

(A) Prevention costs
(B) Appraisal costs
(C) Internal failure costs
(D) External failure costs

159. Which of the following types of payments on an international project are unacceptable?

(A) Payment for mail service.
(B) Offering to pay the country officials for not awarding the project to a particular company.
(C) Payment for policy protection.
(D) Payment for a "foreign workers application license" required in the country.

160. The project charter is created during which life-cycle phase?

(A) Execution
(B) Planning
(C) Closeout
(D) Initiation

161. What type of chart is shown below?

(A) Control Chart
(B) Pareto Chart
(C) Flow Chart
(D) Roving Chart

162. You've been assigned to take over managing a project that should be half-complete according to the schedule. You discover that the project is running far behind schedule, and that the project will probably take double the time originally estimated by the previous project manager. However, upper management has been told that the project is on schedule. Which of the following is the best option in this situation?

(A) Report your assessment to upper management.
(B) Move forward with the schedule as planned by the previous project manager and report at the first missed milestone.
(C) Turn the project back to the previous project manager.
(D) Try to restructure the schedule to meet the project deadline.

163. All the following come after scope definition except?

(A) Activity duration
(B) Resource planning
(C) Cost estimating
(D) Scope planning

164. Your company, a leading provider of project management services through outsourcing, is facing a cash-flow shortage. In an effort to obtain a steady stream of revenue, it bid on an IFB and won a contract issued by the city for trash pickup services. Although management was pleased to win the contract, the garbage trucks your company was planning to buy were sold to someone else. The landfill your company was planning to use was closed, and project managers objected to the new company slogan, "We don't talk trash, we haul it!" Today is Thursday, and work begins next Monday. The CEO recognizes that this is not an opportunity for a successful project and is meeting with the mayor to end the contract because the company cannot perform the work. This is called:

(A) Expiration
(B) Formal acceptance
(C) Cessation
(D) Termination

165. There are several tools and techniques that are useful with integrated change control. Which of the following is used to assess whether variances from the plan require corrective action?

    (A) Project review meetings with key stakeholders
    (B) Earned value management
    (C) A configuration information system (CIS)
    (D) A project management information system (PMIS)

166. It is likely that the _____ estimate is the one that people remember most.

    (A) Summary
    (B) Capital
    (C) Last
    (D) First

167. Which of the following processes is used in risk management to determine which risks might affect the project and documenting their characteristics?

    (A) Risk management planning
    (B) Risk response planning
    (C) Risk identification
    (D) Risk qualitative analysis

168. The technologies or methods that are used to transfer information back and forth between project stakeholders can vary significantly. Which of the following is a communications technology factor for projects?

    (A) Work breakdown structure
    (B) Project scope definition
    (C) Expected project staffing
    (D) Schedule for the project

169. While testing the strength of concrete poured on your project, you discover that over 35% of the concrete does not meet your company's quality standards. You feel certain the concrete will function as it is, and you don't think the concrete needs to meet the quality level specified. What should you do?

    (A) Change the quality standards to meet the level achieved.
    (B) List in your reports that the concrete simply "meets our quality needs".
    (C) Ensure the remaining concrete meets the standard.
    (D) Report the lesser quality level and try to find a solution.

170. Your company, a leading pharmaceutical firm, has more project opportunities to pursue than resources available to complete them. You are leading a team to establish a project selection and prioritization method. The team is considering many different management concerns, including financial return, market share, and public perception. You told the team that the most important of the various criteria for building a project selection model is:

    (A) Realism
    (B) Capability
    (C) Cost
    (D) Ease of use

171. Your organization, a software development firm, has more project opportunities to pursue than resources available to complete them. You are leading a team to establish a project selection and prioritization method. The team is considering different management concerns, including financial return, market share, and public opinion. You told the team the most important of the various criteria for building a project selection model is?

(A) Realism
(B) Capability
(C) Cost
(D) Ease of use

172. You are using earned value progress reporting for your current project in an effort to teach your software developers the benefits of earned value. You plan to display project results so that the team knows how the project is progressing.

PV = $7,500
EV = $5,000
AC = $5,500
BAC = $13,000

What is the CPI for this project, and what does it tell us about cost performance thus far?

(A) 0.91; actual costs have exceeded planned costs
(B) 0.09; actual costs are exactly as planned
(C) 0.09; actual costs have exceed planned costs
(D) 0.91; actual costs are less than planned costs

173. The project manager has just received a change from the customer that does not affect project time and is easy to complete. What should the project manager do first?

(A) Contact the project sponsor for permission.
(B) Evaluate the other components of the triple constraint.
(C) Go to the change control board.
(D) Make the change happen as soon as possible.

174. Which of the following is considered to be a simulation technique?

(A) PDM analysis
(B) GERT analysis
(C) Monte Carlo analysis
(D) Critical path method

175. What doctrine causes a party to relinquish rights under a contract because it knowingly fails to execute those rights?

(A) Material breach
(B) Warranties
(C) Waiver
(D) Assignment of claims

176. You are a project manager working on a project to market a new product. The deliverables of the project have been established, and the project work has begun. A contract to deliver the deliverables has been signed. The customer who has signed the contract has telephoned you to request additional work to be done on the project. This work will affect the budget but not the schedule of the project. This project has a high priority with your company. What should you do next?

(A) Refuse the request and send a memo to your management explaining the situation.
(B) Arrange to meet with the project team to discuss this change.
(C) Respond to the customer's request by explaining the change procedure and asking that he or she submit a request for change.
(D) Do what the customer asks you to do and add the additional requirements to the original contract.

177. Your team is working on an international project to build a regional cellular network in a small in the Middle East. After 2 months of work, a political leader is killed in an unfortunate car accident. His death leads to mass riots throughout the country. Work cannot continue, and your team returns home. A risk such as civil unrest typically requires:

(A) Disaster recovery actions instead of risk management.
(B) A repository or risk database to be established as the basis of a risk lessons learned program.
(C) Periodic risk audit and project risk reviews.
(D) Up front risk management planning with continual review of the plan throughout the project life cycle.

178. You are working on the new oil purification project in a foreign country. A person informs you that you will have to pay him a "transfer fee" for the permit to move heavy equipment through the city. What is the first thing you should do?

(A) Pay the fee but only to the city.
(B) Do not pay the fee.
(C) Make sure the person is really a government official.
(D) Negotiate openly with the city officials.

179. The project manager can have control over _____ costs.

(A) Direct
(B) Indirect
(C) Strategic
(D) Tactical

180. In acceptance sampling the ideal operating characteristic curve would:

(A) Have buyer's risk below the Acceptable Quality Level (AQL).
(B) Have seller's risk below the Acceptable Quality Level (AQL).
(C) Reject all lots that were above the Acceptable Quality Level (AQL).
(D) Accept all lots that were above the Acceptable Quality Level (AQL).

181. Project planning is defined in the PMBOK as:

(A) Using planning techniques to achieve a desired end goal
(B) A structured approach used to guide a project team during development of a project plan
(C) Organizational policies
(D) General management skills

182. Project success depends on a number of interrelated factors, including time, cost, and scope control. However, the success of any project depends primarily on:

(A) Customer acceptance
(B) Customer satisfaction
(C) Customer compromise in defining its needs
(D) Exceeding customer requirements through gold-plating

183. Your company is very excited to work on a major new project. Although the contract is not yet signed, your management wants you to go ahead and begin to staff the project. What should you do?

(A) Wait until the last minute to do so.
(B) Ask the customer for a letter of intent.
(C) Only start to collect resumes and not committee any funds.
(D) Explain to management that this would not be a good idea at this point.

184. A project has a tight budget when you begin negotiating with a seller for a piece of equipment. The seller has told you that the equipment price is fixed. Your manager has told you to negotiate the cost with the seller. What is your best course of action?

(A) Postpone negotiations until you can convince your manager to change their mind.
(B) Make a good faith effort to find a way to decrease the cost.
(C) Cancel the negotiations.
(D) Hold the negotiations but only negotiate other aspects of the project.

185. The diagram that ranks defects in the order of frequency of occurrence and shows the number of defects and the cumulative percentage from the greatest number of defects to the least number of defects is called a:

(A) Bar chart.
(B) Critical path.
(C) Pie chart.
(D) Pareto diagram.

186. All of the following are used in the quality control process except?

(A) Control charts
(B) Gantt charts
(C) Statistical sampling
(D) Pareto charts

187. Historical information is used:

(A) To compare current performance with prospective lessons learned
(B) To prepare the stakeholder management plan
(C) To evaluate the skills and competencies of prospective team members
(D) As an input to project initiation

188. You are currently in the market for a new car. You are debating between two different cars. The Porsche is a highly reliable car with an excellent track record. However, the Ford lacks some premium equipment, such as high-end audio system and sports suspension. On the other hand, the Porsche comes standard with various premium equipment, including a sports suspension and high-end audio system. However, the Ford is much less reliable and would require more frequent maintenance and repairs. How would you characterize the two cars?

    (A) The Porsche is a high grade, high quality car while the Ford is a high grade, low quality car.
    (B) The Porsche is a low grade, high quality car while the Ford is a high grade, high quality car.
    (C) The Porsche is a low grade, high quality car while the Ford is a high grade, low quality car.
    (D) The Porsche is a high grade, low quality car while the Ford is a low grade, high quality car.

189. The management theory that all people can direct their own efforts is:

    (A) Herzberg's theory
    (B) Theory Y
    (C) Theory X
    (D) Maslow's hierarchy

190. The principal sources of project failure are:

    (A) Poorly identified customer needs, a geographically dispersed project team, and little communication with the customer until the project is delivered
    (B) Organizational factors, poorly identified customer needs, inadequately specified project requirements, and poor planning and control
    (C) Lack of a projectized or strong matrix structure, poor scope definition, and lack of a project plan
    (D) Lack of commitment or support by top management, disharmony on the project team, and lack of leadership by the project manager

191. A project team includes five people when the project manager adds two more. How many additional channels of communication are there?

    (A) 7
    (B) 10
    (C) 11
    (D) 21

192. You are the project manager responsible for constructing a new 500-unit apartment building in downtown Los Angeles. As part of the construction project, you are planning to outsource a particular deliverable on your project. You have created a document that described the product and services required in detail and have included the necessary reporting requirements. Which of the following best describes the document you have just prepared?

    (A) Request for Proposal
    (B) Request for Quotation
    (C) Statement of Work
    (D) Procurement management plan

193. In the path convergence example (see image), if the odds of completing activities 1, 2, and 3 on time are 40%, 50%, and 60%, what are the chances of stating activity 4 on day 4?

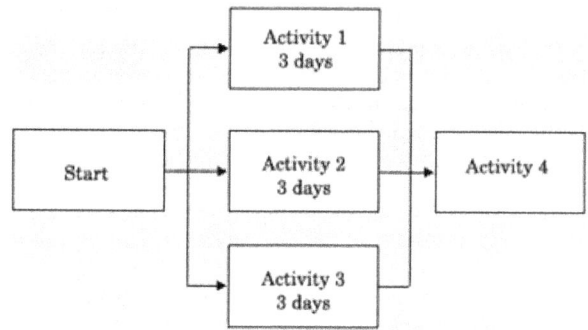

(A) 11%
(B) 12%
(C) 15%
(D) 10%

194. The use of brainstorming as a communications technique encourages which of the following?

(A) Analytical results
(B) Use of the scientific method
(C) Team building and convergent thinking
(D) Divergent thinking

195. You are the program level manager with several project activities underway. In the execution phase, you begin to become concerned about the accuracy of progress reports from the projects. Which of the following would best support your opinion that there is a problem?

(A) Risk quantification reports
(B) Quality audits
(C) Monte Carlo simulation
(D) Regression analysis

196. A family member has a copy of a software program. He offers it to you at no cost because it will solve a business problem you have discussed with him. What should you do?

(A) Refuse the software and notify the owner of the software.
(B) Do not accept the software and advise the family member that such activity is in violation of copyright law.
(C) Accept the software with thanks since the software creator will not find out.
(D) Accept the software and use it until you're able to buy the software yourself.

197. Performance reports are used to provide information to stakeholders on project scope, schedule, cost, and quality. Which statement most accurately describes this process?

(A) Performance reporting focuses on examining earned value analysis to determine whether cost overruns will require budget revisions.
(B) The configuration control board receives performance reports and generates change requests to modify aspects of the project.
(C) Performance reporting includes histograms, flow charts, and bar charts to show network dependencies and relationships.
(D) Performance reporting includes status reports, which detail where the project is now; progress reports, which describe accomplishments; and forecasts, which predict future status and progress.

198. Which of the following is not a measure that determines whether a business practice used by another country is an unfair business practice?

(A) It is a common practice in the other country.
(B) It hurts the right to physical movement.
(C) It discriminates against women.
(D) It does not supply a decent wage for the country and the type of work.

199. Quality seems to be your company motto. First the company obtained certification under ISO 9000. Now the CEO wants to win the Malcolm Baldrige Award. Each project has a quality statement that is consistent with the organization's vision and mission. Both internal and external quality assurance is provided on all projects to:

(A) Provide confidence that the project will satisfy relevant quality standards
(B) Monitor specific project results to note whether they comply with relevant quality standards
(C) Identify ways to eliminate causes of unsatisfactory results
(D) Use inspection to keep errors out of the process

200. Employees who believe their efforts will lead to effective performance and expect to be rewarded for their accomplishments remain productive as rewards meet their expectations. This is called:

(A) The expectancy theory.
(B) A motivational theory.
(C) A perquisite.
(D) A halo effect.

Sample Answer Sheet

	T F		T F		T F		T F
1	Ⓐ Ⓑ Ⓒ Ⓓ Ⓔ	26	Ⓐ Ⓑ Ⓒ Ⓓ Ⓔ	51	Ⓐ Ⓑ Ⓒ Ⓓ Ⓔ	76	Ⓐ Ⓑ Ⓒ Ⓓ Ⓔ
2	Ⓐ Ⓑ Ⓒ Ⓓ Ⓔ	27	Ⓐ Ⓑ Ⓒ Ⓓ Ⓔ	52	Ⓐ Ⓑ Ⓒ Ⓓ Ⓔ	77	Ⓐ Ⓑ Ⓒ Ⓓ Ⓔ
3	Ⓐ Ⓑ Ⓒ Ⓓ Ⓔ	28	Ⓐ Ⓑ Ⓒ Ⓓ Ⓔ	53	Ⓐ Ⓑ Ⓒ Ⓓ Ⓔ	78	Ⓐ Ⓑ Ⓒ Ⓓ Ⓔ
4	Ⓐ Ⓑ Ⓒ Ⓓ Ⓔ	29	Ⓐ Ⓑ Ⓒ Ⓓ Ⓔ	54	Ⓐ Ⓑ Ⓒ Ⓓ Ⓔ	79	Ⓐ Ⓑ Ⓒ Ⓓ Ⓔ
5	Ⓐ Ⓑ Ⓒ Ⓓ Ⓔ	30	Ⓐ Ⓑ Ⓒ Ⓓ Ⓔ	55	Ⓐ Ⓑ Ⓒ Ⓓ Ⓔ	80	Ⓐ Ⓑ Ⓒ Ⓓ Ⓔ
6	Ⓐ Ⓑ Ⓒ Ⓓ Ⓔ	31	Ⓐ Ⓑ Ⓒ Ⓓ Ⓔ	56	Ⓐ Ⓑ Ⓒ Ⓓ Ⓔ	81	Ⓐ Ⓑ Ⓒ Ⓓ Ⓔ
7	Ⓐ Ⓑ Ⓒ Ⓓ Ⓔ	32	Ⓐ Ⓑ Ⓒ Ⓓ Ⓔ	57	Ⓐ Ⓑ Ⓒ Ⓓ Ⓔ	82	Ⓐ Ⓑ Ⓒ Ⓓ Ⓔ
8	Ⓐ Ⓑ Ⓒ Ⓓ Ⓔ	33	Ⓐ Ⓑ Ⓒ Ⓓ Ⓔ	58	Ⓐ Ⓑ Ⓒ Ⓓ Ⓔ	83	Ⓐ Ⓑ Ⓒ Ⓓ Ⓔ
9	Ⓐ Ⓑ Ⓒ Ⓓ Ⓔ	34	Ⓐ Ⓑ Ⓒ Ⓓ Ⓔ	59	Ⓐ Ⓑ Ⓒ Ⓓ Ⓔ	84	Ⓐ Ⓑ Ⓒ Ⓓ Ⓔ
10	Ⓐ Ⓑ Ⓒ Ⓓ Ⓔ	35	Ⓐ Ⓑ Ⓒ Ⓓ Ⓔ	60	Ⓐ Ⓑ Ⓒ Ⓓ Ⓔ	85	Ⓐ Ⓑ Ⓒ Ⓓ Ⓔ
11	Ⓐ Ⓑ Ⓒ Ⓓ Ⓔ	36	Ⓐ Ⓑ Ⓒ Ⓓ Ⓔ	61	Ⓐ Ⓑ Ⓒ Ⓓ Ⓔ	86	Ⓐ Ⓑ Ⓒ Ⓓ Ⓔ
12	Ⓐ Ⓑ Ⓒ Ⓓ Ⓔ	37	Ⓐ Ⓑ Ⓒ Ⓓ Ⓔ	62	Ⓐ Ⓑ Ⓒ Ⓓ Ⓔ	87	Ⓐ Ⓑ Ⓒ Ⓓ Ⓔ
13	Ⓐ Ⓑ Ⓒ Ⓓ Ⓔ	38	Ⓐ Ⓑ Ⓒ Ⓓ Ⓔ	63	Ⓐ Ⓑ Ⓒ Ⓓ Ⓔ	88	Ⓐ Ⓑ Ⓒ Ⓓ Ⓔ
14	Ⓐ Ⓑ Ⓒ Ⓓ Ⓔ	39	Ⓐ Ⓑ Ⓒ Ⓓ Ⓔ	64	Ⓐ Ⓑ Ⓒ Ⓓ Ⓔ	89	Ⓐ Ⓑ Ⓒ Ⓓ Ⓔ
15	Ⓐ Ⓑ Ⓒ Ⓓ Ⓔ	40	Ⓐ Ⓑ Ⓒ Ⓓ Ⓔ	65	Ⓐ Ⓑ Ⓒ Ⓓ Ⓔ	90	Ⓐ Ⓑ Ⓒ Ⓓ Ⓔ
16	Ⓐ Ⓑ Ⓒ Ⓓ Ⓔ	41	Ⓐ Ⓑ Ⓒ Ⓓ Ⓔ	66	Ⓐ Ⓑ Ⓒ Ⓓ Ⓔ	91	Ⓐ Ⓑ Ⓒ Ⓓ Ⓔ
17	Ⓐ Ⓑ Ⓒ Ⓓ Ⓔ	42	Ⓐ Ⓑ Ⓒ Ⓓ Ⓔ	67	Ⓐ Ⓑ Ⓒ Ⓓ Ⓔ	92	Ⓐ Ⓑ Ⓒ Ⓓ Ⓔ
18	Ⓐ Ⓑ Ⓒ Ⓓ Ⓔ	43	Ⓐ Ⓑ Ⓒ Ⓓ Ⓔ	68	Ⓐ Ⓑ Ⓒ Ⓓ Ⓔ	93	Ⓐ Ⓑ Ⓒ Ⓓ Ⓔ
19	Ⓐ Ⓑ Ⓒ Ⓓ Ⓔ	44	Ⓐ Ⓑ Ⓒ Ⓓ Ⓔ	69	Ⓐ Ⓑ Ⓒ Ⓓ Ⓔ	94	Ⓐ Ⓑ Ⓒ Ⓓ Ⓔ
20	Ⓐ Ⓑ Ⓒ Ⓓ Ⓔ	45	Ⓐ Ⓑ Ⓒ Ⓓ Ⓔ	70	Ⓐ Ⓑ Ⓒ Ⓓ Ⓔ	95	Ⓐ Ⓑ Ⓒ Ⓓ Ⓔ
21	Ⓐ Ⓑ Ⓒ Ⓓ Ⓔ	46	Ⓐ Ⓑ Ⓒ Ⓓ Ⓔ	71	Ⓐ Ⓑ Ⓒ Ⓓ Ⓔ	96	Ⓐ Ⓑ Ⓒ Ⓓ Ⓔ
22	Ⓐ Ⓑ Ⓒ Ⓓ Ⓔ	47	Ⓐ Ⓑ Ⓒ Ⓓ Ⓔ	72	Ⓐ Ⓑ Ⓒ Ⓓ Ⓔ	97	Ⓐ Ⓑ Ⓒ Ⓓ Ⓔ
23	Ⓐ Ⓑ Ⓒ Ⓓ Ⓔ	48	Ⓐ Ⓑ Ⓒ Ⓓ Ⓔ	73	Ⓐ Ⓑ Ⓒ Ⓓ Ⓔ	98	Ⓐ Ⓑ Ⓒ Ⓓ Ⓔ
24	Ⓐ Ⓑ Ⓒ Ⓓ Ⓔ	49	Ⓐ Ⓑ Ⓒ Ⓓ Ⓔ	74	Ⓐ Ⓑ Ⓒ Ⓓ Ⓔ	99	Ⓐ Ⓑ Ⓒ Ⓓ Ⓔ
25	Ⓐ Ⓑ Ⓒ Ⓓ Ⓔ	50	Ⓐ Ⓑ Ⓒ Ⓓ Ⓔ	75	Ⓐ Ⓑ Ⓒ Ⓓ Ⓔ	100	Ⓐ Ⓑ Ⓒ Ⓓ Ⓔ

	T F		T F		T F		T F
101	Ⓐ Ⓑ Ⓒ Ⓓ Ⓔ	126	Ⓐ Ⓑ Ⓒ Ⓓ Ⓔ	151	Ⓐ Ⓑ Ⓒ Ⓓ Ⓔ	176	Ⓐ Ⓑ Ⓒ Ⓓ Ⓔ
102	Ⓐ Ⓑ Ⓒ Ⓓ Ⓔ	127	Ⓐ Ⓑ Ⓒ Ⓓ Ⓔ	152	Ⓐ Ⓑ Ⓒ Ⓓ Ⓔ	177	Ⓐ Ⓑ Ⓒ Ⓓ Ⓔ
103	Ⓐ Ⓑ Ⓒ Ⓓ Ⓔ	128	Ⓐ Ⓑ Ⓒ Ⓓ Ⓔ	153	Ⓐ Ⓑ Ⓒ Ⓓ Ⓔ	178	Ⓐ Ⓑ Ⓒ Ⓓ Ⓔ
104	Ⓐ Ⓑ Ⓒ Ⓓ Ⓔ	129	Ⓐ Ⓑ Ⓒ Ⓓ Ⓔ	154	Ⓐ Ⓑ Ⓒ Ⓓ Ⓔ	179	Ⓐ Ⓑ Ⓒ Ⓓ Ⓔ
105	Ⓐ Ⓑ Ⓒ Ⓓ Ⓔ	130	Ⓐ Ⓑ Ⓒ Ⓓ Ⓔ	155	Ⓐ Ⓑ Ⓒ Ⓓ Ⓔ	180	Ⓐ Ⓑ Ⓒ Ⓓ Ⓔ
106	Ⓐ Ⓑ Ⓒ Ⓓ Ⓔ	131	Ⓐ Ⓑ Ⓒ Ⓓ Ⓔ	156	Ⓐ Ⓑ Ⓒ Ⓓ Ⓔ	181	Ⓐ Ⓑ Ⓒ Ⓓ Ⓔ
107	Ⓐ Ⓑ Ⓒ Ⓓ Ⓔ	132	Ⓐ Ⓑ Ⓒ Ⓓ Ⓔ	157	Ⓐ Ⓑ Ⓒ Ⓓ Ⓔ	182	Ⓐ Ⓑ Ⓒ Ⓓ Ⓔ
108	Ⓐ Ⓑ Ⓒ Ⓓ Ⓔ	133	Ⓐ Ⓑ Ⓒ Ⓓ Ⓔ	158	Ⓐ Ⓑ Ⓒ Ⓓ Ⓔ	183	Ⓐ Ⓑ Ⓒ Ⓓ Ⓔ
109	Ⓐ Ⓑ Ⓒ Ⓓ Ⓔ	134	Ⓐ Ⓑ Ⓒ Ⓓ Ⓔ	159	Ⓐ Ⓑ Ⓒ Ⓓ Ⓔ	184	Ⓐ Ⓑ Ⓒ Ⓓ Ⓔ
110	Ⓐ Ⓑ Ⓒ Ⓓ Ⓔ	135	Ⓐ Ⓑ Ⓒ Ⓓ Ⓔ	160	Ⓐ Ⓑ Ⓒ Ⓓ Ⓔ	185	Ⓐ Ⓑ Ⓒ Ⓓ Ⓔ
111	Ⓐ Ⓑ Ⓒ Ⓓ Ⓔ	136	Ⓐ Ⓑ Ⓒ Ⓓ Ⓔ	161	Ⓐ Ⓑ Ⓒ Ⓓ Ⓔ	186	Ⓐ Ⓑ Ⓒ Ⓓ Ⓔ
112	Ⓐ Ⓑ Ⓒ Ⓓ Ⓔ	137	Ⓐ Ⓑ Ⓒ Ⓓ Ⓔ	162	Ⓐ Ⓑ Ⓒ Ⓓ Ⓔ	187	Ⓐ Ⓑ Ⓒ Ⓓ Ⓔ
113	Ⓐ Ⓑ Ⓒ Ⓓ Ⓔ	138	Ⓐ Ⓑ Ⓒ Ⓓ Ⓔ	163	Ⓐ Ⓑ Ⓒ Ⓓ Ⓔ	188	Ⓐ Ⓑ Ⓒ Ⓓ Ⓔ
114	Ⓐ Ⓑ Ⓒ Ⓓ Ⓔ	139	Ⓐ Ⓑ Ⓒ Ⓓ Ⓔ	164	Ⓐ Ⓑ Ⓒ Ⓓ Ⓔ	189	Ⓐ Ⓑ Ⓒ Ⓓ Ⓔ
115	Ⓐ Ⓑ Ⓒ Ⓓ Ⓔ	140	Ⓐ Ⓑ Ⓒ Ⓓ Ⓔ	165	Ⓐ Ⓑ Ⓒ Ⓓ Ⓔ	190	Ⓐ Ⓑ Ⓒ Ⓓ Ⓔ
116	Ⓐ Ⓑ Ⓒ Ⓓ Ⓔ	141	Ⓐ Ⓑ Ⓒ Ⓓ Ⓔ	166	Ⓐ Ⓑ Ⓒ Ⓓ Ⓔ	191	Ⓐ Ⓑ Ⓒ Ⓓ Ⓔ
117	Ⓐ Ⓑ Ⓒ Ⓓ Ⓔ	142	Ⓐ Ⓑ Ⓒ Ⓓ Ⓔ	167	Ⓐ Ⓑ Ⓒ Ⓓ Ⓔ	192	Ⓐ Ⓑ Ⓒ Ⓓ Ⓔ
118	Ⓐ Ⓑ Ⓒ Ⓓ Ⓔ	143	Ⓐ Ⓑ Ⓒ Ⓓ Ⓔ	168	Ⓐ Ⓑ Ⓒ Ⓓ Ⓔ	193	Ⓐ Ⓑ Ⓒ Ⓓ Ⓔ
119	Ⓐ Ⓑ Ⓒ Ⓓ Ⓔ	144	Ⓐ Ⓑ Ⓒ Ⓓ Ⓔ	169	Ⓐ Ⓑ Ⓒ Ⓓ Ⓔ	194	Ⓐ Ⓑ Ⓒ Ⓓ Ⓔ
120	Ⓐ Ⓑ Ⓒ Ⓓ Ⓔ	145	Ⓐ Ⓑ Ⓒ Ⓓ Ⓔ	170	Ⓐ Ⓑ Ⓒ Ⓓ Ⓔ	195	Ⓐ Ⓑ Ⓒ Ⓓ Ⓔ
121	Ⓐ Ⓑ Ⓒ Ⓓ Ⓔ	146	Ⓐ Ⓑ Ⓒ Ⓓ Ⓔ	171	Ⓐ Ⓑ Ⓒ Ⓓ Ⓔ	196	Ⓐ Ⓑ Ⓒ Ⓓ Ⓔ
122	Ⓐ Ⓑ Ⓒ Ⓓ Ⓔ	147	Ⓐ Ⓑ Ⓒ Ⓓ Ⓔ	172	Ⓐ Ⓑ Ⓒ Ⓓ Ⓔ	197	Ⓐ Ⓑ Ⓒ Ⓓ Ⓔ
123	Ⓐ Ⓑ Ⓒ Ⓓ Ⓔ	148	Ⓐ Ⓑ Ⓒ Ⓓ Ⓔ	173	Ⓐ Ⓑ Ⓒ Ⓓ Ⓔ	198	Ⓐ Ⓑ Ⓒ Ⓓ Ⓔ
124	Ⓐ Ⓑ Ⓒ Ⓓ Ⓔ	149	Ⓐ Ⓑ Ⓒ Ⓓ Ⓔ	174	Ⓐ Ⓑ Ⓒ Ⓓ Ⓔ	199	Ⓐ Ⓑ Ⓒ Ⓓ Ⓔ
125	Ⓐ Ⓑ Ⓒ Ⓓ Ⓔ	150	Ⓐ Ⓑ Ⓒ Ⓓ Ⓔ	175	Ⓐ Ⓑ Ⓒ Ⓓ Ⓔ	200	Ⓐ Ⓑ Ⓒ Ⓓ Ⓔ

PMP Sample Exam – Answers

1. (A) Ask for clarification of the intent of adding the resource.

2. (C) A Pareto diagram. A Pareto Diagram is a histogram, ordered by frequency of occurrence that shows how many results were generated by each identified cause.

3. (A) Training.

4. (A) Statement of work. Statement of Work - A narrative description of products, services, or results to be supplied.

5. (C) Differences between or among stakeholders should be resolved in the most cost efficient manner consistent with project objectives.

6. (D) Fast tracking. Fast tracking - A schedule compression technique in which phases or activities that normally would be done in sequence are performed in parallel.

7. (A) Change control system. Change Control System. A collection of formal documented procedures that define how project deliverables and documentation will be controlled, changed, and approved. In most application areas the change control system is a subset of the configuration management system.

8. (B) performing quality control. Perform Quality Control – monitoring specific project results to determine whether they comply with relevant quality standards and identifying ways to eliminate causes of unsatisfactory performance.

9. (B) Allowed.

10. (C) management by objectives. Management by Objectives ("MBO") is a management theory that calls for managing people based on documented work statements mutually agreed to by manager and subordinate. Progress on these work statements is periodically reviewed, and in a proper implementation, compensation is tied to MBO performance.

11. (C) Greater than 75%. Nonverbal cues can be divided into four categories: physical, aesthetic, signs, and symbols. Many studies have demonstrated that most messages are conveyed through such nonverbal cues as facial expression, touch, and body motion, rather than through the words spoken.

12. (D) Passing a quality control inspection.

13. (B) Build trust. Team members who are physically separate from each other tend not to know each other well. They have few opportunities to develop trust in the traditional way, and they tend to communicate poorly with one another. Trust then must become the foundation upon which all team-building activities are built.

14. (D) Contact the employee's manager to arrange a meeting to discuss the matter.

15. (C) Cultural differences will always be an obstacle to be overcome.

16. (C) quality planning. Quality planning involves identifying which quality standards are relevant to the project and determining how to satisfy them. It is one of the key processes when doing the Planning Process Group, and during development of the project management plan, and should be performed in parallel with the other project planning processes.

17. (A) Cost sharing. Where the seller will receive additional value beyond the current project it may be acceptable for the buyer to share in this additional value through a sharing of costs on the current project.

18. (C) Collaborating. Collaborating is an effective technique for managing conflict when a project is too important to be compromised. It involves incorporating multiple ideas and viewpoints from people with different perspectives and offers a good opportunity to learn from others. It provides a long-term resolution.

19. (C) Plan, do, check, and act. In the Shewhart and Deming cycle, an idea is first identified and planned for implementation. Then an experiment is performed to see if the idea will work. The results are checked, and then evaluated. If the evaluation is positive, the idea is fully implemented, and the next idea is planned.

20. (D) Influencing factors that cause change, determining that change has occurred, and managing actual changes as they occur. Integrated Change Control. The process of reviewing all change requests, approving changes and controlling changes to deliverables and organizational process assets.

21. (A) Set international standards for quality conformance in organizations. The International Standards Organization attempts to ensure consistency in organizations that can be relied upon by their customers. To qualify, an organization must meet six requirements regarding the control of documents, control of records, internal audits, control of nonconformance, corrective action, and preventive action.

22. (A) Top-down. This type of estimating looks at the large picture first and gives an overall view of the potential costs.

23. (D) Transfer. Risk transference requires shifting the negative impact of a threat, along with ownership of the response, to a third party. Transferring the risk simply gives another party responsibility for its management; it does not eliminate it. Transferring liability for risk is most effective in dealing with financial risk exposure. Risk transference nearly always involves payment of a risk premium to the party taking on the risk. Transference tools can be quite diverse and include, but are not limited to, the use of insurance, performance bonds, warranties, guarantees, etc. Contracts may be used to transfer liability for specified risks to another party. In many cases, use of a cost-type contract may transfer the cost risk to the buyer, while a fixed-price contract may transfer risk to the seller, if the project's design is stable. (

24. (B) 1.33. EV = 8 and PV = 6, and the formula reads SPI=8/6, which is 1.33.

25. (A) Seven consecutive measurements are ascending, descending, or the same. Consecutive points on a process control chart that are ascending, descending, or the same indicate an abnormal trend in the process and must be investigated.

26. (C) Rule of seven. (See question 26).

27. (B) Follow the bid process and show the vice president why the favored vendor is or is not the best choice.

28. (D) 10. n (n-1) / 2 = 5 (6-1) / 2 - 5 (4) / 2 = 20 / 2 = 10. (PMBOK Guide - page 226)

29. (B) Quality assurance. Quality Assurance – applying the planned, systematic quality activities to ensure that the project employs all processes needed to meet requirements.

30. (C) Hold a project kickoff meeting. An indispensable tool in project management, the kickoff meeting is held at the outset of the project and is designed to get the project rolling. The meeting provides the opportunity not only to present the project charter and discuss the project's goals and objectives but also to establish rapport among team members.

31. (C) 40. If the tasks listed in the WBS are longer than this, it will be very difficult to have control over them.

32. (A) deciding how to approach and plan risk management activities for the project. Risk Management Planning - The process of deciding how to approach, plan, and execute risk management activities for a project.

33. (C) Permanent. The records must be permanent so that they can be referred to after they have been sent and received. This means that you will not use verbal communications as project records unless someone writes down the conversation. In that case, the notes of the conversation or meeting should be circulated to get agreement that what is captured is what was actually said.

34. (B) Report possible violations of the code of conduct to PMI. PMP® Professional Code of Conduct I.A.2

35. (C) Try to get permission from the customer.

36. (D) Cost estimating. This is the directly from the PMBOK.

37. (A) Follow the customs of the country and bring the gift of wine.

38. (C) Degree of authority the project manager has over team resources.
In a strong matrix organization, the balance of power shifts toward the project manager. In a weak matrix organization, the balance of power shifts toward the functional or line manager.

39. (A) Professional engineers. Only people trained in the major engineering types of product analysis should attempt to use these techniques to gain a better understanding of the product of the project. These techniques are not easily learned and require a good background in a variety of mathematical analytics. In other words, if you do not understand how to use them, do not even try.

40. (B) Inputs. These are all inputs into scope verification.

41. (D) An imposed date. Constraint - the state, quality, or sense of being restricted to a given course of action or inaction. An applicable restriction or limitation, either internal or external to the project that will affect the performance of the project or a process. For example, a schedule constraint is any limitation or restraint placed on the project schedule that affects when a schedule activity can be scheduled and is usually in the form of fixed imposed dates. A cost constraint is any limitation or restraint placed on the project budget such as funds available over time. A project resource constraint is any limitation or restraint placed on resource usage, such as what resource skills or disciplines are available and the amount of a given resource available during a specified time frame.

42. (C) Acceptance. Acceptance: A strategy that is adopted because it is seldom possible to eliminate all risk from a project. This strategy indicates that the project team has decided not to change the project management plan to deal with a risk, or is unable to identify any other suitable response strategy. It may be adopted for either threats or opportunities. This strategy can be either passive or active. Passive acceptance requires no action, leaving the project team to deal with the threats or opportunities as they occur. The most common active acceptance strategy is to establish a contingency reserve, including amounts of time, money, or resources to handle known—or even sometimes potential, unknown—threats or opportunities.

43. (B) Value engineering. The planning of the engineering tasks to reduce cost, improve quality and maximize performance of the product is value engineering. Value engineering also helps to give clear data from which good decisions can be made.

44. (D) For paying a bribe to a foreign official.

45. (B) Early in. The earlier you have good plans from which to work the easier it is to control your costs and get good cost planning. If there is no clarity about the work to be done, there will be no clarity about the costs to be incurred.

46. (D) Inclusion. Inclusion, Control and Affection are the fundamental patterns of relationship needs.

47. (B) Progressive elaboration of the product description. The product description documents the characteristics of the product or service that the project was undertaken to create. This description will generally have less detail in early phases and more detail in later ones as the product characteristics are elaborated progressively.

48. (C) Legal. The terms and conditions in any contract are legal requirements that must be adhered to by the parties entering into the agreement.

49. (D) All of the above. Activity Resource Estimating - the process of estimating the types and quantities of resources required to perform each schedule activity.

50. (C) Contact your clients and seek permission to disclose the information.

51. (D) All of the above. The project scope statement is the definition of the project—what needs to be accomplished. The Develop Preliminary Project Scope Statement process addresses and documents the characteristics and boundaries of the project and its associated products and services, as well as the methods of acceptance and scope control. A project scope statement includes: Project and product objectives; Product or service requirements and characteristics; Product acceptance criteria; Project boundaries; Project requirements and deliverables; Project constraints; Project assumptions; Initial project organization; Initial defined risks; Schedule milestones; Initial WBS; Order of magnitude cost estimate and the Project configuration management requirements.

52. (C) Conduct a stakeholder analysis to assess information needs. Stakeholder analysis is used to analyze the information needs of the stakeholders and determine the sources to meet those needs. The analysis should include consideration of appropriate methods and technologies for providing the information needed.

53. (A) Do not make the payment.

54. (D) Critical path method (CPM). Critical Path Method - a schedule network analysis technique used to determine the amount of scheduling flexibility (the amount of float) on various logical network paths in the project schedule network, and to determine the minimum total project duration. Early start and finish dates are calculated by means of a forward pass, using a specified start date. Late start and finish dates are calculated by means of a backward pass, starting from a specified completion date, which sometimes is the project early finish date determined during the forward pass calculation.

55. (D) Reward power. Reward power involves positive reinforcement and the ability to award people something of value in exchange for their cooperation. The project manager's ability to use this power derives from his or her position in the organizational hierarchy and degree of control over the project.

56. (C) Quality control. Quality Control is the process of monitoring specific project results to determine if they comply with relevant standards and identifying ways to eliminate causes of unsatisfactory performance.

57. (B) scope definition. Scope definition is the process of breaking down a deliverable in to smaller manageable parts to ensure better control.

58. (B) Report the issue to management and inform the customer of their decision.

59. (C) Risk identification.

60. (A) Avoidance. Risk avoidance involves changing the project management plan to eliminate the threat posed by an adverse risk, to isolate the project objectives from the risk's impact, or to relax the objective that is in jeopardy, such as extending the schedule or reducing scope. Some risks that arise early in the project can be avoided by clarifying requirements, obtaining information, improving communication, or acquiring expertise.

61. (C) 25.0. Triangular distribution is used only when we know the minimum, maximum and most likely values. It leads to a less conservative estimate of uncertainty. The triangular distribution is useful for stochastic modeling rather than statistical analysis because of its artificial nature. Distribution Formula: Probability (cost < most likely) = (most likely - min) ÷ (max - min).

62. (B) Data. The data are only useful to you when you know how they were derived. It is possible that one case in the data may be so far away from the average data that in fact the entire set of information is not truly useful. This would be the case when a very large company's data was blended in with several companies that were less than one tenth the size of the big company. Ask how the data were derived, and you can save yourself a lot of grief later.

63. (C) 2.5%. Expected value = $ 1,000,000. Standard Deviation (SD) = $ 50,000. Project budgeted for = $ 1,100,000. Probability of completing within budget = the area on the left half of normal distribution + area under 2 sigma right side to normal distribution = 50% + (95/2)% = 97.5%. Probability of not completing within the budget is = 100 – 97.5 = 2.5%.

64. (D) identifies which variables have the most influence on a quality outcome. Design of experiments is a statistical method that helps identify which factors might influence specific variables and is applied most often to the product of the project (for example, automotive designers may wish to determine which combination of suspension and tires will produce the most desirable ride characteristics at a reasonable cost.) It can also be applied to project management issues such as cost and schedule tradeoffs. Example: senior engineers will cost more than junior engineers but will usually complete the assignment in less time. An appropriately designed experiment which computes project costs and duration for various combinations of senior and junior engineers will often yield an optimal solution from a relatively limited number of cases.

65. (D) Greater than 50%. Nonverbal cues can be divided into four categories: physical, aesthetic, signs, and symbols. Many studies have demonstrated that most messages are conveyed through such nonverbal cues as facial expression, touch, and body motion, rather than through the words spoken.

66. (B) Constraints. All of these are constraints that may affect the project and the project manager. The key for the project manager is to check at the beginning of the project to determine whether any of these constraints will affect the project as it is executed.

67. (C) Indexed. In order to search for materials after Administrative Closure has occurred and the project is finished, indexing archives helps make searching for information much faster and simpler.

68. (B) A constraint. Constraints are factors that will limit the team's options.

69. (D) As an input to quality assurance. Quality control measurements are records of quality control testing and measurement in a format for comparison and analysis. These measurements serve as an input to quality assurance, which consists of all the planned and systematic activities implemented within the quality system to provide confidence that the project will satisfy the relevant quality standards.

70. (C) Formal. It's extremely important to have formal acceptance when the project is being brought to Administrative Closure. If the acceptance is formal, you will have a record of it. You can refer to this record at any later time, and it forestalls any arguments about whether the project was done correctly.

71. (D) Estimate and budget controllable and uncontrollable costs separately. To be effective, reward and recognition systems must make and establish the link between performance and reward clear, explicit, and achievable. For example, if a project manager is to be rewarded for meeting the project's cost objectives, he should have the appropriate control over both staffing and procurement decisions. In addition, a reliable method for estimating, budgeting, and tracking controllable costs must be in place.

72. (D) Work with leadership from each area to collaboratively engineer a mutually acceptable solution

73. (B) determining the responses to individual risks. Responses to individual risks are not determined until the risk response planning process.

74. (B) 15. n (n-1) / 2 = 6 (6-1) / 2 = 6 (5) / 2 = 30 / 2 = 15.

75. (C) Create a workaround.

76. (D) Transference. Risk transference requires shifting the negative impact of a threat, along with ownership of the response, to a third party. Transferring the risk simply gives another party responsibility for its management; it does not eliminate it. Transferring liability for risk is most effective in dealing with financial risk exposure. Risk transference nearly always involves payment of a risk premium to the party taking on the risk. Transference tools can be quite diverse and include, but are not limited to, the use of insurance, performance bonds, warranties, guarantees, etc. Contracts may be used to transfer liability for specified risks to another party. In many cases, use of a cost-type contract may transfer the cost risk to the buyer, while a fixed-price contract may transfer risk to the seller, if the project's design is stable.

77. (A) In lieu of formal termination procedures. A no-cost settlement can be used in lieu of formal termination procedures when the seller has indicated that such an arrangement is acceptable, no buyer property has been furnished under the contract, no payments are due the seller, no other obligations are outstanding, and the product or service can be readily obtained elsewhere.

78. (D) Making the most efficient use of the available resources. Resource Leveling - any form of schedule network analysis in which scheduling decisions (start and finish dates) are driven by resource constraints (e.g., limited resource availability or difficult-to-manage changes in resource availability levels).

79. (A) 30%. The likelihood is determined by multiplying the probability of event 1 by the probability of event 2 and the probability of event 3. .50 X .75 X .80 = .30 or 30%

80. (B) Oral communication from key stakeholders. Change Request. Requests to expand or reduce the project scope, modify policies, processes, plans, or procedures, modify costs or budgets, or revise schedules. Requests for a change can be direct or indirect, externally or internally initiated, and legally or contractually mandated or optional. Only formally documented requested changes are processed and only approved change requests are implemented.

81. (B) Procurement management plan. The procurement management plan describes how the procurement processes; from solicitation planning through closing will be managed. This includes the type contracts to be used, preparation of independent estimates, actions to be taken by the procurement department and the project management team, location of standardized procurement documents, management of multiple providers, and coordination of the procurement with other aspects of the project.

82. (C) Total float for the activity is 9 days. Total float is computed by subtracting the early start date from the late start date, or 19-10 = 9. To compute the early finish date given a duration of 4, we would start counting the activity on the morning of the 10th; therefore, the activity would be completed at the end of day 13, not 14 (10, 11, 12, 13). If we started the activity on its late start date on the morning of the 19th, we would finish at the end of day 22, not 25. Insufficient information is provided to determine whether this activity can be completed in 2 days if the resources are doubled.

83. (C) Discuss the issue with the customer.

84. (C) A unit price contract. A unilateral contract takes the form of a purchase order—a standardized form listing routine items at standard (for example, vendor catalog) prices. The seller usually accepts the purchase order automatically. Unilateral contracts issued in this way normally do not involve any negotiation and contain relatively low monetary amounts.

85. (B) Develop alternative solutions to the problem.

86. (A) $700,000. EMV = (3,000,000 X 45%) + (-$1,000,000 X 65%); $1,350,000 + (-$650,000) = $700,000

87. (C) Complete an accurate estimate of the project. In addition, create a risk assessment on why the project budget would be inadequate. It would be inappropriate to bloat the project costs by 25 percent. A risk assessment describing how the project may fail if the budget is not accurate is most appropriate.

88. (D) Making process adjustments as a result of deficiencies. Integrated Change Control. The process of reviewing all change requests, approving changes and controlling changes to deliverables and organizational process assets.

89. (B) E B C D. The critical path is E B C D as it is the longest path to completion at 18 days.

90. (B) Acceptance, correctness. The stakeholders accept what is being done during scope verification, and the correctness of the results is determined during the quality control process.

91. (A) $12,500. EAC is calculated as BAC/CPI in this case $10,000 / .80 or $12,500.

92. (A) Communicate with the vendor in regard to the rumor. The project manager should confront the problem by talking with the vendor about the rumor.

93. (A) Resource assignment matrix. A resource assignment matrix shows who is responsible for the various tasks in your WBS and who are the other participants working on the task.

94. (C) Evaluate failure modes and causes associated with the design and manufacture of a new product. This technique is a method of analyzing design reliability. A list of potential failure modes is developed for each element, and then each mode is given a numeric rating for frequency of occurrence, criticality, and probability of detection. These data are used to assign a risk priority number for prioritizing problems and guiding the design effort.

95. (C) Notify your manager of the probable decreased cost.

96. (B) Work Breakdown Structure. The Work Breakdown Structure is the best choice for this scenario.

97. (C) Financial. Although these are also quantitative types of analysis, the answer that is looked for on the exam is financial.

98. (A) Let the customer know of the issue.

99. (B) A Pareto diagram. In the late 1800s, Vilfredo Pareto, an Italian economist, found that typically 80 percent of the wealth in a region was concentrated in less than 20 percent of the population. Later, Dr. Joseph Juran formulated what he called the Pareto Principle of Problems: only a "vital few" elements (20 percent) account for the majority (80 percent) of the problems. For example, in a manufacturing facility, 20 percent of the equipment problems account for 80 percent of the downtime. Because the Pareto Principle has proven to be valid in numerous situations, it is useful to examine data carefully to identify the vital few items that most deserve attention.

100. (A) Complete the activities as requested. The project manager must respect the delegation of the Functional Manager.

101. (A) Legitimate. Legitimate power is derived from the person's formal position within the organization. The project manager's ability to use this power derives from his or her position in the organizational hierarchy and his or her degree of control over the project, as modified by the organizational climate. Use of this power should be in conjunction with expert and reward power whenever possible.

102. (C) Phase. Waiting until the end of the project to do Administrative Closure may result in loss of important information. The end of each phase is a natural time to gather and archive documentation.

103. (A) Many competing needs and objectives must be satisfied.

104. (D) Market conditions. The procurement planning process must consider what products and services are available in the marketplace, from whom, and under what terms and conditions.

105. (D) Project management methodology. Inputs to the close project process are: project management plan; contract documentation; enterprise environmental factors; organizational process assets; work performance information; and deliverables.

106. (B) Communication barriers. Communication Management Plan - describes the communications needs and expectations for the project; how and in what format information will be communicated; when and where each communication will be made; and who is responsible for providing each type of communication. A communication management plan can be formal or informal, highly detailed or broadly framed, based on the requirements of the project stakeholders. The communication management plan is contained in, or is a subsidiary plan of, the project management plan.

107. (B) 1.5. At the end of two weeks this task is 75% complete. The PV was to be 4 person-weeks, two people working full time for two weeks. The EV is therefore 3 person-weeks, .75 X 4. The AC is 2 person-weeks. The cost performance index is the EV / AC. CPI = 3 person-weeks / 2 person-weeks = 1.5.

108. (D) Progress reporting. When percentage of completion is used in performance reporting, you are doing progress reporting.

109. (A) use the forms from company B and begin to instruct them on ways to upgrade their own.

110. (D) An estimate of the probability that a given risk will occur. Risk event probability—an estimate of the probability that a given risk event will occur.

111. (B) Tell your manager and remove yourself from the selection committee.

112. (C) These are benefit measurement methods. According to the PMI, there are two categories of project selection methods: constrained optimization methods and benefit measurement methods. Constrained optimization methods are complicated mathematical models "using linear, non-linear, dynamic, integer, and multi-objective programming algorithms", and are often referred to as decision models. On the other hand, benefit measurement methods are "comparative approaches, scoring models, benefit contribution, or economic models."

113. (A) Downward communication. Downward communication provides direction and control for project team members and other employees. It contains job-related information, such as actions required, standards, the time activities should be performed, activities to be completed, and progress measurement.

114. (A) p = .003. $0.1 \times .2 \times .15 = .003$.

115. (A) Request the supporting details for the estimate to ensure it has been properly prepared.

116. (C) Inspection. Scope verification is the process of obtaining the stakeholders' formal acceptance of the completed project scope and associated deliverables. Verifying the project scope includes reviewing deliverables to ensure that each is completed satisfactorily. If the project is terminated early, the project scope verification process should establish and document the level and extent of completion. Scope verification differs from quality control in that scope verification is primarily concerned with acceptance of the deliverables, while quality control is primarily concerned with meeting the quality requirements specified for the deliverables. Quality control is generally performed before scope verification, but these two processes can be performed in parallel.

117. (B) Working with the bidders to determine alternative solutions for the project.

118. (C) Benchmarking. Benchmarking involves comparing actual or planned project practices to those of other projects to generate ideas for improvement and to provide a basis by which to measure performance. These other projects can be within the performing organization or outside of it, and can be within the same or in another application area.

119. (B) Scope verification. Scope verification is the process of obtaining the stakeholders' formal acceptance of the completed project scope and associated deliverables. Verifying the project scope includes reviewing deliverables to ensure that each is completed satisfactorily. If the project is terminated early, the project scope verification process should establish and document the level and extent of completion.

120. (B) Opportunities. Opportunity. A condition or situation favorable to the project, a positive set of circumstances, a positive set of events, a risk that will have a positive impact on project objectives, or a possibility for positive changes.

121. (A) Let the customer know of the issue.

122. (D) Sum of the years' digits. Sum of the years' digits is an accelerated depreciation method. Each year of the useful life of the asset is given a sequential number; the numbers are summed and used as the denominator for a fraction of the asset's book value to be taken each year as depreciation. The numerator of the fraction for each year is the reverse of the years' sequence numbers. $1 + 2 + 3 + 4 + 5 + 6 + 7 + 8 + 9 + 10 + 55$. First year use 10/55; second year use 9/55, and so on.

123. (A) Calendar time between the start of A to the finish of B is 11 days. The duration of A, which is 3, is added to the duration of B, which is 4, for a total of 7. The 3 days between the activities is lag and not duration. The lag is a constraint and must be taken into account as part of the network calculations, but it does not consume resources. The total time by the calendar is 11 days as counted from the morning of Monday the 4th. The lag occurs over Thursday, Friday, and Saturday. Sunday is a non-workday, so activity B does not start until Monday the 11th. Therefore, the calendar time is 11 days, and activity B ends on Thursday the 14th. (Project Management: Effective Scheduling - page 49)

124. (D) Triggers. Triggers are indications that a risk has occurred or is about to occur. Triggers may be discovered in the risk identification process and watched in the risk monitoring and control process. Triggers are sometimes called risk symptoms or warning signs.

125. (C) A resource calendar. Project and resource calendars identify periods when work is allowed. Project calendars affect all resources. Resource calendars affect a specific resource or a resource category, such as a labor contract that requires certain workers to work on certain days of the week.

126. (A) Ask the team members how they would divide the money. Probably the best thing to do in this situation would be to divide the money by letting the team decide how to divide it. This is participative management.

127. (C) Postpone the negotiations.

128. (C) Refuse to answer the question and remove the company from consideration for future work.

129. (B) Methods that will be used to gather and store information. The plan should also contain a distribution structure that shows the methods that will be used to distribute various types of information and the individuals or organizations to whom the information will be distributed, production schedules showing when each type of communication will be produced, and methods to access information between scheduled communications. Also included should be a discussion of how the plan will be updated and revised as needs change. The communication plan is a component of the project plan and may be formal or informal, highly detailed or broadly framed, based on the needs of the project.

130. (C) An external dependency. External dependencies are those that involve a relationship between project activities and non-project activities.

131. (D) Respect confidentiality of sensitive information. PMP® Professional Code of Conduct II.A.3

132. (D) 73. According to learning curve theory, the cost of a unit of production, the software module, will decrease by a fixed percentage for each doubling of the units produced. Since from unit 1 to unit 2 there was a 10% change in cost, the fixed percentage of reduction in cost was 90%. For unit 4, cost would be 81 person-hours, 90% of 90 person-hours. For unit 8, it would be 90% of 81, or 73 person-hours.

133. (C) A set of procedures by which project scope may be changed, including the paperwork, tracking systems, and approval levels necessary for authorizing change. A project scope change control system, documented in the project scope management plan, defines the procedures by which the project scope and product scope can be changed. The system includes the documentation, tracking systems, and approval levels necessary for authorizing changes. The scope change control system is integrated with any overall project management information system to control project scope.

134. (D) Project plan execution. The vast majority of the project's budget will be expended in performing the Executing Process Group processes.

135. (A) As a public official you make a decision about a contract award that will benefit you personally.

136. (C) Avoidance. Avoidance. Risk avoidance involves changing the project management plan to eliminate the threat posed by an adverse risk, to isolate the project objectives from the risk's impact, or to relax the objective that is in jeopardy, such as extending the schedule or reducing scope. Some risks that arise early in the project can be avoided by clarifying requirements, obtaining information, improving communication, or acquiring expertise.

137. (C) Indirect. The nature of an indirect cost is such that it is neither possible nor practical to measure how much of the cost is attributable to a single project. These costs are allocated to the project by the performing organization as a cost of doing business.

138. (A) It makes sure the project is on track by ensuring the customer's acceptance of the deliverable. Scope verification is the process of obtaining the stakeholders' formal acceptance of the completed project scope and associated deliverables. Verifying the project scope includes reviewing deliverables to ensure that each is completed satisfactorily. If the project is terminated early, the project scope verification process should establish and document the level and extent of completion.

139. (C) project selection methods. The project-selection method(s) used by an organization should be relevant to the objectives of the company and its managers and should be consistent with the capabilities and resources of the organization. The two methods of project selection are benefit measurement (comparative approach) and constrained optimization (mathematical approach).

140. (C) Grade. Products that are able to perform and function acceptably but are different technically are graded into different categories. For example, wood is graded according to the number of knots that are present in the wood. The wood performs the function of being structurally sound in all grades, but the desirability of knot free wood leads us to higher grades of wood.

141. (C) Tell your sponsor that you want to set up a meeting with the customer to resolve the conflict.

142. (D) Used as required to approve or reject change requests. Change Control Board - A formally constituted group of stakeholders responsible for approving or rejecting changes to the project baselines.

143. (A) Analogous. Analogous estimating uses previous projects as a benchmark for estimating cost.

144. (D) Many competing needs and objectives must be satisfied.

145. (C) The team is gold plating. Simply defined, gold-plating gives the customer more than what was required. Exceeding the specified requirements is a waste of time and money, with no value added to the project. The customer should expect and receive exactly what was specified. This is the underlying philosophy of project quality management espoused by PMI®; it is the process required to ensure that the project will satisfy the needs for which it was undertaken.

146. (A) Forecast remaining time. All activities have baseline start and finish dates once project execution begins. Completed tasks also have an actual start date. Forecast remaining time only has meaning in the context of an activity in progress.

147. (C) Active acceptance. Acceptance means accepting the consequences of a risk. Acceptance can be active, such as developing a contingency plan to execute should the risk occur, or passive, such as accepting a lower profit should some activities overrun.

148. (D) Speak to the visiting engineers and discuss having an informal meeting between your engineers and the visiting engineers. This type of problem occurs frequently. Many times there is a misunderstanding on the part of the customer's engineers, and it can be resolved simply by having an informal meeting and discussing the problem. Later, if the disagreement persists, the customer should submit a request for a change, and a formal investigation can be completed.

149. (A) considering both development and operating costs when evaluating project alternatives. Project Cost Management should also consider the effect of project decisions on the cost of using, maintaining, and supporting the product, service, or result of the project… This broader view … is often called life-cycle costing.

150. (A) All projects, large and small. A system is needed for careful monitoring of changes made to the requirements. Use of written change orders encourages the individuals asking for changes to take responsibility for their requests and reduces frivolous requests that may adversely affect the project.

151. (B) Support the promotion but work with the employee and the employee's new management to develop a good transition plan.

152. (B) Make the link between project performance and reward clear, explicit, and achievable. Reward and recognition systems are formal management actions that promote or reinforce desired behavior. As a tool and a technique for team development, these systems can be very effective.

153. (B) The overall project plan. The quality plan is part of the overall project plan and is an important input to the project plan.

154. (D) Tell the project sponsor about your budget and schedule projections. PMP Code of Conduct.

155. (D) ISO. The ISO is the international organization that controls the standards for quality.

156. (B) Develop a subproject work breakdown structure for the work package that is her company's responsibility. Work packages are items at the lowest level of the work breakdown structure. A subproject work breakdown structure breaks down work packages into greater detail. A subproject work breakdown structure generally is used if the project manager assigns a scope of work to another organization, and the project manager at that organization must plan and manage the scope of work in greater detail.

157. (A) 9%. The likelihood is determined by multiplying the probability of event 1 by the probability of event 2; 20 X .45 = .09 or 9%

158. (A) Prevention costs. Cost of quality refers to the total cost of all efforts to achieve product or service quality. Prevention costs are a category of quality costs. Prevention costs are investments made to keep nonconforming products from occurring and reaching the customer. They include quality planning costs, process control costs, information systems costs, and training and general management costs.

159. (B) Offering to pay the country officials for not awarding the project to a particular company.

160. (D) Initiation. The initiation phase is the process of preparing for, assembling resources and getting work started. May apply to any level, e.g. program, project, phase, activity, task.

161. (A) Control Chart. The chart shown is a control chart. Control chart is a device for describing in a precise manner what is meant by statistical control. Its uses are: 1) It is a proven technique for improving productivity; (2) It is effective in defect prevention; (3) It prevents unnecessary process adjustments; (4) It provides diagnostic information; and (5) It provides information about process capability.

162. (A) Report your assessment to upper management.

163. (D) Scope planning. Scope Planning - this is the process necessary for creating a project scope management plan that documents how the project scope will be defined, verified and controlled, and how the work breakdown structure will be created and defined.

164. (D) Termination. Contracts typically end in one of three ways: successful performance, mutual agreement, or breach. Termination is a word used to define a contract ending through mutual agreement or breach. It is a special case of contract closeout.

165. (B) Earned value management. Earned Value Management (EVM). A management methodology for integrating scope, schedule, and resources, and for objectively measuring project performance and progress. Performance is measured by determining the budgeted cost of work performed (i.e., earned value) and comparing it to the actual cost of work performed (i.e., actual cost). Progress is measured by comparing the earned value to the planned value.

166. (D) First. The first estimate that people see is often the one that they remember the most. Even if you explain the major caveat that you are simply showing a first estimate, it always seems that people remember the first information they receive.

167. (C) Risk identification. Risk Identification. The process of determining which risks might affect the project and documenting their characteristics.

168. (C) Expected project staffing. The expected project staffing is important to the communications technology since it will be necessary for the project staff to be able to use the communications tools effectively.

169. (D) Report the lesser quality level and try to find a solution.

170. (A) Realism. The model should reflect the objectives of the company and its managers; consider the realities of the organization's limitations on facilities, capital, and personnel; and include factors for risk: the technical risks of performance, cost, and time and the market risk of customer rejection.

171. (A) Realism. Project selection methods are used to determine which project the organization will select. These methods generally fall into one of two broad categories: (1) benefit measurement methods that are comparative approaches, scoring models, benefit contribution, or economic models and (2) mathematical models that use linear, nonlinear, dynamic, integer, or multiobjective programming algorithms.

172. (A) 0.91; actual costs have exceeded planned costs. CPI is calculated as EV/AC
$5,000 (EV) / $5,500 (AC) = .909 or .91 (CPI). EV measures the budgeted dollar value of the work that has actually been accomplished, whereas AC measures the actual cost of getting that work done. If the two numbers are the same, work on the project is being accomplished for exactly the budgeted amount of money. In this example, an index of 0.91 means that for every dollar spent on the project only 91 cents worth of work is actually being accomplished.

173. (B) Evaluate the other components of the triple constraint. Triple Constraint - The term used to describe the three key project objectives that must be simultaneously accomplished, namely, the performance specification, the time schedule, and the monetary budget.

174. (C) Monte Carlo analysis. Monte Carlo analysis is a simulation technique that assigns durations to tasks in a schedule and then calculates the schedule information. It repeats this assignment and calculation many times and then reports statistical results, including the percent of time a task is on the critical path.

175. (C) Waiver. Under the doctrine of waiver, a party can relinquish rights that it otherwise has under the contract. If the seller offers incomplete, defective, or late performance and the buyer's project manager knowingly accepts that performance, the buyer has waived its right to strict performance. In some circumstances, the party at fault may remain liable for provable damages, but the waiver will prevent the buyer from claiming a material breach and, thus, from terminating the contract.

176. (C) Respond to the customer's request by explaining the change procedure and asking that he or she submit a request for change. There should be a change procedure in the project to handle changes that might be initiated by customers. The change procedure should include the cost for managing the change and the cost of developing the estimate for the effects of the change.

177. (A) Disaster recovery actions instead of risk management. Examples of external risks include shifting legal or regulatory environment, labor issues, changing owner priorities, country risk, and weather. Unknown risks that cannot be managed, such as earthquakes, floods, and civil unrest are called force majeure risks. They generally require disaster recovery actions rather than risk management.
178. (C) Make sure the person is really a government official.

179. (A) Direct. Costs that are directly incurred because the project is being executed are directs costs. In some cases the project manager has control over the costs and in some cases the organization itself will control the costs. In any case, the costs occur only when the project is going on.

180. (C) Reject all lots that were above the Acceptable Quality Level (AQL). In sampling inspection the ideal operating characteristic curve would correctly pass or reject all lots that were below or above the AQL point. Any lot that truly had more than the allowed AQL would be rejected, and any lot that had less than or equal to the AQL would be accepted.

181. (B) A structured approach used to guide a project team during development of a project plan. Project planning is the identification of the project objectives and the ordered activity necessary to complete the project. The identification of resource types and quantities required to carry out each activity or task.

182. (B) Customer satisfaction. Customer satisfaction, not time or cost, is the primary criterion for measuring project success.

183. (B) Ask the customer for a letter of intent.

184. (B) Make a good faith effort to find a way to decrease the cost.

185. (D) Pareto diagram. The Pareto diagram shows a histogram where the defect classes are arranged in the order of the highest to lowest frequency of occurrence of the defect. It also shows the cumulative percent of defects from the highest to lowest number of defects.

186. (B) Gantt charts. Gantt Chart - a graphic display of schedule-related information. In the typical bar chart, schedule activities or work breakdown structure components are listed down the left side of the chart, dates are shown across the top, and activity durations are shown as date-placed horizontal bars.

187. (D) As an input to project initiation. Reviewing past projects often helps a person prepare cost and schedule estimates and a risk management plan for the current project.

188. (C) The Porsche is a low grade, high quality car while the Ford is a high grade, low quality car. Quality and grade are not the same. Grade is a category assigned to products or services having the same functional use but different technical characteristics. Low quality is always a problem; low grade may not be. For example, a software product can be of high quality (no obvious defects, readable manual) and low grade (a limited number of features), or of low quality (many defects, poorly organized user documentation) and high grade (numerous features). The project manager and the project management team are responsible for determining and delivering the required levels of both quality and grade.

189. (B) Theory Y. With Theory Y assumptions, management's role is to develop the potential in employees and help them to release that potential toward common goals.

190. (B) Organizational factors, poorly identified customer needs, inadequately specified project requirements, and poor planning and control. Organizational problems, such as separation of responsibility and authority, can hinder the work being done and lead to poor quality; poorly identified customer needs and inadequately specified project requirements can result in a product that is unusable or grossly underused; and poor planning and control can create a chaotic environment and poor project results.

191. (C) 11. $n (n-1) / 2 = 5 (5-1) / 2 = 5 (4) / 2 = 20 / 2 = 10$; $n (n-1) / 2 = 7 (7-1) / 2 = 7 (6) / 2 = 42 / 2 = 21$; 21 total - 10 previous = 11 additional channels.

192. (C) Statement of Work. The statement of work (SOW) is a narrative description of products or services to be supplied by the project. For internal projects, the project initiator or sponsor provides the statement of work based on business needs, product, or service requirements. For external projects, the statement of work can be received from the customer as part of a bid document, for example, request for proposal, request for information, request for bid, or as part of a contract.

193. (B) 12%. Probability (starting activity 4 on day 5) = .4 X .5 X .5 = .12 or 12%

194. (C) Team building and convergent thinking. Brainstorming encourages team building if handled properly. Participants feel that they are part of the decision making process and have a sense of participation. In the evaluation part of brainstorming, the participants' thinking converges to a common agreement.

195. (B) Quality audits. A quality audit is a structured, independent review to determine whether project activities comply with organizational and project policies, processes, and procedures. The objective of a quality audit is to identify inefficient and ineffective policies, processes, and procedures in use on the project.

196. (B) Do not accept the software and advise the family member that such activity is in violation of copyright law.

197. (D) Performance reporting includes status reports, which detail where the project is now; progress reports, which describe accomplishments; and forecasts, which predict future status and progress. Information from these reports is valuable only to the extent that the project manager, customer, and other key stakeholders use them to make decisions regarding present and future actions. In the decision-making process, the project manager needs to know the current situation (status reports); the past performance capability that led to the current status (progress reports); and a best estimate of future progress, using past performance as a predictor (forecasts).

198. (A) It is a common practice in the other country.

199. (A) Provide confidence that the project will satisfy relevant quality standards. Quality assurance increases project effectiveness and efficiency and provides added benefits to project stakeholders. It is all the planned and systematic activities implemented within the quality system that provide confidence that the project will satisfy relevant quality standards. It should be performed throughout the project.

200. (A) the expectancy theory. Expectancy theory holds that people will tend to be highly productive and motivated if the following two conditions are satisfied: (1) people believe that their efforts will likely lead to successful results and (2) those people also believe they will be rewarded for their success. Expectancy theory says two things. One, you get what you expect—self-fulfilling prophecy. The other is, if people think that their outcomes are going to be significant, if they think they are going to matter in terms of the organization, and then they do better. People like to be involved in something where they think they are making a difference.